U.S. STAMP YEARBOOK 1991

A comprehensive record of technical data, design
development and stories behind all of the stamps,
stamped envelopes, postal cards and souvenir cards
issued by the United States Postal Service in 1991.

By
George Amick

Published by *Linn's Stamp News*, the largest and most informative stamp newspaper in the
world. *Linn's* is owned by Amos Press, 911 Vandemark Road, Sidney, Ohio 45365. Amos
Press also publishes *Scott Stamp Monthly* and the Scott line of catalogs.
Copyright 1992 by Linn's Stamp News

ISSN 0748-996X

1

With gratitude . . .

It would be impossible to produce the *Linn's U.S. Stamp Yearbook* series without the help of dozens of people across the United States. My associates at *Linn's* and I deeply appreciate the generosity with which they give of their time and information.

For the concept sketches and other art-in-progress developed by the U.S. Postal Service in the creation of 1991's stamp and stationery designs, and for many hours of recollections as to how the stamps and the designs came to be, we thank Donald M. McDowell, director, Office of Stamp and Philatelic Marketing; Jack Williams, Joe Brockert and Terrence McCaffrey of the Design Section, and Bradbury Thompson, Howard Paine, Dick Sheaff, Derry Noyes and Jerry Pinkney, design coordinators for the Citizens' Stamp Advisory Committee.

Production information was furnished by Joseph Y. Peng, general manager, USPS Stamp Manufacturing Division, and his associates Kathy Caggiano and Frank Farrell; Frank Thomas, Jim Murphy, Mike O'Hara, Peter Papadopoulos, Jim Adam and Kim Parks of USPS; Leah Akbar, Leonard Buckley, Ira Polikoff, Cecilia Hatfield and Maureen McGuinness of the Bureau of Engraving and Printing; George Whitman of the Government Printing Office; Richard Sennett, Sandra Lane and Lynda Tilton of Sennett Enterprises; Alan Green of Avery International; Thomas C. Harris and Kelly Keough of the American Bank Note Company, and Dick Salois of Westvaco-USEnvelope Division.

Time, artwork and information were also generously shared by CSAC members Jack Rosenthal, Mary Ann Owens and "Digger" Phelps; stamp designers Don Adair, John Berkey, Higgins Bond, William Bond, Christopher Calle, Paul Calle, Harry Devlin, Sabra Field, Robert Giusti, Nancy Howe, Howard Koslow, Wallace Marosek, Ron Miller, Pierre Mion, Chuck Ripper, Richard Schlecht, Jim Sharpe and Marc Zaref, and Norma Opgrand, Patricia Fisher and Jim Palmer of the U.S. Fish and Wildlife Service.

Requests for specific details and collateral material were willingly answered by Dennis K. Brown, University of Notre Dame; Ken Crilly, Music Library, Yale University; P. Robert Farley, Magazine Publishers of America; Jean Holt, University of Vermont; photographer Paul Kalinian; Bob Lund, Denver, Colorado; John Mankins, NASA; Katherine Metz, Museum of the City of New York; Bruce Mosher and Dr. Douglas B. Quine, the Bureau Issues Association; Dan Myers; Ray C. Noll, Piper Aviation Museum; Joseph O'Brien, Basketball Hall of Fame; Phil Ogilvie, District of Columbia government; William T. Piper Jr., Lock Haven, Pennsylvania; Vicki Y. Saito, University of Texas Medical Branch; Betty Sena, New Mexico State Library; Mary E. Todoric, Professional Photographers of America; Gloria Chavez Tristani, Albuquerque, New Mexico; Carolyn Wilson, The Museum of Fine Arts, Houston, and stamp dealers Dana Okey, Jacques C. Schiff Jr. and Bob Tremaine.

Thanks also to stamp writer Ken Lawrence for again reading the manuscript, correcting errors, offering suggestions and giving us the benefit of his immense philatelic knowledge, and to Wayne Youngblood at *Linn's*, for his ever-available counsel.

My personal thanks, finally, to two Donnas: my editor at *Linn's*, Donna O'Keefe, who is the best stamp book editor in the business, and my wife and computer-resource person, Donna Amick, who steered me through the intricacies of word processing and computer graphics, and tolerated without complaint the hours I stole from household duties to write this *Yearbook*.

— George Amick

CONTENTS

Introduction _____ 6

Commemoratives _____ 8
50¢ Switzerland 700th Anniversary (joint issue), February 22 _____ 9
29¢ Vermont Statehood Bicentennial, March 1 _____ 15
29¢ U.S. Savings Bonds, April 30 _____ 21
29¢ William Saroyan (joint issue), May 22 _____ 27
$5.80 Fishing Flies booklet, May 31 _____ 34
29¢ Cole Porter, June 8 _____ 40
29¢ Desert Storm sheet stamp, July 2 _____ 47
$5.80 Desert Storm booklet, July 2 _____ 56
29¢ Olympic Track and Field strip of five, July 12 _____ 58
29¢ Numismatics, August 13 _____ 64
29¢ Basketball Centennial, August 28 _____ 68
$5.80 Comedians by Hirschfeld booklet, August 29_____ 76
$2.90 World War II souvenir sheet of 10, September 3 _____ 86
29¢ District of Columbia Bicentennial, September 7 _____ 103
29¢ Jan Matzeliger, September 15 _____ 111
$5.80 Space Exploration booklet, October 1_____ 118

Special Stamps _____ 125
29¢ Love sheet stamp (two varieties), May 9 _____ 126
$5.80 Love booklet, May 9 _____ 130
52¢ Love sheet stamp, May 9 _____ 132
Non-denominated Christmas Madonna stamp, October 17 _____ 135
Non-denominated Christmas Madonna booklet, October 17 _____ 140
Non-denominated Christmas Santa sheet stamp, October 17 _____ 142
Non-denominated Christmas Santa booklet, October 17 _____ 146

Definitives_____ 152
F (29¢) sheet stamp, January 22 _____ 153
F (29¢) coil stamp, January 22 _____ 158
F ($2.90, $5.80) booklet, BEP, January 22 _____ 161
F ($2.90) booklet, KCS, January 22 _____ 165
Makeup Rate (4¢) stamp, January 22 _____ 168
F ($2.48) Flag ATM-vended sheetlet, January 22_____ 174
4¢ Steam Carriage coil (two varieties), January 25_____ 177
19¢ Fawn, March 11 _____ 182
29¢ Flag Over Mount Rushmore coil, BEP, March 29 _____ 185
29¢ Flag Over Mount Rushmore coil, ABNC, July 4 _____ 191
35¢ Dennis Chavez, April 3 _____ 194
29¢ Flower sheet stamp (two varieties), April 5 _____ 201

$5.80 Flower booklet, April 5 _____ 204
29¢ Flower coil, August 16 _____ 207
23¢ Lunch Wagon coil, April 12 _____ 212
$2.90 Wood Duck booklet, BEP, April 12 _____ 217
$2.90 Wood Duck booklet, KCS, April 12 _____ 223
$2.90 Flag With Olympic Rings booklet, April 21 _____ 225
$3.80 Hot-Air Balloon booklet, May 17 _____ 229
5¢ Canoe coil, BEP, May 25 _____ 233
5¢ Canoe coil, Stamp Venturers, October 22 _____ 237
10¢ Tractor-Trailer coil, May 25 _____ 239
29¢ Flags on Parade, May 30 _____ 244
52¢ Hubert Humphrey, June 3 _____ 248
1¢ American Kestrel, June 22 _____ 255
3¢ Eastern Bluebird, June 22 _____ 260
30¢ Cardinal, June 22 _____ 263
$5.22 Liberty Torch ATM-vended sheetlet, June 25 _____ 267
19¢ Fishing Boat coil, August 8 _____ 274
23¢ Flag first-class presort rate coil, September 23 _____ 278
$1 USPS Olympic Sponsorship, September 29 _____ 281
Non-denominated (10¢) Eagle & Shield bulk-rate, December 13 _285
Revised definitives and airmail stamps _____ 290

Airmail and Expedited Mail _____ 292
$9.95 Eagle Express Mail, June 16 _____ 293
$14 Eagle Express Mail, August 31 _____ 298
$2.90 Eagle Priority Mail, July 7 _____ 301
50¢ Harriet Quimby airmail, April 27 _____ 306
40¢ William Piper airmail, May 17 _____ 314
50¢ Antarctic Treaty airmail, June 21 _____ 320
50¢ First Americans airmail, October 12 _____ 325

Official Stamps _____ 330
F (29¢) Official Mail coil, January 22 _____ 331
4¢ Official Mail, April 6 _____ 333
19¢ Official Mail, May 24 _____ 335
23¢ Official Mail, May 24 _____ 337
29¢ Official Mail coil, May 24 _____ 339

Migratory Bird Hunting _____ 341
$15 King Eiders duck stamp, July 1 _____ 341

Postal Stationery _____ 348
F (29¢) Official Mail Savings Bond envelope, January 22 _____ 349
29¢ Star Envelope, January 24 _____ 352
29¢ Official Mail envelope, April 6 _____ 357
29¢ Official Mail Savings Bond envelope, April 17 _____ 359
4

11.1¢ Birds non-profit envelope, May 3 _____361
29¢ Love envelope, May 9 _____364
45¢ Eagle aerogram (two varieties), May 17 _____369
29¢ Star Security envelope, July 20 _____373
29¢ Magazine Industry envelope, October 7_____375
29¢ Country Geese envelope, November 8_____381
19¢ Flag postal card, January 24 _____384
19¢ Flag double-reply postal card, March 27 _____386
19¢ Postal Buddy postal card, February 3_____388
19¢ Carnegie Hall postal card, April 1 _____392
19¢ Official Mail postal card, May 24 _____397
19¢ Old Red postal card, June 14 _____399
40¢ Yankee Clipper airmail postal card, June 28 _____404
30¢ Niagara Falls postal card, August 21 _____408
19¢ Bill of Rights Ratification postal card, September 25 _____412
19¢ University of Notre Dame postal card, October 15_____417
19¢ Old Mill, University of Vermont, postal card, October 29 ____422

Souvenir Cards _____426
Stampshow 91 souvenir card (BEP), August 22 _____426
Migratory Bird, July 1_____429

Appendix _____431
The Year in Review_____431
Varieties_____437
Plate numbers _____443
Items withdrawn from sale in 1991_____447

INTRODUCTION

In the nearly a century and a half that the United States has issued stamps, there has never been another year like 1991.

For volume and variety of stamps and stationery, for controversy and confusion and changes of plans, for official errors and embarrassment, 1991 was unprecedented. There was even a congressional investigation.

Collectors, philatelic writers and even officials of the U.S. Postal Service itself were often unable to keep up with what was happening, as new issues by the dozens, many of them produced by suppliers new to the stamp business, came rolling out of USPS.

The total number of those issues by itself would have made 1991 unique. By *Linn's* count, 1991 saw the appearance of 137 collectible varieties of stamps, stamped envelopes and postal cards (including 11 tagging varieties). The figure rose to 138 if you add in the Department of the Interior's duck stamp. It was by far the heaviest one-year program in U.S. stamp history.

The load was weighted with an unusually large helping of se-tenant booklets and strips — although there were no 50-variety commemorative panes of the kind that had helped inflate previous years' counts. One such pane, showing 50 wildflowers, had originally been announced for 1991, but it was withdrawn from the list before the year began and later rescheduled for 1992.

At least three major developments coincided to make 1991 the strange and complicated year it turned out to be for the Postal Service and for stamp collectors.

The first was a general rate overhaul, which brought with it a price increase in every postage category, along with a proliferation of new stamps to meet those rates.

The second was the continuation of the Postal Service's program of diversifying its sources of stamp supply throughout the private sector.

And the third development was the Postal Service's frankly stated intention to use philatelic sales to help defray its costs, including the estimated $122 million expense of sponsoring the 1992 Winter and Summer Olympic Games. Among the byproducts of this policy were four "Olympics" stamps with face values of $1 or more and one with a record-high denomination of $14.

The accelerated pace of Postal Service activity demanded by these and other developments created ideal conditions for Murphy's Law: that what can go wrong will go wrong. In 1991 USPS officials spent much more time than usual explaining and/or apologizing.

Its problems included erroneous or poorly worded information in

6

stamp selvage, poor quality (including stamps with ink that tended to flake away when soaked in water), long delays in making specific new issues available to the public — and, conversely, ahead-of-schedule sale of many items by postal clerks who hadn't gotten the message.

There was also a major controversy over disclosure that a U.S. stamp — and a Great Americans definitive, at that — was being printed in Canada. This Postal Service decision, and the criticism it engendered, was a major reason a House subcommittee held a highly unusual hearing in 1991 into the procurement and production of postage stamps.

But despite all its difficulties, USPS also came up with its share of innovations, high-quality artwork and craftsmanship, and novel formats and production methods. These helped make stamp collecting in 1991 not only challenging, but tremendously interesting.

Recording the events of 1991 has been equally challenging and interesting. To do the task justice, we at *Linn's Stamp News* have produced the biggest, most fact-filled and lavishly illustrated *U.S. Stamp Yearbook* since the annual series began in 1983. We hope collectors will enjoy the 1991 *Yearbook*, and that it will help them better understand all that happened in this extraordinary year.

COMMEMORATIVES

In 1991 the U.S. Postal Service issued 46 commemorative stamps. The total was greater than in any of the preceding three years, when the average output of commemoratives was only 34. It more nearly resembled the annual average of nearly 50 recorded in the five years before that, from 1983 through 1988. And, as usual, the total was boosted by a substantial number of se-tenant multiples.

The commemoratives of 1991 were an interesting lot. They included a booklet of five varieties honoring famous comedians, designed by the renowned caricaturist Al Hirschfeld, and a strip of five Olympic Track and Field stamps that were the first U.S. postal items to be designed on a personal computer. A sheetlet comprising 10 different stamps attached to a historical map was the first installment of what will be a five-year series to mark the 50th anniversary of World War II.

There was also a booklet of 10 varieties, featuring the planets of the Solar System; a booklet of five varieties depicting freshwater and saltwater fishing flies, and a hastily created stamp that was issued in sheet and booklet formats to celebrate the successful end of Operation Desert Storm. The deciding vote on the Desert Storm stamp's design was cast by President Bush himself.

Among single-stamp issues were the first joint issue with Switzerland and the third (and final) joint issue with the former Soviet Union, the latter stamp an addition to the long-running Literary Arts series. Other series that were extended in 1991 were Black Heritage and Performing Arts. A lengthy tradition of statehood anniversary stamps was continued with one for the bicentennial of Vermont. The bicentennial of the District of Columbia was also commemorated.

50¢ SWITZERLAND 700TH ANNIVERSARY (JOINT ISSUE)

Date of Issue: February 22, 1991

Catalog Number: Scott 2532

Colors: special blue, yellow, magenta, cyan, black

First-Day Cancel: Washington, D.C., and Bern, Switzerland

FDCs Canceled: 316,047

Format: Panes of 40, horizontal, 5 across, 8 down. Gravure printing cylinders of 160 (10 across, 16 around) manufactured by Armotek Industries Inc., Palmyra, New Jersey.

Perf: 10.9 (L perforator)

Selvage Markings: "© United States Postal Service 1990." "Use Correct ZIP Code ®." USPS Olympic logo.

Designer: Hans Hartman of Koniz, Switzerland

Art Director and Project Manager: Joe Brockert (USPS)

Typographer and Modeler: Richard Sennett (Sennett Enterprises) for American Bank Note Company

Printing: Printed for American Bank Note Company on a leased Champlain gravure press at J.W. Fergusson and Sons, Richmond, Virginia, under the supervision of Sennett Enterprises, Fairfax, Virginia. Stamps perforated, processed and shipped by ABNC, Bedford Park, Illinois.

Quantity Ordered: 100,000,000 plus 3,648,000

Quantity Distributed: 103,648,000

Cylinder Number Detail: 1 group of 5 cylinder numbers preceded by the letter A alongside corner stamp

Tagging: overall

9

The Stamp

On February 22, USPS took part in its first-ever joint stamp issue with Switzerland. The occasion was the 700th anniversary of Switzerland's founding. Single stamps of near-identical design were issued by each country in Washington, D.C., and Bern, the Swiss capital

The U.S. stamp was a 50-center — the first U.S. non-airmail com-

The Swiss stamp of the joint issue.

memorative to bear that value since the Trans-Mississippi series of 1898. The Swiss stamp's denomination was 1.60 Swiss francs, or the equivalent of $1.25. The 50¢ value coincided with the basic international airmail letter rate that had gone into effect 19 days earlier.

"The stamp's design had to be determined and the stamp committed to production prior to final determination of new U.S. international postage rates," USPS explained in its news release. "Fifty cents was selected because it was the most likely new airmail rate, and even if the subsequent airmail rate was different, 50¢ is a useful U.S. denomination."

The Swiss stamp was available by mail order from the Philatelic Sales Division in Kansas City.

Switzerland is the oldest existing republic in the world. The region it now occupies was made up of petty states and city states when it was taken into the Holy Roman Empire in the 11th century and subjected to feudal taxes.

In August of 1291, leaders of three states, the forest cantons of Uri, Schwyz and Unterwalden, joined to assert control of their rugged land from the Hapsburgs, who had come to dominate the empire. The

On this sketch for the U.S. stamp, the horizontal dimension is longer than on the stamp as issued, and more of the Swiss Bundeshaus is shown.

In this pair of sketches for the joint issue, the two capitols' central domes are side by side and of equal size.

Perpetual League they formed was the core around which the Swiss confederation grew. Swiss independence was recognized after victory over the Empire at Dornach in 1499.

Switzerland is now composed of 20 full cantons, or states, and six half-cantons. Its present status as a federal state was established by the constitution of 1848.

Legislative powers in the Federal Assembly, like those in the U.S. Congress, are based in two chambers. Two hundred deputies are elected to the lower house, or National Council, by popular vote. The upper house, or Council of States, is composed of two representatives from each canton and one from each of the six half-cantons.

The Design

The Citizens' Stamp Advisory Committee made its endorsement of the joint issue contingent on whether an acceptable design could be developed, explained Joe Brockert, project manager and art director for the U.S. stamp.

"We basically put the challenge to Switzerland," Brockert said. "We said, 'Let's see what kind of designs you can come up with.' Had that not worked out we probably would have gone to our own artists and recommended some alternatives. But they gave us something that we felt was very good, and we didn't commission any U.S. artists to do any finished artwork for us."

This pair of Hans Hartman sketches featured a pair of see-through domes to represent the Swiss Bundeshaus.

11

The Citizens' Stamp Advisory Committee was intrigued by this pair of designs that put the two capitol buildings together, base to base, so that one appeared to be a reflection of the other.

Swiss postal officials sent a selection of designs that the committee found appealing, including several by Hans Hartman of Koeniz, Switzerland. The Hartman designs all featured two buildings, the U.S. Capitol and the Bundeshaus in Bern, which houses the Swiss Parliament. "The Swiss wanted to make the point graphically that their legislature was based very much on the U.S. system of government," said Brockert.

One treatment showed the two buildings' principal domes side by side, in equal size. Another featured a see-through pair of Swiss domes in the foreground and a full view of the U.S. Capitol at the rear. CSAC members were strongly attracted to a third pair of concept sketches that showed the buildings linked base to base, as if one were the reflection of the other. The U.S. stamp would have had the U.S. Capitol on top, with the Swiss building in the reflected position; the Swiss stamp would have reversed that arrangement.

But the committee ultimately decided that these designs would confuse the public, and that users putting the stamps on envelopes would be uncertain which side was up.

"Not being able to resolve that, the committee settled on a treatment that showed the U.S. Capitol dome in the foreground, and more of the Swiss Parliament building in the background," Brockert said.

Hartman's design had been executed in the customary dimensions of

This pair of sketches for the joint issue approaches the designs that were finally used, but with different wording and a circus-style typeface on the U.S. stamp.

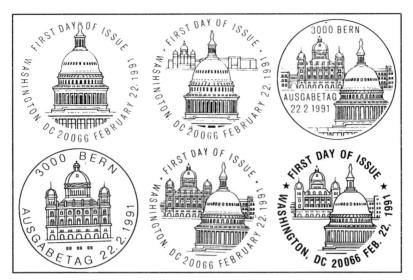

These are some of Hans Hartman's proposed designs for first-day postmarks for the Switzerland stamps.

Swiss stamps. To fit it into standard U.S. commemorative size would have required that it be stretched. USPS officials decided that the design would require less alteration if it was adapted to the more squarish semi-jumbo configuration. Accordingly, the U.S. stamps were printed in that size, 40 to the pane. The stamps turned out to be slightly deeper than the Swiss ones, and showed a little more of the U.S. Capitol.

Among the phrases considered for the U.S. stamp were "Switzerland's Septicentennial," which was proposed by the Swiss artist, and "Switzerland/700 Years." CSAC members dismissed the word "Septicentennial" as being too unfamiliar. Postmaster General Anthony M. Frank himself vetoed the latter on the grounds that it wasn't clear what "700 years" referred to. The wording was then changed to the final version, "Switzerland/Founded 1291." After considering the typefaces suggested by the Swiss, CSAC opted for the face named for Switzerland: Helvetica.

Several of the Hans Hartman sketches for the Swiss version had incorporated the number "700" prominently, followed by the word "years" in each of the four official languages of the country: German, French, Italian and Romansch. In the stamp as issued, however, the Swiss used only the two dates "1291-1991," in the style that USPS had formerly used for anniversary commemoratives. Another difference between the two stamps was the use on the Swiss stamp of the designer's name and the name of the printer, Courvoisier, in small letters below the image area.

As stamp writer Bill McAllister noted in *The Washington Post*, the dearth of information on the finished stamp designs probably produced puzzlement for postal customers in both countries. The Swiss might well have wondered why the U.S. Capitol — assuming they could identify it as such — was shown on their stamp. And the U.S. stamp also contained no explanation as to why the Capitol was there — an omission, McAllister wrote, "that could leave some Americans wondering whether Switzerland happens to have a building that strangely resembles the Capitol."

Swiss artist Hartman also submitted several design proposals for the first-day cancellation, including the one that was ultimately chosen for use. This design, which also featured the domes of the two capitol buildings, was used in a simplified form on the rubber canceling device.

Switzerland's Federal Palace, located near the Aare River in Bern, comprises three wings. The central part with its cupola and corner towers was begun in 1896 by H. Auer, who was also the builder of the building's east wing. The U.S. Capitol, which houses Congress, has appeared on many U.S. stamps, and was most recently depicted on the 15¢ Washington Cityscape postal card of the America the Beautiful series in 1989.

First-Day Facts

Deputy Postmaster General Michael S. Coughlin and Kurt Eichenberger, director of marketing for the Swiss postal agency's philatelic office, dedicated the stamps of their respective countries at a ceremony at the Swiss Embassy in Washington, D.C. Edouard Brunner, Swiss ambassador to the United States, gave the welcome.

At the Bern first-day ceremony, the Postal Service was represented by Assistant Postmaster General Thomas E. Leavey and John N. Griesemer, vice chairman of the USPS Board of Governors.

Collectors were given 90 days, rather than the usual 30, to obtain the first-day postmark by mail. Service was provided for three kinds of cover: those bearing the U.S. stamp and postmark, those bearing the Swiss stamp and postmark (for which customers had to supply addressed stamped envelopes bearing U.S. postage for the return of the covers), and combination covers. Customers preparing their own combination covers were instructed to affix the two stamps so that neither country's handstamped cancellation would touch the other country's stamp.

Later, USPS announced that a standard machine version of the first-day cancellation was available for prestamped covers submitted by mail.

29¢ VERMONT STATEHOOD BICENTENNIAL

Date of Issue: March 1, 1991

Catalog Number: Scott 2533

Colors: yellow, blue, magenta, black

First-Day Cancel: Bennington, Vermont

FDCs canceled: 308,105

Format: Panes of 50, vertical, 10 across, 5 down. Gravure printing cylinders of 200 (10 across, 20 around) manufactured by Armotek Industries Inc., Palmyra, New Jersey.

Perf: 10.9 (L perforator)

Selvage Markings: "© United States Postal Service 1991." "Use Correct ZIP Code ® 36 USC 380." USPS Olympic logo.

Designer: Sabra Field of South Royalton, Vermont

Art Director and Typographer: Bradbury Thompson (CSAC)

Project Manager: Jack Williams (USPS)

Modeler: Richard Sennett, Sennett Enterprises, for American Bank Note Company

Printing: Stamps printed for American Bank Note Company on a leased Champlain gravure press at J.W. Fergusson and Sons, Richmond, Virginia, under the supervision of Sennett Enterprises, Fairfax, Virginia. Stamps perforated, processed and shipped by ABNC, Bedford Park, Illinois.

Quantity Ordered: 181,000,000

Quantity Distributed: 179,990,000

Cylinder Number Detail: 1 group of 4 cylinder numbers preceded by the letter A alongside corner stamp

Tagging: overall

The Stamp

Vermont was "the first of the rest" — the first state to enter the Union after the original 13 colonies had attained statehood by ratifying the U.S. Constitution. The Green Mountain State ratified on January 10, 1791, and on the following March 4 Vermont was admitted as the 14th state.

On March 1, 1991, USPS celebrated Vermont's 200th anniversary by issuing its first commemorative stamp in the new 29¢ first-class rate denomination. The first-day city was Bennington, site of the act of ratification of the Constitution.

The design of the stamp — minus the denomination, which at that time was unknown — was unveiled January 4 as part of a ceremony rededicating the governor's reception room, which is known as the Cedar Creek Room, in the Vermont capitol in Montpelier. Doing the honors were outgoing Governor Madeline M. Kunin and Donald Kelpinski, postmaster of White River Junction, Vermont.

The stamp was the third to mark a significant anniversary in Vermont's history and the second to commemorate its statehood.

In 1927 a 2¢ stamp (Scott 643) was issued for the 150th anniversary of the victory by Vermont patriots over the British general, John Burgoyne, near Bennington on August 16, 1777. Earlier that year, Vermonters had established their own state, independent of its two neighbors, New Hampshire and New York. For that reason the 1927 stamp bore the words "Vermont Sesquicentennial" over its central figure, a Green Mountain Boy holding his musket.

And in 1941 the 150th anniversary of Vermont's statehood was noted

The 1941 Vermont Sesquicentennial stamp showed the state capitol in Montpelier.

with a 3¢ commemorative (Scott 903) depicting the Vermont state capitol. Unlike the 1991 stamp, this one was issued on March 4, the anniversary date, and its first-day city was Montpelier. It was the only commemorative stamp produced by the United States in 1941.

Other stamps that have had a Vermont connection include the 13¢ State Flag stamp of 1976 (Scott 1646), the State Bird and Flower stamp of 1982 (Scott 1997) and the 6¢ Bennington Flag stamp in the Historic Flags set of 1968 (Scott 1348).

Brigham Young, whose leadership of the Mormons into the Valley of the Great Salt Lake was commemorated in 1947 (Scott 950), was born in Vermont. Other Vermont natives depicted on U.S. stamps include Presidents Chester Alan Arthur and Calvin Coolidge, Admiral George

This was Sabra Field's alternative design proposal for the stamp, a collage of a village scene inspired by her hometown of East Bernard.

Dewey, Senator Stephen A. Douglas, John Dewey and Alden Partridge. Ethan Allen, leader of the Green Mountain Boys, who was born in Connecticut but was a Vermont hero, was shown on a 1955 stamp (Scott 1071) marking the 200th anniversary of Fort Ticonderoga in New York.

Vermont has been an individualistic and independent-minded state from the beginning. Its anniversary celebration reflected those characteristics. One of the events scheduled by the Vermont Statehood Bicentennial Commission was a series of debates on whether Vermont should secede from the United States. They brought forth vigorous argument on both sides of the question. The debates were "half whimsical," the commission's Carolyn Crowley Meub told *The New York Times,* but she added: "We thought there was no better way to get people to focus on statehood than to discuss secession."

Vermont's name is a contracted form of the French "Verd-Mont," or "Green Mountain." From July 8, 1777, to March 4, 1791, Vermont was

Field created and marketed this limited-edition wood-block print called "Windrows," based on her collage design for the Vermont stamp.

17

These rough pencil sketches were submitted by one of the artist candidates in a preliminary search for an appropriate design theme for further development.

an independent republic, issuing bills of credit, coining money, establishing post offices, naturalizing citizens of other states and countries and corresponding with foreign governments.

George Washington at one time believed it would be necessary to subdue Vermont with arms, but fortunately he turned out to be mistaken. After the peace treaty with Great Britain was signed, Vermont steadily gained the friendship and confidence of neighboring states. It settled an old dispute with New York over land grants in 1790, compensating those who held Vermont land by deeds issued from New York. This helped clear the way for its admission to the Union.

The Design

The stamp as issued was arranged vertically and depicted a stylized Vermont landscape. The original USPS news release described the scene as showing "rows of tilled soil and a brick-red farmhouse in the foreground." That was all wrong, according to the designer, Sabra Field. The building was actually a hay barn, she said, and the striped pattern represented "windrows of hay piled up, ready to be baled."

Field, a woodcut print specialist from South Royalton, Vermont, and a descendant of the state's first postmaster general, created her design as

18

This color sketch of Mount Mansfield in northern Vermont, the state's highest peak at 4,393 feet, with autumn foliage in the foreground was prepared by one of the stamp's other artist candidates.

a collage. "I did it the way I frequently do commissioned pieces when no multiples are required," she said. "I print pieces of colored paper from woodblocks which have not been cut. I get the effect of a woodcut on paper, and I have the option of shading, for instance, and doing other special effects that might make it look like one of my woodcuts, but in fact what I then do is cut up those papers and assemble them as a collage. So the picture is a one-of-a-kind."

The scene, she said, was "strictly imaginary." She had done many Vermont landscapes before, and she said of the design elements — barn, windrows, mountains — which she used: "I already had all those icons in my bag of tricks!"

As an alternative design, Field offered USPS another collage, showing a slightly rearranged version of her hometown of East Barnard, Vermont. "I was sort of hoping they would choose that one," she said, "for sentimental reasons, and because in the group of buildings was the little store in which we had a post office once upon a time, before the RFDs."

Field's name had been recommended to USPS by the Vermont Bicentennial Commission. When Jack Williams of USPS, the stamp's project manager, took her design to Montpelier in May 1989 to get the approval of Governor Kunin, he was encouraged to see a Field print hanging on the wall of the governor's office. Field was a favorite artist of Governor Kunin, Williams discovered.

Two other artists also submitted concept sketches for CSAC's consideration. The subjects they chose included farm and village scenes, a

A New York artist offered these views of a Vermont covered bridge and dairy cows standing in a pasture.

19

Art director Richard Sheaff created this design for CSAC's consideration using a color photograph of white birches and surrounding woodland in autumn.

covered bridge, a herd of cows and mountain vistas. In addition, art director Richard Sheaff created a design using a color photograph of an autumn woodland scene. The committee also considered adapting an existing painting by a Vermont artist, such as Paul Sample's *Beaver Meadow* or Aldo Hibbard's *Wardsboro Bridge*.

Ironically, before CSAC finally selected Sabra Field's warm daytime summer scene, it seriously considered a sketch by another designer that was its opposite in almost all respects. This one showed a lone farmhouse in a snowy valley with a full moon overhead. Because the original picture was so bleak, the committee members asked for some changes, and the artist, among other things, lit up the farmhouse windows and placed a car on the nearby road. In the end, however, his offering was set aside in favor of the Field design.

First-Day Facts

Postmaster General Anthony M. Frank dedicated the stamp in a ceremony at Greenwald Hall on the campus of Bennington College. Governor Richard A. Snelling gave the welcome, and William Gray, chairman of the Vermont Bicentennial Commission, was the principal speaker. Willie Jones, in period costume, offered a theatrical presentation, "109 Hats to Bennington: A Journey to Statehood."

These are two stages of a concept showing a moonlit Vermont farmhouse in winter. In the second version, the artist added a car on the highway and lit the house windows in an attempt to relieve the loneliness of the scene.

29¢ U.S. SAVINGS BONDS

Date of Issue: April 30, 1991

Catalog Number: Scott 2534

Colors: red (PMS 1795C), process yellow, process cyan, process black, yellow (PMS 125C), blue (PMS 287C)

First-Day Cancel: Washington, D.C.

FDCs Canceled: 341,955

Format: Panes of 50, vertical, 10 across, 5 down. Gravure printing cylinders of 200 subjects (10 across, 20 around).

Perf: 11.2 (Eureka off-line perforator)

Selvage Markings: "© United States Postal Service 1991 36 USC 380." "Use Correct ZIP Code ®." USPS Olympic logo.

Designer and Typographer: Primo Angeli of San Francisco, California

Art Director: Joe Brockert (USPS)

Project Manager: Terrence McCaffrey (USPS)

Modeler: Peter Cocci (BEP)

Printing: printed by BEP on 7-color Andreotti gravure press (601)

Quantity Ordered: 151,000,000

Quantity Distributed: 150,560,000

Cylinder Number Detail: One group of 6 cylinder numbers alongside corner stamp

Tagging: overall

The Stamp

On April 30, USPS marked the 50th anniversary of the World War II-era E Series Savings Bonds with a 29¢ commemorative stamp. In announcing the stamp on December 7, 1990, and in a subsequent news release, USPS said its purpose was to commemorate the 50th anniversary of "U.S. Savings Bonds." Actually, government savings bonds pre-dated 1941 by many years, and later USPS specified that its intent was to honor the E Series bond.

Even so, the design of the stamp carried only the wording: "US Savings Bonds Fiftieth Anniversary," and a few complaints were expressed in the philatelic press about the lack of preciseness in the inscription. However, the exact same amount of information had been carried on an earlier stamp issued to commemorate the E bond program, a 5-center (Scott 1320) that appeared October 26, 1966, to mark the 25th anniversary and also to honor U.S. servicemen.

This 1966 stamp honored U.S. servicemen and also marked the 25th anniversary of Series E bonds.

The new stamp was originally scheduled for dedication in Washington, D.C., May 1, the 50th anniversary of the day that President Franklin D. Roosevelt bought the first E Bond. Later it was moved up to April 30 to allow the stamp to be sold to the general public on the May 1 anniversary date. It was on April 30, 1941, that President Roosevelt went on the radio to announce the creation of a new "Defense" Savings Bond, the Series E, and asked all citizens to join him in "one great partnership" to help finance the nation's defense effort.

The Savings Bond stamp design was unveiled by USPS January 23, 1991, in a small, unpublicized ceremony during the 1991 Campaign Leadership Conference for corporate and government bond campaign coordinators in Washington. Deputy Postmaster General Michael S. Coughlin presided and was assisted by Catalina Vasquez Villalpando, treasurer of the United States.

The Bureau of Engraving and Printing gravure-printed the stamp, its first commemorative to be produced by that process in more than two

This souvenir card, available only to employees of the Bureau of Engraving and Printing as an incentive to participate in the U.S. Savings Bond payroll savings plan, featured an engraved die imprint of the 10¢ Postal Savings stamp of 1941 (Scott PS11).

years. Later in 1991, collectors were surprised to learn that BEP had manufactured — for employees only — a handsome souvenir card, with an uncanceled 29¢ Savings Bond commemorative affixed, marking the 50th anniversary of the Series E bonds. The card bore an intaglio die imprint of the 10¢ Minute Man Postal Savings stamp of 1941 (Scott

These three concept sketches featured the Minuteman motif in red, white and blue against light, dark and striped backgrounds.

PS11) in red ink. The rest of the card, including an enlarged drawing of a Minute Man and a circle of stars, was printed in blue by the offset process, and stamped with gold foil on a letter press.

The card, produced in May, was made available only to BEP personnel who enrolled in the U.S. Savings Bond payroll savings plan or, if they were already enrolled, increased their payroll savings amount. Writer Ken Lawrence reported in *Linn's Stamp News* in August 1991 that BEP spokesman Ira Polikoff had told him that 2,000 cards were printed, but only about 1,400 were distributed to qualified BEP employees, one per employee. The rest were destroyed.

The card wasn't offered to the public, but according to Lawrence, a few copies had reached collectors' hands at $300 apiece. A previous employees-only souvenir card issued by BEP, and given in appreciation to those who had worked on the 25¢ Honeybee coil stamp of 1988, was selling for as high as $850, Lawrence added.

"It's unfair for the Bureau to create desirable collectibles and then not make them available to collectors," *Linn's* editor Michael Laurence complained in his September 2 column. "BEP should rethink its policies here before it creates another privately distributed card."

The Design

Advertising designer Primo Angeli of San Francisco used a computer and stock graphic images to create the Savings Bonds stamp's ornate design, which featured the head of an American bald eagle against a

With these two eagle head designs, Primo Angeli was getting close to the finished product, but CSAC decided it wanted the eagle to appear in natural colors rather than a single tone, as in these sketches.

These are two sketches prepared on the computer by Primo Angeli, using a variety of stock graphic elements.

background of vertical red and silver stripes.

Postal Service officials had wanted the design to evoke the mood of the patriotic posters of the World War II era. They asked Angeli to prepare concept sketches that included minutemen, eagles and other appropriate images. Angeli complied, providing a variety of different treatments of these national icons.

The Citizens' Stamp Advisory Committee examined Angeli's sketches, as well as one created by art director Joe Brockert and incorporating the Treasury Department's logo for the 50th anniversary of the Savings Bond program. That one "didn't hold up well in stamp size," Brockert said.

The committee liked a vertical concept featuring the head and shoulders of an eagle against a striped background, but asked that the eagle be rendered in realistic colors rather than the single-tone versions Angeli had shown them. Thus changed, the sketch became the finished design.

Over the years, the eagle has been used repeatedly as a U.S. stamp subject, both as a specimen of wildlife and as a national symbol (for

This design, with slight modifications, became the design used on the stamp. CSAC worked with low-resolution computer prints, such as this one, in making its design decisions. To create the color separations for the stamp itself, high resolution was used.

example, on the Great Seal of the United States and the Postal Service logo). In 1991 alone it showed up on one commemorative (the Savings Bonds stamp), two definitives (the $1 Olympic Sponsorship and non-denominated bulk mail stamps), two Express Mail stamps, a Priority Mail stamp, five Official Mail stamps, three Official Mail envelopes and an aerogram. A speculative question: If Benjamin Franklin had gotten his way and the wild turkey had been designated the national bird instead of the eagle, would turkey stamps have become equally plentiful?

First-Day Facts

The stamp was dedicated by Postmaster General Anthony M. Frank at a by-invitation-only ceremony at the Treasury Building in Washington. Nicholas F. Brady, secretary of the Treasury, also spoke. The event had been planned for outdoors, but inclement weather forced it inside, where it was held in the historic and newly renovated Cash Room.

For the public, first-day cancellations were available at the Washington post office and the Philatelic Center at USPS headquarters.

29¢ WILLIAM SAROYAN (JOINT ISSUE)
LITERARY ARTS SERIES

Date of Issue: May 22, 1991

Catalog Number: Scott 2538

Colors: line red, magenta, yellow, cyan, black

First-Day Cancel: Fresno, California, and Yerevan, Armenia, USSR

FDCs Canceled: 326,483. Combination joint issue FDCs, 7,890

Format: Panes of 50, horizontal, 5 across, 10 down. Gravure printing cylinders of 200 subjects (10 across, 20 down) manufactured by Armotek Industries Inc., Palmyra, New Jersey.

Perf: 10.9 (L perforator)

Selvage Inscription: "William Saroyan was/an Armenian- American/playwright & novelist." "His 1939 play 'The/Time of Your Life' won/ him a Pulitzer Prize." "This is the third joint/stamp issue by the U.S./and the Soviet Union."

Selvage Markings: "©/United States/Postal Service/1991." "Use Correct/ZIP Code/®/36 USC 380." USPS Olympic logo.

Designer: Ren Wicks of Los Angeles, California

Art Director and Project Manager: Jack Williams (USPS)

Typographer: Bradbury Thompson (CSAC)

Modeler: Richard Sennett, Sennett Enterprises, for American Bank Note Company

Printing: Stamps printed for American Bank Note Company on a leased Champlain gravure press at J.W. Fergusson and Sons, Richmond, Virginia, under the supervision of Sennett Enterprises, Fairfax, Virginia. Stamps perforated, processed and shipped by ABNC, Bedford Park, Illinois.

Quantity Ordered: 161,000,000

Quantity Distributed: 161,498,000

Cylinder Number Detail: 1 group of 5 gravure cylinder numbers preceded by the letter A alongside corner stamp

Tagging: overall

The Stamp

William Saroyan, Armenian-American novelist, playwright and short-story writer, was honored on a 29¢ commemorative stamp issued May 22. The stamp, a part of the USPS Literary Arts series, was also part of a joint issue with the Soviet Union, of which Armenia — at the time the stamps were issued — was still a component republic.

The Soviets issued a 1-ruble stamp with the same basic design. The two stamps were jointly dedicated in ceremonies in Fresno, California, Saroyan's birthplace and hometown, and in Yerevan, Armenia's capital.

The Citizens' Stamp Advisory Committee had received numerous proposals for a Saroyan stamp after the writer's death in 1981. A special CSAC subcommittee assigned to the Literary Arts series had endorsed him as an appropriate stamp subject once the required 10-year waiting period had elapsed. When CSAC finally decided to issue the stamp, one of those who reacted with enthusiasm was Robert Setrakian of San Francisco, chairman of the USPS Board of Governors and an Armenian-American himself, who was also president and chairman of the William Saroyan Foundation. Setrakian later participated with Postmaster General Anthony M. Frank in the unveiling of the stamp design in Fresno February 21, 1991.

In the meantime, Soviet delegates to a Universal Postal Union meeting in Bern, Switzerland, had notified representatives of the USPS International Postal Affairs Department of their interest in cooperating with the United States on a joint stamp issue. Out of this contact came an agreement, formalized at the UPU Congress in Washington, D.C., in 1989, for three such joint issues in consecutive years.

"Not all of our past joint issues have been seen as having equal significance in both the participating countries," said Donald M. McDowell, director of the USPS Office of Stamp and Philatelic Marketing. "In this case, we reached an understanding with the Soviets that we

The Soviet Union's William Saroyan stamp.

would look for subjects that had the potential to be quite popular in both their country and ours. They were very interested in the environment and ecological themes, and they were also interested in anything that had to do with a cultural tie or association with the United States. We looked at what we had pending in our stamp program, and shared the information with them." The first subject chosen for a joint issue was Creatures of the Sea, which was featured on a se-tenant block of four stamps in 1990. The second was Saroyan — a choice that was probably influenced by the fact that the director of the Stamp Issuing and Marketing Bureau of the USSR Ministry of Communications, L.K. Manukian, was Armenian.

The U.S. stamp, like many previous U.S. commemoratives, was printed by the American Bank Note Company on a Champlain gravure press at the J.W. Fergusson and Sons plant in Richmond, Virginia, and was perforated and finished at ABNC's plant in Chicago. This time, however, the manufacturer encountered a major problem.

The perforations were ragged, leaving many hanging and blind perfs, which made the stamps not only unattractive but also difficult to separate. Because the product failed to meet USPS specifications, ABNC was forced to destroy the entire lot of some 160 million stamps and print them again on a paper that would perforate properly. There was no financial loss to the Postal Service, but the mistake cost ABNC some $360,000, which ABNC announced it would try to recover from the paper supplier.

The original paper, USPS told *Linn's Stamp News*, was a DuPont product furnished by Paper Corporation of America, and was too fibrous and soft for the job. The paper used for the second printing was described as a Glatfelter converted IVEX hardwood. Because the paper had fewer fibers, it perforated and separated more cleanly than the DuPont paper.

The Soviet stamp was available for sale through the USPS Philatelic Sales Division for 65¢. Many U.S. collectors bought it for use on combination first-day covers. One who did so was Lloyd A. DeVries, a columnist for *Stamp Collector*, who provided this insight from his experience: "I can state definitively (or perhaps commemoratively) that the U.S. produces better-tasting stamps than the Soviets."

William Saroyan was born August 31, 1908, to immigrants from Armenia. Drawn to writing from boyhood, he sold his first story to a magazine when he was 20 and working at a San Francisco telegraph office. In 1934 his story "The Daring Young Man on the Flying Trapeze" appeared in *Story* magazine and captured national attention. The story's "boyish ebullience," in the words of *Current Biography*, "buoyed up the spirits of American readers." It was followed by hundreds of short stories, essays, novels, plays, autobiographical sketches and miscellaneous items in well over 40 books. "A literary nonconformist, (Saroyan) writes in an original, freewheeling style directly from experience, but turns personal incidents into allegorical events in which his readers are induced to find themselves," *Current Biography* continued. ". . . Saroyan holds a probably secure place in American literature on the strength of several masterpieces, such as his Pulitzer Prize-winning play, *The Time of Your Life*, which express his exuberant personality, his wonder and innocence, his insight into human nature and his love and sympathy for mankind."

In 1959 Saroyan moved to France to seek tax-exemption relief while working to pay off a substantial indebtedness to the Internal Revenue Service. Thereafter he divided his time between a Paris apartment and a Fresno house. He died in Fresno May 18, 1981.

One person who could testify to the robust and mercurial nature of Saroyan's personality was Paul Kalinian, the man who took the photographs used in designing the stamp. Kalinian was a Fresno portrait photographer of Armenian heritage who was born in Lebanon. For years he had been fascinated by Saroyan — not only by his writing ability, but also by his patriarchal appearance: his broad forehead, shaggy gray hair and flamboyant walrus mustache. "As a photographer," Kalinian said, "I wanted to capture his greatness, his natural feelings, and to portray his special genius." One day — March 26, 1976 — the opportunity came.

Kalinian learned from a mutual friend, sculptor Varaz Samuelian, that the writer was in Fresno and was expected to visit Samuelian that afternoon. Samuelian invited Kalinian to set up his lights and cameras in

Some of Kalinian's photos of Saroyan that Ren Wicks used in creating his alternative stamp designs, including the one that was used on the stamp.

the sculptor's studio and try his luck.

Sure enough, Saroyan eventually arrived, pedaling his bicycle. Kalinian nervously introduced himself and asked Saroyan if he would be willing to pose. "He told me to get lost!" the photographer recalled.

Fortunately, Kalinian persisted, and as they talked — in English and Armenian — Saroyan softened. Eventually Saroyan asked Kalinian to sing an old folk song, *Tzangam Desnem Zim Giligia* ("I Wish to See My Armenia"), a sentimental favorite of the writer. "We sang this together," Kalinian said. "It was difficult for him to hold back the tears . . . He wasn't the same man I had met earlier. He said, 'I like you, Paul. Take all the pictures you want.' "

The photographer shot one exposure after another with his Mamiya R.B. 67 camera, using 2¼- by 2¾-inch Kodak color film. To his relief and joy, the pictures turned out well. Saroyan himself would later characterize one of them as the best photo that had ever been taken of him.

Several years later Kalinian formed a non-profit corporation, raised $175,000 from his own funds plus contributions from other Saroyan admirers, and made a one-hour documentary film titled: *William Saroyan: The Man, The Writer*. The film, narrated by actor Mike Connors, premiered at the William Saroyan Theater in Fresno April 13, 1991.

The Design

When the time came to design the stamp, Jack Williams of USPS wrote to Paul Kalinian asking for a selection of photographs for use by the artist whom USPS had commissioned, Ren Wicks of Los Angeles.

Working from the photos Kalinian supplied, Wicks made several concept sketches in color. Of this group, the committee chose a horizontal treatment of a portrait in which Saroyan was leaning his face against his clasped hands. The pose itself was taken from a specific Kalinian photograph, but Wicks borrowed from other pictures to create a face that bore a slight smile, rather than the solemn expression of the original. The

Artist Ren Wicks submitted to USPS these three alternative color sketches of Saroyan, all of them based on Paul Kalinian photographs.

artist placed his subject against a deep red background.

The stamp, the ninth in the Literary Arts series, was the first in the series to be designed in a horizontal format. (Kalinian negotiated a $500 fee from USPS for use of his photograph, and then added a specification that no doubt pleased the Postal Service. The fee, he said, was to be paid in Saroyan stamps.)

The choice of stamp wording is a subjective one, and this has been particularly evident with series like Literary Arts. In 1990, for instance, the Citizens' Stamp Advisory Committee felt that Marianne Moore's picture and name alone weren't sufficient identification, and added the words: "American Poet." The year before, however, the members decided that Ernest Hemingway was familiar enough that his portrait needed only the single word "Hemingway" accompanying it. In Saroyan's case, said Jack Williams, the committee chose the middle road: Use the full name, but allow the name to "stand alone" without the inclusion of "American author" or "Literary Arts."

The Soviet stamp's design was essentially the same as that of the U.S. stamp, but the two portraits differed noticeably in appearance, particularly in the eyes — which had an oddly unnatural look on the Soviet stamp — and the highlights on the hair. James Helzer, president of Unicover Corporation in Cheyenne, Wyoming, the U.S. agent for Soviet stamps, explained that the Soviets had had the portrait repainted for their use by their own artist, one I. Martynov.

Apparently their decision stemmed from national pride. On the two previous U.S.-USSR joint issues — the Apollo Soyuz pair in 1975 and the Creatures of the Sea block in 1990 — the design assignment had been equally divided between the two countries. Each had produced one of the two Apollo Soyuz stamps and two of the four Creatures of the Sea stamps. With only a single stamp involved this time, the Soviets chose to have a Soviet artist create an original piece of art for their stamp. In so doing, Helzer said, Martynov had made use of both Ren Wicks' painting and Paul Kalinian's original photograph.

Unlike the U.S. stamp, the Soviet stamp contained the year of issue, 1991, as per that country's custom. In 1990, with the Creatures of the Sea joint issue, USPS had followed the Soviet practice and placed the year date on its stamps too. It didn't do so this time. Another difference was that the Soviet stamp was printed by four-color process offset lithography rather than gravure.

First-Day Facts

Postmaster General Anthony M. Frank spoke during a dedication ceremony for the two stamps in Yerevan, Armenia, on May 22. Meanwhile, a similar ceremony was taking place at the William Saroyan Theater in Fresno, where Associate Postmaster General Edward E. Horgan Jr. dedicated the U.S. stamp and R.S. Avojan, minister of communications of Armenia, dedicated the Soviet stamp.

Translations were provided for Avojan, who spoke in Russian, and

M.S. Ter-gulanian, chief editor of *Garun* magazine, who spoke in Armenian. Other speakers included Haig Mardikian, vice chairman of the board of trustees of the William Saroyan Foundation, and Karen Humphrey, mayor of Fresno. A number of Soviet postal and philatelic officials were honored guests. Although Paul Kalinian wasn't included in the ceremony, USPS used one of his color photographs of Saroyan on the cover of the first-day program.

Collectors were given 60 days to obtain the first-day postmark by mail. Those wishing to obtain Soviet stamps and postmarks were encouraged

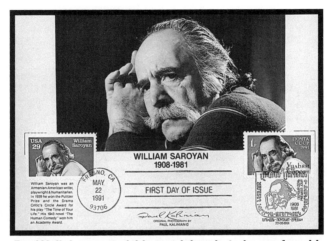

Paul Kalinian created this special cacheted cover from his photo portrait on which the stamp was based. The cover is shown here with first-day cancellations on both the U.S. and Soviet Saroyan stamps.

to buy the stamps by mail from the Philatelic Sales Division at a cost of 65¢ apiece, affix them to addressed envelopes and send them to the postmaster in Fresno along with a larger addressed stamped envelope for the return of the covers. Combination covers, bearing both countries' stamps and their respective postmarks, could also be obtained, but collectors were cautioned that the stamps must be spaced far enough apart so that neither country's cancellation would touch the other's stamp. USPS prepared combination covers on request at a cost of 94¢ per cover.

$5.80 FISHING FLIES BOOKLET

Date of Issue: May 31, 1991

Catalog Numbers: Scott 2545-49 (stamps); Scott 2549a (booklet pane)

Colors: yellow, orange, magenta, cyan, black

First-Day Cancel: Cuddebackville, New York

FDCs Canceled: 1,045,726

Format: 4 panes of 5 different horizontal stamps, arranged vertically. Gravure printing cylinders of 275 subjects (11 across, 25 around).

Perf: 10.9 (L perforator)

Selvage Markings: Cylinder numbers printed on each pane binding stub. Color-bar electric-eye mark remnants on 7.3 percent of all pane binding stubs.

Cover Markings: "© United States Postal Service 1991" and mailing information on inside of front cover. Universal Product Code (UPC) and promotion for USPS Commemorative Stamp Club on outside of back cover. Coupon for Stamp Club on inside of back cover. Position guidemarks at left or right edge of inside front cover on 18.2 percent of all booklets.

Designer: Chuck Ripper of Huntington, West Virginia

Art Director and Project Manager: Jack Williams (USPS)

Typographer: Bradbury Thompson (CSAC)

Printing: Printed by Guilford Gravure Division of George Schmitt and Company, Guilford, Connecticut, for American Bank Note Company on an Andreotti 5-color webfed gravure press. Perforated and formed into booklets at ABNC, Bedford Park, Illinois.

Quantity Ordered: 800,000,000 (40,000,000 booklets)

Quantity Delivered: 753,558,000 (37,677,900 booklets)

Cylinder Number Detail: 1 group of 5 gravure cylinder numbers preceded by the letter A on pane binding stub. Up to 4 different cylinder number sequences can be found on panes in the same booklet.

Tagging: phosphor-coated paper

The Stamps

In 1987 Chuck Ripper, a Huntington, West Virginia, wildlife artist and fisherman, cast a lure at the U.S. Postal Service — and got a bite. Ripper's suggestion was that USPS issue a series of topicals featuring fishing flies.

Fly fishing is centuries old, and is considered by its adherents to be the most artful and sporting method of catching fish. A fly is a wispy imitation insect on a small hook, made of feathers, hair, wool and/or other appropriate material. The fisherman uses a lightweight and flexible fly rod to cast the unweighted fly onto the water and — he hopes — deceive the fish into striking.

The idea of showing flies on stamps was hatched in 1986 when Ripper attended the first-day ceremony in Seattle, Washington, for the Fish booklet stamps, which he had designed. Ripper struck up a conversation with the principal speaker, Senior Assistant Postmaster General Mitchell H. Gordon. They found that fishing was a shared hobby, and agreed that sometime in the future another fishing-related stamp issue would be worth considering. "We had the Fish booklet there under our noses," Ripper recalled, "and I said, 'We could do something with the lures used to catch them.' "

That was as far as it went at the time, but the following year the artist put the proposal in writing. He included with his letter to USPS a copy of a *USA Today* article headlined "The Lure of Fly-Fishing," which described its subject as one of the fastest-growing sports in America, with a million participants and the allegiance of many celebrities, including former President Jimmy Carter.

Ripper also sent an actual Royal Coachman fly that he had tied himself. "I figured I was casting flies on empty water if there was nobody up there in Washington who knew what a fishing fly was," Ripper said.

The idea and presentation appealed to the Citizens' Stamp Advisory Committee, and Ripper was asked to recommend a list of flies to be shown. After some research he chose four that represented a variety of areas and types of fishing: the Royal Wulff, Muddler Minnow, Lefty's Deceiver and Jock Scott. Selecting four wasn't easy, Ripper told CSAC, inasmuch as there were 1,200 or more different patterns.

"I talked with two of the nation's leading experts, Lee Wulff and Bernard 'Lefty' Kreh, as well as the director of the American Museum of Fly Fishing, asking them to comment on my selections," Ripper wrote to the committee. "They said they had no problem with my choices and offered several alternate patterns should others be needed."

In late 1988, CSAC decided that the stamps should comprise another of the five-variety topical booklets that had appeared at least once a year since 1985. The committee specified that the fifth fly should be a saltwater specimen, and Ripper chose the Apte Tarpon Fly.

ROYAL WULFF. Lee Wulff, one of the outstanding innovators and popularizers in modern American fly fishing, developed this dry, or floating, fly in 1929 on New York's Ausable River. It has become one of the most popular flies for pursuing trout or salmon. A variation of an earlier fly called the Royal Coachman, this one used animal hair for wings, a practice that caught on under Wulff's influence.

Ironically, on April 28, less than five weeks before the Fishing Flies booklet was issued, Lee Wulff died at 86. He had gone aloft in his Piper Cub to get his pilot's license renewed and suffered a heart attack at the controls. The plane crashed into a hillside. "Wulff did for American fly-fishing what Ernest Hemingway did for American prose: He saved it from British conventions and mannerisms," Tom Mathews wrote in a *Newsweek* obituary. When Wulff was born, Mathews explained, "you could still find Currier-and-Ives anglers in coats and ties casting along banks shaded with hemlock and mountain laurel. At the beginning of the Depression, Wulff sewed deep pockets onto a vest, crammed them with gear and hit the rivers. He changed the way fly-fishermen fished, what they fished for, even the way they looked."

MUDDLER MINNOW. This wet fly, utilizing hair, is used to imitate

36

sculpin (bullhead) minnows as well as other creatures, including grass-hoppers, stoneflies and crayfish. It was created by Don Gapen of Minnesota in the late 1930s on the Nipigon River in Ontario, a stream renowned for its brook trout. The fly is now used throughout Canada and the United States for trout, grayling, bass and pike in fresh water and for snook, bonefish and channel bass in salt water. It has been called the "one fly to have if you're having only one" and "one of those few flies that almost everyone does have."

LEFTY'S DECEIVER. "Lefty" Kreh, a prominent flycaster, writer and instructor, developed the Deceiver around 1963 for casting for striped bass in the Chesapeake Bay. The fly is now used worldwide for all species of saltwater game fish. The fly is more of a style than a specific color pattern, in that it is tied in the same manner but the colors may be varied to match the baitfish where the fly is to be used.

JOCK SCOTT. Ripper chose this fly to honor the British origins of the sport. To the Citizens' Stamp Advisory Committee, he wrote: "This salmon fly, called 'the utmost triumph in harmony and proportion,' was created by John 'Jock' Scott, born at Branxholme, Roxburgshire, in February 1817. Fishing for salmon dates to the 1400s, and by 1658 many salmon fly patterns were developed, using colorful combinations of feathers from around the world. Any fly fisherman lucky enough to own one of these classic flies would have it framed to hang in his den and be content to use one of the modern-day hair wing flies on his favorite salmon rivers."

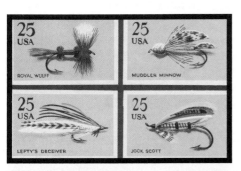

The Fishing Flies stamps originally were conceived as a block of four. Designer Chuck Ripper made these two sets of color sketches, one with plain green backgrounds, the other with the backgrounds of sepia waterscapes, which were used on the stamps as issued.

APTE TARPON FLY. Like the Deceiver, this popular salt-water fly is a style, tied in a number of different color combinations. It was developed in the late 1950s or early 1960s by Stu Apte, a saltwater fisherman and guide. "It's interesting that tarpon, which can weigh well over 100 pounds, are attracted to a four-inch fly," wrote Chuck Ripper. "One of the experts says it suggests a shrimp when brought back to the fisherman in short rapid strips."

The five flies were identified in the stamp designs, which meant that two living individuals — Stu Apte of Florida and "Lefty" Kreh of Maryland — were referred to

37

by name on U.S. postage stamps. The same would have been true of Lee Wulff, of course, if he had lived a few weeks longer. The last previous living person to have been named on a U.S. stamp was artist Thomas Hart Benton, who was identified as the painter of the picture used on the Missouri statehood commemorative of 1971 (Scott 1426).

Most previous U.S. topical-booklet stamps had been printed in the intaglio-offset combination process by the Bureau of Engraving and Printing, but the Fishing Flies were gravure-printed for the American Bank Note Company by Guilford Gravure of Guilford, Connecticut. Guilford Gravure used a printing cylinder layout unlike any that had been used before in U.S. booklet pane production. It incorporated 11 book stamp subjects around the printing cylinder and 25 subjects across the cylinder, for a total of 275 subjects.

The stamps were printed in five colors, the standard process yellow, magenta, cyan and black, plus orange. Thus, a five-digit number sequence preceded by the letter "A" in yellow appeared on each pane's binding stub. The Fishing Flies booklets were unique in U.S. booklet-stamp history in that they contained up to four different cylinder number sequences on the four panes within the same booklet. All previous U.S. folded-pane booklets with numbered panes had contained only a single number or sequence on its panes within a single booklet.

Of the 55 panes on each printed sheet, four had platable electric-eye color bars or blocks in the tabs. The sheets also had long color lines of orange and/or black along both outside columns of stamps, apparently for the purpose of guiding the cutting knives that separated the printed web into sheets of 275 stamps for further processing. If the knife cut too far to the right or the left, the line showed up on each of the adjacent panes, along its long edge.

Bruce Mosher, in a detailed article on the Fishing Flies booklets in the *The United States Specialist*, had this to say about collecting them:

"There appear to be hundreds of possible Fishing Flies booklet varieties issued through the USPS, when considering all the sequence numbers and cylinder position(s) combinations that could exist on the four different booklet panes within a booklet. Thus, we quickly realize that many decisions . . . are very dependent upon how deep one wants to dip into his/her stamp collecting funds."

Complaints were heard from collectors about misregistration of colors, poor centering of stamps, and the folding of some of the booklets in mid-stamp rather than along the perforations. Stamp writer Ken Lawrence reported in *The Philatelic Communicator* that order-fillers at Philatelic Sales Division headquarters in Kansas City had declined to fill a large order for Fishing Flies booklets from an unnamed Eastern dealer "because they knew their supplies didn't meet his quality requirements." Lawrence cited as further evidence of problems a notice in the June 27 *Postal Bulletin* that mentioned "production and distribution delays" on the Fishing Flies booklets.

As a collateral sales item, USPS offered collectors a 7- by 9-inch framed plaque containing a pane of the stamps and a print, in color, of an outdoor fly-fishing scene painted by Chuck Ripper. The cost was $20.

The Designs

Ripper submitted to CSAC two sets of color sketches for a se-tenant block of four stamps that differed only in the background. One set showed the flies against a plain pale-green backdrop; the other backed each one with a sepia view of the kind of fishing scene where the fly would be used — coastal waters with mangrove trees for the Apte tarpon, a rocky, swift-running stream for the Royal Wulff, and so on.

CSAC preferred the second treatment. Ripper made very few changes in the flies or backgrounds in his finished artwork, which he executed in the opaque watercolor called gouache. He used actual flies for models. Lefty Kreh sent the artist a Lefty's Deceiver and an Apte Tarpon Fly that Kreh had tied himself. Dan Bailey's fly shop in Montana sold him a Royal Wulff and a Muddler Minnow, and the American Museum of Fly Fishing in Manchester, Vermont, lent him a Jock Scott from its collection.

Ripper chose sepia for the background scenes because it matched the hues of old photographic prints contained in an album his father had owned. Black and white for the backgrounds would have been "kind of cold looking," Ripper said. Full-color scenic backgrounds would have clashed with the colors of the fishing flies. He painted a shadow beneath each fly, "to try to give the fly a three-dimensional look, as if you had just laid it down on the photograph," he explained.

Ripper also painted the picture that was used on the booklet cover, a square-shaped arrangement of four of the flies on the stamps (the Muddler Minnow was omitted). His original artwork had shown the four flies full-length, but to his disappointment two of the flies were partially cropped out on the finished booklet cover.

First-Day Facts

The booklet was dedicated May 31 at the Never Sink Valley Area Museum on Highway 209 in Cuddebackville, New York, in the heart of trout-fishing country. When rain began just before the scheduled ceremony, the platform, podium and guests were moved from the planned outdoor location to an indoor site about 300 yards away. The room was too small to accommodate all those present, however. Fortunately, the rain stopped before the move was completed, and the ceremony was held outdoors after all, although not on the original spot.

The stamps were dedicated by William T. Johnstone, assistant postmaster general. Speakers included Peter Fiduccia, host of the program "Woods 'n' Water," and Representative Benjamin A. Gilman, R-New York. Graham Skea, commissioner, Orange County Parks, Recreation and Conservation, gave the welcome.

29¢ COLE PORTER
PERFORMING ARTS SERIES

Date of Issue: June 8, 1991

Catalog Number: Scott 2550

Colors: yellow, magenta, cyan, black, gold

First-Day Cancel: Peru, Indiana

FDCs Canceled: 304,363

Format: Panes of 50, vertical, 10 across, 5 down. Gravure printing cylinders of 200 subjects (10 across, 20 around) manufactured by Armotek Industries Inc., Palmyra, New Jersey.

Perf: 10.9 (L perforator)

Selvage Markings: "Use Correct/ZIP Code/®/36 USC 380." "©/United States/ Postal Service/1991." USPS Olympic logo.

Selvage Inscription: "1991 is the centennial/of Cole Porter, famous/American musical comedy/composer and lyricist." "He created music for/many Broadway plays/and films. Among his/ best known songs were:" " 'Night and Day, Begin the/ Beguine, Let's Do It, What/is this thing Called Love/and Don't Fence Me In.' "

Designer: Jim Sharpe of Westport, Connecticut

Art Director and Project Manager: Jack Williams (USPS)

Typographer: Bradbury Thompson (CSAC)

Modeler: Richard Sennett, Sennett Enterprises, for American Bank Note Company

Printing: Stamps printed for American Bank Note Company on a leased Champlain gravure press at J.W. Fergusson and Sons, Richmond, Virginia, under the supervision of Sennett Enterprises, Fairfax, Virginia. Stamps perforated, processed and shipped by ABNC, Bedford Park, Illinois.

Quantity Ordered: 150,000,000

Quantity Distributed: 149,848,000

Cylinder Number Detail: 1 group of 5 gravure cylinder numbers preceded by the letter A alongside corner stamp

Tagging: overall

The Stamp

On June 8, USPS honored Cole Porter, one of the giants of the American musical theater, with a stamp in the Performing Arts series. It was issued in Peru, Indiana, Porter's birthplace, one day before the 100th anniversary of his birth. Plans for the stamp had been announced a year earlier, on what would have been the composer's 99th birthday.

The Performing Arts series was launched in 1978 with stamps honoring Jimmie Rodgers and George M. Cohan. Addition of the Porter stamp raised the number in the series to 12. The others had honored Will Rogers, W.C. Fields, the Barrymores (John, Ethel and Lionel), Douglas Fairbanks, John McCormack, Jerome Kern, Duke Ellington, Enrico Caruso and Arturo Toscanini.

The Porter stamp design was unveiled at the Columbia Club in Indianapolis May 18 after a concert of the composer's music at the nearby Circle Theater. Ann McK. Robinson, consumer advocate for USPS, spoke at the ceremony.

Cole Porter was an unusual member of that small group of composers who converted the American musical comedy from European-style operetta to a unique native art form, with jazz and blues-influenced tunes and sophisticated, vernacular lyrics. His peers — Kern, George Gershwin, Irving Berlin, Richard Rodgers, Arthur Schwartz — were born and/or reared in New York City, in most cases in modest circumstances. But Porter was born into a family of means in Middle America and graduated from Yale (where he wrote two of the school's most famous football anthems, *Bull Dog* and *Bingo*). Through his life he wore the outward appearance of a playboy, who traveled in high society, dressed for dinner and doted on exotic ports of call, yet no craftsman worked harder or to better effect when an opening night was drawing near.

Porter was one of only a handful of top songwriters who wrote both words and music, and he did each with equal skill. Author John Updike wrote of him: "He brought to the traditional and somewhat standardized tasks of songsmithing a great verbal ingenuity, a brave flexibility and resourcefulness, a cosmopolitan's wide expertise in many mundane matters including foreign lands and tongues, and a spirit that has always kept something of collegiate innocence about it." Among the musical plays and movies Porter supplied with songs were *Paris, The Gay Divorcee, Anything Goes, Kiss Me Kate, Can-Can* and *Silk Stockings*.

41

Among his some 400 published songs are *Just One of Those Things, I Get a Kick Out of You, In the Still of the Night, Begin the Beguine, I've Got You Under My Skin, It's De-Lovely, You'd Be So Nice to Come Home To, Night and Day, My Heart Belongs to Daddy* and *You're the Top.*

Robert Kimball, a compiler of show music, had this to say of Porter's life in later years: "Even after the riding accident that crushed both his legs...in 1937, Porter continued to write his amusing, exhilarating, often poignant songs. Despite more than 30 operations over the years, and constant pain for the rest of his life, his courage remained enormous, his spirit indomitable and his creative skill unimpaired. He finally lost the will to write, however, after the amputation of his right leg in 1958. He

In the list of representative Porter songs in the selvage inscription, **What Is This Thing Called Love?** *is randomly capitalized and lacks the question mark that is an integral part of the song title.*

died in Santa Monica, California, six years later." Porter was buried in his hometown of Peru. Although he had never lived there since childhood, he was always proud of his Hoosier background, and came back regularly for visits from his travels to the far corners of the world.

The biographical information on Porter contained in the stamp's selvage included the titles of five of Porter's representative songs. One of them was listed as "What is this thing Called Love" (sic), a reference which was marred by its haphazard capitalization and the absence of the essential question mark.

The Design

Like all its predecessors in the Performing Arts series, the Porter stamp was vertically arranged, gravure printed, and designed by Jim Sharpe of Westport, Connecticut. The Cole Porter design assignment almost went

42

This design by another artist was approved by the Citizens' Stamp Advisory Committee but vetoed by Postmaster General Frank.

to someone else, however.

At the outset, USPS commissioned Sharpe and another artist to prepare concept sketches. (The Postal Service declines to identify designer candidates whose work is submitted but not selected.) The Citizens' Stamp Advisory Committee, following the recommendation of its design subcommittee, gave its approval to one of Sharpe's concepts — the one that ultimately became the stamp design. However, at its next meeting, the subcommittee and the full CSAC unexpectedly reversed themselves and chose a design submitted by the second artist instead.

When the committee's new selection went to Postmaster General Frank for approval, he vetoed it, calling the portrait of a solemn-faced Porter "unsatisfactory in terms of facial expression and general appearance." By now time was growing short; the scheduled public unveiling

Jim Sharpe made these three pencil sketches in the process of working out a design for the Cole Porter commemorative.

of the design was only a few weeks away. Fortunately, the postmaster general solved the problem by giving his blessing to the Sharpe design that CSAC had originally selected.

Sharpe's portraits, whether painted for stamps or for the covers of magazines such as *Time* and *TV Guide*, have a distinctive look to them. They are clean, direct and economical of line. His old friend Stevan Dohanos, a long-time stamp designer, once reminded him that the Performing Arts personalities were in show business, and that should guide him in doing their portraits. "That's what I've always tried to remember, in the highest sense, and I try to give them a little flair, a little spontaneity," Sharpe said. He added, "I always try to compliment the person who is on the stamp. It's a big honor to be on a stamp, and if it was my relative being shown, I would want to be proud of the picture."

On CSAC's instructions, Sharpe showed Porter seated at a piano. He based the composer's face on a photograph he obtained from the Museum of the City of New York, changing the mouth slightly to give it the expression he wanted. He created the rest of the figure — jacket, arm and hand leaning casually on the piano top, polka-dot tie and pocket handkerchief — from his imagination to fit the space available.

Sharpe's previous Performing Arts designs had been executed in inks and acrylics, but he tried a new approach with this one. He painted it in oil on gold-colored clay-coated paper, but left an unpainted gold border and also allowed the gold to show through in spots, such as the tie and handkerchief. Although the painted areas were opaque, the portrait "picked up a kind of an overall tone" from the color of the paper beneath, Sharpe said. "I thought it would be interesting to try something new, as long as it worked," he added. "I felt pleased when I saw the stamp, because it didn't appear gaudy and overly done."

The fragment of sheet music that appears in the background was copied from a photostat of an original handwritten Porter manuscript that Sharpe selected at random from the collection of the Museum of the City of New York. Was it *Night and Day* or *Begin the Beguine* or one of the composer's other world-famous show songs? No: Sharpe by chance chose Porter's very first composition, a piano piece called *Song of the Birds*, which the composer wrote when he was 10 years old and dedicated to his mother, Kate Porter. Bearing such annotations as "mother's cooing," "the young ones learning to sing" and "one birdling falls from the nest," the unpublished song would be dismissed by the grown-up Porter years later as "an obnoxious item."

In copying a small piece of the score onto his painting, Sharpe misread the notation "MF" (for mezzo-forte) on the photocopy as a "VF," and that was how it appeared on the stamp. He also faithfully copied a small arrow or "V" at the top of the score, which the youthful composer had inserted to show where he had inadvertently omitted a measure. One reader of *The American Philatelist*, puzzled by these markings, noted in a letter to the magazine that they bore "no resemblance to any known musical notation" and wondered whether the "VF" was "a misguided philatelic joke? The world's first self-graded stamp?"

When the color separations were made from the original artwork, the printers electronically lightened the shadows that Sharpe had painted on Porter's fingers, making them more clearly visible, and darkened the blue of the composer's jacket to a solid color, eliminating its lapels and other details contained in Sharpe's painting.

Varieties

At least one pane of 50 Porter stamps with all horizontal perforations missing was found in California. The pane was reportedly discovered by a "casual collector" and purchased from the Richmond, California, post office. The error was possible because the stamps were processed on a line perforator, which perforates in one direction at a time. In August, dealer Dana Okey of San Diego advertised a vertical strip of three of the errors for sale for $695.

First-Day Facts

The June 8 first-day ceremony in the Peru High School auditorium received unusual word-and-picture coverage in *The New York Times*, which reported, among other things, that the name of the town where it was held is pronounced "PEA-roo," and that 950 Peruvians attended the event. Among the speakers was James O. Cole, first cousin once removed of the songwriter, who reminded listeners that Porter had Arnold's Fudge

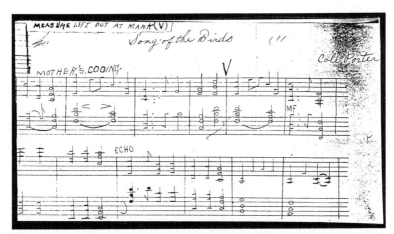

This is the opening section of the 10-year-old Cole Porter's piano composition Song of the Birds, from which artist Jim Sharpe took the musical notations for his stamp design. Sharpe copied parts of the last three measures of the top staff. Probably because of the faintness of the photocopy he was using, he mistakenly copied the letters "MF" (for mezzo-forte) as "VF." The stamp design also faithfully reproduces the V-shaped mark above the top horizontal line, which Porter had used to indicate where he had omitted a measure, as his hand-printed annotation tells us.

This strip of stamps came from a full pane that was imperforate horizontally.

shipped from Peru to wherever he was in the world. "Judging from the samples handed out at the end, it was worth the postage," *The Times* reporter opined.

The Peru High School Swing Choir did song-and-dance renditions of *Another Op'nin', Another Show, An Old-Fashioned Garden* and *Be a Clown,* along with two non-Porter songs, *America the Beautiful* and *Happy Birthday.* Senior Assistant Postmaster General William R. Cummings dedicated the stamp, and Thomas J. Beczkiewicz, executive producer of the Cole Porter Centennial, also spoke. The first-day program cover featured a colorized portrait of Porter at age 4½, prepared especially for USPS by Porter's relatives.

The next day, in New York, Postmaster General Anthony M. Frank opened the Porter centennial birthday concert at Carnegie Hall with a brief speech and presentation of framed Porter stamps to James Cole and to a second cousin of the songwriter, Margaret Cole Richards. Behind Frank was a 16-foot-wide video screen displaying the Porter stamp. Each person in the audience received a first-day cover in his souvenir program.

Lloyd A. DeVries, in his column First Days Today in *Stamp Collector,* pointed out a curious coincidence for collectors who prepared combination first-day covers using the Porter stamp and the 5¢ American Music commemorative (Scott 1252). The American Music stamp had been issued October 15, 1964, the day of Porter's death.

29¢ OPERATION DESERT STORM (SHEET STAMP)

Date of Issue: July 2, 1991

Catalog Number: Scott 2551

Colors: magenta, yellow, cyan, metallic bronze, blue, black, dark blue

First-Day Cancel: Washington, D.C.

FDCs Canceled: 860,455 (includes sheet and booklet)

Format: Panes of 50, vertical, 10 across, 5 down. Gravure printing cylinders of 200 subjects (10 across, 20 around) manufactured by Armotek Industries Inc., Palmyra, New Jersey.

Perf: 10.9 (L perforator)

Selvage Inscription: "This stamp salutes the/members of the U.S./Armed Forces who served/in Operations Desert/Shield & Desert Storm." "The design depicts the/Southwest Asia Service/Medal, established by/Presidential Executive/order in March 1991."

Selvage Markings: "© United States Postal Service 1991." "Use Correct ZIP Code ® 36 USC 380." USPS Olympic Rings logo.

Designer, Art Director and Project Manager: Jack Williams (USPS)

Typographer: John Boyd of Anagraphics Inc., New York, New York

Printing: Stamps printed by Stamp Venturers on a Champlain gravure press at J.W. Fergusson and Sons, Richmond, Virginia. Stamps perforated, processed and shipped by KCS Industries Inc., Milwaukee, Wisconsin.

Quantity Ordered: 180,000,000

Quantity Distributed: 200,003,000

Cylinder Number Detail: 1 group of 7 cylinder numbers preceded by the letter S alongside corner stamp

Tagging: phosphor-coated paper

The Stamp

Operation Desert Storm, the U.S.-led United Nations military operation to drive Iraqi invaders out of Kuwait, was one of the shortest and most decisive wars in American history. The allied coalition seized air supremacy soon after fighting began January 16, 1991, and from then until February 23, round-the-clock air strikes on Iraqi forces in and near Kuwait and on strategic targets deep inside Iraq dealt devastating blows to the enemy's ability to fight. The ground war that followed lasted only 100 hours and ended with Kuwait liberated and the remnants of Iraq's army in full retreat.

The Desert Storm Commemorative Panel identified the wrong printing contractor for the Desert Storm stamps included. The erroneous attribution is shown blown up and inset on the panel.

48

Not long after President George Bush halted offensive operations at midnight February 27, reports began circulating that a commemorative stamp would be issued to honor the U.S. servicemen and servicewomen who had taken part in Operation Desert Storm and the buildup of forces in the area that preceded it, Operation Desert Shield.

On April 12, USPS spokesman Art Shealy told Mark A. Kellner of *Stamp Collector* that a stamp was "definitely under development." And Postmaster General Anthony M. Frank, in a conversation with Kellner April 30, said he hoped the design for the stamp would be unveiled "in some public ceremony during June."

Even before the fighting ended, Frank had told top officials of the Philatelic and Retail Services Department that he would probably order the development of a Desert Storm stamp. As soon as the Iraqis surrendered, he gave the directive, saying in effect, as one official put it, "Let's see if we can set a speed record for getting this produced."

On June 4 USPS confirmed that the design would be unveiled on June 7 — the day before the National Victory Celebration parade in Washington — and that the stamp would be released "sometime in July." The design was leaked to the newspaper *USA Today*, which published it first, and the following day USPS formally released details of the design and the information that the stamp would be issued July 2 in two forms: panes of 50 and booklets of 20.

The sheet version was contracted to Stamp Venturers and printed on the gravure press of J.W. Fergusson and Sons of Richmond, Virginia. The booklet version was printed by the Multi-Color Corporation for another private firm, the American Bank Note Company.

The fact that there were two contractors confused even USPS. Along with the stamp, the Postal Service marketed what it called an American Commemorative Print — actually, part of the American Commemorative Panel series — that included a block of four Desert Storm stamps from the sheet version. However, a small line at the bottom of the panel read: "Stamps printed by the American Bank Note Company." "It's

These stamps commemorating Operation Desert Storm were issued by Palau ($2.90 Priority Mail stamp) and the Marshall Islands (29¢ stamp).

49

Stevan Dohanos and Jack Williams had improvised the design for the 1979 Vietnam Veterans' stamp (Scott 1802) during a quick meeting in Connecticut.

purely a mistake," USPS spokesman Shealy told *Linn's Stamp News*, which had questioned him about the error.

The commemorative panels were normally available only by subscription from the USPS Philatelic Sales Division at $4.95 each. This one, however, was offered to non-subscribers at a price of $9.95, plus 50¢ handling per order. The offer was carried on the back cover of the booklet version of the stamp, and in the division's *Philatelic Catalog* for July-August 1991, where the item was described as "a one-time, limited edition art print perfect for framing."

The offer was made "due to overwhelming interest," USPS said in its press release (although, as Gary Griffith of *Linn's* pointedly noted, the booklet covers carrying the offer were printed before the general public even knew for certain that a Desert Storm stamp would be issued). A total of 22,000 panels were ordered, compared to the normal press run of 12,000 for the American Commemorative Panel series.

The Desert Storm stamp represented by far the quickest postal tribute ever afforded veterans of a U.S. war. Veterans of World War II were honored the year after their conflict ended with the Honorable Discharge Emblem ("Ruptured Duck") stamp (Scott 940). Vietnam veterans waited four years, until 1979, for their stamp (Scott 1802). And the troops of Korea and World War I had to mark time 32 and 67 years, respectively, for the 1985 stamps that commemorated their service (Scott 2152, 2154).

Operations Desert Shield and Desert Storm were served by the largest concentrated postal operation in the history of USPS and the armed

One artist proposed the ever-popular American flag image for a Desert Storm stamp. Jack Williams later tried a modification of the design, adding the Desert Storm service ribbon.

forces. During the conflict, postal employees collected, sorted and processed up to 600,000 pounds of mail each day for delivery to the more than 500,000 U.S. military men and women serving in the Gulf. By the end of the war, nearly 60 million pounds of mail from home had been delivered. Outgoing letters and audio cassettes from service personnel traveled postage-free. A total of 214 new Army (APO) and fleet post office (FPO) numbers were assigned, in addition to 11 that had previously existed in the area. Many ships with their own post offices also served in the Gulf.

Among other countries postally celebrating the Gulf War victory were Palau, which issued a sheetlet of nine stamps, a $2.90 Priority Mail stamp and a souvenir sheet containing that stamp; the Marshall Islands, which produced a 29¢ commemorative, and, naturally, Kuwait.

The Design

Design credit for the Desert Storm stamp went to a veteran USPS staff member who had helped plan literally hundreds of stamps but had never

designed one himself. He was Jack Williams, 63, of Baileys Crossroads, Virginia, a program manager in the Office of Stamp Development and a former Army lieutenant colonel.

When the word came down that a Desert Storm stamp would be issued, Williams remembered taking part in a hurry-up project 12 years earlier in which he and Stevan Dohanos, a CSAC design coordinator, put together the stamp for Vietnam veterans, using Williams' own Vietnam service ribbon as the centerpiece. A similar approach, using the newly minted decoration for Operation Desert Shield and Desert Storm, might meet the needs of this project too, Williams thought.

He went to the Army's Institute of Heraldry in Cameron Station, Alexandria, Virginia, where medals are designed, and picked up a copy of the new medal, along with a color photograph of it and a letter granting permission to reproduce the decoration on a stamp. Then, on April 8, he sat down and made some rough sketches, trying out various wordings and arrangements of design elements.

This is the obverse and reverse of the Southwest Asia Service medal, issued to those who served in the Persian Gulf conflict.

John Boyd of Anagraphics Inc. in New York phototoset the type and translated Williams' sketches into more formal artwork. Several different background colors were tried, including a dark charcoal and dark blue, before it was decided that the light blue showed the medal to best advantage.

Meanwhile, USPS had invited another artist to

51

submit sketches incorporating yellow ribbons, the symbols of remembrance of the troops overseas that had decorated the country coast to coast during the war. And Richard Sheaff of Needham, Massachusetts, a CSAC design coordinator, tried an altogether different design approach, creating two designs that combined the image of the Desert Storm medal with scenes of flag-bedecked streets in New York City. The pictures Sheaff used weren't contemporary, however; they were reproductions of 1917 paintings by the American impressionist Childe Hassam showing patriotic demonstrations in World War I.

In the end, Postmaster General Frank took the medal design conceived by Williams, a yellow-ribbon design and one of the designs incorporating a Hassam painting to the White House, where President Bush pronounced the first one his choice.

The side of the medal shown on the stamp was the obverse, a somewhat cluttered design that incorporated the words "Southwest Asia Service" and images of tanks, helicopters, jet aircraft and a warship. Much of this detail was lost in the process of reducing, screening and reproducing the image in metallic bronze ink on the stamp. An option that USPS

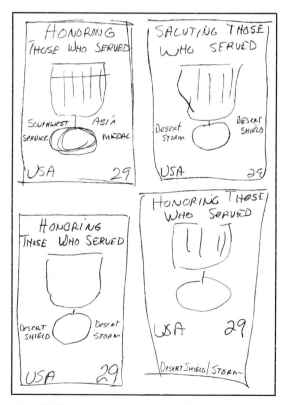

Jack Williams made these pencil sketches as he developed his idea to use the Desert Storm service medal as the stamp's design subject.

These two concept sketches incorporated yellow ribbons, the universal home-front symbol of the Persian Gulf war.

considered but turned down was to show the medal's reverse side, which bore a simpler image of a sword and olive branch.

At a press conference in San Jose, California, July 10, Postmaster General Frank said that neither he nor President Bush knew the official Gulf War global address until they met to decide on the stamp design.

"I was a little bit bemused to see 'Southwest Asia' on the stamp," Frank said, according to the Associated Press. "I'd never connected it with Iraq.

"(President Bush) said, 'Why does it say "Southwest Asia"?' I said, 'I think I missed that day in geography.'"

Jack Williams' earlier design experience with the Vietnam Veterans stamp (Scott 1802) is worth recording. "Bill Bolger was postmaster general at that time," Williams recalled. "He had told us that he wanted to do something to honor Vietnam veterans, because they had never been honored. Of course, at that time neither had World War I or Korean veterans, but the Vietnam issue was important to him, and he told us to

Richard Sheaff combined the Desert Storm service medal with two Childe Hassam paintings of World War I parades in New York City in a somewhat anachronistic design concept.

Jack Williams also tried out this horizontal design treatment, borrowing a U.S. flag image from the Olympic Rings definitive booklet stamp issued earlier in the year.

start thinking about it.

"We did think about it. We looked at concepts and kicked it around, but we always ran into the same thing: If you single out any one service or any one piece of military hardware, it just doesn't work. Then we got a call from Mr. Bolger's office, saying that the White House had called, and President Carter wanted to unveil the design of a stamp during Vietnam Veterans' Week, which was three weeks away.

"So Don McDowell (then general manager of the Stamps Division) and I were talking about it, and I finally remembered my service ribbon. I had to go home and dig it out; it was buried in among a lot of old mementos. I called Steve Dohanos and hopped on a plane and went up to Westport, Connecticut, to his studio. Steve had found a piece of khaki-colored burlap for background, and he found a strip of red, white and blue bunting and laid it across one corner of the burlap as a patriotic touch, and then he took my ribbon and quickly painted a replica of it on a piece of cardboard and raised it up so it was three-dimensional; it cast a little shadow. Then he took some grocery-store lettering — white letters, like you see in a supermarket — and put wording on the thing, including the date it would be issued, 'Nov. 11, 1979,' Veterans' Day, and then I brought the whole thing back here, carrying it on my lap on the airplane.

"We took it to the Bureau and had it modeled. There weren't any changes made in it. And we took it up to Mr. Bolger, and he liked it, and

This proposed design, similar to the one used on the stamp, featured the reverse of the medal and placed the entire decoration against a white background.

54

President George Bush and Postmaster General Anthony Frank are shown at the dedication ceremony for the Desert Storm stamp at the White House July 2.

took it to the White House, and they liked it, and it was unveiled and issued on schedule. So this stamp (Desert Storm) was an easy one, for me, remembering that one."

First-Day Facts

The first-day ceremony for the stamp was a closed event at the White House. Nevertheless, USPS produced a program for the ceremony and sent it to subscribers to the first-day program subscription service. The program was small in size, bore a color photograph of an American flag fluttering against a deep blue sky on the cover, and listed only two participants: President Bush, the speaker, and Postmaster General Frank, to dedicate the stamps.

$5.80 OPERATION DESERT STORM BOOKLET

Date of Issue: July 2, 1991

Catalog Number: Scott 2552 (single stamp); Scott 2552a (booklet pane of 5)

Colors: light blue, tan, dark blue, red, green, metallic bronze, black, medium blue

First-Day Cancel: Washington, D.C.

FDCs Canceled: 860,455 (includes sheet and booklet)

Format: Four panes of 5 vertical stamps arranged horizontally in a row of 5. Gravure printing cylinders of 275 subjects (11 across, 25 around).

Perf: 10.9 (L perforator)

Selvage Markings: cylinder numbers printed on each pane binding stub

Cover Markings: "© United States Postal Service 1991" on inside of front cover. Universal Product Code (UPC) and advertisement for Desert Shield/Desert Storm art print on outside of back cover. Coupon for art print on inside of back cover. Position guidemarks at left or right edge of inside of front cover on 18.2 percent of all booklets.

Designer, Art Director and Project Manager: Jack Williams (USPS)

Typographer: John Boyd of Anagraphics Inc., New York, New York

Printing: Printed by Multi-Color Corporation, Scottsburg, Indiana, for American Bank Note Company on a Schiavi 10-color webfed gravure press. Perforated and formed into booklets at ABNC, Bedford Park, Illinois.

Quantity Ordered: 200,000,000 (10,000,000 booklets)

Quantity Distributed: 200,000,000 (10,000,000 booklets)	
Cylinder Number Detail: 1 group of 8 cylinder numbers preceded by the letter A on each pane binding stub	
Tagging: phosphor-coated paper	

The Stamp

The Desert Storm stamp was the first regular-mail commemorative stamp to appear in both sheets and booklets, although as far back as 1928 a commemorative airmail — the Lindbergh (Scott C10) — had been issued in those two formats.

Multi-Color Corporation in Scottsburg, Indiana, printed the Desert Storm booklet for the contractor, the American Bank Note Company. The sheet version was printed by J.W. Fergusson for Stamp Venturers.

The design was the same in both cases, but some differences were readily apparent. Although USPS reported that both companies had used the same seven colors, Multi-Color actually used eight on the booklet stamps. The extra color was a green and was used on the ribbon of the medal. Fergusson, with the sheet stamps, had created its green out of process colors by printing cyan over yellow.

On the booklet stamp, the details shown on the medal — lettering and images — were much clearer than they were on the sheet stamp. The booklet stamp had thinner vertical bars on the ribbon, but its lettering was a trifle heavier. And, of course, the booklet stamp had straight edges at top and bottom (and, for the end stamp on the pane, at the right side as well).

Shortly after the booklet was released, a Virginia collector found a used copy of the booklet stamp without the red vertical lines normally found on the ribbon. *Linn's Stamp News* reported that no traces of red color dots could be found under magnification, and that there was no evidence of tampering.

For first-day covers of the booklet stamps that were fully serviced by USPS, only full panes were affixed at a cost of $1.45 per pane.

The used copy of the Desert Storm stamp (far left) has a color-omitted error. The vertical red stripes in the service ribbon are missing. A normal copy is shown at left.

57

29¢ OLYMPIC TRACK AND FIELD (STRIP OF FIVE)

Date of Issue: July 12, 1991

Catalog Numbers: Scott 2553-2557 (stamps); Scott 2557a (strip of five)

Colors: magenta, yellow, cyan, black, green

First-Day Cancel: Los Angeles, California

FDCs Canceled: 886,984

Format: Panes of 40, horizontal, 5 across, 8 down. Gravure printing cylinders of 160 (10 across, 16 around) manufactured by Armotek Industries Inc., Palmyra, New Jersey.

Perf: 10.9 (L perforator)

Selvage Markings: "Use Correct ZIP Code ® 36 USC 380." "© United States Postal Service 1991." USPS Olympic logo.

Designer and Typographer: Joni Carter of Los Angeles, California

Art Director and Project Manager: Joe Brockert (USPS)

Modeler: Richard Sennett (Sennett Enterprises)

Printing: Stamps printed for American Bank Note Company on a leased Champlain gravure press at J.W. Fergusson and Sons, Richmond, Virginia, under the supervision of Sennett Enterprises, Fairfax, Virginia. Stamps perforated, processed and shipped by ABNC, Bedford Park, Illinois.

Quantity Ordered: 171,000,000

Quantity Distributed: 170,025,600

Cylinder Number Detail: 1 group of 5 gravure cylinder numbers preceded by the letter A alongside corner stamp

Tagging: overall

The Stamps

On July 12, at the Olympic Festival in Los Angeles, California, USPS issued its second set of five stamps celebrating its sponsorship of the 1992 Olympic Games. The stamps were issued in a se-tenant pane of 40 consisting of eight horizontal rows of five different stamps each, with each vertical row containing identical stamps.

This configuration was chosen to match one that had been improvised the year before when the first Olympics set of five stamps, honoring past U.S. Olympic gold medalists, was issued.

USPS had originally announced that the five Olympic medalists stamps of 1990 would be issued in booklet form. Then postal officials were informed by the Bureau of Engraving and Printing that BEP couldn't schedule production of the booklet on the short notice it had been given. The Postal Service quickly changed plans.

It converted the format from booklet to sheet, and reassigned the printing job to the American Bank Note Company, which had a standing contract with USPS to produce commemorative stamps in sheets. To get five varieties onto a pane, USPS adopted the arrangement by which all five were lined up side by side on each horizontal strip of stamps.

All concerned were pleased with the result. And because the USPS Office of Olympic Marketing wanted a consistent format for the various stamp sets that were yet to come to publicize the 1992 Summer and Winter Games, the decision was made to issue these sets, too, in panes containing five-variety strips. The second such set, featuring Olympic track and field events, was unveiled by Postmaster General Anthony M. Frank May 14 at the National Postal Forum in Chicago, Illinois, and was issued July 12 in Los Angeles.

Like the 1990 series, the new stamps were produced by the American Bank Note Company and were of the size USPS calls semi-jumbo. There was only one significant difference in layout. The 1990 stamps had been issued in panes of 35 (seven horizontal rows of five) to leave room for wide margins at the top or bottom of each pane containing biographical information on the athletes who were honored. The 1991 Track and Field set focused on events rather than individuals, however, and selvage notes (and wide margins) weren't deemed necessary this time.

The five events depicted were the pole vault, the javelin throw, a sprint race, a hurdle race and the discus throw. The Office of Olympic Marketing had specifically requested the first four events, and offered the option of either the discus or shot put for the fifth stamp. Each of these events had been depicted at least once, and some several times, on U.S. Olympic Games commemoratives dating back to 1932.

The athletes shown in the designs were to be generic and not to be associated with any individual or team. Olympic Marketing left it to the Citizens' Stamp Advisory Committee and the artist to decide which stamps would show male athletes and which would show females. It asked only for a reasonable male-female balance, as well as a reasonable racial balance, over the entire Olympics series.

USPS used full-color, full-page advertisements in major magazines, including *Time* and *Newsweek*, to promote the sale of full panes of the Olympic Track and Field stamps. Describing U.S. Olympians as "first-class heroes," the ad copy invited readers to "share in their glory" by buying stamps "that capture all the color and drama of competition." For $13.10, a purchaser got a pane of stamps (face value $11.60), plus a transparent protective sleeve that USPS called a "commemorative saver page." The price also included a 50¢ service charge.

USPS also offered for sale a number of merchandise items related to the Track and Field stamps. One was a matted "U.S. Olympic Festival stamp print," created by Joni Carter, the designer of the stamps. It incorporated a variation of the discus thrower design against a backdrop of the American flag, the Olympic torch and the Los Angeles skyline, and contained a strip of five stamps affixed within a die-cut section of the mat. The item sold for $20. Another was a set of five "collectors' cards," each featuring an enlarged reproduction of one of the stamp designs surrounded by a graphic border. On the reverse was information about the stamp's production, a screened image of a Los Angeles postmark and an area for affixing the appropriate stamp. The cards sold for $2.50 per set.

The Postal Service used this full-page magazine advertisement to promote its Olympic Track and Field stamps. For $13.10, a buyer could get a pane of the stamps and a "commemorative saver page."

60

Artist Joni Carter is shown here with the computer equipment she used to design the Olympic Track and Field commemorative stamps.

The Designs

The five stamps were the first U.S. stamps to be designed entirely on a personal computer. Their creator was Joni Carter, a Los Angeles artist, whose live-action computer sports paintings had been seen by millions of viewers of televised Super Bowls, baseball playoffs, the U.S. Tennis Open, the Kentucky Derby, the Indianapolis 500, and the 1984 and 1988 Olympic Games.

"We discovered that she was very much respected in her field," said Joe Brockert, the project manager and art director. "For this issue, we were looking for something a little different, a bit flashier, something with a lot of color and appeal, and her artwork tended to be very bright and colorful. So we decided to see if that would translate into stamps."

This sketch of a male sprinter charging out of the blocks was considered too close in appearance to the Jesse Owens stamp of 1990, which showed the sprinter crouched at the starting line.

61

This sketch of the javelin thrower is close to the final design. The dropped shadows on the Olympic Rings were eliminated, stripes were added to the athlete's jersey and the color streaking in the background was altered.

Carter electronically painted on her computer screen, setting her human figures against backgrounds brightly splashed and streaked with color. Writer Jim Strothman described her equipment and methodology this way in *Computer Pictures* magazine:

"Carter's multimedia studio includes two IBM PS/2s, one a Model 80 with IBM's M-Motion Video Adapter/A and Audio Visual Connection. She uses Time Arts' Lumena painting software, Truevision Targa+Micro Channel board, Wacom tablet with pressure-sensitive pen, Panasonic Color Video Printer and Kodak XL7700 Digital Thermal Printer.

"Carter programmed videos and photos from past Olympics into the M-Motion system, where she could freeze frames. These, in effect, became her 'models.' Using the other PS/2, Lumena and Wacom tablet, she sketched her own version of the sport, painted it, made video prints and sent them off to the Citizens' Stamp Advisory Committee."

These prints were low-resolution prints, in contrast to the high-resolution art that the computer system would produce for the finished versions. Because of the speed and versatility of the computer, Carter was able to provide dozens of sketches, showing many different background colors and textures and a variety of details in the figures. She also was able to make changes swiftly: major ones, such as converting her sprinters and hurdlers from men to women at the committee's request; minor changes,

In these preliminary concept sketches, the hurdlers and sprinter were male. Their gender was changed to give the Olympics stamp set better balance between the sexes.

62

On this sketch, Joni Carter mistakenly drew the nearest hurdler with right arm and right leg extended — the wrong way to clear a hurdle.

such as adding stripes to athletes' jerseys and removing a wristwatch from one hurdler's wrist because Brockert and others assured her that the accessory would disappear when the design was reduced to stamp size.

After changing the hurdlers' sex, she discovered that she had mistakenly drawn one of the competitors with right arm and right leg extended forward at the same time, a major breach of hurdling form. The required correction was easily made.

"It was sort of a happy coincidence," said Joe Brockert, "that by the time we were nearing the final selection of background colors, we saw that we had an opportunity to pick up on the five colors of the Olympic rings — blue, yellow, black, green and red. That wasn't the original intention of the design project, but we came to define it that way.

"Otherwise, the color selection for background would have been very arbitrary, and we could have spent months trying to decide what color looked better with any given image. The pole vault, for example, was much more purple originally, and we simply converted that more toward the blue end. The sprint background was originally a maroon color, and we converted that to black, because that was one of the variations Joni had shown us originally. We simply selected alternatives that needed just a little 'push' to get them to the Olympic colors."

First-Day Facts

John Krimsky Jr., deputy secretary general of the U.S. Olympic Committee, was the main speaker at the first-day ceremony at Drake Stadium on the campus of the University of California at Los Angeles. Other speakers were past Olympians Al Oerter, Greg Steward and Bob Seagren. The welcome was extended by Charles E. Young, chancellor of UCLA. The stamps were dedicated by Kenneth J. Hunter, associate postmaster general.

USPS provided a pictorial first-day handstamp showing a hurdle and the five Olympic rings. In servicing collectors' first-day covers by mail, USPS affixed either a strip of five or a single stamp chosen at random. Requests for specific singles were declined.

29¢ NUMISMATICS

Date of Issue: August 13, 1991

Catalog Number: Scott 2558

Colors: yellow (PMS 110), yellow (PMS 116), cyan, gold (PMS 872), green (PMS 554), brown (PMS 469) (offset); green (intaglio)

First-Day Cancel: Chicago, Illinois

FDCs Canceled: 288,519

Format: Panes of 50, vertical, 10 across, 5 down. Offset printing plates of 200 subjects (10 across, 20 around); intaglio printing sleeves of 400 subjects (10 across, 40 around).

Perf: 11.2 (Eureka off-line perforator)

Selvage Markings: "© United States Postal Service 1990 36 USC 380." "Use Correct ZIP Code ®." USPS Olympic Rings logo.

Designer and Typographer: V. Jack Ruther (BEP)

Art Director: Leonard Buckley (BEP)

Project Manager: Jack Williams (USPS)

Engravers: Thomas Hipschen (BEP, vignette); Richard Everett (BEP, lettering and numerals)

Modeler: Peter Cocci (BEP)

Printing: printed by BEP on 6-color offset, 3-color intaglio D press (902)

Quantity Ordered: 152,000,000

Quantity Distributed: 150,310,000

Plate/Sleeve Number Detail: 1 intaglio sleeve number alongside corner stamp; 1 group of 6 offset plate numbers in selvage of adjacent stamp.

Tagging: overall

The Stamp

More than 14 years after a postmaster general first approved a design for it, USPS issued a stamp honoring the hobby of numismatics — coin and currency collecting. The stamp was dedicated August 13, 1991, in Rosemont, Illinois, a Chicago suburb, at the opening of the centennial convention of the American Numismatic Association.

Back in 1977, after the Citizens' Stamp Advisory Committee had given the go-ahead, Bureau of Engraving and Printing artist V. Jack Ruther began work on a numismatic stamp design. Postmaster General Benjamin Bailar OK'd Ruther's artwork August 3. Models were made in the 13¢ denomination and, after the 1978 rate change, in the 15¢ denomination, and a 15¢ die proof was approved in April 1979.

"Shortly after the die proof was made, the Postal Service decided not to include the commemorative in its 1980 program," recalled Leonard Buckley, foreman of designers at BEP. "It sort of languished until 1990, when the Postal Service wanted to look at it again."

CSAC approved the stamp for the 1991 program, and a revised and updated design was unveiled August 22, 1990, by Donald M. McDowell, director of the USPS Office of Stamp and Philatelic Marketing. The place was the Seattle, Washington, convention of the American Numismatic Association, whose executive director, Robert J. Leuver, was a past director of the Bureau of Engraving and Printing and was well known to USPS officials and members of CSAC, on which he had served. The Numismatics stamp was the first of the many stamps of 1991 to have its design made public.

The ANA had held its first convention in Chicago in 1891. Even though the centennial convention was held in Rosemont, which was part of the Des Plaines, Illinois, Post Office delivery area, the first-day postmark read "Chicago, IL 60607." This was done in recognition of the first convention site, USPS explained.

The Design

In 1975 the BEP's V. Jack Ruther had designed a pair of stamps honoring Banking and Commerce that had depicted a group of four classic U.S. coins. When he undertook a Numismatics design two years later, he followed a similar tack.

From the Smithsonian Institution, Ruther borrowed two more coins prized by collectors: a 1907 gold Double Eagle and an 1857 1¢ Flying Eagle. From BEP's vaults, he obtained two pieces of paper money, a $10

Designer V. Jack Ruther had used a similar money theme in the design of the Banking and Commerce stamps of 1975 (Scott 1577-1578).

65

National Currency, Series 1902, bill from the Third Charter Period and a $1 United States Note, Series 1875. These were laid together in an aesthetically attractive arrangement and photographed. BEP engraver Thomas Hipschen then engraved the four items onto a stamp die.

When the design was brought out and reviewed by CSAC some 13 years later, the committee's art subcommittee asked that a new, flat background be provided for the coins and currency. To create the new stamp, modeler Peter Cocci scanned a proof of Hipschen's original engraving into the Bureau's Electronic Design Center, and the offset color separations were made electronically. The two coins and the background weren't engraved again, but were reproduced this time by offset. The two pieces of currency, however, were re-engraved by Hipschen. In the redesign process, the word "Numismatics" was moved from the top, where it had been dropped out of the background, to the bottom of the stamp.

One of the offset colors BEP used was a metallic gold. "We didn't want to overdo it, but we wanted to give a little glitter to the $20 gold piece," said Leonard Buckley. "There was a very slight tone of color, one of the yellow colors, that was put under the currency note itself, to give it an old-paper look."

The original (1978) version of the stamp, if it had been issued, would have been printed in two stages, using BEP's sheetfed I-8 intaglio press and offset press. Now, however, the stamp could be produced in one operation on BEP's webfed D press.

Its design featured portions of the obverse, or "heads," sides of the two coins and the reverse sides of the two notes. (USPS, in two separate news releases on the stamp, mistakenly described the obverse as the "back" side of a coin. The back, or "tails," side is known to numismatists as the reverse.)

The 1907 Double Eagle, or $20 gold piece, was designed by sculptor Augustus Saint-Gaudens at the request of President Theodore Roosevelt. Its obverse, pictured on the stamp, showed a walking figure of Liberty; the reverse, not shown, bore an eagle in flight. A total of 11,250, with

These are models of the never-issued Numismatics stamp made in 1977 and 1979, when the first-class rates were 13¢ and 15¢. The coins were engraved in making the dies for these versions, but were reproduced by offset on the version that was finally issued, in 1991.

Roman numerals (MCMVII), were struck in high relief for general circulation and are especially valued by collectors. Later 1907 coins, and the coins of subsequent years through 1932, bore the dates in Arabic numerals. The portion of the coin shown on the stamp doesn't contain the date.

The Flying Eagle cents were copper-nickel or "white" cents and showed on the reverse a wreath of corn, wheat, cotton and tobacco. Authorized by Congress in 1857, they were the first of the present-day small-sized cents. A total of 24.6 million 1858s were made and are relatively inexpensive today except in proof condition.

United States Notes of the design of the Series of 1875 were current for many years, being replaced in 1923. The obverse bore a portrait of George Washington and a view of Christopher Columbus in sight of land. The reverse included a small interlocking "U" and "S"; this is the design element shown on the stamp.

The National Currency bank notes were issued from 1863 to 1929 by many thousands of banks in the United States and territories, in many denominations and in three charter periods. They form the most plentiful and extensive series of American paper money. The $10 Series 1902 bore a portrait of the recently assassinated President William McKinley on the front and, on the reverse, an allegorical female figure, which is partly shown in the stamp design along with the words "National Currency."

The 10¢ Banking and Commerce stamps that Ruther had designed earlier (Scott 1577-1578) had depicted an Indian Head Penny, a Morgan-type Silver Dollar, a Seated Liberty Quarter and a Gold Double Eagle. The Indian Head Penny had also been featured on a miniature stamp of 1978 (Scott 1734). Augustus Saint-Gaudens, designer of the 1907 Double Eagle, was portrayed on a 3¢ Famous Americans stamp of 1940 (Scott 886).

First-Day Facts

Donald McDowell dedicated the stamp at the ANA convention opening ceremonies in the Rosemont/O'Hare Exposition Center in Rosemont, Illinois. McDowell replaced the official listed for this honor, Assistant Postmaster General Gordon C. Morison. Principal speakers were Catalina V. Villalpando, treasurer of the United States, and Edward Rochette, president-elect of the ANA. Kenneth L. Hallenbeck, the organization's president, gave the welcome.

Collectors submitting orders by mail for first-day postmarks were instructed to address them to the Des Plaines, Illinois, Post Office.

29¢ BASKETBALL CENTENNIAL

Date of Issue: August 28, 1991

Catalog Number: Scott 2560

Colors: magenta, cyan, yellow, black

First-Day Cancel: Springfield, Massachusetts

FDCs Canceled: 295,471

Format: Panes of 50, vertical, 10 across, 5 down. Gravure printing cylinders of 200 subjects (10 across, 20 around).

Perf: 11.2 (Eureka off-line perforator)

Selvage Markings: "©/United States/Postal Service/1991/36 USC 380." "Use Correct/ZIP Code/®." USPS Olympic logo.

Designer: Lon Busch of Ellisville, Missouri

Art Director and Typographer: Richard Sheaff (CSAC)

Project Manager: Jack Williams (USPS)

Printing: printed by BEP on 7-color Andreotti gravure press (601)

Quantity Ordered: 150,000,000

Quantity Distributed: 149,810,000

Cylinder Number Information: 1 group of 4 gravure cylinder numbers alongside corner stamp

Tagging: overall

The Stamp

On August 28, USPS issued a stamp commemorating the 100th anniversary of the invention of the game of basketball, the only major sport strictly of U.S. origin. The place of issue was Springfield, Massachusetts, where James Naismith created the game in 1891 and where the Basketball Hall of Fame is located.

Earlier, on January 6, 1991, Postmaster General Anthony M. Frank had unveiled the stamp's design in Springfield's Civic Center. The occasion was the Centennial Classic basketball game between the University of Notre Dame and the touring Soviet National Team. Joining Frank at the unveiling ceremony before the game was Joseph O'Brien, executive director of the Basketball Hall of Fame, and Richard "Digger" Phelps, a member of the Citizens' Stamp Advisory Committee and Notre Dame's head basketball coach (a post he would resign later in the year).

The stamp came about after O'Brien reminded Phelps in 1989 of the upcoming centennial and asked for his help in obtaining postal commemoration for it. Phelps, who was chairman of CSAC's sports subcommittee, persuaded his fellow committee members of the merits of the proposal. One talking point was the fact that several other countries planned to issue stamps to mark the anniversary of this international game that was invented in the United States.

Nearly 30 years before, the U.S. Post Office Department had issued its first stamp with a basketball theme. That one (Scott 1189) had marked the 100th anniversary of James Naismith's birth, and was inscribed: "Naismith 1861-1961." And in 1983, women's basketball was the subject of one of the 12 airmail stamps (Scott C103) issued as a prelude to the Summer Olympic Games in Los Angeles the following year.

Other sports had also been honored on their centennials with U.S. stamps. Baseball was the subject of a 3¢ commemorative in 1939 (Scott 855), issued for the 100th anniversary of its alleged invention in Cooperstown, New York. The birth of professional baseball in 1869 — a more reliably documented event — was marked by a 6¢ stamp in 1969 (Scott 1381). The centennial of the first intercollegiate football game was

A similar design theme — a hand, basketball and net — was used on this 1961 stamp that was issued to commemorate the centenary of the birth of basketball's inventor, James A. Naismith.

69

also the subject of a 1969 commemorative (Scott 1382).

James Naismith was born in Almonte, Ontario, Canada, November 6, 1861. As a young man he became a physical-education instructor at the International YMCA Training School (now Springfield College) in Springfield, Massachusetts. One day in 1891 his department head, Luther Halsey Gulick, assigned him the task of creating a new team sport that could be played indoors in the winter.

Naismith decided to adapt the game of football, or American rugby, to indoor play, using a soccer ball. Because of space limitations and the desire to avoid injuries, he ruled that the man holding the ball couldn't run, which would obviate the need to tackle him. He recalled from his Canadian boyhood the game of duck on the rock, in which a player lobbed a stone in an effort to knock a large stone (the "duck") off the top of a boulder, and he concluded that a similar throwing style, aiming at an elevated horizontal goal, would fit his new game.

On the December morning that he was scheduled to unveil his new

second, and Maggie Lobus, 99, third. Time—1:08¼.

A NEW GAME OF BALL.

A SUBSTITUTE FOR FOOTBALL WITHOUT ITS ROUGH FEATURES.

At the opening of the Athletic Grounds of the Young Men's Christian Association on Saturday a new athletic game—basket ball—was introduced. The game has been started as a substitute for football, with an attempt to eliminate the roughest features of that sport.

The game is played with an ordinary association football, and the object of each team is to get the ball into its opponent's goal. The field is 150 feet long by about 60 feet wide, and at each end is a post with a basket on top just large enough to conveniently hold the ball. The top of the basket is about nine feet above the ground, and a ladder is necessary to take the ball out after a goal has been made.

When a player gets the ball he is not allowed to run with it, but must stand and pass it to some other member of his own team within fifteen seconds after he touches it. The time for a match is about forty minutes, played in "halves" of fifteen minutes each, with a rest of five or ten minutes between.

On Saturday afternoon a match was played between the Twenty-third Street Branch of the Young Men's Christian Association and a team composed of members of the Students' Club. The students won by a score of 1 to 0. Next Saturday there will be two matches of basket ball at the association's grounds—one between the Students' Club and the Eighty-sixth Street Branch of the Young Men's Christian Association, and the other between the Twenty-third Street Branch and the Harlem Branch of the Young Men's Christian Association.

PREPARING FOR THE REGATTA.

A meeting of the Harlem Regatta Association was held last night at the Grand Union Hotel. Presi-

Four months after the game of "basket ball" had been invented in Springfield, it had spread to New York City and was considered worthy of this report on page 2 of The New York Times for April 26, 1892.

Richard Sheaff sent these rough "instructional sketches" to one of the artist-candidates in August 1988 as a guide to him in developing the design approach utilizing the first basketball game as the subject.

game, Naismith asked the YMCA janitor for two boxes about 19 inches square. Instead, the janitor produced two small peach baskets, about 15 inches across at the top. Naismith nailed them to the lower rail of a balcony-running track that circled the gymnasium at a level about 10 feet above the floor. He read to his students the 13 rules he had drafted and appointed two team captains, who divided the 18-man class into two nine-man teams.

The historic first game was played in a basement gymnasium with a playing area of approximately 35 by 50 feet. The players wore long trousers and some of them sported the then-fashionable beards or walrus mustaches. Most of the shots at the baskets were attempted from a crowded area directly in front of the goal, where much fouling occurred. Before play began, Naismith asked the janitor to get a stepladder and retrieve any balls that reached their target. He had little to do. Although the men ran and shot with enthusiasm, only one player, William R. Chase, succeeded in dropping the ball into a peach basket, and the game ended in a 1-0 score.

"Basketball," a name coined by one of the first players, was an immediate hit. The 19 students went home for Christmas vacation and carried the news and the rules of the new sport to their hometown YMCAs. Later, Naismith took a nine-man team on an exhibition tour to play other local teams.

In time, refinements evolved. Peach baskets gave way to woven-wire baskets and, finally, rims with suspended nets; removing the bottom from the net removed the need for a ladder. Backboards were introduced to prevent spectators from leaning over the balconies and interfering with the shots. Dribbling, or bouncing, the ball was permitted, giving players an alternative to standing still while searching for a teammate to pass to.

And team size was fixed at five for men, six for women.

Basketball grew in time to become one of the most popular sports in the world. Naismith himself went from Springfield to become a professor of physical education at the University of Kansas. In 1936 he was in Berlin to see basketball officially become an Olympic Games sport. He died of a heart attack in Lawrence, Kansas, in 1939 at the age of 78.

The Design

The airbrush painting that Lon Busch of Ellisville, Missouri, developed for the Basketball stamp was reminiscent of Charles R. Chickering's design for the 1961 Naismith centennial stamp. Both were vertically arranged and both featured a basket, a ball and upstretched hands. But the differences between the two designs reflected the changes that had taken place in the game in 30 years.

Whereas Chickering, back in 1961, had shown a side view and a single hand, pushing the ball up for a layup shot, Busch's 1991 airbrush painting looked down on the hoop and depicted the hands and forearms of two players reaching high above the basket: a white player's hand holding the ball, as if ready to dunk it, and a black player's hand, raised as if to block the shot.

The 1991 design acknowledged the powerful role that black athletes had come to play in basketball. It proclaimed that much of the game's combat was now waged in the rarefied altitudes above the 10-foot basket level by the towering, high-leaping players of today. And its vertical perspective was one that had become familiar to television viewers through the use of "skycam" cameras positioned over the hoops.

Two *Linn's Stamp News* readers wrote the paper to declare that the stamp depicted defensive goaltending, which is illegal and results in an automatic basket for the shooting team. However, as Joseph O'Brien of the Basketball Hall of Fame confirmed, goaltending doesn't occur until a defensive player touches the ball in the imaginary vertical "cylinder"

Lon Busch also offered the committee this airbrush rendering incorporating portions of a basketball, rim and net.

In these two pencil sketches for the Basketball stamp, the artist tested the idea of placing James Naismith in the Springfield gymnasium with the peach basket hanging from the balcony behind him.

above the hoop. If the hand on the right is that of an offensive player trying to dunk the basketball and the hand on the left is a defensive player's hand, as the letter writers assumed, no illegal contact has yet been made.

Besides, as Digger Phelps pointed out to the *Yearbook*, in international basketball goaltending is a legal maneuver as soon as the ball has struck the rim of the basket. "Once the ball hits the iron you can do anything to it above the rim — knock it in or knock it away — and that's the thing we were trying to depict," he said. "We Americans think basketball's our game, but the game has become international. In the design we were trying to simulate a situation where the ball has hit the rim, it's in the air and the players are allowed to go after it."

A slightly different interpretation came from the stamp's art director, Richard Sheaff. "The hands were drawn to be absolutely ambiguous," he said. "It could be someone about to stuff it and someone defending. It could be a rebound coming off the rim that two guys are going up for. It could be any of a number of things."

In this sketch, James Naismith is shown holding the soccer ball and peach basket. The sketch was prepared by an artist who worked for the Basketball stamp's art director, Richard Sheaff.

73

These four concept sketches show the evolution of the first-game theme to the point where it was virtually a finished piece of artwork (upper right). The committee almost approved it for the stamp, but finally chose the modern vignette instead.

Before the final design was chosen, CSAC considered some other design ideas. Some of the sketches featured James Naismith himself, with his soccer ball and peach basket. Another approach, which the committee came close to approving, attempted to show what that first basketball game in Springfield must have looked like, with mustachioed pioneers caught up in the action. The committee asked for various alterations, adding and subtracting a stepladder, fine-tuning the appear-

In this concept, which didn't get beyond the pencil-sketch stage, the 1891 soccer ball-and-peach basket combination is paired with a modern basketball, basket and backboard.

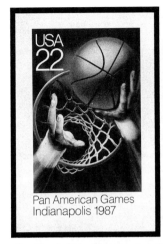 

On the left is the design that Lon Busch originally proposed for the Pan American Games stamp of 1987 and which he adapted for the 1991 Basketball commemorative. At right is Busch's first version of the adaptation. For the finished stamp, colors were altered and the typography changed.

ance of the players and their uniforms, before abandoning the concept in favor of a design representing basketball as it is played today.

Lon Busch submitted two designs showing close-ups of rim, net and basketball. One was a stylized view from the side, with no hands in the picture. The other, which was ultimately chosen for the stamp, was a modification of a concept sketch that Busch had created several years earlier while working on the 1987 Pan American Games commemorative — the only previous stamp he had designed. He revised the colors and other details of that sketch to CSAC's specifications, and it became the 1991 Basketball stamp.

One of the other artists' concept sketches, Jim Lamb's painting of the first basketball game, was also put to good use. USPS placed it on the cover of the first-day ceremony program.

First-Day Facts

Principal speakers at the August 29 first-day ceremony in Springfield were "Digger" Phelps and Tom Heinsohn, former Boston Celtics player and coach and a member of the Basketball Hall of Fame. Joe O'Brien, executive director of the Hall, gave the welcome. The stamp was dedicated by Michael S. Coughlin, deputy postmaster general.

$5.80 COMEDIANS BY HIRSCHFELD BOOKLET

Date of Issue: August 29, 1991

Catalog Numbers: Scott 2562-2566 (stamps); Scott 2566a (booklet pane of 10)

Colors: purple, red, black (offset); purple, red (intaglio)

First-Day Cancel: Hollywood, California

FDCs Canceled: 954,293

Format: 2 panes of 10 horizontal stamps each arranged horizontally 5 by 2. Five varieties on each pane. Offset printing plates of 200 subjects (10 across, 20 around); intaglio printing sleeves of 400 subjects (10 across, 40 around).

Perf: 11.2 (Eureka off-line perforator)

Selvage Markings: Sleeve number on binding stub of each pane

Cover Markings: "© United States Postal Service 1991" and mailing information on inside of front cover. Universal Product Code (UPC) and promotion for USPS Souvenir Pages on outside of back cover. Coupon for Souvenir Pages on inside of back cover.

Designer: Al Hirschfeld of New York, New York

Engraver: Deborah Alexander (BEP, denomination)

Art Director and Typographer: Howard Paine (CSAC)

Project Manager: Jack Williams (USPS)

Modeler: V. Jack Ruther (BEP)

Printing: printed by BEP on 6-color offset, 3-color intaglio D press (902)

Quantity Ordered: 700,000,000 (34,450,000 booklets; 1,100,000 unfolded panes)

Quantity Distributed: 699,978,000 (33,945,900 booklets; 2,106,000 unfolded panes

Sleeve Number Detail: 1 intaglio sleeve number on each pane binding stub

Tagging: overall

The Stamps

In an interview published in *Stamp World* in November 1981, Howard Paine, who had recently been named a design coordinator for the Citizens' Stamp Advisory Committee, was asked what he planned to do in his new post. ''I'd like to try some adventurous things,'' he said. ''I'd like to see some of the great caricaturists design stamps. Al Hirschfeld could do theater people . . .''

Ten years later, Paine's ''adventurous'' idea became a reality. On August 29, 1991, Postmaster General Anthony M. Frank dedicated a booklet of five stamp designs featuring 20th-century American comedians, with portraits created especially for USPS by famed show-business caricaturist Albert Hirschfeld.

The comedians were: Stan Laurel and Oliver Hardy; ventriloquist Edgar Bergen and his wooden dummy, Charlie McCarthy; Jack Benny; Fanny Brice, and Bud Abbott and Lou Costello. They were the first of 25 show-business personalities and teams for whom Hirschfeld had created

This self-portrait by Al Hirschfeld was used in USPS promotional material for the Comedians booklet.

77

stamp art, with the others in line to appear on stamps in future years.

So proud was USPS to obtain Hirschfeld's work that for the first time it gave a stamp designer an official credit line — not on the stamps themselves, as some countries do, but on the booklet cover, which bore the title: ''Comedians by Hirschfeld.''

Because of the artist's prominence, USPS waived an unwritten rule that prohibits so-called secret marks on U.S. stamps. A Hirschfeld tradition, which began when his daughter Nina was born in 1945, was that he hide her first name somewhere in each of his drawings. It was Postmaster General Frank himself who asked that the Ninas be included in the stamp designs as well, Hirschfeld said.

''I squeezed them in somehow after I finished the drawings,'' he told a National Public Radio interviewer.

Frank explained it in a prepared statement. ''We felt that 'Nina' has become such a distinctive element in Al Hirschfeld's art that our stamp designs would not be true Hirschfelds without them,'' he said.

In fact, at one point Frank suggested that some kind of contest be organized in which postal customers would find the Ninas. ''That fell through,'' said Howard Paine, ''because there wouldn't have been that much for them to do.''

But USPS did launch a major campaign to promote the secret marks and the fun of searching them out. A full-page ad in the September 14 issue of *TV Guide* magazine showed Frank and Hirschfeld in front of blowups of the five stamps, with Frank holding a magnifying glass that revealed the ''Nina'' on Bud Abbott's necktie. Headed ''There's Something Funny About These Stamps,'' the ad proclaimed:

''Al Hirschfeld captures character in a single stroke of the pen. And he sneaks his daughter's name into almost every illustration. Now this master of the pure line celebrates eight masters of the punchline. And because our Postmaster General relishes a good mystery, each stamp has that secret twist. All the fun is waiting for you at your local post office. So come find out how many NINAs Hirschfeld hid.''

After all the hoopla, it must be reported that ''Ninas'' could be found on only four of the five stamps, and on only two of them were they clear and umistakable. In a letter to Howard Paine dated February 16, 1991,

Inset in each of the lower stamps of this pane is a blowup of the word "Nina," with the location of each mark also shown. Not shown is the second, partial "Nina" on Jack Benny's tie. No "Nina" appeared on the Laurel and Hardy stamp.

Hirschfeld revealed the location of what he called the "Ninas and near-Ninas in my drawings." In the artist's words, these locations were:

"Laurel and Hardy: None. Bergen and McCarthy: One (in hair). Jack Benny: One (misspelled in tie) and one in violin scroll. Fanny Brice: One in left sleeve. Abbott and Costello: One in Abbott's tie."

Hirschfeld elaborated on the "misspelled" Nina. "The 'I' in this one is missing," he wrote. "If possible, have one of your master craftsmen put it in. If not, leave this as is to further mystify our audience!"

In fact, as Paine noted, the first "N" of the "necktie Nina" also seemed to be partially absent. In any case, Paine opted not to have Bureau artists touch the master's work.

The use of a living person's name on a U.S. booklet cover, or even on a stamp itself, wasn't without precedent. Charles Lindbergh's solo flight from New York to Paris in 1927 was commemorated with a 10¢ airmail stamp (Scott C10) that bore the word "Lindbergh." The Missouri Sesquicentennial stamp of 1971 (Scott 1426) depicted a mural by Thomas Hart Benton and included Benton's full name. And two of the Fishing Flies booklet stamps issued earlier in 1991 carried the last name or nickname of the flies' inventors (see Fishing Flies chapter).

However, no stamp designer is permitted to "sign" his work, and Hirschfeld wasn't allowed to do so either. (In his commercial caricatures, Hirschfeld customarily included his name and with it a number indicating how many Ninas could be found in the picture.)

It was in early 1987 that Howard Paine telephoned Hirschfeld to see whether he would be interested in doing some stamp designs. He was pleased to accept the commission, Paine recalled, and Paine began sending the artist names of stars of Broadway, Hollywood, vaudeville, radio and television selected by the Citizens' Stamp Advisory Committee. As the caricatures came back, Paine said, "the committee loved them. They said, keep them coming."

USPS had originally intended to issue the Comedians booklet in 1990, along with another booklet of stamps depicting U.S. Olympic Games gold medalists. However, the notice it gave BEP was too short for the Bureau to meet the desired timetable. As a result, the Olympians stamps were converted to sheet stamps and assigned to a private contractor, and the Comedians booklet was deferred to 1991.

The booklet's actual issuance, however, came with relatively little advance notice. For many months, USPS had said only that it would appear sometime in September. Then, on August 7, it was announced that the booklet would be dedicated August 29 in a ceremony at Mann's Chinese Theatre in Hollywood, California. The change in scheduling came after USPS decided to push quickly for a further increase in the first-class letter rate, which, if it was granted, would sharply reduce the demand for 29¢ stamps.

The postmaster general unveiled the stamp designs July 15 at the 10th annual convention of the Video Software Dealers Association in Las

Vegas, Nevada. Joining him was Robert Blattner, president of MCA/Universal Home Video. The ceremony launched a joint promotional campaign between USPS and MCA/Universal to sell assorted merchandise. Besides the stamp booklets, the goods were: an 11- by 14-inch matted print of the Abbott and Costello stamp design that included a copy of the stamp with a first-day postmark, which USPS sold for $14.95, and two new Abbott and Costello video-cassette films released by MCA/Universal, which included inserts plugging the stamps and art print.

"These comedians have made immeasurable contributions to American culture and, through the magic of radio and film, have brought laughter and joy to millions of people throughout the world," Frank said at the unveiling ceremony.

USPS received permission from the comedians' families and estates to use the names and images without charge, but in some cases private cachetmakers wishing to depict the celebrities were required to pay licensing fees. Lloyd A. DeVries, writing in *Stamp Collector*, described the required procedures.

The rights to Laurel and Hardy were owned by Larry Harmon Pictures Corporation in Los Angeles. Harmon — who was television's original "Bozo the Clown" — had been working for years to persuade USPS to issue a Laurel and Hardy stamp. A spokesman for the company told DeVries that "the basic percentage we have discussed is 10 percent," but that deals were negotiable. Cachet art also had to be approved in advance by Larry Harmon Pictures.

The Curtis Management Group of Indianapolis, Indiana, administered the rights for Abbott and Costello on behalf of the comedians' estates. Again, the cost was negotiable and would depend on quantity of cachets and selling prices, DeVries found, but he was assured by John Appuhn, vice president of Curtis, that it would be "fair and equitable." The major concern of agencies such as his was protecting the property and its image, Appuhn told him, adding: "We don't make money on $2 or $5 agreements . . . We do it to be consistent, to protect the integrity of the rights."

Curtis was familiar with cachetmakers' requirements, having also represented the estates of Jesse Owens, Lou Gehrig and Judy Garland, three other Americans whose portraits had appeared on stamps in recent years. In fact, the identities of the five comedians and comedy teams to be honored in the booklet were first disclosed in the March 1991 issue of the company's newsletter, *The Curtis Report*. USPS confirmed the names in an official announcement of the names April 16.

For the other three comedians, there was no cost involved for cachetmakers. Frances and Candice Bergen, represented by the William Morris Agency of Beverly Hills, California, didn't even require advance inspection of the Edgar Bergen and Charlie McCarthy artwork before production. Those administering the rights for Jack Benny (Rosenfeld, Meyer & Susman of Beverly Hills) and Fanny Brice (Frances Stark and William Brice of Beverly Hills) told DeVries they wanted to see the art to make sure it was in good taste and not defamatory.

"(In 1990), the rights for the Classic Films stamps were terribly confused and confusing," DeVries wrote. "The Postal Service seems to have done a much better job in educating the rights-holders and administrators this time about the economics of first-day covers. Only four groups need to be contacted, and only two are charging cachet makers."

LAUREL AND HARDY. "In terms of sheer laugh content and brilliance of comic invention and construction, Stan Laurel and Oliver Hardy take second place to no one," wrote film historian William K. Everson. Indeed, the misadventures of eager-to-please Stan (the "thin one") and blustering Ollie (the "fat one") have grown steadily in popularity in the 40 years since their last film.

Laurel, born Arthur Stanley Jefferson in Ulverston, England, June 16, 1895, made his music-hall debut at the age of 16. He came to America with Fred Karno's famed theatrical troupe in 1910, understudying Charlie Chaplin. On his own, he toured U.S. vaudeville houses as a comic and pantomimist, and made his first film in 1917. Oliver Norvelle Hardy was born in Harlem, Georgia, January 18, 1892. Fascinated by the movies — he opened a small theater in 1910 — he began acting in comic films in Florida in 1913. Eventually, both he and Laurel joined producer Hal Roach, and in 1926 Roach teamed them in a two-reeler called *Forty-Five Minutes From Hollywood*. Over the next 20 years, they made a total of 99 shorts and feature-length films together, including such classics as *Sons of the Desert, Babes in Toyland, Way Out West* and *Blockheads*.

Hardy died in 1957; Laurel, in 1965. (Hal Roach, who had brought them together, turned 100 in 1991).

EDGAR BERGEN AND CHARLIE McCARTHY. America's most famous ventriloquist was born Edgar John Bergren, February 16, 1903, in Chicago. As a boy he became interested in voice tricks and sleight-of-hand, and in high school he created his lifetime companion and alter ego, "Charlie McCarthy," a dummy patterned after a tough Irish newsboy.

Dropping out of Northwestern University, he entered vaudeville under the name Edgar Bergen, and as the popularity of Bergen and McCarthy grew, they played nightclubs, musical comedy and, finally radio. Their own program, which began in 1937, became one of America's most popular, as the saucy and precocious Charlie indiscriminately insulted Bergen and the prominent personalities who appeared as guests on the show. Several Hollywood films also featured Bergen, McCarthy and Bergen's other wooden creations, yokel Mortimer Snerd and bachelor maid Effie Klinker.

Bergen and his wife Frances were the parents of actress Candice Bergen, television's "Murphy Brown." Edgar Bergen died in 1978 in Las Vegas, during what he had billed as a final engagement. Charlie went to the Smithsonian Institution.

JACK BENNY. Jack Benny, one of the major stars of the Golden Age of Radio, was born Benny Kubelsky in Waukegan, Illinois, February 14,

1894. As a sailor in World War I, he toured with a Navy revue and discovered his flair for comedy, using his violin (which he actually could play respectably) as a prop. Later he became a successful vaudeville monologuist, Broadway entertainer, master of ceremonies and motion-picture star, appearing in more than 20 films.

In 1932 he launched his long-running radio career with an appearance on Ed Sullivan's broadcast. The humor in his weekly radio comedy show derived not from gags but from his talented cast playing off the star's established character and traits: his stinginess, his vanity, his inability to control events. His TV show, which began in 1950, was an extension of the radio program. He died in 1974.

FANNY BRICE. Although radio listeners in the 1940s knew Fanny Brice as the voice of a naughty, mouthy 4½-year-old named "Baby Snooks," older Americans remembered her as one of the greatest comediennes of the 1920s and 1930s, a singer, satirist and mimic who starred in Florence Ziegfeld's Follies and made the torch song *My Man* her personal trademark. In the 1960s, it was that Fanny Brice who became known to the public again through the Broadway musical *Funny Girl* and its film version.

Fannie Borach was born October 29, 1891, on New York's Lower East Side. She began her acting career at 13 by winning $10 in an amateur contest, and went on to play small roles in small stage productions. In 1910 she made a hit singing an Irving Berlin dialect song and was signed by Ziegfeld, thereafter appearing in most of his annual Follies. She appeared in several movies and in 1936, with Hanley Stafford as "Daddy," introduced Baby Snooks — a character she had invented at a party in 1921 — to delighted radio listeners. She died in 1951.

ABBOTT AND COSTELLO. This team of New Jersey-born clowns made their mark successively in burlesque, vaudeville, radio, theater, movies and television. Bud Abbott (the thin one) was born William Abbott October 2, 1900; Costello was born Louis Francis Cristello March 6, 1908. The two met in 1929 when Costello, a burlesque comedian booked into Brooklyn's Empire Theatre, needed a straight man when his regular partner took sick, and Abbott, working in the box office, volunteered to fill in.

They subsequently teamed up on the burlesque and vaudeville circuits, working without a script, clowning, getting off ancient jokes, knocking each other around. Their best-known routine was a zany baseball dialogue known universally as "Who's on first?" In 1938 they began regular appearances on Kate Smith's radio program, where Costello, to enable listeners to tell the two apart, adopted the high-pitched voice that became his trademark. Eventually they reached Hollywood, where their appearance in the film *Buck Privates* (1940) made them overnight box-office hits. Costello died in 1959; Abbott, in 1974.

AL HIRSCHFELD. Hirschfeld, who turned 88 in June 1991, first began creating his caricatures in the 1920s for New York newspapers after moderate success in sculpture and painting. His flowing line drawings were influenced by the art of Bali, which he visited in the 1930s, and the Japanese print master Hokusai.

He has written that if there were such a word he would be "more comfortable being classified as a 'characterist' than as a caricaturist." "My primary interest," he explained, "is in producing a drawing capable of surviving the obvious fun of recognition or news value . . . For the subject which turns me on is people." Brooks Atkinson observed that Hirschfeld wasn't interested in anatomical distortions or in exaggerations of his subjects' deficiencies: "Instead of burlesquing people, he joins them on their own terms, adding his own gaiety for good measure." Dancer Ray Bolger told the artist that for years he had tried to imitate Hirschfeld's drawings of him.

Until November 1990, Hirschfeld's caricatures appeared weekly in the Friday theater section of *The New York Times*, but since then his work has been seen less frequently in the newspaper.

The identities of two of the performers whom Hirschfeld had drawn for future U.S. stamps were disclosed by *The Evening Sun* of Baltimore. As confirmed by the Margo Feiden Galleries, the artist's representative in New York, they were opera singer Rosa Ponselle and silent movie star Mary Pickford.

The Designs

Hirschfeld's original drawings were about 8 by 10 inches, a size that was smaller than he was used to working in. He was forced to leave out his customary detail and produce drawings that were "almost calligraphic," as he told a National Public Radio interviewer. For instance, with the thin Laurel and the rotund Hardy, "one is like a figure one, the other like a zero," Hirschfeld told the interviewer.

Hirschfeld did his first drawings in color, but art director Howard Paine told him to keep them in black and white; color would be provided elsewhere on the stamps. Paine specified to the Bureau of Engraving and Printing that the faces should be reproduced by photo-offset rather than engraved. The only intaglio portion would be the "USA 29." "An engraver trying to reproduce a Hirschfeld caricature might miss the fluidity of it," he explained.

Paine chose his typography and color scheme with the idea that the

In this early Laurel and Hardy essay, the typography was carried by torn paper and ticket stubs superimposed on the portraits. Note that the 22¢ first-class rate was still in effect when this essay was made.

83

This alternative typography was considered before art director Howard Paine decided to go with a posterlike all-capitals type.

stamps should look "theatrical." "USA 29" was placed on a torn ticket stub; a single engraving of this device was used for all five stamps. The names of the performers appeared in one of two ways: dropout lettering on backgrounds that suggested torn strips of paper, or colored lettering standing alone. They were done in all capitals, in a sans-serif typeface called Machine Bold, to give what Paine called a "poster effect" or "marquee effect."

Paine experimented with multiple colors, orange and green and brown, in addition to the black. In the end, he settled on just two: a bright red, and a purple whose subdued tint was balanced by the boldness of the type.

The stamps were laid out on the pane in the format that originated with the 25¢ Indian Headdresses booklet of 1990: 10 stamps consisting of five varieties in matching vertical pairs. Thus each variety could be found with a straight edge at either the top or bottom. Each of the two Abbott and Costello stamps, the outermost stamps on the pane, also had a straight edge on its right side.

Paine arranged the design elements and colors so that not only would each individual stamp be interesting and attractive, but that a full pane would have a logical and balanced appearance, with colors and typographical devices (dropout or solid lettering) alternating.

Varieties

A number of booklet panes were printed without the intaglio red and purple ticket-stub designs containing the denominations. Some of these were intercepted by postal clerks, but others were sold to postal customers and reached the hands of dealers and collectors.

The first report of the two-missing-color error came from a Chapel Hill, North Carolina, couple, Merri and David Wright, who told *Linn's Stamp News* they had found several error booklets in mid-September at the main branch of the Chapel Hill post office. The husband was buying stamps for postage when he noticed the color omission. Realizing that his find would be of interest to Merri, a stamp collector, he bought additional booklets, some of which turned out to contain error panes as well.

On returning to the post office the next day to purchase more, David Wright was told that the booklets had been temporarily removed from sale after a customer had returned a faulty booklet, alerting the clerks to check their stocks. They found many more. "I went through my first

This strip is the two-color-missing error. The engraved red denomination is missing from the first, third and fourth stamps in the strip. The engraved purple denomination is missing from the second and fifth stamps.

batch of 25 (booklets) and they were fine,'' postal clerk Steve Shipp told *The News and Observer* of Raleigh, ''but in the second batch almost every single one had the misprint.''

First-Day Facts

Postmaster General Frank, an alumnus of Hollywood, California, High School, dedicated the Comedians booklets at the Hollywood post office August 29. Johnny Grant, honorary mayor of Hollywood, gave the welcome. The scheduled speaker, Brooke Knapp, president of the Hollywood Chamber of Commerce, was unable to attend.

Brief remarks were delivered by members of the families of the honored comedians, including Bud Abbott Jr., Chris Costello and Frances Bergen, wife of Edgar Bergen. Actors Ed Asner and Morey Amsterdam were among those on hand. After the ceremony, the postmaster general presented an enlarged replica of the Edgar Bergen stamp to the comedian's daughter Candice Bergen.

Postmaster General Frank presents Edgar Bergen's daughter Candice with a blown-up reproduction of the Bergen and McCarthy stamp.

85

$2.90 WORLD WAR II SOUVENIR SHEET

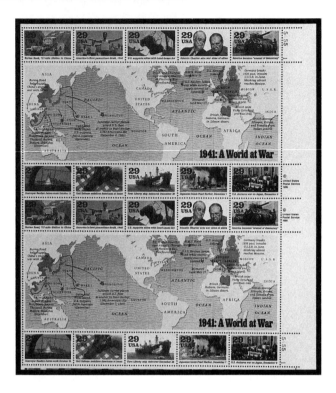

Date of Issue: September 3, 1991

Catalog Number: Scott 2559 (souvenir sheet); 2559a-j (individual stamps)

Colors: magenta, yellow, cyan, black (offset); black (intaglio)

First-Day Cancel: Phoenix, Arizona

FDCs Canceled: 1,832,967

Format: Miniature sheets of 10 different horizontal varieties, arranged in two strips of 5, 1 strip across top of sheet, 1 strip across bottom of sheet, with world map between. Issued in post-office panes containing 2 miniature sheets abutting vertically so that bottom strip of 5 stamps of upper miniature sheet is se-tenant to top strip of 5 stamps of lower miniature sheet. Offset printing plates of 8 miniature sheets (2 across, 4 around); intaglio printing sleeves of 8 miniature sheets (2 across, 4 around).

Perf: 11.2 (Eureka off-line perforator)

Selvage Markings: "©/United States/Postal Service/1990" in selvage adjacent to each miniature sheet of 10; inscription appears twice on each pane of two miniature sheets.

Designer: William H. Bond of Arlington, Virginia

Art Director and Typographer: Howard Paine (CSAC)

Project Manager: Jack Williams (USPS)

Engraver: Deborah Alexander (lettering, BEP)

Modeler: Peter Cocci (BEP)

Printing: printed by BEP on 6-color offset, 3-color intaglio D press (902)

Quantity Ordered: 160,000,000 stamps (16,000,000 sheets)

Quantity Distributed: 152,180,000 stamps (15,218,000 sheets)

Plate/Sleeve Number Detail: One group of 4 offset plate numbers and 1 single-digit intaglio sleeve number in corner of selvage adjacent to each miniature sheet of 10; numbers appear twice on each pane of two miniature sheets.

Tagging: overall, large block covering stamps

The Sheet

On December 18, 1990, an ex-U.S. Navy pilot who had been shot down over the Pacific Ocean in World War II helped launch the first installment of a major postal commemoration of that conflict.

The ex-flyer was President George Bush. At the White House with Postmaster General Anthony M. Frank, the president unveiled the design of a mini-sheet, captioned "1941: A World at War," that bore a global map and 10 stamps illustrating events of the first year of active war participation by the United States. The sheet would be issued in 1991, USPS explained, and would be followed by similar sheets in the 50th-anniversary years of 1992, 1993, 1994 and 1995, for a total of five sheets and 50 stamps.

The 1991 mini-sheet, which USPS originally had called a "souvenir sheet" and later termed a "commemorative sheet," was issued September 3 in ceremonies at the American Legion's national convention in Phoenix, Arizona.

The overall plan had been years in the making.

By the mid-1980s, requests and suggestions for World War II stamps were already appearing in the Citizens' Stamp Advisory Committee's mail. It was clear to then-Postmaster General William F. Bolger and to CSAC that, when the anniversaries began arriving, a major Postal Service response would be expected and appropriate. Later on, Postmaster General Frank put down in writing why this was so.

"The historical significance of World War II on the United States and the world was profound," Frank wrote. "The war and how it evolved historically as the direct result of the rise and fall of Hitler's Germany and Japan's territorial expansion thrust the United States and its 132 million people into a total, global conflict.

"During the war, 16 million Americans served in the Armed Forces; another 20 million worked in war-related industries, hospitals and government agencies. As a result of the war, the United States altered its role in the free world, maintained its armed forces abroad on permanent status, and thrust its capitalist system outward, providing goods and services to every continent and nation.

"So profound were the changes wrought by World War II that the history and direction of the United States and virtually every other combatant nation were altered permanently."

What the Postal Service had to devise, explained Donald M. McDowell, director of the Office of Stamp and Philatelic Marketing, was "as comprehensive a treatment as possible without expanding the stamp program to 100 issues every year for all those consecutive years." A careful and credible selection process would be needed. The country was full of those people Anthony Frank had mentioned — men and women who had helped win the war on the land and sea, in the air and on the home front — and they would have very firm ideas about what, or whom, should be depicted.

In 1985 CSAC appointed a three-member World War II Subcommittee consisting of Clinton Andrews, John Foxworth and, as chairman, Robert J. Leuver, then director of the Bureau of Engraving and Printing, to determine how to select the subjects and themes for commemoration and how best to do the job. The subcommittee, in turn, sought the help of

Postmaster General Frank shows President Bush the design of the first 10-stamp sheetlet commemorating the 50th anniversary of World War II.

the historians for the Army, Navy, Air Force and Marines and the historian at the U.S. Department of State. Its aim, in Leuver's words, was ''to establish an unassailable group that was politically insulated from outside pressure and technically competent.''

The armed services' historians met jointly under the leadership of Brigadier General William A. Stofft, chief of military history for the Army, and produced a proposal for stamps that, as Stofft put it, would ''properly recognize and honor all facets of national endeavor that contributed to victory.'' William Z. Slany, the State Department historian, filed a separate report on significant wartime diplomatic events and personalities. Working with their findings, the subcommittee by April 1986 had devised the general outline of what would become the USPS plan for commemorating World War II.

As the subcommittee saw it, there would be five souvenir sheets, one each year from 1991 through 1995. Each sheet would have an appropriate theme: 1941 (1991), Global Conflict; 1942, Full Mobilization; 1943, Turning the Tide; 1944, Road to Victory; 1945, Victory. The base image for each sheet would be a world map, appropriately annotated. The stamps on the sheet would depict significant events of the year.

The CSAC subcommittee had originally thought that the best way to commemorate the many and varied facets of World War II would be with a mixture of single stamps, se-tenant blocks of four and souvenir sheets. The group had also considered starting the series in 1989, the 50th anniversary of the outbreak of World War II in Europe, with recognition of such 1939-1940 events as the escorting of neutral shipping by the U.S. Navy, the start of U.S. rearmament, the Army's training maneuvers in Louisiana, the destroyers-for-bases agreement with the British and the

This early sketch by William Bond envisioned a five-stamp souvenir sheet. At this point, the stamp subject matter, map annotations and border inscriptions were still very much unsettled. In this design approach, the ocean color bleeds into the stamp backgrounds. (Note that there are two Australias on the map.)

Battle of Britain between the British RAF and the German Luftwaffe.

Even after the subcommittee had settled on the basic idea of five souvenir sheets, 1991 through 1995, its members had thought that the sheets could contain as few as "three or four" stamps each, covering "the more significant events which are easier to depict," as Robert Leuver put it. "Starred on each year's souvenir sheet (map) would be the various campaigns and diplomatic conferences," Leuver explained to CSAC. "Bulleted items could be arranged in various locations on the sheet which would identify important personages, events or issues not depicted as stamps or starred on the map."

In April 1986 the subcommittee submitted to CSAC this proposal for the five souvenir sheets:

1991 (1941): Global Conflict. Four stamps would depict the U.S. neutrality patrols, the Lend-Lease agreement with Great Britain, the Atlantic Charter meeting between President Franklin D. Roosevelt and Prime Minister Winston Churchill, and the U.S. Selective Service System. Starred on the map would be the Japanese attack on Pearl Harbor. Noted elsewhere on the sheet would be the U.S. declaration of war on the Axis Powers.

1992 (1942): Full Mobilization. Four stamps would depict "Rosie the Riveter," the symbolic representative of home-front defense workers; the naval battles of Midway and the Coral Sea; the Joint Chiefs of Staff, who devised and coordinated global military operations, and the B-25 raid on Tokyo led by Lieutenant Colonel James Doolittle. Starred would be the Casablanca conference of Roosevelt and Churchill and the Allied campaign in North Africa. Otherwise noted would be Civil Defense operations at home and the breaking of the Japanese Imperial Fleet's operational code by U.S. Navy cryptographers.

In this sketch, designer William Bond has more fully developed the five-stamp sheet concept, with the stamp subjects more closely paralleling those that ended up on the sheet that was issued.

1993 (1943): Turning the Tide. Four stamps would show cartoonist Bill Mauldin's "Willie and Joe," the weary, wisecracking foot soldiers who spoke to and for GIs everywhere in *Yank* magazine; the B-17 Flying Fortress, workhorse of the U.S. strategic air war in Europe; the Allied campaign in Italy, and a scene on the home front. Starred on the map would be the war in the Aleutian Islands and meetings of Allied leaders in Cairo and Teheran. Noted would be Ernie Pyle as a representative of war correspondents, and "Kilroy," the mysterious personality who existed only in graffiti that proclaimed that no matter where U.S. GIs might venture, Kilroy had been there first.

1994 (1944): Road to Victory. Three stamps would show the Allied invasion of Normandy, the naval battles of the Philippine Sea and the Battle of the Bulge, in which the Allies overcame a desperate German counterattack in Belgium. Starred would be the conferences at Dumbarton Oaks in Washington, D.C., and Bretton Woods, New Hampshire, where plans for organizing the postwar world were prepared. Otherwise noted would be the role of science in advancing the U.S. war effort.

1995 (1945): Victory. Three stamps would mark V-E (Victory in Europe) Day, with a view of the schoolhouse at Rheims, France, where the Germans surrendered; V-J (Victory over Japan) Day, with the signing of the surrender agreement aboard the *USS Missouri*, and a home-front celebration scene, such as the famous *Life* magazine photo of a sailor kissing a girl in Times Square, New York. Starred would be the conferences of Allied leaders at Yalta and Potsdam and the organizing meeting of the United Nations in San Francisco. Otherwise noted would be the role of non-combatants such as medical corpsmen, nurses, Red Cross workers and war correspondents.

CSAC discussed and debated the subcommittee's report, and eventually accepted it in substance. However, the committee decided that five stamps per sheet wouldn't be enough. At one time in the artistic evolution of the sheets, as many as 16 stamps on each sheet was considered. Ultimately, the figure was set at 10.

Postmaster General Anthony M. Frank, who closely monitored the planning process after he took office in 1988, came up with the key idea that the central map on the souvenir sheet should vary with each year's addition to the set. "In the concept we showed him, we had the same map five times," recalled Don McDowell. "He said, 'We didn't have a static world during World War II. Let's move this map back and forth so that its center is the focus of where the war was in each year.' So his contribution was that the map would roll back and forth like a strip map to keep the central focus more prominent."

In June 1990 the first word of the souvenir-sheet plan reached the public when USPS hosted a private-industry conference on stamp production and distributed solicitations for stamp printing contracts, including one for the five World War II souvenir sheets.

"One of the things that was crucial," said McDowell, "was a

recommendation by the subcommittee that we shouldn't launch this thing with the 1941 design in hand and hope that 1942 and 1943 and so on would somehow work out. The entire thing had to be done as a comprehensive whole, with one printer, one artist and one art director. We're still adding small details to the sheets for the subsequent years, but basically they are in place.''

The specification that the printing process be a combination of offset and intaglio was tailor-made for the Bureau of Engraving and Printing's D press, and ultimately BEP received the order. BEP prepared offset plates and intaglio printing sleeves of eight sheets (80 stamps) each. The eight were cut into post-office panes, each containing two souvenir sheets, or sheetlets, one above the other.

The fact that the bottom row of stamps from the top sheetlet and the top row of stamps from the bottom sheetlet directly abutted each other meant that se-tenant blocks or vertical pairs of stamps could be obtained. (A similar situation had occurred with the CAPEX 78 souvenir sheets of 1978, in which the panes contained six sheetlets, each bearing eight different stamps.)

Collectors found they had several options with the World War II souvenir sheets. They could collect complete panes of two sheetlets; individual sheetlets of 10; horizontal blocks of 10 that spanned both sheetlets on a pane, and/or 10 single stamps. Either a 10-stamp sheetlet or a 10-stamp horizontal block could be used on a piece of Priority Mail, since either would exactly cover the $2.90 rate.

Because each post-office pane contained only 20 usable stamps instead of the normal 50 or 100, the cost of production per unit was unusually high. On the other hand, the Postal Service expected that

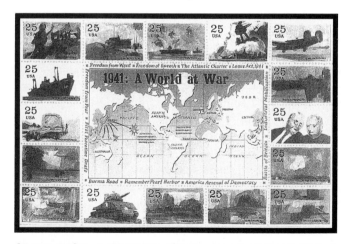

At one point, a 16-stamp sheet was considered. This is Bond's color sketch showing how it might look. Some of the individual stamp sketches have recognizable links to stamps that appeared on the finished sheet.

Americans would keep a large proportion of the sheets as souvenirs rather than use them on mail.

"It's not the most efficient way to make stamps," Don McDowell acknowledged. "It's expensive — not prohibitively so, but it is expensive.

"But once in a while the hobby of stamp collecting gets challenged to really be what it says it is: educational. When an opportunity like that comes along, the committee thought it should be maximized."

Moreover, the World War II sheetlet was made to be distributed to every post office in the country. The last souvenir sheets before this one — the Ameripex (presidential) sheets of 1986 — had gone automatically to the 8,000 largest post offices (Cost Accounting Group A through G), while smaller offices were given the option of ordering them. The World War II souvenir sheet would go to all offices, from CAG A to CAG L. "That way they will reach all the people who served in the war, and their families," McDowell said.

As the process of selecting the 10 stamp subjects for the 1941 sheet developed, eight subjects became firm choices. These were: The Lend-Lease Act, a Liberty Ship, the Atlantic Charter, the Burma Road, America as the "Arsenal of Democracy," the first peacetime draft, the Japanese attack on Pearl Harbor and the U.S. declaration of war.

A ninth stamp would show either an Atlantic convoy or the sinking of a convoy escort, the U.S. destroyer *Reuben James*; the final choice was the *Reuben James*. It was proposed that the tenth stamp depict the Japanese conquest of Wake Island, but the committee decided that this subject was too close, topically and geographically, to the Pearl Harbor attack, and so the final subject became Civil Defense.

As the planning moved into its final stages, USPS sought and obtained the cooperation of the Defense Department in heading off expected pressures to add more stamps and more subjects. Early in 1990, a group of USPS and CSAC officials met with Pete Williams, assistant secretary of defense for public affairs, to explain the project and the problem. Postmaster General Frank followed up the meeting with a letter to Williams in which he reviewed the long and careful planning process for the series, and then got to the point.

"... (T)he Postal Service increasingly is becoming the focus of intense lobbying efforts by advocates of stamps that would honor the individual services, specific units, military specialties and particular kinds of weaponry, specific land battles and naval engagements, and individual heroes," Frank wrote. "...(S)uch lobbying was predicted in 1985 by the Joint Services Committee and the members urged that it be resisted lest the careful balance they had recommended be lost.

"We greatly appreciate the support we have received from you and Secretary (Dick) Cheney as we strive to preserve the concept of our souvenir sheets by saying 'no' to requests to single out specific services, units, organizations and individuals. We believe strongly that the five

93

souvenir sheets with their total of 50 stamps will portray vividly the pivotal events of the war in a manner bringing understanding to Americans too young to have experienced them.''

It wasn't until August 15 that USPS finally announced the date and place of issue of the inaugural souvenir sheet: September 3, at the American Legion's national convention in Phoenix, Arizona.

In addition to the souvenir sheet, USPS offered for sale a 44-page book titled: *A World At War: 1941*, describing the events of that year in text and pictures, with an introduction by James Michener, a popular novelist and former member of CSAC. The book's creative director was Howard Paine, who also served as art director for the souvenir sheet, and the editor and project manager was USPS' Bill Halstead. The item sold for $15.95, plus 50¢ handling per order, which included two sheets for mounting in the book, one intact and the other as individual stamps.

The events depicted on the 10 stamps, and their captions, were:

BURMA ROAD, 717-MILE LIFELINE TO CHINA. From 1937 to

Burma Road, 717-mile lifeline to China

1939, some 160,000 Chinese and Burmese laborers toiled to build a road from Lashio in Burma over rugged mountains and through jungles to Kunming in southwestern China. The road served as a ''back door'' to China for vital war supplies, and avoided Japan's blockade of the Chinese coast. In 1942, however, Japanese troops closed the Burmese part of the road. In 1945, near the end of the war, Allied forces under U.S. General Joseph W. Stilwell linked the Burma Road with a new road, the Ledo Road from Ledo, India, to create a supply route more than 1,000 miles long from India to China.

AMERICA'S FIRST PEACETIME DRAFT, 1940. President

America's first peacetime draft, 1940

Roosevelt asserted that the job of building up the Army couldn't wait on voluntary enlistments, and Congress approved the Selective Service Act in September 1940, over strong opposition. All men aged 21 through 35 were required to register. The Army planned to enroll 900,000 annually from this pool of 17 million, train them for a year and hold them subject to call for 10 years. Draftees couldn't be used overseas. In 1941, with war nearing, Congress extended the draft law, approving it in the House by a single vote.

U.S. SUPPORTS ALLIES WITH LEND-LEASE ACT. President Roosevelt's Lend-Lease Act, which he likened to lending a garden hose to a neighbor whose house was on fire, was introduced in Congress

U.S. supports allies with Lend-Lease Act

January 10, 1941, and signed into law March 11. It authorized the president to procure ''any defense article for the government of any country whose defense the president deems vital to the defense of the United States.'' It was ultimately used to send enormous amounts of arms and other material to Great Britain and the Soviet Union.

ATLANTIC CHARTER SETS WAR AIMS OF ALLIES. Roosevelt and Prime Minister Winston Churchill met face to face for the first time at Placentia Bay, Newfoundland, from August 9 to 12, 1941. At conferences aboard the U.S. cruiser *Augusta* and the British battleship *Prince of Wales*, the two leaders agreed on an eight-point Atlantic Charter, which held out the hope of liberation to the Axis-occupied nations and advocated universal peace, ''freedom from fear and want,'' and freedom of the seas, all to be established through ''a wider and permanent system of general security.''

Atlantic Charter sets war aims of allies

AMERICA BECOMES ''ARSENAL OF DEMOCRACY.'' America's role as the great maker of armaments of World War II began a year before Pearl Harbor. ''We must be the great arsenal of democracy,'' President Roosevelt said in a fireside chat, calling on America to supply its allies and build its own defenses with planes, tanks, guns and ships. The country didn't hit its stride until after it had entered the war, when civilian output yielded to military under the direction of a federal War Production Board with far-reaching powers.

America becomes "arsenal of democracy"

DESTROYER REUBEN JAMES SUNK OCTOBER 31. Through much of 1941, American warships convoyed merchant vessels carrying lend-lease materials to the British Isles through waters infested with Hitler's U-boats. At daybreak of October 31, the U.S. destroyer *Reuben James* was torpedoed by the German submarine *U 552* some 600 miles west of Ireland. The ship sank after about five minutes, taking with it some 115 officers and men. It was the only American warship sunk by Hitler's navy during the so-called neutrality period from Sep-

Destroyer Reuben James sunk October 31

tember 1939 to December 1941.

(The commander of the *U 552*, Lieutenant Commander Erich Topp of the German Navy, was shown on a German semipostal stamp, Scott B260, issued in 1944. The picture of Topp peering into a periscope eyepiece, unidentified by name, was adapted from newsreel footage of

This 1944 German semipostal (Scott B260) depicted Lieutenant Commander Erich Topp, commander of the U-boat that sank the Reuben James October 31, 1941.

him taken during a war patrol. Long after the war, Topp served as the West German representative to NATO in Washington. He was deputy commander-in-chief of the West German Navy when he retired in 1969.)

CIVIL DEFENSE MOBILIZES AMERICANS AT HOME. The

Civil Defense mobilizes Americans at home

Office of Civil Defense was organized in mid-1941 to plan and direct the protection of civilians against air attack. The agency prepared mass-evacuation plans and recruited millions of volunteers to serve as airplane spotters, air-raid wardens, messengers and ambulance drivers. Virtually every U.S. community was organized down to the block level, where the air-raid warden, identifiable by helmet, arm band and whistle, was in charge of keeping all lights turned off during the periodic nighttime blackouts.

FIRST LIBERTY SHIP DELIVERED DECEMBER 30. In Septem-

First Liberty ship delivered December 30

ber 1941 the nation launched a crash shipbuilding program. The 441-foot Liberty Ships — homely adaptations of a British tramp steamer — were built at the low cost of $2 million each by contractor Henry J. Kaiser, who had built Boulder, Bonneville and Grand Coulee dams ahead of schedule. At the peak of the effort, workers could build a ship in 80½ hours. The joke was told of a woman who stepped up with a champagne bottle to christen a new vessel whose keel had not yet been laid. ''Just start swinging,'' Kaiser instructed her.

JAPANESE BOMB PEARL HARBOR, DECEMBER 7. Just before dawn on Sunday, December 7, a Japanese air armada of bombers and

Japanese bomb Pearl Harbor, December 7

fighters took off from five aircraft carriers north of Oahu, heading for the U.S. naval base at Pearl Harbor, where the U.S. Pacific Fleet lay like a sitting duck in an area not three miles square. When the surprise attack was over, more than 3,500 Americans had been killed or wounded; five warships had been lost and 13 others badly damaged, and 188 aircraft had been destroyed. The battleship *Arizona*, which sank with more than 1,000 men aboard, still lies on the floor of Pearl Harbor. Its superstructure jutting above the water now houses a national memorial, and it was at this spot that President Bush led a moving 50th anniversary memorial service December 7, 1991.

U.S. DECLARES WAR ON JAPAN, DECEMBER 8. The day after Pearl Harbor, President Roosevelt addressed a joint session of Congress.

U.S. declares war on Japan, December 8

Labeling December 7 ''a date which will live in infamy,'' he asked for recognition of the state of war that had suddenly been thrust upon the country. Both houses acted at once with only a single dissenting vote. Three days later, Germany and Italy declared war on the United States, and again Congress was called on for the appropriate response; this time the vote was unanimous.

The Designs

The art director assigned to the project was Howard Paine, a long-time design coordinator for CSAC and the art editor of *The National Geographic* magazine. For his designer, Paine chose an old colleague, William H. Bond of Arlington, Virginia. Bond, an Englishman by birth who served in the Royal Navy during World War II, was a *National Geographic* staff artist known for his versatility. In this assignment, which would call for examples of virtually every type of art — portraits, still lifes, landscapes, pictures of battles and weapons — versatility would be an essential requirement.

In developing a design treatment that would remain constant through the five-year life of the project, Bond and Paine worked from a basic concept they called their ''placemat.'' This was a Mercator-projection world map, with stamps in various numbers on one or more sides of the map and, in some versions, a decorative ribbon border bearing slogans and other words that evoked the year being commemorated. Each year's

97

sheet would have an appropriate title. For the first one, the designers and CSAC tried out ''1941: Global Conflict'' before settling on ''1941: A World at War.''

Once the number of stamps was finally fixed at 10, the design treatment could also be made final. The ribbon with words was eliminated, and every subject or event to be recognized on a sheet was either developed into a full-fledged stamp design or marked by a phrase on the map.

No previous U.S. stamp artist had faced challenges of the kind that Bill Bond now confronted in his first venture in the field. Bond had to produce 50 different stamps over a five-year period. Each had to illustrate, in miniature but in an immediately recognizable way, a specified event or a phenomenon of World War II. The stamps had to be varied in their approach to their subject matter; too many look-alike battle scenes, for instance, wouldn't do. Furthermore, the artist was told, the emphasis had to be on American subjects. He should avoid troops or weaponry of the Allies, and certainly of the Axis.

The pictures had to be accurate, because millions of people who remembered World War II would be examining them critically. The stamps also had to be colorful. Those two requirements weren't always easy to reconcile, because much of the photographic reference material Bond had to work with was black and white. The colors themselves had to vary from stamp to stamp on a given sheet, but they had to be distributed in a balanced way across the entire sheet. The stamps also had to be arranged chronologically by subject matter, so that on the 1941 sheet, for instance, the raid on Pearl Harbor and U.S. declaration of war would be the last items. Working within these constraints, Bond created skies and other backgrounds of deep blues, sunset oranges and yellows,

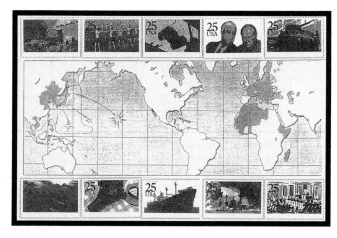

This sketch shows the 10-stamp layout that was ultimately adopted for the World War II souvenir sheet. Most of the stamp designs also have acquired their final form.

blank whites, and even greens — and distributed them so that no two stamps with similar background colors were side by side.

"If I had known what I was getting into," Bond laughed, "I'm not sure I would have accepted Howard's invitation."

The artist and art director worked closely together over the long period of design development, with Paine providing suggestions and comments, often illustrated with pencil sketches, and relaying to Bond the reactions and requests of CSAC.

Bond tested various artistic styles, but "it ended up that I should be fairly realistic," he said. He did most of his finished paintings, as well as his rough color sketches, in acrylic on designer board, at five times stamp size. In some cases, his original paintings were cropped to focus more closely on the central subject, so that the usable artwork was actually only three times up. Each individual stamp design presented its own unique problems of approach and execution.

The Burma Road design had to suggest the tortuous mountain terrain of the road. Bond tried a picture based on a well-known aerial photograph, showing the road zigzagging up a mountain in a dizzying series of switchbacks, but finally opted for a closeup of a truck towing an artillery piece up a steep grade. The Peacetime Draft design was "a tough one," for which he considered showing draftees signing up, or taking the oath of allegiance, before he settled on a picture of men in their undershirts doing calisthenics. For reference, he used photographs — and his own arms-extended image in a mirror.

The picture of Roosevelt and Churchill in a conversational mode at the Atlantic Charter conference was based on several individual photographs of the two men. The Churchill portrait, for instance, shows the influence of the Yousuf Karsh photograph on which the 1965 U.S. Churchill Memorial stamp (Scott 1264) was based. For his Liberty Ship design,

This is the U.S. Navy photo on which Bond based his Pearl Harbor stamp design. Nearest the viewer is the battleship West Virginia, sunk but still upright. Behind it is the Tennessee, less seriously damaged.

Bond used photographs, but also went "on location" to Baltimore, Maryland, where one of two surviving Liberty Ships was docked. "I added a seagull to the picture to try to soften it a little bit, and add some interest," he said.

The Civil Defense picture was perhaps the most difficult. Bond originally painted a night scene during an air-raid drill. Two people stood near a blacked-out street lamp; nearby were a house with blinds drawn, and a vintage-1941 automobile with its headlights shielded. "It was too dark," Bond said. "It didn't blend with the rest of the stamp layouts." He and Paine discussed the problem at a lunchroom table, and hit on the idea of depicting Civil Defense equipment — a gas mask and a CD helmet — on a red and white checked tablecloth. Bond modeled the tablecloth on one in his own kitchen. The solution had a double benefit: It forced some bright color into the sheet, and it showed how essentially domestic Civil Defense was. "Kitchen table stuff," Howard Paine said.

For the Pearl Harbor scene, Bond decided against showing the stricken battleship *Arizona*, the best-known casualty of the attack, choosing instead to depict the battleships *West Virginia* (foreground) and *Tennessee*, moored side by side in "Battleship Row," against a backdrop of flame and black smoke. His source was a widely published Navy photograph. Although the *West Virginia* was sunk and the *Tennessee* damaged in the attack, both were salvaged and saw action later in the war.

Bond's picture of the House of Representatives, with President Roosevelt addressing a joint session of Congress, was based on contemporary photographs. Before settling on a long-range view from the right,

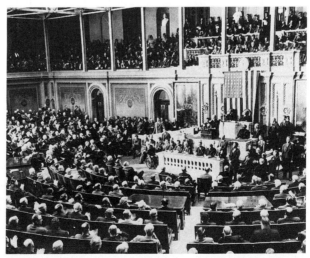

William Bond based his painting of President Roosevelt asking Congress for a declaration of war on this photograph taken in a packed House of Representatives, which is under scaffolding for ceiling repairs. USPS used the photograph in its book 1941: A World at War.

adapted from a photo in the National Archives, Bond had experimented with closeups of FDR at the podium and views from other angles. "I felt this one said what I wanted," he said.

Finally, Bond painted the map. Although not a cartographer, he had painted numerous map and map segments in his career with *The National Geographic*, and this part of the job was relatively easy.

For the sheet's typography, Howard Paine chose a variety of faces. "1941: A World at War" was a type called Egyptienne Bold Condensed F67. "29 USA" on each stamp was Clarendon Bold. The captions across the bottom of each stamp were in Stempel Schadow Italic, and the map notes were in Egyptienne F56 Italic. The type was set by an Arlington, Virginia, type house called Carver Photocomposition.

The wording on the stamps and map underwent changes as USPS researchers got into their work. For example, they found that the first Liberty Ship was launched in September 1941 for sea trials, but wasn't delivered until December 30. Because sources differed over the date of the U.S. occupation of Iceland, the October date that originally had been listed in the map reference was eliminated. And, after it was pointed out that Vichy France was nominally in control of part of North Africa, the color of that area on the map was changed to yellow from the red that denoted occupation by the Axis powers.

Although the map on the sheetlet bore the year "1941," the individual stamps did not. Postal officials conceded that this omission was unfortunate. The *Reuben James* stamp, for instance, carried the inscription "Destroyer Reuben James sunk October 31," but didn't say which October 31 it was. "We had to write these 'headlines' to very tight dimensions," said Jack Williams, USPS project manager for the sheet. "However, considering that the stamps were meant to be broken loose and used separately, there should have been a year on them. For the future sheets, we'll make sure a year date is given where it's necessary."

As USPS expected, critics were quick to find fault. A *Linn's Stamp News* reader challenged the accuracy of the map note that read: "Japan invades Philippines, Borneo, Thailand, Burma, Malaya, Shanghai (December)." The reader suggested that the entry should have been "Singapore" instead of "Shanghai," and *Linn's*, in an editor's note, agreed that the inclusion of Shanghai was "certainly a mistake," in that the Japanese had captured Shanghai from the Chinese back in 1937.

But other readers then wrote to defend the Postal Service. They pointed out that although the Chinese section of Shanghai did fall in 1937, the International Settlement and the French Settlement in Shanghai weren't occupied by Japanese forces until much later. The International Settlement was seized December 8, 1941, and the small U.S. garrison in the American section may have been the first American prisoners of war taken by the Japanese. *Linn's* acknowledged that its information had been faulty and apologized to its readers and USPS.

There wasn't room on the map to explain that Shanghai had been captured in stages, explained project manager Williams. "We probably would have been better advised leaving off the reference to Shanghai," he added. "But we didn't."

Another objection was raised by Eric C. Rust of Waco, Texas, who had translated into English the memoirs of Erich Topp, the skipper of the German U-boat that sank the *Reuben James*. Rust told *Linn's* that the design of the *Reuben James* stamp, showing a torpedo exploding against the hull of the U.S. destroyer as seen through a periscope, was "long on imagination and short on historical accuracy."

"First, *U 552* attacked on the surface with no need for Topp to use a periscope," Rust said. "Second, even if it had been a submerged attack, German periscopes used different optical crosswires than the ones shown on the stamp. Third, the *Reuben James* broke in half and sank well before daylight illuminated the scene.

"As Topp wrote me earlier this year, the scene as depicted on the stamp never could have occurred."

Said Jack Williams: "We used some artistic license to highlight a significant event. We had to show it at dawn, in some kind of light. And we picked a common grid for a periscope. There again, the expert is right, but we're not necessarily wrong."

Finally, another *Linn's Stamp News* reader pointed out that on the map the island of Sjaelland, on which Copenhagen, Denmark, is located, was colored yellow, instead of red, even though it was occupied during the war by Nazi Germany.

First-Day Facts

Postmaster General Frank and American Legion National Commander Robert S. Turner dedicated the sheet during the opening-day ceremonies for the Legion convention at the Phoenix Civic Plaza Convention Center. Among those on hand to autograph sheets, stamps, covers and books was designer William Bond.

Collectors of first-day covers had several options. They could affix complete 10-stamp sheets or individual stamps or multiples to addressed envelopes and send them to the postmaster at Phoenix for canceling. They could send addressed envelopes along with appropriate remittance and have the Postal Service affix sheets or individual stamps (selected at random) to receive the postmark. Or they could purchase USPS-made first-day covers bearing either a 10-stamp sheet or a full 20-stamp pane bearing the first-day cancellation. Service charges of $1 and $2, respectively, were assessed for these covers in addition to the face value.

29¢ DISTRICT OF COLUMBIA BICENTENNIAL

Date of Issue: September 7, 1991

Catalog Number: Scott 2561

Colors: magenta, yellow, cyan, black (offset); black (intaglio)

First-Day Cancel: Washington, D.C.

FDCs Canceled: 299,989

Format: Panes of 50, horizontal, 5 across, 10 down. Offset printing plates of 200 subjects (10 across, 20 around); intaglio printing sleeves of 400 subjects (10 across, 40 around).

Perf: 11.2 (Eureka off-line perforator)

Selvage Markings: "©/United States/Postal Service/1991." "Use Correct/ ZIP Code/®." USPS Olympic logo.

Designer: Pierre Mion of Lovettsville, Virginia

Art Director and Typographer: Derry Noyes (CSAC)

Project Manager: Jack Williams (USPS)

Engraver: Gary Slaght, lettering (BEP)

Modeler: Ronald C. Sharpe (BEP)

Printing: printed by BEP on 6-color offset, 3-color intaglio D press (902)

Quantity Ordered: 150,000,000

Quantity Distributed: 149,260,000

Plate/Sleeve Number Detail: 1 intaglio sleeve number alongside corner stamp; 1 group of 4 offset plate numbers in selvage of adjacent stamp.

Tagging: overall

The Stamp

USPS marked the bicentennial of the naming of the city of Washington and the District of Columbia with a 29¢ commemorative stamp issued in the nation's capital September 7.

Early in the stamp's development stages, individuals in the District of Columbia government apparently contacted representatives of the French government with the idea that the anniversary should be commemorated with a joint stamp issue by the United States and France. The proposed stamps would feature a portrait of Pierre L'Enfant, the French-born engineer who fought with the Americans in their Revolution and later created the plan for the city of Washington. Among the suggestions were that the stamps be diamond-shaped, matching the original shape of the District, and bear a District map, with L'Enfant's picture superimposed. One published report even had it that the joint issue was a *fait accompli.*

But neither the Postal Service nor the French postal administration ever showed any interest. "There was no French tie to that act of Congress establishing the District of Columbia," explained Donald McDowell, director of the USPS Office of Stamp and Philatelic Marketing. "To have had a joint stamp issue would have required that we get away from the theme of the D.C. Bicentennial and get it over into a shared interest between the United States and France in Pierre L'Enfant, which was a different thing."

The District of Columbia staged a series of bicentennial events beginning with the stamp-issuing ceremony, but it was not an elaborate birthday party, or even a universally popular one among Washington's citizens. "The District had a difficult time organizing even this modest bicentennial celebration," *The Washington Post* reported. "Because of the city's financial woes, the volunteer D.C. Bicentennial Commission never had any funds of its own and recently began relying on the mayor's office and private groups and businesses to organize or contribute to bicentennial theme events." And *Post* columnist Courtland Milloy called the celebration "inappropriate." It marked only "the beginning of political impotence" for the District, whose citizens have no voting representation in Congress, Milloy wrote.

Controversy over District affairs wasn't new. From the beginning, locating the nation's capital had been a matter of political dispute between Northern and Southern interests. In a compromise worked out by the North's Alexander Hamilton with the help of the South's Thomas Jefferson, the northern states — still burdened by heavy Revolutionary War debts — agreed to a site on the Potomac River incorporating portions of Virginia and Maryland. In return, the South would share in repaying the debts by allowing the federal government to assume and pay the state obligations. As a result of the bargain, President George Washington signed the Residence Act July 16, 1790, placing the Federal District on the Potomac and allowing 10 years to prepare the new capital city.

The following January Washington himself selected the specific site,

104

a four-sided tract 10 miles on each side bisected by the river and including the towns of Alexandria, Virginia, and Georgetown, Maryland. He sent surveyors Andrew Ellicott and Benjamin Banneker to fix the borders and named L'Enfant, whom he had known from Revolutionary War days, to draw up a plan for the city proper. On September 9, 1791, Secretary of State Thomas Jefferson and the three federal building commissioners sent a brief letter to L'Enfant announcing: "We have agreed that the federal district shall be called 'The Territory of Columbia,' and the federal city 'The City of Washington.' "

L'Enfant's plan, which he delivered to President Washington in August 1791, was the basis on which the city was built. Today's motorists and pedestrians see Washington as L'Enfant envisioned it, with its grid of streets overlaid and opened up by wide diagonal boulevards, with spacious parks at the boulevards' intersections, with the Capitol on a hill and the "Presidential palace" about a mile away along the tree-lined Pennsylvania Avenue, and with a broad Mall linking the grounds at the foot of Capitol Hill with those south of the president's home.

In the summer of 1800, however, when the federal government moved to town from Philadelphia, nothing was complete. Only one wing of the

Pierre Mion based his painting for the stamp on this 1903 photograph of Pennsylvania Avenue looking toward the Capitol from the Treasury Department. Mion found the picture in an illustrated history of Washington. The negative is owned by the Library of Congress.

Capitol was up, the single federal office building near the president's residence wasn't fully usable, and the "Presidential palace" itself — later to be called the White House — was without fencing or landscaping, and with interior plaster still wet. Abigail Adams, the first First Lady to live here, hung her wash in the unfinished East Room.

In 1846 the Virginia part of the District, on the west bank of the Potomac, was ceded back to the state. Finally, in 1895, Congress consolidated Washington and Georgetown and turned the entire area east of the Potomac into one large city with the boundaries as they are today, congruent with the District lines.

The original L'Enfant plan of 1791, yellowed and faded, is in the Library of Congress. During the bicentennial year of 1991, it was mounted in a new hermetically sealed case and put on public view for the first time in a quarter of a century. At the same time, the Library offered for sale copies of a computer-generated black-on-white reproduction of the plan, which brought out the lines with satisfying clarity and even revealed such hidden details as penciled notations made by Jefferson, who crossed out the "w" in L'Enfant's "Potowmac River."

Many stamps and postal cards have been issued depicting Washington scenes and landmarks and persons identified with the capital city. Two issues associated with the city's founding were the National Capital Sesquicentennial issue of 1950, consisting of four 3¢ stamps issued to mark the 150th anniversary of the move of the seat of government from Philadelphia to Washington (Scott 989-992), and a 1980 Black Heritage stamp honoring Benjamin Banneker (Scott 1804).

The Design

Although the stamp celebrated the District of Columbia's bicentennial, and its design subject was Pennsylvania Avenue, the centerpiece of Pierre L'Enfant's grand vision for the city, the period shown was a later period in the District's history: the first decade of the 20th century.

Artist Pierre Mion's painting, which he described as "stylized realism," showed Pennsylvania Avenue as it was in 1903, looking east from the Department of the Treasury toward the Capitol building. Trees line the avenue, two green and yellow trolley cars are in the foreground and a third car is seen in the distance, and pedestrians and horse-drawn carriages dot the pavement. On either side of the avenue are buildings, some of which still stand today. Willard's Hotel is at the extreme left, the turreted Apex Building at Seventh Street and Pennsylvania Avenue is in the middle distance on the left, and the Old Post Office (its Romanesque tower cut off by the top of the picture frame) can be seen on the right.

The small size of the stamp, and the complexity of the scene, forced Mion to keep his artwork simple, limit the number of people to a relative few, and stylize such features as the building windows. "If I had tried to show all the windows, they would have all run together in the reproduction," Mion said. "I felt this approach would work better at stamp size, rather than trying to make it photographically realistic." For the same

106

The only likeness of Pierre L'Enfant that is believed to be authentic is this silhouette, made around 1785 by Sarah DeHart.

reason, he used "very flat, postery type colors," he said.

The decision to use this particular image was reached only after a long and laborious process involving the Citizens' Stamp Advisory Committee, Mion and another artist who also worked on the project.

After preliminary talks with art director Derry Noyes, Mion prepared several sketches in which an outline map of the District served as a backdrop for various combinations of objects, including the Capitol dome and a profile of George Washington. The committee looked at these sketches and suggested that Mion take another tack, involving Pierre L'Enfant's original plan of the city and a portrait of L'Enfant.

Philip Ogilvie, public records administrator for the District of Columbia, conducted a long search and finally located what he was convinced was the only existing true likeness of L'Enfant. It was a profile silhouette that was cut around 1785 by one Sarah DeHart of Elizabethtown, New Jersey. The silhouette, the most striking feature of which was a prominent aquiline nose, was given to the Fine Arts Committee of the State Department in 1973 and now hangs in the department's lavish diplomatic reception rooms. Despite Ogilvie's lengthy and ultimately successful search, the idea of depicting L'Enfant on the stamp was dropped.

These two concept sketches by Pierre Mion showed a late 19th-century view of Washington as seen across the Potomac River from Virginia and a scene along the Chesapeake and Ohio Canal in Georgetown.

107

CSAC then asked that Mion work up some period sketches of the city. He prepared three such pieces. One was a view down the Chesapeake and Ohio Canal toward old Georgetown, with Georgetown University on an elevation at the left. A second, set around 1884, looked across the Potomac River from the Virginia shore. In the foreground were a paddle-wheel steamboat and (square-rigged) sailing ships. Behind them were the newly completed Washington Monument, with the Capitol dome in the far distance. The third scene was the one that eventually became the stamp design.

But before CSAC made its final choice, it returned to the idea of a design incorporating Pierre L'Enfant's city plan, and commissioned another artist to prepare some sketches. In the end, the committee abandoned this idea, and asked each of the two artist candidates to prepare a final painting. Mion's was to incorporate the Pennsylvania Avenue scene, and the other artist's was to show the District of Columbia flag, a red and white banner based on George Washington's coat of arms. The flag idea appealed to some CSAC members because the District had been left out when the 50-stamp pane depicting State Flags had been issued in 1976.

"At that point, we were just spinning wheels," said art director Noyes, "because we couldn't come up with an image that everybody thought was appropriate for saying 'the city' without being just totally 'the federal government,' which doesn't give the impression of the District of Columbia itself. All the icons in Washington are really not of the District of Columbia, but evoke the whole country. So the historical route was really the only way to go."

But to go all the way back to the original year, 1791, would have been futile, she added. There were no buildings then, only undeveloped land. So the decision was made to choose a representative scene from a recognizable period in the city's history, which led the committee back to Mion's Pennsylvania Avenue painting.

Mion based his picture on a photograph in a book, *The City of Washington: An Illustrated History* by the Junior League of Washington (1977, Alfred Knopf), and supplemented this reference with photographs of the present-day Pennsylvania Avenue, which he shot from the same

An attempt was made to develop a design using Pierre L'Enfant's city plan, but it was obviously too detailed and not readily recognizable.

District of Columbia Bicentennial
USA 25
★ ★ ★

This sketch by another artist of the red and white District of Columbia flag was passed over in favor of Pierre Mion's more lively street scene.

vantage point at the Treasury. He made some changes in his picture for artistic purposes. He removed some tree foliage and overhead utility wires, simplified the building lines, and — making full use of artistic license — changed the angle of the Capitol so that it seemed to meet Pennsylvania Avenue head-on rather than at an angle.

The trolleys in the original photograph had open sides, but Mion enclosed them, after consulting experts at the National Capital Trolley Museum in Wheaton, Maryland, and examining pictures in a library book about vintage Washington trolley cars. A colored illustration in that

Pierre Mion's original concept sketch of the Pennsylvania Avenue scene was later adapted to a finished painting and used on the District of Columbia stamp.

volume confirmed that the trolleys were green and yellow, and he used these colors for the cars in his own picture.

Mion originally made the scene deeper — showing, for example, more of the old Post Office tower at the right — and superimposed the commemorative inscription on the sky at the top. But the committee decided it wanted a somewhat shallower picture with the typography placed outside the frameline.

The stamp was printed on BEP's combination offset-intaglio D press, with only the "USA 29" inscription in intaglio.

Varieties

Several small finds were made of District of Columbia stamps missing the intaglio portion, which consisted only of the black typography at the lower right corner of the design.

First-Day Facts

Samuel Green Jr., Eastern regional postmaster general, dedicated the stamp at a public ceremony at the Pavilion of the Old Post Office, 1100

109

District of Columbia Bicentennial

Pennsylvania Avenue, circa 1903

The intaglio portion, which consisted only of the black typography at the lower right corner of the design, is missing on this District of Columbia stamp.

Pennsylvania Avenue. Robert G. Stanton, director of the National Capital Region of the National Park Service, extended the welcome, and Washington Mayor Sharon Pratt Dixon was the principal speaker. "You see Pennsylvania Avenue in all its glory," Mayor Dixon said of the stamp design. "But you won't see the District Building. That came later." It was completed in 1908.

Two actors, dressed as Pierre L'Enfant and Benjamin Banneker, were on stage and autographed programs and covers afterward — staying in character during the entire exercise.

USPS provided a pictorial handstamp first-day postmark featuring the District of Columbia's bicentennial logo.

29¢ JAN MATZELIGER
BLACK HERITAGE SERIES

Date of Issue: September 15, 1991

Catalog Number: Scott 2567

Colors: tan, brown, yellow, magenta, cyan, black

First-Day Cancel: Lynn, Massachusetts

FDCs Canceled: 289,034

Format: Panes of 50, vertical, 10 across, 5 down. Gravure printing cylinders of 200 subjects (10 across, 20 around) manufactured by Armotek Industries Inc., Palmyra, New Jersey.

Perf: 10.9 (L perforator)

Selvage Markings: "©/United States/Postal Service/1991." "Use Correct/ ZIP Code/®/36 USC 380." USPS-Olympic Logo.

Marginal Inscription: "Jan E. Matzeliger/(1852-1889) came/to the U.S. from/ Dutch Guiana in 1870." "Working as a cobbler/in Lynn, MA, Jan/invented and patented/a shoe lasting machine." "His invention cut/cost and improved/ working conditions/in the shoe industry."

Designer: Barbara Higgins Bond of Teaneck, New Jersey

Art Director: Jerry Pinkney (CSAC)

Project Manager: Jack Williams (USPS)

Typographer: Bradbury Thompson (CSAC)

Modeler: Richard Sennett, Sennett Enterprises, for American Bank Note Company

Printing: Printed for American Bank Note Company on a leased Champlain gravure press at J.W. Fergusson and Sons, Richmond, Virginia, under the supervision of Sennett Enterprises, Fairfax, Virginia. Stamps perforated, processed and shipped by ABNC, Bedford Park, Illinois.

Quantity Ordered: 152,000,000

Quantity Distributed: 148,973,000

Cylinder Number Detail: 1 group of 6 cylinder numbers preceded by the letter A alongside corner stamp

Tagging: overall

The Stamp

The 14th stamp in the Black Heritage series honored Jan Matzeliger, the inventor of the first practical machine for lasting (shaping) shoes. The stamp was issued on his birthday, September 15, in Lynn, Massachusetts, where Matzeliger lived for most of his adult life.

The September release date was the latest for any stamp in the series. Most previous Black Heritage stamps had been timed to appear in or around February, which is observed annually as Black History Month. Because of the uncertainty over what the first-class rate would be in February 1991, however, it would have been impossible for USPS to have prepared a stamp with the appropriate denomination in time for the beginning of the month.

Once again a marginal inscription produced problems for USPS, as it had done earlier in the year with the Hubert Humphrey definitive stamp (see Humphrey stamp chapter). The inscription, one of three paragraphs about Matzeliger printed in the selvage, was this: "Working as a cobbler in Lynn, MA, Jan invented and patented a shoe lasting machine."

Barth Healey, stamp writer for *The New York Times,* took note of the wording as it was reported in the official USPS news release on the stamp and sought comment from Ethelbert Miller, whom he described as a researcher in Afro-American history at Howard University. Miller told Healey the use of the first name "Jan" was "a major error" and was "like misspelling someone's name."

Miller cited the long history of whites' using only first names to address blacks, who as slaves did not have last names. "But by using 'Mr.' or 'Mrs.' the speaker acknowledges that the black is an adult," Miller said, "and the use of first names is a sign of a certain power relationship, that the black is kept subservient."

Healey reported this conversation in a *Times* article August 4 that was headed: "Post Office Goofs Again and Some Cry Racism." In the article he also quoted Art Shealy, of USPS, as saying: "It was more of an editorial slip. I don't think it was intentional. Some of our writers here are not used to using journalistic style, and they might have been uncomfort-

112

able using 'Mr. Matzeliger' or just 'Matzeliger,' so they used 'Jan.' "

To a *Linn's Stamp News* writer, Shealy explained that the use of the first name "wasn't caught" in the normal approval process. "If we could run everything by everybody we would catch these things," he said.

Donald M. McDowell, director of the Office of Stamp and Philatelic Marketing, told the *Yearbook* that one of the reasons USPS had had problems with the accuracy and style of its marginal inscriptions was that up until then these paragraphs had been "retrofitted" to stamps that had already been through the research and design process. As a result, the inscriptions were prepared in haste and without independent review.

"It's kind of a headline writing exercise," McDowell said. "You can put the selvage message adjacent to only three stamps. You have a restricted number of characters and lines to work with. (The Matzeliger mistake) happened the same way that an unfortunate headline might happen in a newspaper. I don't know what we could say about it other than we were aghast that we had inadvertently done something that anyone would interpret the way *The Times* pictured some people as interpreting it. We regret it.

"But the Matzeliger stamp was the last one in which the marginal inscription was added retroactively. From this day forward the inscription will be a part of the basic design process. It will proceed with all the research and the same careful review that the design gets from the researchers and the Citizens' Stamp Advisory Committee and the staff. The inscription will be as much a part of the design as a piece of art."

Jan Ernst Matzeliger (pronounced mat-ZELL-eh-ger) was born in 1852 in Dutch Guiana (now Surinam), the son of a Dutch father and a

A source contacted by The New York Times *raised an objection to the reference to Matzeliger as "Jan" in the stamp selvage.*

native mother. At the age of 10, he was apprenticed to the government machine shop, where he developed an interest in mechanics and showed an aptitude for machine work.

When he was about 20, Matzeliger came to the United States. As a black man in post-Civil War America, and a foreigner who spoke only rudimentary English, he found the search for skilled employment extremely difficult, but he persevered, taking odd jobs to survive. In 1877 he obtained work at the Harney Brothers shoe factory in Lynn, running a McKay sole-stitching machine.

It was the Golden Age of machinery, when ingenious inventors everywhere were finding ways to make steam- or combustion-driven gears, pistons, wheels and cables do the work of men. Machines had been developed for all the shoe-making functions except lasting — connecting the upper part of the shoe to the inner sole. Stretching the leather over the last (a wooden model of the foot) and tacking the finished shape into place took great skill. Matzeliger heard the hand lasters boast that no one would ever create a machine to do their work. He resolved to prove them wrong.

Matzeliger carefully watched the hand lasters' technique. In a rented room, using what scrap material he could lay his hands on, he worked alone and at night for many months to design and build a model of a machine that would imitate the skilled craftsmen's motions. He took a job at another shoe factory, Beal Brothers, where his new employer had the forge and lathe necessary for building a full-size working machine and was willing to let Matzeliger use them for that purpose.

By 1882 he had his scrap-metal prototype completed. Though crude, it proved capable of pleating the leather around the toe of the sole. The inventor's success became known, and though he was very poor, he refused an offer of $1,500 for the device. With the financial support of two Lynn businessmen, he set to work on a third machine — one made with precision, of new parts. This he completed in 1883 and patented, receiving patent number 274,207 on March 20. In one minute, the machine could hold the last in place to receive the leather, move it forward step by step so that the other parts could draw the leather over the heel, punch and grip the upper and draw it down over the last, lay the leather properly at the heel and toe, feed the nails and hold them in position for driving, and then eject the completed shoe.

New investors came aboard, and the Consolidated Hand Method Lasting Machine Company was formed, with Matzeliger receiving a block of stock in return for his patent rights. Shoe manufacturers were eager to obtain the new machine, which could turn out up to 700 pairs of shoes in a 10-hour day, compared to the 50 that a good hand laster could produce. The machine also could be adapted to differing shoe styles. "People who could have never been able to afford shoes before suddenly found them affordable," wrote a biographer, Barbara Mitchell. "Jan Matzeliger had quietly revolutionized the shoe industry."

Unfortunately, Matzeliger didn't live to prosper from his invention.

114

Matzeliger's portrait on the stamp was based on this photograph, the only likeness of the inventor that could be found.

He contracted tuberculosis and died at the age of 37. He left a bequest of stock to North Congregational Church in Lynn, which later enabled the church to pay off its mortgage. Children from the Sunday School still place flowers on his grave at Pine Grove Cemetery each year.

The Design

An artist new to stamp design, Barbara Higgins Bond of Teaneck, New Jersey, designed the Matzeliger commemorative. She was only the third artist to work in the Black Heritage series. Jerry Pinkney and Tom Blackshear had created all the previous designs.

Bond, who uses the name Higgins Bond professionally, is an illustrator whose credits include books, magazines, record albums, posters, calendars, advertisements, collectors' plates and individual painting commissions. She had known Jerry Pinkney, a CSAC design coordinator, from work they had done together on a series of paintings of the "Great Kings of Africa" commissioned by the Anheuser-Busch Company. She had been a stamp collector herself as a child, and she wrote to Pinkney asking how she could apply for a stamp-designing assignment. Pinkney showed samples of her work to CSAC and the USPS staff, and in 1990 the Postal Service's Jack Williams telephoned Bond and asked her to submit concept sketches for a Jan Matzeliger commemorative.

The only photograph of Matzeliger that could be found was one showing the young man in a coat and polka-dotted bow tie. Culver Pictures owned the photograph. USPS obtained the rights to reproduce it from Culver. Bond based her acrylic painting for the stamp inventor on that image. But because the original picture was black and white, she had to guess at skin tones when she translated it into color.

"I tend to work very dark, in rich colors," Bond said. "Jerry kept saying, 'When the painting is reduced to stamp size it's going to get muddy. You need to lighten it up.' I think we changed that bow tie a dozen times before I got it light enough so that it would show contrast." The polka-dotted tie was originally a deep burgundy shade, and it ended up

115

lavender. "Everything had to be light enough and airy enough so that when it was reduced it wouldn't just turn to a blob of color," she said.

The biggest problem Bond and Jerry Pinkney faced was finding a way artistically to link Matzeliger to the invention of a shoe-lasting machine. "It wasn't like doing Martin Luther King, where you can show people marching and you know what he's about," she said. "We tried using a small figure of Matzeliger working on a shoe, different views like that, to place in the foreground, in front of the portrait."

Eventually they decided to make artistic reference to the 1883 patent that marked Matzeliger's great achievement. They first tried incorporating in the design a hypothetical patent tag of the kind that would have been attached to Matzeliger's lasting machine at the Patent Office. "That didn't work," said Jack Williams, the stamp's project manager. "It left empty space in the design, and we were afraid the details on the tag would get lost in the reduction, and it wouldn't really tell the story."

Finally, they turned to the schematic drawing of the machine that had accompanied the patent — a drawing that was reproduced in a number of books and articles about the inventor. The drawing was too detailed to use without modifications, however. Accordingly, it was photographed and then retouched by John Boyd of Anagraphics Inc. in New York to remove extraneous letters and numbers, lighten dark areas and generally improve legibility. A print was made in the sepia color that had been chosen for the stamp, and this print was spread horizontally behind the portrait in the stamp design to provide a balanced arrangement of the machine elements on either side of the face.

First-Day Facts

The first-day ceremony for the Matzeliger stamp was held at the Heritage State Park in Lynn and was open to the public. The ceremony

The artist and art director tried combining the portrait with the actual patent drawing and two versions of a Patent Office tag, but these approaches were unsatisfactory.

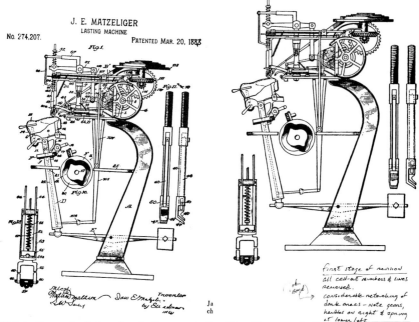

J. E. MATZELIGER
LASTING MACHINE

No. 274,207.

PATENTED MAR. 20, 1883

This is the patent drawing before and after it had been artistically simplified for use on the stamp. The numbers, letters and lines that keyed parts of the drawing to a list of machine parts were eliminated. Dark areas were lightened.

was part of a series of activities honoring Matzeliger, which included a 30-minute television documentary produced by WGBH in Boston that was broadcast nationwide.

Gladys Haywood and Robert Smith, a Matzeliger historian, were the principal speakers. The stamp was dedicated by Elwood A. Mosley, assistant postmaster general.

$5.80 SPACE EXPLORATION BOOKLET

Date of Issue: October 1, 1991

Catalog Numbers: Scott 2568-2577 (stamps); 2577a (booklet pane of 10)

Colors: magenta, cyan, yellow, black, light brown, blue

First-Day Cancel: Pasadena, California

FDCs Canceled: 1,465,111

Format: 2 panes of 10 horizontal stamps each, arranged horizontally, 5 across by 2 down. Gravure printing cylinders of 200 subjects.

Perf: 11.2 (Eureka off-line perforator)

Selvage Markings: cylinder numbers printed on each pane binding stub

Cover Markings: "© United States Postal Service 1991" and promotion for USPS Commemorative Stamp Club on inside of front cover. Universal Product Code (UPC) and promotion for Stamp Club on outside of back cover. Coupon for Stamp Club on inside of back cover.

Designer: Ron Miller of Fredericksburg, Virginia

Art Director and Typographer: Howard Paine (CSAC)

Project Manager: Jack Williams (USPS)

Printing: printed by BEP on Andreotti 7-color gravure press (601)

Quantity Ordered: 701,000,000 (33,750,000 booklets; 2,600,000 unfolded panes

Quantity Distributed: 333,948,000 (15,392,400 booklets; 2,610,000 unfolded panes

Cylinder Number Detail: 1 group of 6 gravure cylinder numbers on each pane binding stub

Tagging: overall

The Stamps

Late in 1988, Howard Paine, a design coordinator for the Citizens' Stamp Advisory Committee, pointed out that the following August the *Voyager 2* unmanned space probe would pass Neptune and head out of the Solar System after a 12-year trip from Earth. Paine suggested that USPS issue a booklet of commemorative stamps featuring all nine planets, plus Earth's Moon, to mark the occasion.

Stamps showing the planets had been discussed by CSAC from time to time over the years, and Paine was given the go-ahead to have the artwork prepared. But lack of time, plus technical problems, made it impossible to issue the stamps in August 1989. It wasn't until October 1, 1991, that the booklet made its appearance, to help launch the 11th annual USPS-sponsored Stamp Collecting Month. The theme of the campaign: "Journey to a New Frontier — Collect Stamps!"

The booklet contained 10 different varieties, each depicting one of the nine planets that orbit the Sun, plus the Moon. Also shown were the U.S. unmanned spacecraft that journeyed to them (with the exception of Pluto, which hasn't yet been explored).

To promote the stamps themselves, USPS joined with Paramount Studios, which was marking the 25th anniversary of its popular television and movie series *Star Trek*. The arrangement was similar to the Postal Service's 1989 joint promotion with MCA Home Video of the Prehistoric Animals block of four.

According to the Postal Service, the new joint campaign was proposed by Paramount in 1990 after USPS had announced its 1991 stamp program. On July 3, 1991, Postmaster General Anthony M. Frank unveiled the designs of the 10 space stamps at Paramount Studios on the bridge of the *Starship Enterprise*, the space vehicle featured in *Star Trek*. With him were Mel Harris, president of Paramount Television Group, and Leonard Nimoy, who played *Star Trek's* Mr. Spock.

The joint promotion included not only the stamps but 10 *Star Trek* stickers and a stamp-sticker holder produced by Paramount. Posters and counter cards featuring those items were displayed in post offices, video stores and other retail stores. In addition, Paramount included an insert promoting the stamps and *Star Trek* items in 1.3 million video cassettes.

The Postal Service attempted to deflect potential criticism of these joint promotions with a news release containing endorsements by Keith A. Wagner, executive director of the American Philatelic Society, and Joseph B. Savarese, executive officer of the American Stamp Dealers' Association. Both men noted that joint promotions attract new people to

119

stamp collecting.

Said Gordon C. Morison, assistant postmaster general: "Based on our experience in 1989 (with the Prehistoric Animals joint promotion), we knew we could expand awareness and sales of selected stamps through carefully planned joint promotions which enable us to reach large, targeted audiences. That was our first experience with it, and we waited two years before agreeing to more joint promotions in order to thoroughly evaluate and analyze the results ... Since we are competing for the leisure time and budget of our audience, we believe targeted joint promotions are one of the best vehicles to convey our message (to that audience)."

In promoting stamp collecting during October, USPS was joined by five co-sponsors: the Benjamin Franklin Stamp Clubs, the Council of Philatelic Organizations, the American Library Association, the Girl Scouts and the National Association of Elementary School Principals.

USPS created a pictorial first-day postmark for the Space Exploration stamps that featured the ringed planet Saturn; a National Stamp Collecting Month pictorial postmark from Washington, D.C., and a special cancellation featuring the *Starship Enterprise* and the National Stamp Collecting Month slogan. This special machine cancellation die was authorized for use from September 1 through October 31 at 151 post offices throughout the country.

MERCURY. The Mercury stamp depicted *Mariner 10*, launched in November 1973. It passed Venus the following February and Mercury in March. Venus gave *Mariner 10* a gravity boost, the first time one planet's gravity was used to whip a spacecraft toward another. The thousands of photographs the spacecraft transmitted were the first detailed pictures of Mercury and Venus. *Mariner 10* and the two planets it visited were depicted on a 10¢ commemorative stamp of 1975 (Scott 1557).

VENUS. The Venus stamp showed *Mariner 2*, NASA's earliest major space probe. *Mariner 2* was launched August 27, 1962, and passed within 22,000 miles of Venus the following December 14.

EARTH. The Earth stamp depicted one of the *Landsats*, formally known as Earth Resources Technology Satellites (ERTS). Three *Landsats*

These are the three special postmarks authorized by USPS in connection with the Space Exploration stamps and National Stamp Collecting Month.

were launched between 1972 and 1978 to orbit the Earth at an altitude of about 560 miles and collect information about the location of mineral resources, monitor atmospheric and oceanic conditions and detect variations in pollution levels and other ecological changes. In 1982 a new *Landsat D* series was introduced with *Landsat 4*, followed by *Landsat 5* in 1984. A U.S. aerogram issued in 1985 (Scott UC58) saluted the *Landsat* program.

THE MOON. The vehicle featured on the Moon stamp was a Lunar Orbiter, five of which were launched in 1966 and 1967. Instead of surveying very specific, small areas of the lunar surface, as the *Surveyor* probes had done, *Lunar Orbiters* presented all-encompassing views of the Moon and the Earth. As they circled the Moon, each of the first three Orbiters photographed in detail the equatorial landing sites for the forthcoming Apollo manned missions.

MARS. The Mars stamp featured a *Viking Orbiter*. *Vikings 1* and *2* were launched in 1975 and went into orbit around Mars in 1976. Their landers separated from the orbiting craft and touched down on the planet, enabling a tiny laboratory on board to test soil samples for signs of life. The Viking missions to Mars were saluted on a 15¢ commemorative stamp of 1978 (Scott 1759).

JUPITER. Jupiter was shown with *Pioneer 11*, which was launched in 1973 and swept past the planet in December 1974, measuring its radiation levels. The gravity boost the spacecraft received sent it on its way to a rendezvous with Saturn in 1979. *Pioneer 11* and Saturn were depicted on one of the stamps in the se-tenant Space Achievement block of 1981 (Scott 1916). *Pioneer 11's* predecessor, *Pioneer 10*, the first unmanned probe to be launched toward the outer planets, left Earth orbit in 1972 and flew by Jupiter in December 1973. It was pictured on a 10¢ commemorative stamp of 1975 (Scott 1556).

SATURN, URANUS, NEPTUNE. *Voyager 2* was shown on the stamps featuring these three planets. This probe and its companion, *Voyager 1*, were launched in 1977, and both flew by Jupiter in 1979 before heading for Saturn. *Voyager 2* continued on to encounter Uranus in 1986 and Neptune in 1989. Both carried 11 instruments, including video cameras, antennae and instruments to study planetary magnetic fields and atmospheres.

PLUTO. The outermost planet and the only one that hasn't been visited

Previous U.S. space commemoratives marked the **Pioneer 10** *(Scott 1556),* **Mariner 10** *(Scott 1557) and* Viking *(Scott 1759) missions.*

by a space vehicle from Earth was pictured alone on its stamp.

The Designs

Ron Miller of Fredericksburg, Virginia, whose paintings were reproduced on the stamps, is a free-lance artist, illustrator and science-fiction writer specializing in space topics. Until 1977, he had been an illustrator at the Smithsonian Institution's National Air and Space Museum, doing everything from the panoramas projected on the planetarium dome to artwork for museum publications. The Space Exploration booklet was his first stamp design assignment.

After Howard Paine commissioned Miller to develop artwork for the stamps, Miller painted a set of 10 horizontal pictures showing each heavenly body as seen over the horizon of a satellite or neighboring planet, or from a point in outer space.

Mercury, viewed from behind, was a crescent, lit by the brilliant sun beyond it. The Moon stamp depicted a small, glowing globe hanging over a blue, cloud-shrouded Earth; on the Earth stamp, the two bodies were in the opposite relationship. Neptune was a blue orb seen over the blue and

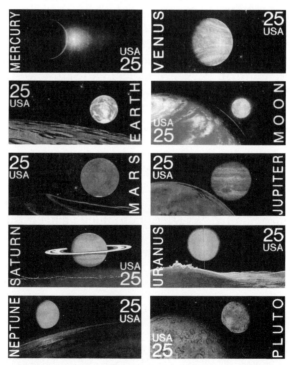

Ron Miller's original paintings didn't contain space vehicles, and most of them showed the featured planet as seen from a neighboring heavenly body. These images, if used on stamps, would have been too dark to allow a good phosphorescent signal from the tagging to the automatic postal equipment.

122

frozen landscape of one of its moons, and dark and remote Pluto hovered behind its single satellite, Charon.

Miller painted the heavenly bodies against the black of outer space, and Howard Paine used dropout white for all the typography. However, this approach presented a technical problem. The designs were deemed too dark for the taggant — whether it was applied before or after the printing ink — to properly activate post office facer-cancelers.

So Paine cropped the paintings to show more white. In the process he added some informational typography to each design: the diameter of the planet, its distance from the sun, and the length of its year. But CSAC members and/or USPS staff turned down the idea, on grounds that the type would be too small to be effective.

At this point, Postmaster General Anthony M. Frank asked that a U.S. spacecraft be incorporated in each painting to make the issue in part a salute to American technological achievement. Possibly, Paine and Miller thought, the spacecraft could be painted separately and then be electronically photo-composed into the original paintings. But this proved to be impractical, so the artist "heaved a sigh," as he said, returned to his drawing board and created completely new artwork.

Miller selected the spacecraft himself for each planet, and referred to pictures from his own library to make sure he was accurately representing the strange-looking vehicles with their multiple panels, booms and antennas. CSAC advised Miller, through Paine, that the paintings should show only the planets and spacecraft, and not include any moons or other neighboring heavenly bodies. "They thought it would be confusing," Miller said. "For that reason, poor Pluto is on its stamp all by itself. I originally had put Pluto's moon in the picture to take up some of the excess space. They didn't want that."

Miller painted his pictures in acrylic on illustration board. Although stamp artists normally work at no more than five times stamp size, Miller

These essays show different ways in which art director Howard Paine cropped the Mercury and Venus pictures to allow white space to show. Paine also hoped, in the process, to provide technical information on the planets, but the typography would have been too small for easy legibility.

Mercury, Mariner 10   USA 30

This is the design format that was finally adopted for the Space Exploration stamps, but a different view of Mercury and Mariner 10 was used. Also, the type was an all-caps Univers face rather than the uppercase and lowercase Galliard shown here.

had a "special dispensation," he said, to work at 10 times stamp size because of the amount of detail in the spacecraft ("They're such spindly little things").

The final decision was to place the vignette in a long rectangle and strip the type across the white space beneath it: the name of the planet and spacecraft, the denomination and "USA." Howard Paine experimented with a typeface called Galliard, using uppercase and lowercase letters, before settling on all capitals in a type with the appropriate name of Univers (spelled without a finishing e).

Because Pluto's stamp was the only one without a space vehicle in the design, the planet's name stood alone at first. But the blank area looked out of place next to the other nine stamps. So Paine added the word "Unexplored," finally changing it to "Not Yet Explored."

Jack Williams, the project manager, took the finished artwork to NASA, where John Mankins, manager of the Exploration Technology Program for the Office of Aeronautics and Space Technology, confirmed that the spacecraft images and the inscriptions were accurate. Postmaster General Anthony M. Frank approved the designs January 4, 1991.

The stamps were printed on BEP's Andreotti gravure press. Afterward, some persons expressed disappointment at the result. Paine, for one, called the stamps "grim and dim." "They should have had much more contrast," Paine said. "Sunlight shining on the moon's surface is luminous, almost like snow. That kind of quality should have come through on the stamps. The gold Mylar wrappings of the spacecraft should have shone brightly."

First-Day Facts

Postmaster General Frank dedicated the stamps during the October 1 first-day ceremony at the Jet Propulsion Laboratory in Pasadena, California. Edward C. Stone, director of the Jet Propulsion Laboratory, and Fred W. Bowen, manager of the Laboratory's NASA Resident Office, were the speakers. The ceremony was televised over the NASA Network and patched to all USPS divisions

An unofficial second-day ceremony, with USPS participation, was held October 2 at the Christa McAuliffe Planetarium on the campus of the New Hampshire Technical Institute in Concord, New Hampshire. The planetarium was named for the schoolteacher-astronaut who died in the explosion of the space shuttle *Challenger* in 1986.

SPECIAL STAMPS

Special stamps are issued for specific mailing purposes, are printed in greater quantities than commemoratives and are on sale for longer periods. The year 1991 saw a record high number of 13 specials, two of which were surprises — to the Postal Service as well as to collectors.

One of the surprises was an extra perforation variety on the 29¢ Love sheet stamp, the result of an equipment breakdown at the private company producing the stamp. This variety was not discovered until several months after it had appeared, and was made available to collectors through the Philatelic Sales Division only after *Linn's Stamp News* had called the attention of USPS officials to its existence.

The other was an extra design variety on the contemporary Christmas stamp booklet. The booklet was supposed to contain five collectible designs, but actually contained six because the printer — another private subcontractor — created two slightly different gravure images of one of the designs and placed them side by side on the same booklet pane. Nothing quite like it had ever happened before in U.S. stamp production.

29¢ LOVE (SHEET STAMP)

Date of Issue: May 9, 1991

Catalog Number: perf 12.75 by 13, Scott 2535; perf 11, no number assigned

Colors: yellow, magenta, cyan, black, blue

First-Day Cancel: Honolulu, Hawaii

FDCs Canceled: 336,132. Combination Love FDCs, 3,744.

Format: Panes of 50, horizontal, 5 across, 10 down. Gravure printing cylinders of 300 subjects (15 across, 20 around).

Perf: 12.75 by 13 (Ormag rotary perforator); 11 (L perforator).

Selvage Markings: "© USPS 1991." "USE CORRECT ZIP CODE ®."

Designer: Harry Zelenko of New York, New York

Art Director and Project Manager: Jack Williams (USPS)

Typographer: Bradbury Thompson (CSAC)

Printing: printed by Jeffries Banknote Division of United States Bank Note Corporation, Los Angeles, California, on 8-color combination Andreotti-Giori gravure-intaglio webfed press

Quantity Ordered: 928,000,000

Quantity Distributed: 928,000,000 (669,000,000, Ormag perforator; 259,000,000 L perforator)

Cylinder Number Detail: 1 group of 4 cylinder numbers preceded by the letter U alongside corner stamp

Tagging: phosphor-coated paper

The Stamp

Four different Love postal items made a simultaneous debut May 9 in Honolulu, Hawaii, a popular honeymoon destination. They were a 29¢ stamp in sheet and booklet form, a 52¢ stamp to cover the two-ounce letter rate, and a 29¢ stamped envelope.

None of the four items represented a new Love format for USPS, but this marked the first time all four types had been issued together.

Late in the year, the existence of a fifth Love item — a perforation variety of the 29¢ sheet stamp — was discovered. It had been quietly created when the printer's original perforator broke down, requiring the use of backup equipment to finish the job.

Following tradition, the design of the basic Love stamp — the one bearing the first-class rate — was unveiled in Washington, D.C., as the New Year of 1991 arrived. But this time the setting was different.

Since 1983, at the major outdoor party staged each New Year's Eve by the city of Washington, a giant illuminated copy of the next Love stamp design had been lowered at midnight from the 310-foot spire of the Old Post Office on Pennsylvania Avenue. Former Washington Mayor Marion Barry was confident, he said, that the falling Love stamp would become a tradition akin to the annual descending orb in New York City.

But by New Year's Eve of 1988, Barry's Washington had ceased its official participation in the event, being unable any longer to afford the musical entertainment, promotional costs and overtime pay for police and other city officials that the party required. Only an estimated 750 people watched the Love design descend that year. The turnout was similarly small to welcome 1990 (when USPS lowered a replica of its already-issued Love envelope of 1989).

So, for 1991, USPS changed venue. A smaller version of the next Love stamp was lowered inside the Old Post Office Pavilion via the National Park Service elevator in the Pavilion's atrium during a party for some 2,500 people sponsored by the Pavilion. The design lacked a denomination because the new first-class rate hadn't yet been set.

The Postal Service dropped the outdoor drop because of the small turnout and the big expense, spokesman Jim Murphy told *The Washington Post.* Murphy was unable to provide cost estimates, but said that previous Love stamp replicas had weighed two tons, featured neon lights and measured 20 by 30 feet.

USPS issued its first Love stamp in 1973, with no indication that the stamp was the forerunner of a continuing series. The next Love stamp didn't appear until 1982. They have since become popular with the public and have remained a constant in the U.S. stamp program.

The 29¢ and 52¢ Love stamps of 1991 bore the 10th and 11th designs in the series. Past designs have featured the word "Love" in various styles and configurations, as well as hearts, flowers, birds and a cartoon puppy.

As was the case in 1990, the sheet version of the basic Love stamp was printed by the United States Bank Note Corporation at its Jeffries Banknote Company plant in Los Angeles, and the booklet version was produced by the Bureau of Engraving and Printing. The gravure process was used by both printers.

In December 1991, officials of the American Bank Note Company, another subsidiary of United States Bank Note, responded to a request by *Linn's U.S. Stamp Yearbook* for printing information about the Love stamp. They told the *Yearbook* that the 29¢ Love stamp had been perforated by two different types of equipment: an Ormag rotary perforator and an L perforator.

Because this same combination at Jeffries had produced two distinctly different varieties of the 29¢ Flower sheet stamp earlier in the year, it now seemed likely that there were two different Love stamp varieties in circulation as well, rather than the single type — perf 12.75 by 13, with bull's-eye perforations — that collectors had known about.

Linn's Stamp News made further inquiries at ABNC and also launched a search of hundreds of pieces of mail at *Linn's* to try to find an example of the L-perfed Love stamp. The search produced one specimen, on a December 2 cover postmarked in Utica, New York. Unlike the Ormag-perfed variety, the stamp was perf 11 and its perforations met randomly

This early version of the Love stamp used dark-on-white typography and a futuristic typeface.

at intersections, leaving a ragged look at the corners.

Jeffries Bank Note's Ormag perforator, which the company used at the beginning of production of both the Flower sheet stamp and the Love stamp, was an on-line harrow perforator that was retrofitted onto the company's Andreotti gravure press. Stamps coming off the press were perforated in full printing sheets.

During the summer, the Ormag broke down, and in September, production of the remaining Love stamps had to be switched to an L perforator, which perforates in one direction at a time. Of a total printing of about 928 million Love stamps, some 259 million, or 28 percent, were produced on the L perforator, an ABNC spokesman told *Linn's*.

Assistant Postmaster General Gordon Morison, asked whether the L-perfed Love stamps would be sold through the Philatelic Sales Division, said he hadn't been aware that the stamps existed, but that they would be placed on sale if possible. Early in 1992, it was announced that the variety would be made available to collectors.

The Design

At its December 1988 meeting, the Citizens' Stamp Advisory Committee examined several potential Love stamp designs. Among those it approved for eventual use was Harry Zelenko's heart-shaped blue Earth with multicolored continents against a dark blue, starry sky, which was the design that finally reached the public via the 1991 29¢ Love stamp.

Zelenko, who headed a creative design firm in New York City, was also the designer of the Special Occasions booklet stamps of 1988 and the experimental stamps that were issued in 1990 and 1991 for dispensing by automatic teller machines.

For his Love design, he invented a map projection with gracefully curving lines of latitude and longitude to go with his invented Earth shape. At the center of the projection, connecting the dip at the top of the heart with the point at the bottom, was the Meridian of Greenwich; the Americas were to the left, Eurasia and Africa to the right. The design prompted one postal customer, M.C. Simatovich of Arlington, Texas, to write an eloquent fan letter.

"I wish to compliment the artist," Simatovich wrote. "I would love to know what prompted the design, and what spirit the artist chose to express in its development . . . I am a writer and photographer, and celebrate the creative nature in every human being. In a world that seems torn from every side by violence, there is a gentle thread of love binding the heart of mankind — encircling the globe. The stamp speaks differently to each person who cares to think about it. Thanks again for your selection. May it be available like love — forever."

Zelenko wrote back: "Thanks for your words and thoughts. We all agree that love is here to stay (sad to say along with the pain and heartaches one reads about every day in the newspapers). I'd like to know what prompted the design, also. Seems that the creative process is not easily definable."

First-Day Facts

The 29¢ Love sheet and booklet stamps, along with the 52¢ Love stamp and the 29¢ Love stamped envelope, were dedicated May 9 at the Honolulu Zoo. "Mari," a Zoo elephant, was called on to unveil the designs at the ceremony.

Bert H. Mackie, a member of the USPS Board of Governors, spoke, and the welcome was tendered by Kaiulani DeSilva, director of the Hawaii Governor's Office of Children and Youth, and Jeremy Harris, managing director of the City and County of Honolulu. Joseph R. Caraveo, regional postmaster general, dedicated the postal items.

Collectors were allowed 60 days to obtain first-day postmarks by mail. USPS offered to affix stamps to prepared covers or provide stamped envelopes, along with first-day cancel, in return for the proper remittance. However, any collector desiring a complete combination cover — stamped envelope plus the three stamp varieties — was required to obtain and prepare the cover or covers himself and send them to the postmaster in Honolulu for canceling.

$5.80 LOVE BOOKLET

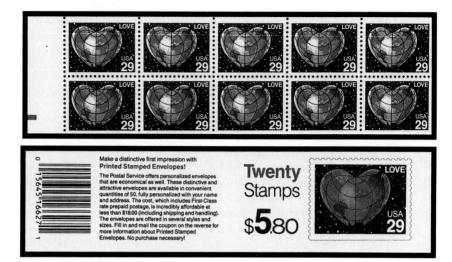

Date of Issue: May 9, 1991

Catalog Number: Scott 2536 (single stamp); 2536a (booklet pane of 10)

Colors: magenta, yellow, cyan, blue

First-Day Cancel: Honolulu, Hawaii

FDCs Canceled: 43,336

Format: 2 panes of 10 horizontal stamps each arranged horizontally, 5 across by 2 down. Gravure printing cylinders of 300 subjects (15 across, 20 around).

Perf: 11.2 (Eureka off-line perforator)

Selvage Markings: Cylinder numbers printed on each pane binding stub. Color bar electric-eye mark remnants on 16.7 percent of all pane binding stubs.

Cover Markings: "© United States Postal Service 1991" and mailing information on inside of front cover. Universal Product Code (UPC) and promotion for personalized stamped envelopes on outside of back cover. Coupon for information on personalized envelopes on inside of back cover.

Designer: Harry Zelenko of New York, New York

Art Director and Project Manager: Joe Brockert (USPS)

Typographer: Bradbury Thompson (CSAC)

Modeler: Clarence Holbert (BEP)

Printing: Stamps printed by BEP on 7-color Andreotti gravure press (601). Booklet covers printed on a 6-color Goebel Optiforma offset press (043) in magenta, yellow, cyan and black. Booklets formed on standard bookbinding equipment.

Quantity Ordered: 1,306,000,000 (65,300,000 booklets; 600,000 unfolded panes)

Quantity Distributed: 601,548,000 (29,748,900 booklets; 657,000 unfolded panes

Cylinder Number Detail: 1 group of 4 cylinder numbers on each pane binding stub

Tagging: overall

The Stamps

Stamps from the Love booklet were distinguishable from sheet stamps by the fact that they had at least one straight edge. There also were perforation differences, although the perf 11.2 of the booklet stamp was very close to the perf 11 used on the later printings of the sheet stamps.

Because the two varieties were made by different printers, there were also subtle differences in appearance. The Jeffries Banknote Division of American Bank Note Company, which made the sheet stamp, used a fifth process color — a blue in addition to the standard cyan. On the booklet stamp, printed at the Bureau of Engraving and Printing, the blue shade of the ocean was less uniform and the continents were not quite so strongly outlined as on the sheet stamp.

The dimensions of the booklet stamp were slightly larger, and at the top of the design, some of the stars were inside the frame, whereas on the sheet stamp the same stars broke the frameline. Also, the figures "29" were closer to the lower right corner on the booklet stamp.

Collectors of first-day covers who wanted the Postal Service to affix the stamps could obtain the booklet version on their covers in full panes only, at a cost of $2.90.

52¢ LOVE

Date of Issue: May 9, 1991

Catalog Number: Scott 2537

Colors: yellow, red, blue

First-Day Cancel: Honolulu, Hawaii

FDCs Canceled: 90,438

Format: Panes of 50, vertical, 10 across, 5 down. Gravure printing cylinders of 200 subjects (10 across, 20 around) manufactured by Armotek Industries Inc., Palmyra, New Jersey.

Perf: 10.9 (L perforator)

Selvage Markings: "© United States Postal Service 1991." "Use Correct ZIP Code ®." "36 USC 380." USPS Olympic logo.

Designer: Nancy L. Krause of Solvang, California

Art Director and Project Manager: Joe Brockert (USPS)

Typographer: Bradbury Thompson (CSAC)

Modeler: Richard Sennett, Sennett Enterprises, for American Bank Note Company

Printing: Stamps printed for American Bank Note Company on a leased Champlain gravure press at J.W. Fergusson and Sons, Richmond, Virginia, under the supervision of Sennett Enterprises, Fairfax, Virginia. Stamps perforated, processed and shipped by ABNC, Bedford Park, Illinois.

Quantity Ordered: 200,000,000

Quantity Distributed: 200,000,000

Cylinder Number Detail: 1 group of 3 gravure cylinder numbers preceded by the letter A alongside corner stamp

Tagging: overall

132

The Stamp

Although the Postal Service had issued a new Love stamp at the first-class rate every year but one since 1984, it apparently felt no need to replace its two-ounce-rate Love stamp so frequently.

The two-ounce-rate stamp that was issued in Honolulu May 9, bearing the 52¢ denomination, was only the second such stamp in the Love series. It replaced the 45¢ stamp depicting a bouquet of roses that was issued August 8, 1988.

USPS explained at the time the 1988 stamp appeared that it was in response to many requests for a stamp for mailing wedding invitations. Most invitations include at least two envelopes and often an RSVP card as well, putting them well over the one-ounce weight.

The 1991 stamp was produced for USPS by the American Bank Note Company. During the House subcommittee hearing of June 3 into stamp production and procurement it was disclosed that USPS had reduced its payment to ABNC by $1,531.20 after it determined that a shipment of the 52¢ Love stamps contained a mixture of "field-quality" and "philatelic-quality" stamps instead of 100 percent "philatelic-quality." The sum represented the amount USPS had been overcharged.

The Design

The stamp, in commemorative size and vertically arranged, depicted a pair of Fischer's Lovebirds (Agapornis fischeri) huddled together affectionately against a palm-frond background. It was the first stamp design project for Nancy L. Krause, an illustrator from Solvang, California. Krause had sent samples of her work to the Postal Service on the advice of fellow Californian Tom Blackshear, who had designed several stamps himself. USPS officials liked her bright, colorful greeting-card type art and asked her in 1989 to submit Love stamp concept sketches.

The birds she chose, a type of parrot native to Africa, were brightly colored, with orange heads, yellow breasts, green wings and underparts and red beaks. The Citizens' Stamp Advisory Committee questioned whether a male and female would have identical coloration, and Krause assured the members in a letter that the picture was accurate. "Please refer

This is Nancy Krause's original sketch of a pair of lovebirds, done in the small-stamp size.

Nancy Krause's finished design, which she painted on clear vinyl, is shown here cropped to the small size for possible use on the one-ounce rate stamp.

to 'The T.F.H. Book of Lovebirds' by Georg A. Radtke, copyright 1981, pages 30, 31, 32 and 33," she wrote. "Males and females have the same coloration. As a parrot owner myself, I understand the concern for a precise representation."

The finished stamps had a kind of luminous quality to them, which may have resulted from the unique way Krause painted her picture. "We emphasized to her," said Joe Brockert, art director and project manager for the stamp, "that we wanted her to use a flexible surface, something that we could easily wrap around a scanner cylinder. We sometimes have a difficult time getting artists to do this.

"She went to the extreme. She said she wanted to see if she could paint on plastic. She made her painting directly on a clear sheet of acetate. You could hold it up to the light and almost see through it. But it was very fragile. She warned us about it; she said, if you bend this too hard or fold it you're going to destroy it, so be very careful. But it worked."

Krause recommended that the typography be in white and dropped out of the design rather than in a dark color printed over it. "Normally, we don't like to use dropout type with process colors because it's harder to work with," Brockert said. "In this case, the printer assured us that it would be reasonably easy, and that we wouldn't even have to outline the type to help trap any slight misregistration of colors."

First-Day Facts

Information on the first-day ceremony can be found in the chapter on the 29¢ Love sheet stamp.

Although USPS officials at first intended to offer combination covers bearing 29¢ and 52¢ Love sheet stamps for 81¢, or the two Love stamps on a number 10 Love stamped envelope for $1.15, they apparently concluded that this would present too many complications, and announced that they would service only one type of item per cover. However, collectors providing their own stamps and/or stamped envelopes could create any combinations they wished for the first-day cancellation.

NON-DENOMINATED (29¢) CHRISTMAS MADONNA AND CHILD SHEET STAMP

Date of Issue: October 17, 1991

Catalog Number: Scott 2578

Colors: red, blue, yellow, gold (offset); red, brown (intaglio)

First-Day Cancel: Houston, Texas

FDCs Canceled: 226,369 (includes sheet and booklet)

Format: Panes of 50, vertical, 10 across, 5 down. Offset printing plates of 300 subjects (15 across, 20 around) and intaglio printing sleeve of 600 subjects (15 across, 40 around).

Perf: 11.2 (Eureka off-line perforator)

Selvage Markings: "USE CORRECT ZIP CODE ®." "© UNITED STATES/ POSTAL SERVICE 1991."

Designer, Art Director and Typographer: Bradbury Thompson (CSAC)

Project Manager: Jack Williams (USPS)

Engravers: Thomas Hipschen (vignette, BEP); Gary Slaght (lettering and numerals, BEP)

Modeler: Peter Cocci (BEP)

Printing: printed by BEP on 6-color offset, 3-color intaglio D press (902)

Quantity Ordered: 401,000,000

Quantity Distributed: 401,000,000

Plate/Sleeve Number Detail: Single-digit intaglio sleeve number in selvage above or below left or right corner stamp, with 1 group of 4 offset plate numbers in selvage of adjacent stamp (outer panes), or single-digit intaglio sleeve number in selvage alongside upper left or upper right corner stamp, with 1 group of 4 offset plate numbers in selvage of adjacent stamp (middle panes).

Tagging: overall

The Stamp

The 1991 Christmas stamps posed a problem for USPS. Experience had shown that several months were required to prepare, print and distribute the more than two billion stamps needed for the holiday season. But as the time neared to begin printing the 1991 traditional and contemporary Christmas stamps, the Postal Service was still hoping for a 30¢ first-class rate before the end of the year — either through a reversal by the Postal Rate Commission of its earlier rate verdict, or a unanimous vote of the USPS Board of Governors overriding the PRC.

Accordingly, as collectors learned in July, USPS decided to print the Christmas stamps without denominations and announce the price later, after the rate case had been resolved.

But on October 4, the PRC rejected the Postal Service's appeal of the 29¢ rate. And the Board of Governors, meeting October 7 and 8, took no vote on whether to raise the rate on its own. Shortly afterward, USPS announced that the Christmas stamps would cost 29¢ when they were placed on sale October 17.

Despite the fact that non-denominated stamps normally are unacceptable for use on international mail, USPS gave post offices clearance to allow use of 1991's Christmas stamps on mail to foreign destinations.

Although the policy wasn't announced, it was communicated to employees in internal memoranda in at least two areas. *Linn's Stamp News* quoted from identically worded memos that were circulated in the Seattle, Washington, and Louisville, Kentucky, divisions:

"Ordinarily, Universal Postal Union rules forbid non-denominated stamps on international mail. However, UPU countries have been contacted and asked to accept mail bearing non-denominated stamps during the holiday mailing season.

"The six non-denominated stamps for the 1991 holiday season are each valued at 29¢. International mail bearing these stamps should NOT be returned to sender as long as adequate total postage has been paid."

The memos then listed first-class postage rates for letters and letter packages to Mexico and Canada and the airmail rate to other countries.

Despite this clear intent on the part of headquarters, many postal workers in the field — and in foreign countries — didn't get the word. Some window clerks immediately rejected mail addressed to points abroad and stamped with Christmas stamps. One postal customer reported that his mail had been accepted at his local post office, only to be sent back several days later from Indianapolis, which insisted that such frankings weren't allowed.

1991 wasn't the first year in which USPS had issued non-denominated Christmas stamps. It had done so twice before.

The first time was in 1975, when the Postal Service was seeking a rate increase from 10¢ to 13¢. The increase was granted, but not until December 31, so the stamps ended up being sold for 10¢. The second time was in 1981, when the USPS Board of Governors overruled the Rate

136

Commission and raised the first-class rate from 18¢ to 20¢. This time the higher rate went into effect November 1, and so the stamps were sold for the higher price. The 1975 Christmas stamps (Scott 1579-1580) were the first non-denominated postage stamps issued by the United States, and were in effect the forerunners of the non-denominated "alphabet" definitive stamps that have accompanied every rate change since 1978.

The so-called "traditional" Christmas stamps in recent years have featured artwork of the Madonna and Child. The last five pieces chosen, and eight of the last nine, had been from the National Gallery of Art in Washington, and the Citizens' Stamp Advisory Committee felt the need to vary its sources and "look very carefully at madonnas from other museums," said Jack Williams, project manager for the stamps.

For its 1991 madonna, USPS turned to the Southwest, to the Museum of Fine Arts of Houston, Texas. The work chosen was *Madonna and Child With Donor* by Antoniazzo Romano, a 15th-century Roman artist. It was painted circa 1475-1480 in tempera and gold leaf on a panel and measures 39 by 28¾ inches. The complete painting contains in the lower left corner the figure of a praying man; he was omitted from the detail chosen for the stamp design.

The Antoniazzo work was nominated for stamp use by Carolyn C. Wilson, adjunct curator for Renaissance art at the Houston museum. Before coming to Houston in 1983, Wilson had served five years as assistant curator of sculpture at the National Gallery of Art, where she became familiar with the process of selecting stamp designs and the particular requirements for Christmas stamps. In 1988 she wrote her former colleague, Douglas Lewis, the National Gallery's curator of sculpture and a member of the Citizens' Stamp Advisory Committee, suggesting the use of a madonna from the Houston museum's collection and enclosing four slides of Renaissance paintings that might be suitable.

Her nominees were *Madonna and Child* by the Master of the Straus Madonna; *Madonna and Child with St. Jerome, St. Bernardino and Six Angels* by Sano di Pietro; *Virgin and Child* by Rogier van der Weyden; and the Antoniazzo painting. All four pieces were part of a collection donated to the museum in 1944 by Percy S. Straus, former president and board chairman of Macy's in New York, and his wife Edith A. Straus.

Wilson suggested these particular works, she said, because the faces of the mother and child are close together on each one, making it easier for a designer to fit the detail into the small stamp size. CSAC picked the Antoniazzo work with the concurrence of Bradbury Thompson, the design coordinator and typographer who had made the task of designing the traditional Christmas stamp an annual personal project.

Wilson wrote the following description of the artist and his work:

"Antonio di Benedetto Aquilio, known as Antoniazzo Romano (c. 1430-d. before September 6, 1512) was the major native painter active in Rome during the second half of the Fifteenth Century. He was influenced by the revolutionary new style developed in Florence during the first half

137

of the 1400s and imported to Rome in the 1440s by Fra Angelico and in the 1450s by Piero della Francesca. This is clearly evident in the Houston painting in the use of realistic portraiture, a unified source of golden light, and deep, long shadows cast by the three-dimensional forms of the pyramidally-arranged composition . . .

"The Houston painting was almost certainly commissioned by the gentleman portrayed kneeling in prayer at lower left. We can be sure that the composition was a popular one, since there are still in existence several copies or variations derived from it. Eight were known previously, and I have recently discovered three more. These variants do not include a portrait. They were probably produced in Antoniazzo's workshop, possibly for a ready market. The carved tabernacle frame on our painting is not original to the work, but its original frame was probably very similar to this one."

The Design

With the approval of the Museum of Fine Arts, the institution's name in the inscription on the stamp was truncated to "Houston Museum."

Madonna and Child With Donor, *by Antoniazzo Romano.*
(The Museum of Fine Arts, Houston, the Edith A. and Percy S. Straus Collection)

138

Peter Marzio, director of the Museum of Fine Arts, told *The Houston Chronicle* that he suspected people would connect the painting with the correct museum anyhow. If they thought of another Houston museum, "that's not all bad," he told the newspaper.

The stamp also bore the approximate date of the painting, "c.1480." That was the first time the artwork had been dated on the traditional Christmas stamp, although the 1983 stamp, depicting a Raphael madonna, also saluted the 500th anniversary of the artist's birth with the dates "1483-1983," and the 1976 contemporary stamp, which was based on Nathaniel Currier's *Winter Pastime*, bore the date of the lithograph, 1855.

The 1991 Christmas stamps, both traditional and contemporary, also contained in their designs the year of issue, 1991. The reason, of course, was to help postal clerks in the future remember that the face value of the non-denominated items was 29¢.

First-Day Facts

The two versions of the Madonna stamp, sheet and booklet, were dedicated by Richard J. Strasser Jr., senior assistant postmaster general, October 17 at the Houston museum's Brown Auditorium. Speakers were Carolyn C. Wilson, the curator who had nominated the Antoniazzo work for the stamp, and LeGree S. Daniels of the Postal Service Board of Governors. Peter C. Marzio, director of the museum, extended the welcome, and Alfred C. Glassell Jr., chairman of the museum's board, was an honored guest.

First-day cover collectors wishing covers bearing some combination of traditional and contemporary Christmas sheet and booklet stamps were required to affix the stamps themselves. USPS applied either the Houston, Texas, cancellation or the cancellation from Santa, Idaho (the first-day site for the contemporary sheet and booklet stamps) according to the customer's request. All combination-cover requests were required to be sent to the postmaster in Santa, Idaho.

NON-DENOMINATED ($5.80) CHRISTMAS MADONNA AND CHILD BOOKLET

Date of Issue: October 17, 1991

Catalog Number: Scott 2578; full pane, Scott 2578a

Colors: red, blue, yellow, gold (offset); red, brown (intaglio)

First-Day Cancel: Houston, Texas

FDCs Canceled: 226,369 (includes sheet and booklet)

Format: 2 panes of 10 stamps each, arranged vertically 2 across by 5 down. Offset printing plates of 300 subjects (15 across, 20 around) and intaglio printing sleeves of 600 subjects (15 across, 40 around).

Perf: 11.2 (Eureka off-line perforator)

Selvage Markings: sleeve number on binding stub of each pane

Cover Markings: "© United States Postal Service 1991" on inside of front cover. Universal Product Code (UPC) and advertisement for 1991 Commemorative Stamp Collection on outside of back cover. Coupon for collection on inside of back cover.

Designer, Art Director and Typographer: Bradbury Thompson (CSAC)

Project Manager: Jack Williams (USPS)

Engravers: Thomas Hipschen (vignette, BEP); Gary Slaght (lettering and numerals, BEP)

Modeler: Peter Cocci (BEP)

Printing: Printed by BEP on 6-color offset, 3-color intaglio D press (902). Booklet covers printed on a 6-color Goebel Optiforma offset press (043) in magenta, yellow, cyan and black. Booklets formed on standard bookbinding equipment.

Quantity Ordered: 300,000,000 (14,700,000 booklets; 600,000 unfolded panes)

Quantity Distributed: 300,000,000 (14,700,000 booklets; 600,000 unfolded panes)

Plate/Sleeve Number Detail: 1 intaglio sleeve number on each pane binding stub

Tagging: overall

The Stamp

The booklet version of the traditional Christmas stamp was identical to the sheet version except that each booklet stamp had at least one straight edge.

This difference was accurately reflected in the enlarged full-color reproduction of the stamp that appeared on the booklet cover; it had a straight edge along the left side. The previous two Christmas stamp booklets had inaccurately shown fully perforated stamps on the covers.

The 1991 traditional Christmas stamp in booklet form was conventionally tagged with overall tagging. The year before, the booklet stamp was issued with block tagging over prephosphored paper, a unique combination made necessary when BEP printers determined that the dense offset-intaglio stamp image was blocking the phosphor signal that the paper emitted.

Information on the Houston, Texas, first-day ceremony can be found in the preceding chapter. For first-day covers of the booklet stamp that were completely serviced by USPS, only full panes of 10 stamps were affixed at a cost of $2.90.

NON-DENOMINATED (29¢) CHRISTMAS SANTA CLAUS SHEET STAMP

Date of Issue: October 17, 1991

Catalog Number: Scott 2579

Colors: red, yellow, blue

First-Day Cancel: Santa, Idaho

FDCs Canceled: 169,750

Format: Panes of 50, horizontal, 5 across, 10 down. Gravure printing cylinders of 300 subjects (15 across, 20 around) manufactured by Armotek Industries, Palmyra, New Jersey.

Perf: 10.9 (L perforator)

Selvage Markings: "© United States/Postal Service 1991." "® Use Correct/ZIP Code."

Designer: John Berkey of Minneapolis, Minnesota

Art Director and Typographer: Howard Paine (CSAC)

Project Manager: Jack Williams (USPS)

Modeler: Richard Sennett, Sennett Enterprises, for American Bank Note Company

Printing: Printed for American Bank Note Company on a leased Champlain gravure press at J.W. Fergusson and Sons, Richmond, Virginia, under the supervision of Sennett Enterprises, Fairfax, Virginia. Stamps perforated, processed and shipped by ABNC, Bedford Park, Illinois.

Quantity Ordered: 900,000,000

Quantity Distributed: 900,000,000

Cylinder Number Detail: 1 group of 3 gravure cylinder numbers preceded by the letter A on selvage alongside upper left or right or lower left or right corner stamp (outer panes), or above or below upper left or lower left corner stamp (middle panes)

Tagging: phosphor-coated paper

The Stamp

The Christmas contemporary stamp, like the traditional stamp, was produced in two versions: sheet and booklet. There were five basic designs used, all featuring Santa Claus. The sheet stamp employed only one of the designs. But the booklet contained stamps bearing the same design as the sheet stamp, plus stamps of four other designs as well.

Both versions were gravure printed and produced by the American Bank Note Company, but different subcontractors were used. The sheet stamps were printed by J.W. Fergusson and Sons; the booklet stamps were printed by the Multi-Color Corporation at its Scottsburg, Indiana, plant. (For details on the booklet, see next chapter).

The Design

The designer of all five Santa stamps — the single design common to the sheet and booklet, and the four other designs used in the booklet — was John Berkey. Berkey, who lived on the appropriately named Christmas Lake Road in Excelsior, Minnesota, had previously designed the contemporary Christmas stamp of 1983, which had also depicted a Santa Claus. He had also done the artwork for the Hubert Humphrey stamp of the Great Americans series that was issued earlier in 1991.

When Berkey was signed to do concept sketches for a new Christmas stamp, the Postal Service intended that it be for a single design only. He submitted a commemorative-size vertical sketch showing Santa seated atop a chimney. By the time USPS was ready to use the design, however, it had adopted its new in-between size for Christmas and Love stamps, and Howard Paine, art director for the project, asked Berkey to revise his Santa sketch to fit into the new format, horizontally arranged.

Accordingly, Berkey produced a painting of Santa waving as he descends the chimney, with only his head, shoulders, hands and the top

John Berkey's original sketch for the Christmas stamp was for a commemorative-sized stamp, vertically arranged.

143

Howard Paine sent Berkey this sketch showing how the original design concept should be adapted to the new Christmas stamp size, arranged horizontally.

of his bag visible above the snow-covered chimney top.

This design was the only design used on the sheet stamp, but it also did extra duty as one of the five designs in the booklet. The two stamps, sheet and booklet, that shared the common design differed in appearance when placed side by side, which was understandable, given the fact that they were made by two different printers.

J.W. Fergusson and Sons, in making the sheet stamps, employed only three colors — red, yellow and blue. For the booklet stamps, Multi-Color Corporation used the four standard process colors — yellow, magenta, cyan and black — and added red for the lettering. In addition, the design size of the sheet stamp was .77 inches by 1.05 inches, slightly larger than the equivalent stamp in the booklet, which measured .725 inches by .99 inches.

On the sheet stamp, the image appeared somewhat sharper, as though a finer screen had been used. More snowflakes were visible against the sky, and they were more distinct than the snowflakes on the booklet stamp. Also, the larger size of the sheet stamp permitted the wording in the lower right corner to be positioned farther from the chimney than the wording in the booklet.

This design, plus the four Santa Claus designs that appeared only in the booklet, bore the wording "1991 USA CHRISTMAS." This marked the first time in 11 years that the word "Christmas" had appeared on a contemporary Christmas stamp. Since 1980, USPS had used the words "Season's Greetings" or simply "Greetings" to avoid a reference to the religious holiday on the stamp that it was offering as an alternative to a religious-oriented one.

However, Art Shealy, a USPS spokesman, told *Linn's Stamp News*: "There has been no formal policy to abandon the use of the word, and it was agreed upon by the Citizens' Stamp Advisory Committee and the postmaster general that it was appropriate."

Varieties

Dealer Jacques C. Schiff Jr., a specialist in errors, reported the discovery of a vertically imperforate full pane of 50 stamps in eastern North Carolina. According to Schiff, a postal customer bought the error

144

pane, removed the bottom selvage, and then returned to the post office for a refund on what seemed to the customer to be unusable stamps. A collector standing in line offered to purchase the pane and save the other customer time, Schiff said. The pane's plate number was A111.

First-Day Facts

The Santa sheet and booklet stamps were placed on sale October 17 in Santa, Idaho, which is located in Benewah County in the state's northern panhandle. (The better-known American town that bears the name of the Christmas saint, Santa Claus, Indiana, had already been the site of a first-day ceremony, for the contemporary Christmas stamp of 1983.)

Michael J. Shinay, executive assistant to the postmaster general, dedicated the Santa stamps. A speaker at the ceremony was Santa Claus himself, as played by Greg Gresham. Cy Chase, a retired Idaho state senator, extended the welcome.

The Postal Service's first-day ceremony program contained six single stamps — the sheet stamp and one each of the booklet varieties — tied to the program page by a first-day postmark.

NON-DENOMINATED ($5.80) CHRISTMAS SANTA CLAUS BOOKLET

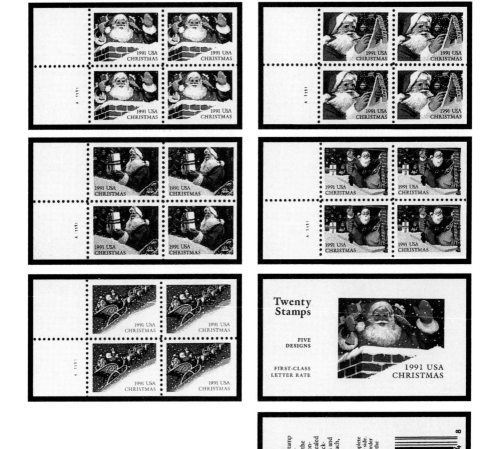

Date of Issue: October 17, 1991

Catalog Numbers: Top pane, single from left side, Scott 2580; single from right side, Scott 2581; horizontal pair, 2581a; full pane, 2581b. Other panes, singles, Scott 2582-2585; full panes, 2582a-2585a.

Colors: yellow, magenta, cyan, black, red

First-Day Cancel: Santa, Idaho

FDCs Canceled: 168,794

Format: 5 panes of 4 stamps each, 1 design per pane, panes laid out in blocks of 4. First pane contains 2 design variations. Gravure printing cylinders of 400 subjects (20 across, 20 around). Each cylinder printed 20 panes (80 stamps) of each of the 5 designs.

Perf: 10.9 (L perforator)

Selvage Markings: cylinder numbers printed on each pane binding stub

Cover Markings: "© United States Postal Service 1991" and postal information on inside of front cover. Universal Product Code (UPC) and advertisement for 1991 Christmas Stamp ornaments on outside of back cover. Coupon for ornaments on inside of back cover. Vertical cut marks at top or bottom of outside or inside of front cover on undetermined percentage of booklets.

Designer: John Berkey of Minneapolis, Minnesota

Art Director and Typographer: Howard Paine (CSAC)

Project Manager: Jack Williams (USPS)

Printing: Printed by Multi-Color Corporation, Scottsburg, Indiana, for American Bank Note Company on a Schiavi 10-color webfed gravure press. Perforated and formed into booklets at ABNC, Bedford Park, Illinois.

Quantity Ordered: 500,000,000 (25,000,000 booklets)

Quantity Distributed: 560,000,000 (28,000,000 booklets)

Cylinder Number Detail: 1 group of 5 gravure cylinder numbers preceded by the letter A on each pane binding stub

Tagging: phosphor-coated paper

The Stamps

With the 1991 contemporary Christmas stamp, USPS tried something new. The sheet version of the stamp consisted of a single Santa Claus design (see preceding chapter). But the booklet contained five different Santa Claus designs: the design that was used on the sheet stamp, plus four others. And instead of placing all five designs se-tenant on each pane, USPS put five little four-stamp panes in the booklet, with each pane consisting of stamps of a single design arranged in a block.

The five designs, examined in sequence from the top pane of the booklet to the bottom one, told a night-before-Christmas story. They showed Santa Claus descending a chimney, Santa beside the Christmas tree checking his list, Santa taking gifts from his bag, Santa preparing to ascend the chimney and, finally, Santa in his reindeer-drawn sleigh, rising skyward through the snowy night.

The two chimney varieties on the top pane of the booklet are shown in these inset enlargements.

After the booklets were issued, it was found that they actually contained at least six collectible stamp varieties rather than five. The extra variety occurred on the top pane (Santa descending the chimney) and was the result of a minuscule difference in appearance between the two stamps on the left and the two on the right. Among the first to discover this curiosity were employees of the Scott Publishing Company, whose editorial director, Richard L. Sine, quickly announced that the Scott catalog would assign each design variant a major catalog number.

The difference could be seen near the topmost chimney brick at the left edge of the stamps. The design on the right-hand vertical pair of stamps with right-side straight edges showed a shaded portion of mortar at the left edge of the stamp. But the design on the left-hand stamps (next to the booklet tab) showed a complete section of mortar near the left edge of the stamp, with a very small part of another brick at the extreme edge of the design. Compensatingly, on the two stamps with the extra brick there was slightly less blue sky visible on the right side between Santa's furry cuff and the edge of the stamp than on their companion stamps.

The variety was created during the process of making the color separations and gravure printing cylinders at Multi-Color Corporation, American Bank Note Company's printing subcontractor. It came about because the etched subjects from which the stamps were printed were made four at a time instead of one at a time, as is customary.

As Thomas C. Harris, vice president for government sales of ABNC, explained in a letter to *The Yearbook*:

''The two versions of the chimney were a result of the cropping and positioning function. The four positions in the booklet were laid out in the Scitex Assembler Plus computer graphics system without any image or copy. These positions are called 'windows.'

''The Santa Claus-and-chimney oversized image was then positioned in those four windows and 'cropped' or cut down to finished stamp size.

''The computer apparently positioned the oversized image in a slightly different location in two of the four windows. When the Scitex cropped the image to size, the slight difference in window location (relative to the larger image) caused the discrepancy in the brick and mortar detail.''

148

Because each of the five panes in the booklet was made in the same way, there were minute differences of cropping on each of the other panes as well, although none was as pronounced as the chimney variety on the top pane. Whether any of these other differences would be noted by Scott was unknown at the time of this writing.

Interestingly, the sheet version of the stamp, printed by ABNC's Jeffries Banknote Division, displayed features of both design varieties on the booklet pane. It had the portion of extra brick at the left, but it also had a relatively wide strip of blue sky next to Santa's cuff on the right side.

Not every collector was delighted with the idea of treating the two chimney varieties as different stamps. ''I could never see spending good money collecting the mistakes and poor craftsmanship of the U.S. Postal Service,'' one reader wrote to *Linn's*. To give catalog listing to ''two chimney varieties,''the reader added, was ''the ultimate absurdity.''

Even though the panes themselves included unusually wide tabs, the fact that they had only four stamps made them small as booklet panes go: 3.15 inches long by 1.74 inches wide. However, the booklets they filled were large enough to be sold from post-office vending machines.

USPS explained that by limiting each pane in the booklet to a single design, ''customers will be able to select a particular design without separating other stamps to get to it.'' Given the overall similarity of the designs, it was questionable how useful most users would find this feature. More relevant, as far as booklet-pane collectors were concerned,

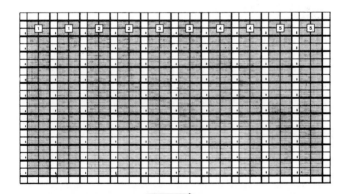

This simplified diagram shows the sheet layout used to print the Santa Claus booklet stamps. Each vertical column contains stamps of a single design: The number 1 represents the first design in the booklet (Santa on the rooftop), 2 represents the second design, and so on. Bold lines indicate where the sheet was cut into booklet panes, and light lines indicate perforations. The dashes in the blank columns show the location of cylinder numbers, one set of numbers for each booklet pane binding stub. The arrow shows the direction the web traveled in the press. No registration marks or other selvage markings are shown.

was the fact that whereas they normally would need only a single pane of a booklet containing multiple designs, they now had to obtain five panes to receive one specimen of each design.

The booklet panes, being uniquely configured, had to be printed in a unique way. Each printing cylinder of 400 subjects contained 80 stamps (20 panes) of each of the five basic designs. The subjects were arranged in double rows, 20 subjects per row, across the cylinder, starting with two double rows of the first design (Santa on the rooftop), then two double rows of the second design, two double rows of the third design, two double rows of the fourth design and two double rows of the fifth design. To the left of the first double row was a wide selvage. Between all the remaining double rows, blank strips extended across the cylinder. The selvage and blank strips would become the binding stubs when the printed sheets were perforated and cut into four-stamp panes. Therefore, each blank strip contained a set of cylinder numbers next to every other stamp in the adjacent row.

The Designs

As described in the last chapter, artist John Berkey's original design submission, showing Santa descending a chimney, was used on the sheet stamp and also the top stamp of the booklet pane. When Berkey was asked early in 1991 to create additional designs for a multi-design booklet, he offered USPS several choices.

John Berkey made these alternative color sketches for additional designs in the Christmas booklet. Although they weren't used, the Raggedy Ann doll in the bag was prominent in two of the accepted Santa Claus designs.

150

The Santa Claus in Berkey's 1983 Christmas stamp (Scott 2064), shown here, closely resembled Berkey's list-checking Santa in the 1991 booklet.

Four of his color sketches, like the original, featured Santa Claus. These were ultimately chosen by CSAC to be made into finished art. But Berkey made other little paintings as well: a candle beside a plate of cookies with a note reading: ''For Santa''; a bag of toys; closeup views of the heads of two of Santa's reindeer, and stockings hanging by a fireplace. These still-life-type paintings weren't used, but some of their elements, such as a Raggedy Ann doll, showed up in the Santa designs.

Berkey didn't use a human model for his stamp Santas. The face common to all of them, he said, was a ''made-up face.'' One of them — the Santa examining a list — bore a close resemblance, in features, beard and cap, to the Santa that Berkey had created for his 1983 Christmas stamp. Interestingly, however, the 1991 Santa produced a reaction that hadn't occurred with the Santa of 1983.

Friends and relatives told Berkey that the face reminded them of his youngest son, John, when the boy was small. Berkey himself hadn't noticed the similarity, he said. However, he added, one of the other Santas — the Santa preparing to ascend the fireplace — ''looked familiar. He looked like somebody that I knew.'' Obviously, it was his own son — who by now was 27, stood about 6 feet, 3 inches tall, and, as Berkey described him, was a ''very handsome man, although he doesn't look like Santa Claus now!'' ''Afterward,'' the artist added, ''I thought it was kind of nice that people would find that Santa Claus looked like a little child.''

The booklet cover showed, in color, the Santa-in-the-chimney stamp that was featured on the top pane of the booklet. (The variety depicted on the cover was the extra-brick variety similar to the two stamps on the left side of the top pane.)

First-Day Facts

Details on the first-day ceremony are given in the preceding chapter. For first-day covers of the booklet stamp that were processed completely by USPS, only a random single stamp from the booklet was affixed. USPS declined to honor requests for a specific design or for a full pane of four stamps.

DEFINITIVES

How much difference a rate change makes in terms of numbers of stamps issued was dramatically demonstrated in 1991, when 33 definitives, or regular, stamps were issued. This total didn't include 10 tagging varieties. The year before, when rates were unchanged, only seven new definitives appeared.

For the first time, a non-denominated rate-change item was issued and then reissued later in the year bearing the first-class rate denomination. This was the Flower stamp, which was produced first with an F and later with a 29¢ marking. Also without precedent was the non-denominated Makeup Rate item issued in connection with the rate change, with a design made up exclusively of words.

Collectors did get one big break. Instead of issuing numerous fractional-value stamps to cover specific types of presorted mail, as it had done in the past, USPS produced three denominated coil stamps and, later, a non-denominated coil stamp. These were all for the purpose of false franking, which is the use of stamps with face values that don't represent the actual amount of postage paid per item.

The Transportation coil series grew to 52 face-different varieties, and the Great Americans series of sheet stamps was increased to 50. Until 1991, both these long-running sets had been printed exclusively on the intaglio presses of the Bureau of Engraving and Printing, but in 1991 one new stamp in each series was produced by a private contractor. A Transportation stamp depicting a canoe was printed by the gravure process, and a Great Americans stamp honoring Senator Dennis Chavez was subcontracted — in a controversial move — to a Canadian printer.

The Postal Service's experiment with the vending of stamps through automatic teller machines (ATMs) continued, and produced two varieties. The first was a non-denominated version of 1990's plastic self-adhesive ATM stamp, issued to meet the new first-class rate. The second, developed to respond to the concerns of environmentalists, was made of paper. Both stamps were produced and sold in dollar-bill-sized sheetlets.

F (29¢) SHEET STAMP

Date of Issue: January 22, 1991

Catalog Number: Scott 2517

Colors: yellow, magenta, cyan, black

First-Day Cancel: Washington, D.C. (no first-day ceremony)

FDCs Canceled: 106,698

Format: Panes of 100, vertical, 10 across, 10 down. Gravure printing cylinders of 400, 20 across, 20 around.

Perf: 13 by 12.75 (Ormag rotary perforator).

Selvage Markings: "© United States Postal Service 1991." "Use Correct ZIP Code ®."

Designer: Wallace Marosek of Boston, Massachusetts

Art Director and Typographer: Bradbury Thompson (CSAC)

Project Manager: Jack Williams (USPS)

Modeler: Peter Cocci (BEP)

Printing: printed by Jeffries Banknote Division of United States Bank Note Corporation, Los Angeles, California, on 8-color combination Andreotti-Giori gravure-intaglio webfed press

Quantity Ordered: 1,700,000,000

Quantity Distributed: 1,700,000,000

Cylinder Number Detail: 1 group of 4 cylinder numbers preceded by the letter U beside corner stamp

Tagging: phosphor-coated paper

The Stamp

Since 1978, USPS has accompanied each change in the first-class letter rate with the issuance of non-denominated sheet, coil and booklet stamps, prepared long in advance, on which a letter of the alphabet represented the new rate. Their purpose was to meet customer demand until new definitives bearing the actual rate designation could be printed and distributed.

Thus there were the A stamp in 1978 (15¢), the B in 1981 (18¢), the C, also in 1981 (20¢), the D in 1985 (22¢) and the E in 1988 (25¢). By the inexorable progression of the alphabet, the increase in the first-class rate to 29¢, effective February 3, 1991, brought forth the F stamp. It was issued in sheet, coil and booklet forms in Washington, D.C., on January 22 — the day the new rate structure was approved by the USPS Board of Governors — and was available throughout the country the next day.

With the E stamp in 1988, USPS had made a change in design policy. The first four lettered stamps had been printed in single colors and had shared a common design, the Postal Service's stylized eagle. For the fifth, however, the Citizens' Stamp Advisory Committee found a design subject to match the letter E. The multicolor gravure-printed stamp depicted a picture of a cloud-flecked Earth as seen from outer space.

The fact that the subject of the next non-denominated stamp, the F stamp, would be a flower was an ill-kept secret. Stamp writers had speculated for some time that this would be the case, and on August 20, 1990, *The Washington Post* reported that USPS was making it a point to call the non-denominated stamp that was then in storage awaiting the next rate change "the flower stamp." "Postal officials are fearful of what hordes of customers — not to mention (comedians) Jay Leno and David Letterman — will say about 'that F-stamp,' " *The Post* explained.

Under Universal Postal Union rules, non-denominated stamps can be used only for mail going to addresses within the United States. The A and B stamps had carried no reference to that restriction. The C and D stamps had carried the wording "Domestic Mail"; the E stamp bore the single word "Domestic." On the F stamp the inscription was more explicit: "For U.S. addresses only."

"It was brought to our attention," explained Donald M. McDowell, director of the Office of Stamp and Philatelic Marketing, "that someone in Sheboygan mailing a letter to someone in Germany might say to himself: 'I'm standing here in Sheboygan mailing this. This is domestic. There's no problem.' So we're using the wording: 'For U.S. addresses only.' We hope that will make the point that, yes, if you mail it in Sheboygan, Sheboygan is domestic, but the transaction isn't, if the letter is going to go overseas."

The A through E stamps had been printed, in all their various forms, by the Bureau of Engraving and Printing. This time, however, USPS spread its printing contracts among three different security printers.

The United States Bank Note Corporation was assigned to produce the

154

sheet stamps. BEP printed the coils of 100, 500 and 3,000, and also printed booklets of 10 and 20. And KCS Industries Inc. of Milwaukee, Wisconsin, a subsidiary of the Banta Corporation of Menasha, Wisconsin, also printed booklets of 10.

Each used the same design and typography, and each employed the gravure printing process. Nevertheless, the result of the division of work was a group of varieties that were distinguishable from one another, not only by the standard differences along the edge that exist among sheet, booklet and coil stamps, but also by subtle differences in the appearance of the printed image.

The blossom and leaves on the United States Bank Note Corporation's sheet stamp were lighter than on the other varieties. The KCS booklet stamp was somewhat darker, with apparently a higher concentration of black throughout the design, and its dot pattern appeared to be smaller than that of the other stamps. The green on its leaf was much brighter than the green used on the BEP booklet stamp. The BEP coil and booklet stamps used the heaviest concentration of black, and their details, such as the veins on the leaves, were more distinct.

One of the disclosures that came out of the June 5 congressional hearing into stamp production and procurement was that USPS had reduced its payment to USBNC by 10 percent ($187,000) when its inspectors determined that 10 percent of the F sheet stamps weren't perforated properly.

The F stamps had been in the works for nearly two years. On April 3, 1989, USPS had placed an advertisement in *Commerce Business Daily* notifying private printers of its intention to seek bids for the printing of 1.7 billion F stamps, by rotogravure or some combination involving gravure and/or intaglio.

The Design

The design, showing a large red tulip and the tip of a single green leaf

Two inscriptions incorporating the word "Domestic" were proposed before it was decided to use the more straightforward "For U.S. addresses only" in a down-style (without capitalized words).

155

against a yellow background, was the work of Wallace Marosek of Boston, Massachusetts, and was the result of a student assignment at the Yale University School of Art and Architecture.

In 1985 Bradbury Thompson, long-time design coordinator for CSAC and an instructor at Yale, assigned the 18 students in his graphic design class the job of creating designs and choosing typography for the non-denominated F stamp that USPS would need some time in the future. They could pick a subject in either the "flower" or "fruit" category, Thompson told his students, and when their artwork was completed he would take it to CSAC for its consideration. If one of the pieces was chosen and used for a stamp, the student would receive the standard fee USPS pays all its stamp designers.

Marosek, a graduate student, chose a flower for a sentimental reason. Some of his fondest boyhood memories were of visiting his grandmother, Catherine Dodge, at her Victorian cottage on Lake Otsego in Cooperstown, New York, where she had a garden full of red and pink tulips as well as stained-glass windows featuring tulip images. Mrs. Dodge died in 1960, and the stamp project "was a nice way to remember her," Marosek said.

Marosek's only submission was a quick colored-pencil sketch, although some of his fellow students turned in several drawings. In all, Thompson took more than 60 stamp designs to Washington. CSAC chose eight finalists, and sent the art back with instructions to the students to make various revisions.

By now it was spring, and tulips were blooming in Cooperstown. Marosek went to his grandmother's home, which his mother now used as a summer cottage, to work from the actual tulips that had inspired him. "I did several sketches, and then several finished paintings, after I had come up with a composition I thought worked well," he said. "I used a combination of mediums, including watercolor, acrylic, dye, colored pencil and graphite. The paintings went in, and months went by, and then I was told by Brad that my design had been selected.

"I think they liked the clarity of the design, and the simplified, pared-down composition. It was a very well-studied composition, I was told."

Marosek chose Galliard for the typeface, because it "married" well with the flower, and also because it was designed by Matthew Carter, another of his professors. "The F itself was so heavy, though, it kind of crushed the flower," Marosek said. "So Brad adapted a lighter form, and that's what we used."

Still later, in 1988, some time after Marosek's graduation from Yale, Thompson informed him that the committee wanted one final change. The tulip's background had to be in color instead of the white setting Marosek had given it. The artist responded with two finished paintings, one on which he airbrushed in a yellow background, the other with a light blue, which, he said, "seemed to me a more logical choice."

The next year, Marosek and his wife, Anne Sheridan, moved to Boston, where he took a job as a graphic designer with the Retail Sales

Department of the Boston Museum of Fine Arts. By now the E stamp had been issued, and Marosek knew the next rate change would bring his own design to the forefront.

A few days before that rate change was scheduled, the artist recalled, "I was watching Dan Rather on TV, and my mother called me from New York and told me to switch to Tom Brokaw because he was carrying the news of the rate-increase stamp.

"The next morning I ran to the post office," he continued. "They had just gotten the stamps in but they weren't ready for sale yet, and the clerk told me to go to the newsstand and I'd find a picture of the stamp in *The New York Times*. When I found it, it was in black and white, and I still didn't know which background color they had used. So I went to the public-relations office of the Museum of Fine Arts, and they had a *USA Today*, which showed the stamp in color. That's how I found out they had chosen the yellow background."

Varieties

A vertical margin pair of the stamps, imperforate, was sold at auction June 28 by Michael M. Karen of North Woodmere, New York. Karen said the pair realized $775.

First-Day Facts

No first-day ceremony was held.

Collectors wishing to combine the four major varieties of the F stamp on one cover with the Washington, D.C., first-day postmark were required to prepare their own envelopes in advance. USPS would not mix and match on covers on which it affixed stamps.

The announcement giving first-day postmark ordering instructions listed four different addresses at the Washington post office on Brentwood Road, one for each of the varieties. Each had its own ZIP-plus-four number. USPS allowed collectors 60 days rather than the normal 30 to submit first-day cancellation requests.

F (29¢) COIL STAMP

Date of Issue: January 22, 1991

Catalog Number: Scott 2518

Colors: red, cyan, yellow, black

First-Day Cancel: Washington, D.C. (no first-day ceremony)

FDCs Canceled: 39,311

Format: Coils of 100, 500 and 3,000. Printing cylinders of 432 subjects (18 across, 24 around) for coils of 500 and 3,000. Printing cylinders of 480 subjects (20 across, 24 around) for coils of 100.

Perf: 10.2

Designer: Wallace Marosek of Boston, Massachusetts

Art Director and Typographer: Bradbury Thompson (CSAC)

Project Manager: Jack Williams (USPS)

Modeler: Ronald C. Sharpe (BEP)

Printing: Printed by BEP on 7-color Andreotti gravure press (601). Coils of 500 and 3,000 processed on Huck coiling equipment. Coils of 100 processed on Goebel equipment.

Quantity Ordered: 3,614,400,000 (2,746,800,000 in coils of 100; 570,000,000 in coils of 500; 297,600,000 in coils of 3,000)

Quantity Distributed: 3,614,400,000 (2,746,800,000 in coils of 100; 570,000,000 in coils of 500; 297,600,000 in coils of 3,000)

Cylinder Number Detail: 1 group of 4 cylinder numbers on every 24th stamp

Tagging: phosphor-coated paper

The Stamp

The Bureau of Engraving and Printing produced the F stamp for USPS in coils of 100, 500 and 3,000. Like the previous non-denominated coil stamp, the E stamp of 1988, the F was printed on BEP's seven-color Andreotti gravure press. Five cylinder number combinations were reported: 1111, 1211, 1222, 2211 and 2222. However, those combinations didn't necessarily reflect the printing history of the stamp for plate number coil collectors, as Ken Lawrence explained in his Plate Number Coils column in *Linn's Stamp News.*

''An F stamp PNC, numbered 1111, taken from a 100-stamp coil was probably not printed from the same set of gravure cylinders as a stamp bearing the same digits from a 500- or 3,000-stamp coil,'' Lawrence wrote. ''Stephen G. Esrati, editor of *The Plate Number*, was the first reporter to learn from Postal Service sources that four sets of F coil cylinders were manufactured, even though only two sets of numbers, Nos. 1 and 2, are shown (one digit for each color of ink). Charles Yeager's sources at the Bureau confirmed Esrati's finding.

''One group of Nos. 1 and 2 cylinders exists with 432 subjects — 18 rows across, and 24 in circumference. The second group, also Nos. 1 and 2, has 480 subjects per cylinder — 20 across and 24 in circumference.

''The 18-row printings were processed on the Bureau's Huck coiling equipment into coils of 500 and 3,000. The 20-row printings were processed on the Bureau's Goebel equipment into coils of 100.''

This duplication of cylinder numbers wasn't unprecedented, Lawrence added, but it contradicted the policy announced by USPS in December 1980, which introduced the single-digit plate numbering system. Under that policy, single-digit suffixes were to be printed instead of the unique five- and six-digit serial numbers that actually define printing bases, and the suffixes were to be assigned consecutively for each stamp design.

Collectors noted a characteristic of the F coil stamp that had also been seen in the previous non-denominated coil stamp, the E stamp. On many rolls, one or more stamps at the beginning bore parallel raised white lines across the design. These lines were residue from the white tape used to seal the coils. The tape had been in place for a long period while the stamps awaited the call to service and, during that time, had dried out and adhered to the paper.

The Design

For a discussion of the subtle printing differences among the F stamps produced by different printers, see the chapter on the F sheet stamp.

Varieties

An early report of imperforate F coil stamps came from Tom Freeman of Erie, Pennsylvania, who told *Linn's Stamp News* he bought a coil of 100 containing 38 imperfs in mid-February. Freeman, an architect who bought the stamps for his business, told *Linn's* he noticed the error after

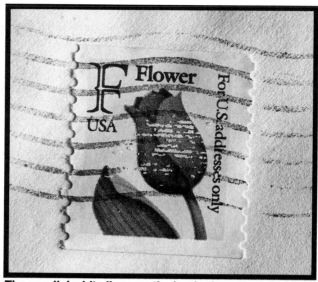

The parallel white lines on the beginning stamps of each roll were tape residue.

tearing the first imperf stamp off to mail a Valentine's Day card to his girlfriend. After dropping the card in the slot, Freeman realized what he had found, he said. "I hope she understands how much her card really cost me," he wrote in a letter to *Linn's*.

In May, Sam Houston Philatelics of Houston, Texas, advertised a pair of the imperforates for $50 and a line strip of six with cylinder number 1111 for $325.

First-Day Facts

For information on first-day covers for the F coil stamp, see the chapter on the F sheet stamp.

F ($2.90, $5.80) BOOKLET, BEP

Date of Issue: January 22, 1991

Catalog Number: Scott 2519 (single stamp); 2519a (booklet pane of 10)

Colors: red, cyan, yellow, black

First-Day Cancel: Washington, D.C. (no first-day ceremony)

FDCs Canceled: 32,971 (includes BEP and KCS versions)

Format: 2 booklet formats, 1 with 1 pane of 10 stamps, the other with 2 panes of 10 stamps, arranged vertically, 2 across by 5 down. Gravure printing cylinders of 800 subjects (10 across, 80 around).

Perf: 11.2 (Goebel booklet machine stroke perforator)

Selvage Markings: Cylinder numbers printed on each pane binding stub. Red electric-eye mark remnants (diagonal-end or rectangle-end) on 10 percent of all binding stubs.

Cover Markings: "© United States Postal Service 1991" on inside of front cover. Universal Product Code (UPC) and mailing reminders on outside of back cover. F stamp information on inside of back cover. 10-stamp booklets have yellow background on front cover; 20-stamp booklets have white background.

Designer: Wallace Marosek of Boston, Massachusetts

Art Director and Typographer: Bradbury Thompson (CSAC)

Project Manager: Jack Williams (USPS)

Modeler: Ronald C. Sharpe (BEP)

Printing: printed by BEP on 7-color Andreotti gravure press (601)

Quantity Ordered: 2,511,000,000 (202,500,000 in booklets of 10; 2,308,500,000 in booklets of 20)

Quantity Distributed: 2,534,840,000 (202,500,000 in booklets of 10; 2,332,340,000 in boolets of 20)

Cylinder Number Detail: 1 group of 4 cylinder numbers on each pane binding stub

Tagging: phosphor-coated paper

The Stamp

The F stamp booklets were produced by two printers. The Bureau of Engraving and Printing made booklets of 10 and 20 stamps, while KCS Industries Inc. of Milwaukee, Wisconsin, a subsidiary of Banta Corporation of Menasha, Wisconsin, made 10-stamp booklets only.

It was the Postal Service's intention that the 10-stamp booklets have white covers and the 20-stamp books have yellow covers, so stamp clerks could easily tell them apart. The covers that KCS put on its 10-stamp booklets were white, as planned. But the arrangement was frustrated when BEP switched colors and made its 10-stamp booklet covers yellow, USPS spokesman Art Shealy told *Stamp Collector's* Mark A. Kellner.

The two printers' stamps themselves differed somewhat in appearance (see chapter on the F sheet stamp). The BEP booklet stamps were perforated 11.2 and were printed on hard, brittle paper, whereas the KCS stamps were perforated 10¾ and were printed on a soft, porous paper.

The cylinder numbers on the pane binding stubs were also a distinguishing element. The KCS cylinder numbers were much larger than the BEP numbers, and were preceded by the letter "K." A "K" also appeared on the inside of the front cover of the KCS booklet, beside the USPS copyright line.

162

Twenty USA Stamps

F Series

Domestic Mail Only
First-Class Letter Rate

Ten USA Stamps

F Series

Domestic Mail Only
First-Class Letter Rate

Please, always use:
☑ Complete address
☑ Return address
☑ Correct ZIP code

These booklet cover designs, featuring tulips, were turned down in favor of designs that prominently displayed the number of stamps in each booklet.

Please, always use:
☑ Complete address
☑ Return address
☑ Correct ZIP code

F Series Twenty USA Stamps

Domestic Mail Only ✢ First-Class Letter Rate

Please, always use:
☑ Complete address
☑ Return address
☑ Correct ZIP code

F Series Ten USA Stamps

Domestic Mail Only ✢ First-Class Letter Rate

BEP used the same printing base layout for its F stamp booklet pane that it had used for the 15¢ Beach Umbrella booklet pane gravure cylinders of 1990 and the Jack London 10-stamp booklet pane intaglio sleeves of 1988. The gravure cylinders were formatted 10 subjects across by 80 subjects around, with alternating rows of panes inverted. Ten percent of the printed F stamp panes showed the tip of a rectangular or diagonal electric-eye mark in red on the binding stub.

In a break with recent practice, the Philatelic Sales Division made no unfolded panes of either the BEP or KCS booklet stamps available to collectors. However, unfolded panes were provided for all subsequent booklets in 1991.

The Design

The design on the outside cover of the booklets was the work of Bradbury Thompson, the veteran designer, typographer and design coordinator for the Citizens' Stamp Advisory Committee. The design was vertically arranged for the 10-stamp booklets and horizontally arranged for the 20-stamp booklets.

Thompson's early versions of the booklet covers, both vertical and horizontal, showed fields of tulips, with the number of stamps inside the booklet expressed in words rather than figures. However, officials soon realized that the most important function of an F stamp cover was to make it as easy as possible for stamp clerks to know whether they were selling a 10-stamp booklet or a 20-stamp booklet. Therefore — in addition to the color difference that was planned but not carried out — a design was selected that gave prominent display to the number of stamps inside the booklet: 10 or 20. On both cover varieties the single-blossom-and-leaf design of the F stamp was tucked inside the large numeral ''0.''

USPS employed a message on the covers to try to soften the impact of the rate increase. ''This is the first increase in First-Class stamp prices since April 1988,'' the covers reminded customers.

First-Day Facts

For first-day covers fully serviced by USPS, only full panes of the booklet stamps were affixed at a cost of $2.90. Collectors were told to use one of two addresses and ZIP-plus-four numbers at the Washington, D.C., post office on Brentwood Road, depending on whether they wanted BEP or KCS panes.

F ($2.90) BOOKLET, KCS

Date of Issue: January 22, 1991

Catalog Number: Scott 2520 (single stamp); 2520a (booklet pane of 10)

Colors: yellow, black, magenta, cyan

First-Day Cancel: Washington, D.C. (no first-day ceremony)

FDCs canceled: 32,971 (includes BEP and KCS versions)

Format: 1 pane of 10 stamps arranged vertically, 2 across by 5 down. Gravure printing cylinders of 400 subjects (20 across, 20 around), manufactured by Armotek Industries Inc., Palmyra, New Jersey.

Perf: 10.7 (L perforator)

Selvage and Other Markings: Cylinder numbers printed on each pane binding stub. Also, 20 percent of all panes show magenta cut mark at outer edge of third stamp down (10 percent on left stamp, 10 percent on right stamp).

Cover Markings: "© United States Postal Service 1991 K" on inside of front cover. Universal Product Code (UPC) and mailing reminders on outside of back cover. F stamp information on inside of back cover. White background on front cover.

Designer: Wallace Marosek of Boston, Massachusetts

Art Director and Typographer: Bradbury Thompson (CSAC)

Project Manager: Jack Williams (USPS)

Modeler: Richard Sennett, Sennett Enterprises

Printing: By Sennett Enterprises on Champlain gravure press at J.W. Fergusson and Sons, Richmond, Virginia, for KCS Industries Inc. Formed into booklets at KCS.

Quantity Ordered: 161,000,000 (16,100,000 booklets)

Quantity Distributed: 157,173,750 (15,717,375 booklets)

Cylinder Number Detail: 1 group of 4 cylinder numbers preceded by the letter K on each pane binding stub

Tagging: phosphor-coated paper

The Stamp

The 10-stamp booklet of F stamps made by KCS Industries was the first booklet to be supplied under a five-year booklet contract signed in 1990 between USPS and Banta Corporation of Menasha, Wisconsin, the KCS parent company. Banta was described by USPS as one of the nation's leading graphic arts companies, offering diverse printing and

The F stamp booklet printed by KCS (far left) had larger cylinder numbers on the binding stub than the booklet printed by BEP (left).

166

graphic/video services.

This booklet and subsequent booklets produced by KCS in 1991 — the denominated Flower, Wood Duck and Flag With Olympic Rings booklets — contained a printing mark that hadn't been seen on any booklet pane previously printed by the Bureau of Engraving and Printing or American Bank Note Company. It was a thin, short cut mark that appeared on 20 percent of the KCS booklet panes.

These marks, as described by Bruce Mosher, modern-issues chairman of the Bureau Issues Association's Booklet and Booklet Panes Committee, were about 0.2 millimeters wide by 4.8mm long and were always located at the outer edge in the middle of the third stamp in the pane, relatively close to the stamp design. In half the examples, the marks were at the left and in the other half at the right. The booklets containing these cut marks are believed to have been cut from the right and left ends of each strip of 10 uncut booklets,'' Mosher reported.

Other differences between the KCS and BEP-produced booklets, plus other details, are discussed in the preceding chapters on the F stamp.

MAKEUP RATE (4¢) STAMP

This U.S. stamp, along with 25¢ of additional U.S. postage, is equivalent to the 'F' stamp rate

Date of Issue: January 22, 1991

Catalog Number: Scott 2521

Colors: gold, red

First-Day Cancel: Washington, D.C. (no first-day ceremony)

FDCs Canceled: 51,987

Format: Panes of 100, vertical, 10 across, 10 down; offset printing plates of 600 (20 across, 30 down).

Perf: 10.9 (L perforator)

Selvage Markings: "© USPS 1990." "Use Correct ZIP Code ®."

Designer and Typographer: Richard Sheaff (CSAC)

Art Director and Project Manager: Jack Williams (USPS)

Printing: printed by American Bank Note Company on a 2-color Harris offset sheetfed press at ABNC, Bedford Park, Illinois

Quantity Ordered: 1,850,000,000

Quantity Distributed: 1,850,000,000

Cylinder Number Detail: 1 pair of cylinder numbers preceded by the letter A alongside corner stamp

Tagging: untagged

The Stamp

The so-called "Makeup Rate" stamp that was issued as part of the new-rate package January 22 was as purely functional a stamp as the United States had ever produced.

Its purpose was to cover the 4¢ gap between the new 29¢ first-class rate that would take effect February 3 and the 25¢ face value of the millions of old first-class-rate stamps that postal customers would still have in their possession on that date.

Like the "F" stamps and stamped envelopes that accompanied it, the stamp bore no denomination. It had been printed long before the appropriate denomination for a makeup rate stamp could have been known.

More unusual, however, was the fact that it bore no picture of any kind. Because it was intended for a very specific use, that use had to be communicated fully and accurately to the customer. Consequently, the design space was occupied by this message, in six lines of uppercase and lowercase red lettering:

"This U.S. stamp,/along with 25¢/of additional/U.S. postage,/is equivalent to/the 'F' stamp rate."

The only other graphic element on the stamp was a rectangular border, printed in gold and made up of alternating solid and blank dashes.

The design — or absence of one — drew considerable comment. Syndicated advice columnist Abigail Van Buren, asked by a reader what she thought of the stamp, replied: "It looks like the preamble to the Constitution of the United States." A writer to *Linn's Stamp News* said the design "comes straight from the 'FOR TEST PURPOSES ONLY' coil" and added: "I can only imagine that the stamps accompanying the next rate change will be inscribed 'G' for 'Generic.'" And another *Linn's* letter writer, an English teacher, criticized the punctuation in the message. "The commas separating the phrase 'along with 25¢ of additional U.S. postage' make it non-restrictive, thereby having no real bearing on the message in the sentence," she wrote. "To be correct, the stamp needs a simpler statement: 'This U.S. stamp plus 25¢ additional U.S. postage is equivalent to the "F" stamp rate.' Please note the period at the end of my sentence. The post office has evidently stopped using periods in its mad dash — no pun — to use all the commas it can!"

On five previous occasions, USPS had preprinted and stockpiled non-denominated stamps to cover a pending new first- class rate. This was the first time, however, that it had ever made advance arrangements to cover the makeup rate. The Postal Service had always depended before on denominated stamps to fill the makeup function.

Thus, when the first-class rate increased in 1979, 1981 (twice), 1985 and 1988 — the increases that were covered by the A, B, C, D and E stamps, respectively — postal patrons wanting to use their old first-class-rate stamps had to search out and purchase supplies of 2¢, 3¢, 2¢, 2¢ and 3¢ stamps, respectively, to go with them.

Donald M. McDowell, director of the Office of Stamp and Philatelic Marketing, explained why this time USPS did it differently.

"Progressively, we've worked out the kinks of changing the rates, to the point where in the 1988 rate change we were down to just one problem," he said. "That problem involved the makeup rate.

"We found out on March 22, 1988, that the new first-class rate would be 25¢ and the makeup rate would be 3¢. We put the new rates in on April 3, and needed almost two billion 3¢ stamps. But we couldn't gamble on preproduction, because the makeup rate could have been 1¢, 2¢, 3¢ or 4¢.

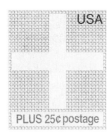

PLUS 25¢ postage

PLUS any 25¢ stamp

25¢ POSTAGE PLUS THIS STAMP EQUALS 'F' RATE

25¢ POSTAGE PLUS THIS STAMP EQUALS 'F' RATE

25¢ POSTAGE PLUS THIS STAMP EQUALS 'F' RATE

ADD TO ANY 25¢ STAMP

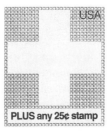

PLUS any 25¢ stamp

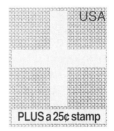

PLUS a 25¢ stamp

25¢ POSTAGE PLUS THIS STAMP EQUALS 'F' RATE

25¢ POSTAGE PLUS THIS STAMP EQUALS 'F' RATE

25¢ POSTAGE PLUS THIS STAMP EQUALS 'F' RATE

25¢ POSTAGE PLUS THIS STAMP EQUALS 'F' RATE

25¢ POSTAGE PLUS THIS STAMP EQUALS 'F' RATE

25¢ POSTAGE PLUS THIS STAMP EQUALS 'F' RATE

25¢ POSTAGE PLUS THIS STAMP EQUALS 'F' RATE

25¢ POSTAGE PLUS THIS STAMP EQUALS 'F' RATE

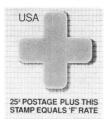

25¢ POSTAGE PLUS THIS STAMP EQUALS 'F' RATE

25¢ POSTAGE PLUS THIS STAMP EQUALS 'F' RATE

25¢ POSTAGE PLUS THIS STAMP EQUALS 'F' RATE

Pluses of all styles, sizes and proportions; pluses with backlighting and shadows; pluses against solid, grilled and patterned backgrounds; pluses accompanied by various combinations of wording — all were studied by the Citizens' Stamp Advisory Committee and USPS staff. This is a sample of the dozens of plus designs that were reviewed before the idea was abandoned.

170

"We decided then that next time we would do a non-denominated Makeup Rate stamp that we could ship with the F stamps, in predetermined ratios."

The stamp was printed by American Bank Note Company, in sheet form only, by the offset process. In an advertisement in the April 3, 1989 issue of *Commerce Business Daily*, the Postal Service had notified private printers of an intention to seek bids not only for the F stamp, but also for a "makeup stamp" in the quantity of 1.85 billion, with "printing by the offset or flexographer (sic) processes." Because the stamp would have a low value and be in use only a relatively short time, officials reasoned, the security feature of gravure or intaglio wouldn't be essential.

No tagging was applied to the stamp, because it was meant to be used with denominated stamps that would be tagged. Its use wasn't restricted to the new letter rate, however. It could be used just as any other 4¢ stamp could be used, as long as the destination of the mail was within the United States. And, although USPS didn't say so specifically, the stamp could even be used by itself in multiples of appropriate size (five to mail a postcard, eight to mail a one-ounce letter).

The Design

For a design that turned out to be as simple and functional as this one was, the Makeup Rate stamp required a remarkable amount of time, effort, trial and discard on the part of the Citizens' Stamp Advisory Committee, USPS staff and Richard Sheaff, the designer-typographer.

"The real question was, how do you get the public to understand what

Richard Sheaff produced a similarly large selection of designs incorporating ampersands for the committee and staff to review. The verdict was that the ampersand, although a graceful and aesthetically pleasing design subject, would prove to be even more puzzling to the stamp-buying public than a plus sign.

171

that stamp is?" Sheaff recalled. "Don McDowell and I, in kicking it around, came up with what I thought was absolutely the perfect idea. That was to call it the 'Plus' stamp. You could mark it with a plus sign, and advertise it so that people would very easily understand that this, plus the old stamp, would equal the new stamp. There would be only a minimum of wording. The promotional campaign, including magazine advertising and ads in other places, would make known what it was.

"Everybody thought it was a great idea. But then we spent perhaps a year in committee trying to make it work. I did what seemed like 400 different sketches. We had pluses of every description — fat pluses, skinny pluses, blue ones, green ones, orange ones, you name it, done in various techniques, by computer, by hand, by photo process. Infinite pluses. And they found something objectionable about all of them: 'It looks like the Red Cross,' for instance. 'It looks like the Blue Cross.' 'It's too skinny like that; it doesn't look like a plus.' 'It looks like a religious symbol.' It went on and on. We tried every kind of plus known to man.

"Finally we gave up on the pluses. The committee wanted something different. Then someone suggested that we do an ampersand; that this would be more interesting than a plus. I said, 'Yes, they're more interesting, but the public isn't going to understand the Ampersand stamp. The 'And' stamp? That won't mean anything to anyone.' Nevertheless, I did a number of ampersands.

"And, by then, words were beginning to come in. So we had ampersands with an increasing number of words sharing the stamp. And along the way we looked at eagles, we looked at all sorts of symbols of one sort or another that had nothing to do with anything except that we needed to come up with something. But words were beginning to creep in. Upper-management people were recognizing that the problem hadn't been solved and were scratching their own heads. They began to say: 'Well, you know, it's really got to say at least this much,' and the wording got longer and longer and longer, to the point where management and Don McDowell and I and others just threw up our hands and said, 'Look, there isn't room for anything BUT these words on the stamp any more.'

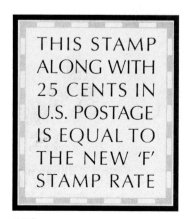

THIS STAMP
ALONG WITH
25 CENTS IN
U.S. POSTAGE
IS EQUAL TO
THE NEW 'F'
STAMP RATE

In this version, the message is still brief enough to allow the use of the Optima type in all capitals, which art director Richard Sheaff considered more attractive than an uppercase-and-lowercase combination. Later, when USPS officials prescribed a longer message, the all-caps typography had to be abandoned.

"So, although we hated to do it, we said, 'Let's think about doing a purely functional, all-words stamp.' And then we went on to 20 or 30 variations. At every meeting I'd come in with six or seven copy alternatives. It was sort of like headline writing. You had to edit it character by character to make it fit, and I was doing this, but trying to make it fit elegantly, in sort of an all-capitals, nice classic typeface with an even number of characters per line so it could be letter-spaced nicely. We did that over and over, and every time we would bring it in everybody would get out their pencils and say, 'Oh, no, it's got to say this,' or 'You'd better change that word.' So through several meetings we tried to make something elegant out of an increasingly cumbersome pile of words.

"Finally, we got to something that still wasn't all that bad. It went further up in postal management somewhere, and it was decided that it had to have another word or two, and it had to have some commas — which, grammatically, weren't necessary, and which the philatelic press subsequently had some fun with.

"By then, there were too many characters, and the Postal Service had decided that it wanted exactly these words in that order and I couldn't shift them around to make the effect a little more attractive. I had originally wanted to set it in Optima. I picked that typeface for its capitals. I don't really like lowercase Optima all that much, but all-cap Optima can be quite elegant. But then they added words, and those commas, and it wouldn't fit in all capitals any more, the message would have been too small. So I had to go to upper and lowercase."

Varieties

A single pane of 100 stamps with all horizontal perforations missing was discovered by a collector from Brooklyn, who purchased it, separated it in half vertically and began to tear the stamps apart before he realized what he had found. The broken pane was sold privately through the firm of Jacques Schiff. Of the total 50 imperforate-between pairs on the pane, 49 survived, Schiff said.

First-Day Facts

Collectors were given 60 days to get the first-day postmark. Those preparing their own covers were instructed to affix, in addition to the Makeup Rate stamp, "additional denominated postage of 21¢ to equal the first-class rate of 25¢ on the date of issue." Taken literally, this would have meant that collectors couldn't pay more than 4¢ of the postage for each cover with Makeup Rate stamps, even if they affixed blocks or strips.

Curiously, collectors who had their covers fully serviced by USPS had to pay 29¢ postage rather than 25¢. USPS affixed one Makeup Rate stamp and one 25¢ Flag Over Yosemite stamp to each cover.

F ($3.48) FLAG (ATM-VENDED SHEETLET)

Date of Issue: January 22, 1991

Catalog Number: Scott 2522 (single stamp); 2522a (sheetlet of 12)

Colors: red, dark blue, black (front); light blue (reverse liner)

First-Day Cancel: Washington, D.C. (no first-day ceremony)

FDCs Canceled: 48,821

Format: Made of polyester film, self-adhesive. Unfolded pane of 12 horizontal stamps arranged horizontally, 4 across, 3 down. Gravure printing cylinders of 180 units, 12 around, 15 across. All marginal markings removed in processing.

Perf: die cut, no perforations

Reverse Liner Markings: "DO NOT WET," "EXTRAordinary Stamp™ for ATM", "Self-adhesive * Do not moisten," "Patent Pending * © USPS 1990," all in repeating patterns.

Designer: Harry Zelenko of New York City

Art Director: Joe Brockert (USPS)

Project Manager: Joseph Peng (USPS)

Typographer and Modeler: John Boyd of Anagraphics Inc., New York, New York

Printing: photogravure by Avery International, Pasadena, California, on USPS-owned Chesnut press

Quantity Ordered: 26,000,000

Quantity Distributed: 25,500,000

Tagging: overall

The Stamp

When the first-class rate increased to 29¢ February 3, USPS was still in the midst of an experimental program with the Seattle First National Bank (Seafirst) to determine the market appeal and practicality of

174

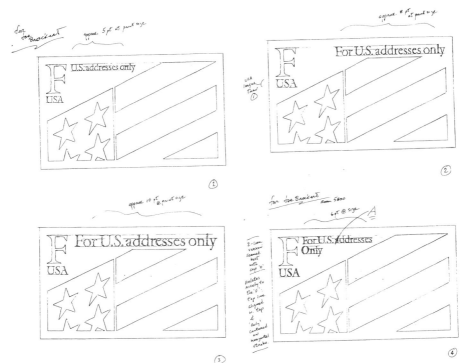

These sketches by John Boyd represent attempts to find the best way to integrate the F denomination symbol and the "For U.S. Addresses Only" message with the original design. Number 4 is close to the final choice, with only a capital "A" necessary to replace the lowercase letter in "Addresses." Boyd's marginal note to Joe Brockert reads: "2-line version seemed best with cap 'O.' Relates nicely to the 'F': top line aligned w. top and 'Only' centered on horizontal stroke."

dispensing stamps from bank automatic teller machines (ATMs). To launch the program in 1990, USPS had developed a unique self-adhesive stamp made of a polyester material that afforded the consistent thickness, or caliper control, that ATMs required.

Now a 29¢ ATM stamp was needed to replace the original, so-called "plastic" stamp, which bore a 25¢ face value. Waiting in the wings was an all-new ATM stamp made of paper, which the USPS Stamp Manufacturing Division was developing in conjunction with its manufacturing contractor, the Avery International Corporation of Pasadena, California, to meet the objections of environmentalists that the polyester stamp couldn't be recycled. But the paper stamp wasn't quite ready to be moved into the experimental program.

"The decision was made to keep the polyester stamps in production with as simple a change as possible, to give us a few months to come out with the replacements," said Joe Brockert, art director for the ATM stamp project. "We decided to upgrade them, so to speak, to the new first-class rate by giving them an F in place of the denomination."

As it happened, F, which stood for Flower on the conventional non-denominated stamps that were issued for the rate change, also stood for Flag, which was the design subject of the original ATM stamp. But this was pure coincidence.

Like the original, the ATM F stamp was issued in dollar-bill-sized sheetlets of 12, die-cut for separation. It was printed for USPS by Avery, a leading manufacturer of pressure-sensitive labels, on laminated material made at Avery's Fasson Division plant in Painesville, Ohio. The printing was done on a six-color webfed gravure press manufactured by Chesnut Engineering Company of Fairfield, New Jersey, which was purchased by USPS and installed at Avery's Pasadena plant.

The sheetlets were dispensed like currency from the ATMs being used in the experimental program, and the cost of each sheetlet, $3.48, was automatically deducted from the customer's bank account.

The new stamp was issued without prior notice January 22 in Washington, D.C., along with the conventional F stamps in sheets, booklets and coils, and the Makeup Rate stamp. After that, it was available only in the Seattle area and from the Philatelic Sales Division.

The Design

Harry Zelenko's original ATM stamp design had shown a portion of the stars and stripes of a stylized American flag in red and blue, with the inscription "25 USA" in red in the upper-left corner. The only change made on the new variety was to replace that inscription with the letter "F," a small "USA" beneath it, and, in two lines of type, the words "For U.S. Addresses Only." The lettering on the new stamp was in black.

The change was preceded by much discussion between Brockert and John Boyd of Anagraphics Inc. in New York, the Postal Service's graphics consultant. "We talked about cutting off the top of the red bars, and running the inscription along the top," Brockert said. "We decided the best and easiest thing to do was leave as much of the design alone as possible, and replace the '25 USA' with new information."

The color of the inscription was changed to black "to make sure that it was absolutely distinct from the earlier version," Brockert said. "We discovered that the printer could do a perfectly good job with more than two colors, so we added one to help avoid confusion."

The original stamp had also been printed from three different color cylinders: one for the blue, one for the red stripes and a third, with a finer screen, for the "25 USA," to give the best possible resolution along the edges of the letters and numbers. The latter cylinder was replaced with a black cylinder for the new version.

First-Day Facts

As with the other rate-change items issued January 22, there was no first-day ceremony. First-day postmarks were made available. Collectors were given 60 days to submit their covers for canceling.

4¢ STEAM CARRIAGE COIL
TRANSPORTATION SERIES

Date of Issue: January 25, 1991

Catalog Number: Scott 2451 (tagged version); Scott 2451b (untagged version)

Color: maroon (PMS 209U)

First-Day Cancel: Tucson, Arizona

FDCs Canceled: 100,393

Format: Coils of 500 and 3,000. Printing sleeve of 936 subjects (18 across, 52 around).

Perf: 9.8 (Huck stroke perforator)

Designer: Richard Schlecht of Arlington, Virginia

Engravers: vignette, Gary Chaconas (BEP); lettering, Michael J. Ryan (BEP)

Art Director and Project Manager: Jack Williams (USPS)

Modeler: Clarence Holbert (BEP)

Typographer: Bradbury Thompson (CSAC)

Printing: BEP's three-color intaglio B press (701)

Quantity Ordered: 533,000,000 (275,000,000 in coils of 500; 258,000,000 in coils of 3,000)

Quantity Distributed: 508,000,000 (250,000,000 in coils of 500; 258,000,000 in coils of 3,000)

Sleeve Number Detail: single-digit intaglio sleeve number on every 52nd stamp

Tagging: two varieties: overall tagging and no tagging

The Stamp

The first Transportation coil stamp of 1991 depicted one of the earliest surviving self-propelled vehicles in America: an 1866 steam carriage made by Richard Dudgeon of New York City. The 4¢ stamp was issued January 25 at Aripex, the annual stamp show sponsored by the Arizona Federation of Stamp Clubs.

The stamp was the 48th face-different variety in the long-running Transportation series — counting two that were later re-engraved with larger denomination numbers — and the second to cover the 4¢ rate. The first, showing an 1890s stagecoach, was issued in 1982.

The Steam Carriage stamp arrived just in time to see service as a make-up rate stamp. Nine days after its issuance, the first-class rate rose from 25¢ to 29¢, and postal customers needed 4¢ stamps to affix to their envelopes alongside their leftover 25-centers.

The denomination on the new stamp appeared as "04," in the new USPS style of expressing whole-number values of 9¢ or less. This style was begun in 1990 with the 5¢ Luis Munoz Marin (Great Americans) and 5¢ Circus Wagon (Transportation) stamps.

The new stamp was produced in two varieties: with and without phosphorescent tagging. This was the result of a USPS policy change, effective January 1, 1991, under which all U.S. stamps with face values of less than 8¢ would be untagged. Any current stamps going back to press thereafter were produced without tagging. Because the Steam Carriage stamps were in production on January 9, when the Bureau of Engraving and Printing was notified of the new policy, both tagged and untagged types were available when the stamp was released January 25. First-day covers exist with both varieties.

Collectors weren't aware of what was going on until after stamp publications began receiving reports of untagged Steam Carriage stamps — and also of the discovery of untagged specimens of other low-denominated definitives (see chapter on Revised Definitives). Suspecting that the omissions were intentional rather than the result of error, *Linn's Stamp News* inquired at USPS and was told of the new policy.

The decision to change was primarily related to revenue protection, said Donald M. McDowell, director of the Office of Stamp and Philatelic Marketing. In recent years, USPS had become aware of organized scams under which letters with insufficient postage were being posted and reaching their destination without being detected. Because all U.S. stamps were tagged, the presence of a single stamp of any denomination on an envelope was sufficient to send the item through an automatic facer-canceler machine. When an untagged stamp passes through automated equipment, however, it is rejected and often is examined by what USPS refers to as a "nixie clerk." Thus, withholding the tagging from low-value stamps would ease the problem, USPS believed.

The Office of Stamp and Philatelic Marketing set 8¢ as the cutoff point for tagging after conferring with the Postal Inspection Service, McDowell said. This breakpoint would help ensure that fewer short-paid mail pieces were processed. At the same time, the added security feature that tagging brings to stamps wouldn't be missed, because it is generally unprofitable to counterfeit low-value stamps anyway.

The USPS decision was similar to a decision made by Canada Post several years earlier. Canada Post not only ceased tagging low-value stamps, but high values as well. With low values, the policy served the same function as the USPS policy: revenue protection. With high values it served a dual function. First, since untagged stamps receive more visual scrutiny, high-value stamps that were being illegally re-used were more likely to be detected. Second, the policy helped ensure that special-service mail pieces actually received the special service that was paid for.

The idea of depicting the Dudgeon steam carriage on a Transportation coil grew out of USPS' frequent consultations about the series with transportation specialists at the Smithsonian Institution. John White, who then was a transportation curator at the Smithsonian and has since retired, suggested that this particular vehicle in the museum's collection be used as a subject.

Richard Dudgeon was a transplanted Scot who had a successful business building hydraulic jacks of his own invention. In 1853, in his machine works in New York, he began work on a steam wagon because, in his words, he wanted "to end the fearful horse murder and numerous other ills inseparable from their use."

By 1857 the vehicle was finished and successfully tested. It was only slightly different from a railway engine. There were no flanges on its

This photograph of the Dudgeon steam carriage, taken in a basement corridor of the Smithsonian Institution, was used by Richard Schlecht as a guide in preparing his pen-and-ink drawing for the Steam Carriage stamp.

wooden, iron-tired wheels, and it was steerable. Otherwise, it was a locomotive, even to its smokestack and the exposed cylinders at the forward end of its cylindrical boiler. The bodywork consisted of a wide wooden framework mounted across the top of the horizontal boiler barrel with shallow water tanks running fore and aft on either side. These tanks formed bench seats that would hold 10 passengers, five to a side. There were slatted back-rests behind the seats, with footboards below to keep the passengers' feet from being caught in the connecting rods.

The first Dudgeon carriage was exhibited in New York City's Crystal Palace, and was destroyed when the Palace was leveled by fire on October 5, 1857. In 1866, however, the inventor built a second machine, similar to the first one, and this is the carriage that is shown on the stamp.

"It is quite obvious that the Dudgeon was not an enjoyable vehicle," one historian wrote. "The crusty mayor of New York, Daniel F. Tiemann, and his police raised objections to the unholy racket of the fire-spitting, smoking street locomotive. Can you imagine the rumble of those iron-shod wheels on Manhattan's cobblestoned streets? Further, the passengers must have had an even worse time than the noise-ridden New Yorkers. They, poor fellows, were asked to sit on wooden benches set parallel to the steaming boiler. The driver and his fireman perched on a pair of seats aft of the rear wheels. Everybody must have suffered from cinders in their eyes."

The vehicle was later owned by private collectors and in 1981 was given to the Smithsonian as a gift. At the time the stamp was issued, it was on display in the Road Transportation Hall of the Smithsonian's National Museum of American History.

In designing the Transportation coil stamp, Schlecht also referred to this 19th-century engraving of the Dudgeon steam carriage, as seen from the rear.

180

The Design

Richard Schlecht, an Arlington, Virginia, artist, designed the Steam Carriage stamp. It was his fourth Transportation coil design assignment; he had previously designed the 3¢ Conestoga Wagon, the 7.6¢ Carreta and the 15¢ Tugboat stamps, all in 1988.

Schlecht based his ink drawing on two items furnished to him by the

This early sketch by Richard Schlecht showed the carriage from a different angle and with its front wheels turned.

Postal Service: an old engraving, and a photograph of the steam carriage taken at the Smithsonian Institution. He changed the angle of the carriage so it was more of a frontal view, and turned the front wheels slightly "to make it a little less static," he said.

Varieties

A number of imperforate specimens of the Steam Carriage stamp were found, including a roll that a Texas collector named Curt Taylor reportedly purchased at the philatelic window of the Amarillo, Texas, post office, on January 25, two days before the stamp's scheduled sale date.

First-Day Facts

For the second straight year, Aripex was the site of a Transportation coil first-day event. In 1990 the $1 Seaplane stamp was dedicated at the Aripex show in Phoenix.

USPS held no formal ceremony for the Steam Carriage stamp. In lieu of a program, the Postal Service produced a generic blue folder, and let it be known that the same folder would be used in the future whenever a new stamp was released at a stamp show and no official ceremony was planned. The cover bore a gold-embossed USPS eagle, and the inside contained a general statement about stamp collecting, along with the new stamps canceled with the first-day date.

19¢ FAWN

Date of Issue: March 11, 1991

Catalog Number: Scott 2487

Colors: magenta, cyan, yellow, black, green

First-Day Cancel: Washington, D.C. (No first-day ceremony)

FDCs Canceled: 100,212

Format: Panes of 100, vertical, 10 across, 10 down. Gravure printing cylinders of 400 subjects (20 across, 20 around).

Perf: 11.2 (Eureka off-line perforator)

Selvage Markings: "© U.S. Postal Service 1991." "Use Correct ZIP Code ®."

Designer, Typographer and Modeler: Peter Cocci (BEP)

Art Director: Leonard Buckley (BEP)

Project Manager: Joe Brockert (USPS)

Printing: printed by BEP on 7-color Andreotti gravure press (601)

Quantity Ordered: 815,000,000

Quantity Distributed: 778,220,000

Cylinder Number Detail: one group of 5 cylinder numbers alongside corner stamp

Tagging: overall

The Stamp

On March 11, with only a week's public notice, USPS issued a sheet stamp with a 19¢ denomination to cover the new postcard rate. The design of this stamp could easily have been chosen instead of a flower to decorate the non-denominated F stamps that had appeared a few weeks earlier; it featured another subject beginning with F, a fawn.

The Fawn stamp gave mailers a multicolor stamp with a popular nature theme, in sheet form, to use on postcards. No such stamp had been provided for the 15¢ rate that had been in effect from 1988 through 1990. During that period the 15¢ Buffalo Bill (Great Americans) stamp had filled the need for a postcard-rate sheet stamp.

At the time of the February 3 rate change the 10-year-old 19¢ Sequoyah stamp was still available in limited quantities, but many mailers of postcards simply made do until Fawn stamps came along by combining Buffalo Bills with the new 4¢ Make-up Rate stamps. (Coincidentally, the Sequoyah stamp, the first stamp of the Great Americans series, had originally been issued for postcard use — for international postcards.)

Collectors soaking used Fawn stamps from envelopes reported that in some cases the ink tended to flake away from the wet paper. (See chapter on the Wood Duck booklet, BEP version.)

The Design

The Fawn stamp was designed by Peter Cocci, the veteran Bureau of Engraving and Printing artist who had designed two of the four Creatures of the Sea stamps jointly issued with the Soviet Union the year before. It

Peter Cocci painted his fawn in these three poses — two lying down, one standing beside its mother — before he hit on the spraddle-legged standing pose that the committee chose for the stamp design.

was printed on BEP's vintage-1970 Andreotti gravure press.

BEP officials had submitted the idea of a fawn as the subject for a new definitive, pointing out that this was a kind of wildlife that hadn't been shown on U.S. stamps before and one that should appeal to the stamp-using public. It was agreed at the outset that the stamp would be printed by gravure, but USPS wasn't certain at first whether it preferred that the stamp be issued in sheets, coils or booklets.

The fawn on the stamp was a white-tailed deer, a familiar species in Maryland, where Cocci lived. The artist's first idea was to have the animal nestling in the grass, with its head down, as if hiding. The Citizens' Stamp Advisory Committee wasn't satisfied with this pose, and asked for others. Cocci sketched one fawn lying down, but with its head erect, and sketched another fawn accompanied by its mother. The artwork that the committee ultimately approved depicted a fawn in the act of rising, its legs spraddled and shaky.

Cocci used acrylic paints for this finished version. He included yellow flowers, of no particular variety, to provide color. In the background he placed a blue-green forest shrouded in mist, which set off the bright hues of the foreground to good advantage. For the "19 USA" he selected an unusual typeface, called Romic. "Peter liked it because it had a woodsy quality to it, with projections like little branches," explained Leonard Buckley, BEP design chief and art director for the stamp.

In addition to the four basic process colors, magenta, cyan, yellow and black, BEP used a green self-color to heighten the impression of forest greenery in the picture's setting.

First-Day Facts

There was no first-day ceremony for the Fawn stamp. With rate-change definitives that were urgently needed, USPS officials said, the policy was to get the stamps out rather than take the time to organize a ceremony. However, first-day cancellations were available at the Washington, D.C., main post office and by mail order. Collectors were given 60 days to submit envelopes or postcards for canceling.

In cases in which USPS affixed the stamps to envelopes, a 10¢ Canal Boat stamp from the Transportation series was combined with a Fawn stamp to make up the 29¢ first-class rate.

29¢ FLAG OVER MOUNT RUSHMORE COIL, BEP

Date of Issue: March 29, 1991

Catalog Number: Scott 2523

Colors: red, blue, brown (PMS 497U)

First-Day Cancel: Mount Rushmore (Keystone), South Dakota

FDCs Canceled: 233,793

Format: Coils of 100, 500 and 3,000. Intaglio printing sleeves of 960 subjects (20 across, 48 around) and 864 subjects (18 across, 48 around).

Perf: 10.2 (Huck rotary and Goebel stroke perforators)

Designer, Modeler and Typographer: Clarence Holbert (BEP)

Art Director: Leonard Buckley (BEP)

Project Manager: Joe Brockert (USPS)

Engravers: Thomas Hipschen (BEP, vignette); Michael J. Ryan (BEP, lettering and numerals)

Printing: printed on BEP's 3-color intaglio C press (901) and the 3-color intaglio station of BEP's offset-intaglio D press (902)

Quantity Ordered: 9,948,000,000 (8,100,000,000 in coils of 100; 1,287,000,000 in coils of 500; 561,000,000 in coils of 3,000)

Quantity Distributed: 7,520,536,000 (6,258,000,000 in coils of 100; 701,800,000 in coils of 500; 560,736,000 in coils of 3,000)

Sleeve Number Detail: one sleeve number on every 48th stamp

Tagging: phosphor-coated paper, prephosphored paper

The Stamp

The Postal Service had planned to release its definitive Flag coil stamp for the 29¢ rate sometime in April. However, the American military victory in the Persian Gulf stirred patriotic feelings and led to an "overwhelming" demand from postmasters and stamp buyers for a Flag stamp, USPS spokesman Michael O'Hara told *Linn's Stamp News*. As a result, USPS moved up the first day of sale to March 29.

"The Flag has always been a popular subject," O'Hara said, "but with

Operation Desert Storm, it has become more popular than ever."

The stamp was another in a long-running series of first-class rate definitives that showed the Stars and Stripes waving over a national landmark. The first landmarks were buildings, but with the Flag Over Yosemite stamp of 1988 (Scott 2280) the Postal Service turned for subject matter to scenery. Following that example, USPS chose for its 1991 Flag stamp the Mount Rushmore National Memorial, one of the world's most readily recognizable locales.

The Flag Over Mount Rushmore stamp, like the Flag Over Yosemite, was produced in coil form only. In its original version, it was printed in intaglio by the Bureau of Engraving and Printing and issued in rolls of 100, 500 and 3,000 on phosphor-coated paper.

Later, a second variety, on prephosphored paper, was reported. As Wayne Youngblood, writing in *Linn's,* described the difference, the (more common) variety on phosphor-coated paper had a splotchy appearance under shortwave ultraviolet light, and the paper surface was slightly rough. On the prephosphored paper, the tagging was "crisp, uniform and bright," Youngblood wrote, and the paper was smooth and appeared to have a coated surface similar to that used for offset-intaglio stamps. The new tagging variety was first reported by Joan Lenz of Sterling Heights, Michigan.

In January, as soon as USPS notified the Bureau of Engraving and Printing of the new 29¢ first-class rate, engraver Michael J. Ryan added "29" to the Mount Rushmore master die. The completed design was taken up on a transfer roll, which siderographers used to make intaglio printing bases for the Bureau's C and D presses.

To print the huge number of stamps initially ordered by USPS, BEP prepared a number of printing bases over a period of several weeks. Collectors reported finding six sleeve numbers within two weeks of the March 29 issue date.

As Charles Yeager, editor of *The United States Specialist*, noted in an article in the magazine's July 1991 issue, it's unusual for modern BEP presses to require so many printing sleeves so rapidly. "There had to be a reason why an inordinate number of printing bases were needed in such a short period of time," Yeager wrote. "With the help of cooperative USPS and BEP personnel, I was able to learn part of the reason why so many printing sleeves were used." This is what Yeager was told: For a time, both presses were used simultaneously for Mount Rushmore stamp production, with sleeve 1 used on the C press and sleeve 2 on the D press. But the printers discovered they couldn't run the presses at more than 200 feet per minute (fpm). When they tried to increase press speed, the inks didn't dry properly. While production continued at 200 fpm, Bureau personnel investigated the problem and found a solution.

"The problem was determined to be the depth of the engraved designs (90 microns) on printing bases 1 and 2," Yeager explained. "Too much ink was being deposited on the paper, more than the drying ovens could

These are the commemorative coins produced by the U.S. Mint for the 50th anniversary of the Mount Rushmore National Memorial. Top, the $5 gold coin, obverse designed by John Mercanti, reverse by Robert Lamb. Center, the $1 silver coin, obverse by Marika Somogyi, reverse by Frank Gasparro. Bottom, the half dollar, obverse designed by Marcel Jovine, reverse by James Ferrell.

dry at normal press running speeds.

"Siderographers went back to the transfer roll and filed down at least one of the designs by hand to a depth of about 55 microns. New printing sleeves (3 and 4) were made from the filed-down transfer roll and tried on the C press. Now printing from sleeves whose stamp designs were not as deep, the printers were able to increase press speed to 400 fpm and print stamps that could be dried properly. Beginning with sleeve 5, no ink drying problems were encountered, and Flag coil stamp production was soon back on schedule."

The Mount Rushmore stamp was unofficially released in many locations before its March 29 issue date. One business firm in New York told *Linn's* that it had used 70,000 of the stamps in a March 22 mailing. The earliest known use of the stamp as of this writing was March 8, three weeks early, from a New Jersey location.

Mount Rushmore, in South Dakota, is crowned by gigantic carvings in the mountain's granite of the heads of four U.S. presidents: George

Washington, Thomas Jefferson, Theodore Roosevelt and Abraham Lincoln. Work on the massive project took 14 years and ended in 1941, making the new stamp, in effect, a 50th anniversary commemorative, although it wasn't billed as such.

The U.S. Mint did, however, produce a set of coins in 1991 directly commemorating the anniversary. It sold the coins at a surcharge to benefit the Mount Rushmore National Memorial. A $5 gold coin showed an eagle in flight over Mount Rushmore, a $1 silver coin depicted the memorial surrounded by a laurel wreath, and a half dollar featured another view of the memorial with a sunburst. Pre-issue price of a proof-quality set was $225.

Mount Rushmore has been described as the dream of one man, made a reality by another. In 1923 Doane Robinson, 66, South Dakota's state historian, conceived the idea of creating a major tourist attraction in the Black Hills by carving a gigantic monument, perhaps the likenesses of Lewis and Clark, Red Cloud, John C. Fremont, or other heroes of Western history. In 1924 he and others persuaded the noted sculptor, Gutzon Borglum, to come to their state and look over the landscape.

Borglum's imagination was fired by the project, and he agreed to take it on. He chose a massive gray monolith called Mount Rushmore, accessible only by horseback or on foot. He persuaded Robinson and other local sponsors that the theme should be national in scope.

Borglum's first thought was of a Washington bust or statue, honoring the "father of the nation." Then Lincoln, preserver of the Union, was added; and then Jefferson, who expanded the nation westward. Not until work had actually begun at the site in 1927 was the fourth subject chosen. Theodore Roosevelt, builder of the Panama Canal, was added at the urging of President Calvin Coolidge, who argued that Teddy Roosevelt was the first president to actively work to protect the rights of workers.

Borglum not only designed the monument, but also invented most of the blast-drill-and-chisel techniques ("carving with dynamite") for executing the plan. Work began August 10, 1927, and was the principal object of the sculptor's time and attention for the rest of his life. Money came at first from private gifts, then from gifts matched by the federal government, and finally exclusively from federal appropriations.

This concept sketch by Clarence Holbert showed the presidential sculptures from a point closer to the base of Mount Rushmore. It also incorporates a flat flag rather than the fluttering banner shown on the finished stamp.

An earlier stamp depicting Mount Rushmore was this 3¢ commemorative of 1952 that marked the 25th anniversary of the start of work on the mountain (Scott 1011).

In 1930 the as-yet-unfinished Washington face was formally unveiled; in 1936, Jefferson; in 1937, Lincoln, and in 1939, Roosevelt. The dimensions of the faces were colossal, set to the scale of men 465 feet tall. Washington's face was 60 feet long; Roosevelt's mustache was 20 feet across; Lincoln's mole, 16 inches wide. As Borglum planned the project, the figures were to be completed to the waists, including such details as period clothing and hands, and the immense pile of rubble from the blastings was to be removed.

But after his death in 1941 at 74, funds — and work — came to an end. Because of the imminence of war, a planned dedication ceremony was abandoned. The total cost of carving the mountain had been just under one million dollars.

Mount Rushmore had been shown twice before on U.S. stamps. A 3¢ stmap of 1952 (Scott 1011) marked the 25th anniversary of the beginning of work on the mountain, and a 26¢ airmail stamp of 1974 (Scott C88) carried a simple black-line drawing of the four presidential heads against a blue, white and red background. One of three 6¢ postal cards issued in 1972 for the Tourism Year of the Americas showed Mount Rushmore and other U.S. tourist attractions on the reverse side (Scott UX61).

Other Gutzon Borglum works have also been stamp subjects. His pioneer group, "Colonization of the West," in Marietta, Ohio, was depicted on the Northwest Territory Settlement commemorative of 1938 (Scott 837). His massive head of Lincoln in the U.S. Capitol was shown on a Lincoln Sesquicentennial stamp in 1959 (Scott 1114). Another commemorative (Scott 1408) marked the 1970 dedication of the Confederate Memorial on Stone Mountain, Georgia, which Borglum designed.

The Design

Clarence Holbert of BEP was the only artist assigned to prepare concept sketches for the Mount Rushmore stamp. Holbert worked from photographs supplied by the National Park Service and some snapshots that the stamp's art director, Leonard Buckley of BEP, had taken during a visit to the site several years earlier.

The view Holbert chose for the painting that became the final design was similar to what a tourist would see from the visitors' lodge at the base

189

of the mountain. He also sketched a less conventional view, from a point closer to the base, looking upward at a sharper angle. "While it was dramatic as a photo, it didn't interpret well. There was no justification for the drama," Leonard Buckley said. "People wouldn't readily recognize the monument."

On the actual monument, the lighting on the faces changes during the day as the sun moves. "The light produces good things at one time and other good things at another time," Buckley said. "The artist put some of those good things together to bring out the four faces properly at stamp size." Between Lincoln and Roosevelt, for example, Holbert darkened the shadow in order to make the adjacent faces stand out. After completing his painting, he used BEP's Electronic Design Center to make some final minor modifications.

The previous Flag stamp had carried the word "Yosemite," but CSAC felt that Mount Rushmore was so familiar that no space need be taken to tell what it was. Engraver Ryan executed the "29 USA" so it appeared in a darker tone over the lighter mountain surface. This balanced the dark space between the Lincoln and Roosevelt heads and "helped give the design a base," Buckley explained. The committee considered various colors for the mountain, beginning with black, the color that had been used for the Flag Over Supreme Court (1981) and Flag Over Capitol (1985) definitives, but finally opted for the shade USPS called maroon.

Varieties

In December, copies of the Mount Rushmore stamp began appearing with the mountain and sculpted heads printed in a color markedly different from the original. The original color was described by USPS as "maroon" and by BEP as "brown" with a Pantone number of 497U. The new color was brown with no maroon tone, and was described by Wayne Youngblood in *Linn's* as being "much like a brown paper bag" and "absolutely consistent, something not possible with an ink contamination freak." All specimens originally reported were from sleeve number 7, which had also produced normal-colored stamps.

The normal-colored stamps were also found in imperforate form, a common occurrence with modern U.S. coils. In October a Florida dealer advertised imperforate pairs for sale at $75 per pair.

First-Day Facts

Snow swirled around the speakers and guests at the outdoor first-day ceremony March 29 at the Memorial, and a few minutes after the program began, fog moved in to hide from view the giant faces on the mountain. Nevertheless, the ceremony went on as scheduled, with speeches by Governor George S. Mickelson of South Dakota; James Ridenour, director of the National Park Service, and Susan E. Alvarado, a member of the USPS Board of Governors, and dedication of the stamp by John G. Mulligan, regional postmaster general. Tom Roberts offered a theatrical presentation entitled "A Gutzon Borglum Retrospective."

29¢ FLAG OVER MOUNT RUSHMORE COIL, ABNC

Date of Issue: July 4, 1991

Catalog Number: Scott 2523A

Colors: medium brown, light brown, dark brown, red, blue

First-Day Cancel: Mount Rushmore (Keystone), South Dakota

FDCs Canceled: 80,662

Format: Coils of 10,000. Gravure printing cylinders of 456 subjects (19 across, 24 around).

Perf: 10.2 (platen perforator, designed and built by Guilford Gravure Division of George Schmitt and Company, Guilford, Connecticut)

Designer and Typographer: Clarence Holbert (BEP)

Art Director: Leonard Buckley (BEP)

Project Manager: Joe Brockert (USPS)

Printing: Printed by Guilford Gravure on an Andreotti 5-color webfed gravure press for American Bank Note Company. Perforated and coiled by Guilford Gravure.

Quantity Ordered: 150,000,000,000 (15,000,000 coils), reduced to 50,000,000,000 (5,000,000 coils)

Quantity Distributed: 50,000,000,000 (5,000,000 coils)

Cylinder Number Detail: 1 set of 5 cylinder numbers preceded by the letter A on every 24th stamp

Tagging: phosphor-coated paper

The Stamp

On July 4, USPS issued a gravure version of the 29¢ Flag Over Mount Rushmore coil stamp that originally had been issued as an intaglio-printed stamp the preceding March 29.

The stamp, furnished by the American Bank Note Company, was the first U.S. coil stamp to be printed outside the Bureau of Engraving and Printing. Its issuance also marked the first time since the emergency offset printings of World War I that a U.S. stamp originally produced in intaglio had later been printed by another process.

The new stamp was available only in coils of 10,000, for use primarily by large business mailers. It was printed for ABNC on an Andreotti press by George Schmitt and Company's Guilford Gravure Division of Guilford, Connecticut. Guilford Gravure also did the perforating and coiling.

Stephen Esrati, writing in *Stamp Collector*, reported that dealers and collectors couldn't find the stamps for more than two weeks after the issue date. The *Postal Bulletin* of June 13 had announced that every regional accountable-paper depository would receive 240 of the jumbo rolls, but a collector who called USPS in Washington after a fruitless search was told the stamps had been shipped only to St. Paul and Denver, as well as to the Philatelic Sales Division in Kansas City.

The Design

The design of the stamp had been created by Peter Cocci, Bureau of Engraving and Printing artist, for adaptation by engravers to the intaglio printing process. For the gravure stamp, BEP, at the request of USPS, used its Electronic Design Center to make continuous-tone color photo prints of the stamp design, which it then turned over to the Postal Service for use by its private contract printer, along with the type mechanical or overlay. The design was in the Design Center's electronic memory because BEP had scanned it during the preparation of the intaglio version to make a stamp-sized model to show to USPS and the Citizens' Stamp Advisory Committee.

The gravure-printed stamp, with its image created by dots, had a muddier appearance than its engraved predecessor, and its colors were darker. In addition, the ''29 USA'' on the gravure stamp wasn't outlined in white, as it was on the original stamp, and was farther from the bottom of the design than on the original.

First-Day Facts

John G. Mulligan, central regional postmaster general, dedicated the stamp at Mount Rushmore National Memorial, Keystone, South Dakota. He had performed the same service when the intaglio stamp was issued March 29. Tom Roberts again impersonated Mount Rushmore sculptor Gutzon Borglum, as he had done at the earlier ceremony. Music was furnished by a band from Denmark, home of Borglum's forbears.

The day before the stamp dedication, on July 3, President George Bush

192

was guest of honor at a 50th-anniversary ceremony attended by some 3,500 people at the foot of the memorial. In a speech, the president called on Americans to "express our undiminished devotion to the ideals of Washington, Jefferson, Lincoln and Roosevelt, ideals as towering and solid as the monument that honors them."

Although the actual first-day post office was Keystone, the postmark bore the name "Mount Rushmore." Collectors were originally given 30 days to submit covers for canceling, but the deadline was later extended another 30 days because of difficulties in distributing the stamp.

35¢ DENNIS CHAVEZ
GREAT AMERICANS SERIES

Date of Issue: April 3, 1991

Catalog Number: Scott 2185

Color: black

First-Day Cancel: Albuquerque, New Mexico

FDCs Canceled: 285,570

Format: Panes of 100, vertical, 10 across by 10 down. Printing plate of 600 subjects, 20 across, 30 down.

Perf: 10.9 (L perforator)

Selvage Inscription: "Dennis Chavez/Born, Apr. 8, 1888/Died, Nov. 18, 1962." "U.S. Representative/from New Mexico./Served 1931 to 1935." "Became U.S. Senator/1935. Served until/his death in 1962."

Selvage Markings: "© United States Postal Service 1991." "Use Correct ZIP Code ®."

Designer: Chris Calle of Ridgefield, Connecticut

Art Director and Project Manager: Jack Williams (USPS)

Typographer: Bradbury Thompson (CSAC)

Engraver: Yves Baril (Canadian Bank Note Company)

Modeler: Yves Baril (Canadian Bank Note Company)

Printing: printed by Canadian Bank Note Company, Ottawa, on a TA-2 intaglio press for Stamp Venturers of Fairfax, Virginia

Quantity Ordered: 200,000,000

Quantity Distributed: 480,000,000

Plate Number Detail: 1 plate number preceded by letter S in selvage at left or right of corner stamp (outer panes) or above or below right corner stamp (middle panes)

Tagging: phosphor-coated paper

194

The Stamp

Dennis Chavez, first American-born Hispanic to serve in the U.S. Senate, was depicted on a 35¢ Great Americans stamp that was issued April 3 in Albuquerque, New Mexico. Chavez, who represented New Mexico in Congress from 1931 to 1962, had once practiced law in Albuquerque.

The stamp was printed by the intaglio process by the Canadian Bank Note Company of Ottawa for Stamp Venturers, a partnership based in Fairfax, Virginia. It was the first Great Americans stamp to be made by a printer other than the Bureau of Engraving and Printing, and the first intaglio-process stamp since the Overrun Countries commemoratives of 1943-1944 to be privately produced.

It was also the first U.S. stamp to be printed outside the United States — a fact that created much controversy, and enough adverse reaction from members of Congress to cause the postmaster general to promise not to continue the practice.

More than a year before the issue date, on February 23, 1990, USPS had announced that a Chavez stamp would be part of its 1991 program. At that time, the denomination was undetermined, but USPS said it would correspond to one of the new rates anticipated for 1991.

The 35¢ denomination selected for the stamp, as it turned out, covered the new half-ounce rate to Mexico that went into effect February 3. Frank Thomas of USPS told *Linn's Stamp News* that the depiction of a Hispanic-American on a stamp that would be used extensively on mail to Mexico was "a happy coincidence."

"Chavez was chosen for a design long before we knew we would have a new rate to Mexico," he said. "When we knew that the timing of the new rate and the issue of the Chavez stamp would be close, someone said, 'Let's put the two together.' "

Chavez was the 49th person to be honored in the Great Americans series, and the second of Hispanic descent. Luis Munoz Marin, the first elected governor of Puerto Rico, had been the first in 1990.

The senator's appearance in the series was the result of a campaign launched more than four years earlier by his daughters, Gloria Chavez Tristani and Ymelda Chavez Dixon. The two women had originally hoped for a stamp in 1988 on the 100th anniversary of their father's birth.

They submitted extensive information on Chavez to the Citizens' Stamp Advisory Committee, and enlisted in their effort a large number of influential supporters, including New Mexico's two U.S. senators, Pete Domenici and Jeff Bingaman. One of the campaign's strongest backers was Representative Edward Roybal, D-California, who, as chairman of the Treasury, Postal Service and General Government Subcommittee of the House Appropriations Committee, was in a good position to get the Postal Service's attention. Roybal, whose grandmother was a member of the Chavez family, told New Mexico newsman Jay Miller that as a youth in Albuquerque he had been encouraged by

195

Senator Chavez to continue his education, and that the senator had campaigned for him when he ran for political office.

The disclosure that the Chavez stamp was being printed in Canada was preceded by mixed signals from USPS.

The first details of the stamp to be made public were published in the March-April 1991 issue of the Philatelic Sales Division's *Philatelic Catalog*. This issue included a picture of the stamp, a notation that it would be available April 4, and a footnote saying that the item would be produced by Stamp Venturers, a company whose name at that time was unfamiliar to collectors. However, the official USPS news release, dated March 21, reported that BEP would be the printer.

This was straightened out in the March 28 *Washington Post*, which reported that the stamp was indeed being supplied by Stamp Venturers and was being manufactured in Canada. Stamp Venturers, it turned out, was a partnership among Sennett Enterprises of Fairfax, Virginia; J.W. Fergusson Inc. of Richmond, Virginia, where many U.S. stamps have been gravure-printed under private contract; and KCS Industries of Milwaukee, Wisconsin.

Assistant Postmaster General Gordon C. Morison told the *Post* that Stamp Venturers had subcontracted the job to the Canadian firm because few private American printers offered the intaglio process that USPS had been using for Great Americans stamps. (USPS later disclosed that Stamp Venturers had also subcontracted the printing of another Great Americans stamp, for Earl Warren, to Canadian Bank Note.)

The arrangement didn't violate the so-called "Buy America" Act, which directs government agencies to give preference to products made in the United States, Morison said, because at least two-thirds of the work on the stamps would be done in this country. He explained that the stamps were printed on paper that was made in the United States and shipped to Ottawa for printing. They were then returned to the United States for perforating and boxing (at Banta in Milwaukee) and forwarding to USPS.

The United States and Canada are historic good neighbors and had recently signed a major free-trade agreement. Canada's own first stamp — the 3-penny Beaver of 1851 — was printed in the United States, by the New York firm of Rawdon, Wright, Hatch and Edson. Nevertheless, the Chavez stamp disclosure touched off a vigorous debate, which began with a strongly critical editorial in the April 15 issue of *Linn's*.

Linn's called the printing of the stamp in Canada a "shameful spectacle" and pronounced itself "outraged" at this "colossal embarrassment" and "fiasco" that "makes our nation a philatelic laughingstock." "One of the philatelic hallmarks of colonies and second-class nations has been that they have foreign firms print their stamps," *Linn's* asserted.

This was followed by numerous letters in the philatelic press, pro and con. Those who were "pro" the arrangement pointed to the high quality of work done by some overseas printers (with some citing specifically the beautiful, detailed engraving that Canadian Bank Note's Yves Baril had

196

created for the Chavez stamp), and deplored what they called isolationist and economic protectionist attitudes on the part of the policy's critics. Those who were "con" cited the U.S. trade deficit and national pride as reasons for keeping stamp printing work at home.

In its May 6 issue, *Linn's* published a full-page debate on the subject between *Los Angeles Times* stamp columnist Barry Krause and Larry McInnis, *Linn's* monthly Canada columnist. Krause used his space to deplore not only the idea of sending stamp-printing jobs abroad but also the use of any printer other than BEP and any printing technique other than intaglio. McInnis, for his part, ridiculed the notion that printing a U.S. stamp in a friendly neighboring country "is a serious threat to America." "Hey — we were on your side in the Persian Gulf war, although you wouldn't know it from any of the U.S. coverage," McInnis wrote. "We just shrug and go on to another day."

In the end, Postmaster General Anthony M. Frank yielded to "serious concerns" expressed to him by several members of the House Committee on Post Office and Civil Service in a letter April 10.

"That a 'Great Americans' series stamp should be printed outside the United States is particularly disturbing," the members wrote. "Regardless of whether the printing of this stamp complied with applicable procurement law and regulations, it seems highly inappropriate for postage stamps, which are, in effect, legal tender of the United States Postal Service, to be printed outside of the United States." The committee hinted that it might go even further: "If legislation is necessary to ensure that future printing is done domestically, we will work with you to develop that legislation."

The postmaster general, in a written reply to the committee April 12, informed the members that a second stamp would also be printed in Canada, but assured them that it would be the last, at least for some time.

"Even though stamp printing outside the United States is permitted by law," he wrote, "the Postal Service would prefer to keep its stamp sourcing in the United States. American stamps are an important cultural tradition in which this country, including its 20 million stamp collectors, rightly takes pride.

"With the exception of these two stamps, we intend to ensure that all stamps are printed in the United States through fiscal year 1992. Beyond that we will do everything reasonably possible to develop and sustain United States stamp sources."

Committee members reacted with satisfaction to Frank's letter. Representative Frank McCloskey, D-Indiana, for one, welcomed the decision to bring Great Americans stamp production "home." "That was one 'stamp tax' the American people should not have suffered," he told *Stamp Collector*.

Whereas BEP prints its definitive-size intaglio stamps from sleeves of 400 subjects, divided into four 100-stamp panes for post office distribution, Canadian Bank Note printed Chavez from plates of 600 subjects, divided into six 100-stamp panes. This meant there were plate-number blocks available in six different positions.

Long after the stamp was issued, complaints were heard that it was unavailable at post offices and philatelic centers. A *Linn's* reader from New Orleans, Louisiana, reported in a letter in the September 2 edition that although the 35¢ stamp should sell well in his city, with its many ties to Latin America, it still hadn't arrived at the philatelic window of the city's main post office.

Dennis Chavez (the name is pronounced with the accent on the first syllable) was born April 8, 1888, in Los Chavez, in what would later be part of the state of New Mexico. One of eight children in an impoverished household, he dropped out of the eighth grade at 13 to drive a grocery wagon. He became active in Democratic Party politics, and in 1918-1919 clerked for U.S. Senator Andrieus Jones in Washington, where Chavez studied law at Georgetown University, after passing a special entrance examination required because he had never been to high school.

Chavez returned to Albuquerque, where he practiced law, was elected to the New Mexico Legislature, and in 1930 became New Mexico's sole U.S. representative. He was appointed to a U.S. Senate vacancy in 1935, was elected to the seat in 1936 and re-elected four successive times.

As a senator, Chavez generally supported President Franklin D. Roosevelt and his New Deal legislation. He won national attention by his long fight for establishment of a permanent Fair Employment Practices Commission that would enforce antidiscrimination requirements in government work or interstate commerce — a fight that wasn't won until two years after his death, with passage of the Civil Rights Act of 1964. He was a strong supporter of reciprocal trade agreements, notably with Latin America, and a sponsor of federal aid for maternal and child care.

Chavez died November 18, 1962, at the age of 74. New Mexico honored him after his death by placing his statue in the U.S. Capitol's Statuary Hall. Its inscription was in three languages — English, Spanish and Navajo — and read: "We have lost our voice forever."

The Design

The Chavez family asked that the stamp design be based on a painting of the senator that had been given to the state of New Mexico after the senator's death. The painting had hung in the state capitol in Santa Fe. But at the time the stamp was issued, the capitol was being renovated and the painting was in the custody of Gloria Chavez Tristani in Albuquerque.

The painter, whose identity was unknown to the family, had based his work on a photograph of Chavez seated at his desk. Although the photograph showed Chavez' right hand resting on the desk and holding a fountain pen, the painting depicted him with arms folded, a cigar in his right hand. The family supplied USPS with a photograph of the painting, which was turned over to Christopher Calle, the artist commissioned to prepare the stamp design.

198

Calle had designed several previous Great Americans stamps, most recently the 40¢ Claire Chennault stamp of 1990. His pencil portraits contain detailed line patterns for the guidance of the engravers. He likes to collect as much pictorial reference information as possible before beginning an assignment, so he obtained some additional Chavez photographs from a library. But he knew that the portrait he would draw had to be quite faithful to the painting that the family had furnished.

"It wasn't a very realistic painting," Calle recalled. "It had a kind of 'painterly' quality which I had to translate into line artwork. Fortunately, Chavez had strong facial features that I could get hold of and provide a directional flow of pencil lines to help the engraver get it on a plate."

Calle was pleased with the stamp that resulted. The Canadian engraver, he said, had done a "super job" of turning his artwork into intaglio. "He even captured the fine lines that soften the background," the artist said. "He kept the lines in the face crisp and clean, not thick."

Though the early Great Americans stamps had light backgrounds, most of the later ones have used fully or partially shaded backgrounds to provide contrast and help bring out the subject's features. This practice was begun by Calle's father, Paul Calle, with the 5¢ Pearl Buck stamp of 1983, and followed by Chris Calle with his own Great Americans design debut, the 20¢ Harry Truman stamp of 1984, and with most of his subsequent designs in the series.

The Chavez stamp design followed the USPS policy, ordered by Postmaster General Anthony M. Frank and first implemented with the two Great Americans stamps issued in 1990, of carrying a line of type that

At left is the painting of Senator Dennis Chavez, by an unidentified artist, on which Chris Calle based his drawing for the stamp. At right is the photograph of Chavez at his desk, which was used as a model for the painting.

referred to the subject's area of distinction. In this case, the words "United States Senator" ran vertically to the right of the portrait. With this stamp, USPS added still more factual information: Chavez' dates of birth and death, "1888- 1962," in vertical dropout white type, were tucked into the lower left corner of the portrait area.

First-Day Facts

The first-day ceremony was held at the Center for Southwest Research, located in the Zimmerman Library of the University of New Mexico in Albuquerque. William T. Johnstone, assistant postmaster general, dedicated the stamp.

New Mexico Governor Bruce King told the audience he owed his career to the man being honored. "I probably would never have been governor if it had not been for Senator Dennis Chavez," he said, explaining that Chavez taught him to remember people and vote his conscience. Albuquerque Mayor Louis E. Saavedra said Chavez had "blazed a path that made it so much easier for the rest of us (Hispanic-Americans) to seek public office."

Other speakers included Senators Domenici and Bingaman, Representative Roybal and Dr. Richard Peck, president of the University of New Mexico. Guests included several members of the Chavez family.

At the end of the ceremony, according to the Associated Press, Chavez's daughter, Gloria Tristani, exclaimed: "Mission accomplished."

29¢ FLOWER SHEET STAMP

Date of Issue: April 5, 1991

Catalog Number: perf 11, Scott 2524; perf 13 by 12.75, no number assigned

Colors: yellow, magenta, cyan, black

First-Day Cancel: Rochester, New York

FDCs Canceled: 132,233

Format: Panes of 100, vertical, 10 across, 10 down. Gravure printing cylinders of 400 subjects (20 across, 20 around).

Perf: 13 by 12.75 (Ormag rotary perforator); 11 (L perforator)

Selvage Markings: "© USPS 1991." "USE CORRECT ZIP CODE ®."

Designer: Wallace Marosek of Boston, Massachusetts

Art Director and Typographer: Bradbury Thompson (CSAC)

Project Manager: Jack Williams (USPS)

Printing: printed by Jeffries Banknote Division of United States Banknote Corporation on 8-color combination Andreotti-Giori gravure-intaglio webfed press

Quantity Ordered: 1,500,000,000

Quantity Distributed: 1,500,000,000 (643,870,400, Ormag perforator; 856,129,600, L perforator)

Cylinder Number Detail: 1 group of 4 cylinder numbers preceded by the letter U alongside corner stamp

Tagging: phosphor-coated paper

The Stamp

For the first time since USPS began creating non-denominated rate-change stamps, it converted one of these temporary stamps into a long-term definitive by simply changing the letter in the design to a number. On April 5, the Flower stamp that had been originally issued January 22 was reissued with ''29'' in place of the F and without the inscription ''For U.S. addresses only.''

201

The impending arrival of the denominated Flower stamp was first signaled in the March-April issue of the Philatelic Sales Division's *Philatelic Catalog*. The catalog reported that sheet, booklet and coil versions would all be "available mid-April." However, the USPS news release of April 1 announced only two versions, sheet and booklet. The coil version didn't show up until August.

All three versions were gravure-printed, but by three different private firms: United States Banknote Corporation for the sheet, KCS Industries Inc. for the booklet and Stamp Venturers for the coil. And, as with the F stamp, there were subtle differences in appearance. For example, the 1992 *Scott Specialized Catalogue of United States Stamps* noted that the flower on the sheet version had a "grainy appearance" and the inscriptions looked "rougher" than on the booklet stamp.

USPS plate-activity reports, cited by Stephen G. Esrati in *Stamp Collector*, indicated that at least some of the sheet stamps were printed with gravure cylinders left over from production of the F stamp. The exception was the black cylinder, which carried the "F" and "For U.S. Addresses Only" slogan and was canceled in February 1991.

Unannounced by USPS, the sheet stamp appeared in two different perforation varieties. Collectors didn't learn of this significant fact until the release of the July-August issue of the Philatelic Sales Division's *Philatelic Catalog*, when two types were listed for sale: PSD order number 5534, "perforated on 'L' perforators," and number B5534, "perforated on 'bullseye' perforators." In the previous catalog, only number 5534, with no description, had been listed.

The bull's-eye perf variety, the original version of the stamp, had a perforation-gauge measurement of 13 by 12.75. The holes were small and met perfectly at intersections. The L-perf variety, which was perf 11,

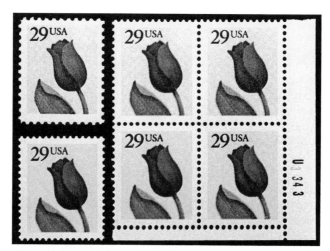

At upper left is the L-perf version; at lower left is the bull's-eye perf version, processed by a comb perforator. The plate block shows how the bull's-eye perforations meet.

had holes that crossed at the intersections in unpredictable patterns, leaving corners that were somewhat ragged-looking.

Joseph Y. Peng, general manager of the USPS Stamp Manufacturing Division, explained what had happened. Jeffries Banknote in Los Angeles, the United States Bank Note Corporation subsidiary that printed the stamps, had an on-line Ormag rotary perforator that failed during the press run. The perforating drum had to be sent to Italy for repairs, a process that would take an estimated eight months. Because USPS needed the stamps, Jeffries was allowed to finish printing them, sheet them out and move them to an off-line L perforator to finish the job.

A spokesman for the American Bank Note Company, another United States Banknote subsidiary, said the 1.5 billion press run of Flower stamps broke down this way: 643,870,400 were bull's-eye perforated (Ormag) stamps, and 856,129,600 were L-perforated.

Late in 1991 it was revealed that the same two kinds of perforation varieties also existed for another Jeffries-printed stamp, the 29¢ Love stamp, sheet version (see 29¢ Love Stamp chapter).

The Design

The red tulip, green leaves and yellow background that Wallace Marosek had created for the F stamp were duplicated on the 29¢ version. Marosek had conceived the tulip design while a graduate student of design at Yale University, studying under Bradbury Thompson, Citizens' Stamp Advisory Committee design coordinator. The artist had no idea that his tulip painting would get a long-term lease as a denominated stamp design until he was notified by a friend in Rochester, New York, the first-day city, who had heard the news on television.

First-Day Facts

The sheet and booklet versions of the Flower stamp made their debut in Rochester, New York, at the Ropex 91 stamp show. USPS suggested in its news release that Rochester was chosen for the honor because of its nickname, "The Flower City." Interestingly, Rochester was originally known as "The Flour City," for its many mills. Later it changed homonyms as milling moved out and nurseries and botanical gardens became featured attractions.

No first-day ceremony was held. Collectors were originally given until June 4 to submit covers for first-day cancellations. Later, because of stamp distribution difficulties, the deadline was extended another 60 days, to August 3.

Date of Issue: April 5, 1991

Catalog Number: Scott 2527 (single stamp); 2527a (booklet pane of 10)

Colors: yellow, magenta, cyan, black

First-Day Cancel: Rochester, New York

FDCs Canceled: 16,975

Format: 2 panes of 10 vertical stamps each arranged vertically, 2 across by 5 down. Gravure printing cylinders of 400 subjects (20 across, 20 around) manufactured by Armotek Industries Inc., Palmyra, New Jersey.

Perf: 10.7 (L perforator)

Selvage and Other Markings: Cylinder numbers printed on each pane binding stub. Also, 20 percent of all panes show magenta cut mark at outer edge of third stamp down (10 percent on left stamp, 10 percent on right stamp).

Cover Markings: "© United States Postal Service 1991 K" on inside of front cover. Universal Product Code (UPC) on outside of back cover. Domestic U.S. postage rates and other mailing information on inside of front cover and both sides of back cover.

Designer: Wallace Marosek of Boston, Massachusetts

Art Director and Typographer: Bradbury Thompson (CSAC)

Project Manager: Jack Williams (USPS)

Modeler: Richard Sennett, Sennett Enterprises

Printing: By Sennett Enterprises on Champlain gravure press at J.W. Fergusson and Sons, Richmond, Virginia, for KCS Industries Inc., Milwaukee, Wisconsin. Formed into booklets at KCS.

Quantity Ordered: 2,200,000,000 (109,650,000 booklets; 700,000 unfolded panes)

Quantity Distributed: 1,880,688,000

Cylinder Number Detail: 1 group of 4 cylinder numbers preceded by the letter K on each pane binding stub

Tagging: phosphor-coated paper

The Stamp

General information on the denominated Flower stamps can be found in the preceding chapter.

Unlike the F booklet stamps, the denominated Flower booklet stamps were made available in unfolded panes by the Philatelic Sales Division.

The Design

The cover of the booklet showed an enlarged replica of one of the stamps inside. The replica was an accurate representation, showing the stamp perforated on three sides and with a straight edge on the left side. Previous stamp booklets that had illustrated the stamps they contained had inaccurately shown the stamps perforated all around.

Subsequent booklets, such as those containing Wood Duck, Flag With Olympic Rings, Love and Hot-Air Balloon stamps, depicted the straight-edge feature accurately.

Varieties

A few booklet panes without vertical perforations surfaced soon after

This imperf-between booklet pane in a KCS-produced booklet has no outer perforations as most imperf booklet panes do. It is a true error of omission.

the booklet was issued. The Jack Nalbandian firm of Warwick, Rhode Island, handled three of the panes, which Nalbandian said were the top panes of three booklets found in the Boston, Massachusetts, area. All had the cylinder numbers K1111 on the binding stubs. In July, dealer Dana Okey of San Diego, California, advertised a full pane for $895 and a horizontal pair imperforate between for $249.

The panes had no outer perforations, suggesting that the error was a true error of omission rather than a paper shift. Because most types of booklet production involve the perforating of every other row of stamps, with the slitting that separates the panes being done along the imperforate row, most imperf-between booklet stamps are created by a shift that leaves perforations on the outer edges but not in the center.

In addition, Bill Langs, a New Jersey dealer specializing in errors, showed *Linn's Stamp News* a foldover freak on a Flower booklet pane that produced an imperforate-between pair. Outer perforations surrounded the imperf-between pair.

First-Day Facts

For first-day covers fully serviced by USPS, only full panes of 10 stamps were affixed at a cost to the customer of $2.90.

29¢ FLOWER COIL STAMP

Date of Issue: August 16, 1991

Catalog Number: Scott 2525

Colors: yellow, magenta, cyan, black

First-Day Cancel: Rochester, New York

FDCs Canceled: 144,750

Format: Coils of 100, issued individually and also in "sticks" of 10 coils stacked vertically with slit perforations between the coils. Gravure printing cylinders of 429 subjects (13 across, 33 around) manufactured by Armotek Industries Inc., Palmyra, New Jersey.

Perf: 9.5 slit perforated (rouletted)

Designer: Wallace Marosek of Boston, Massachusetts

Art Director and Typographer: Bradbury Thompson (CSAC)

Project Manager: Jack Williams (USPS)

Modeler: Richard Sennett of Stamp Venturers

Printing: Printed on a Champlain gravure press and slit perforated by Stamp Venturers at J.W. Fergusson and Sons, Richmond, Virginia. Coiled and finished at KCS Industries Inc., Milwaukee, Wisconsin.

Quantity Ordered: 1,000,000,000

Quantity Distributed: 1,000,000,000 (647,160,000 in sticks; 352,840,000 in individual coils)

Cylinder Number Detail: 4 cylinder numbers preceded by the letter S on every 33rd stamp

Tagging: phosphor-coated paper

The Stamp

The 29¢ Flower stamp in coil format, which was officially issued August 16 after a lengthy delay and not a little confusion, turned out to be unique in two ways.

It had what USPS called "slit perforations" and what collectors call rouletting. Straight-line cuts were made between stamps to allow them to be separated, and no paper was removed in the process. Although some revenue stamps in the past had been rouletted, the principal use of the method with U.S. postage stamps in the past had been to facilitate separation of the backing paper on the experimental pressure-sensitive 10¢ Christmas stamp of 1974 (Scott 1552).

Also, the coil rolls were distributed to post offices for dispensing to the public in a new format that stacked 10 connected coils into what USPS called "stamp sticks." In these sticks, each containing 1,000 stamps, the individual coil rolls remained attached to one another, but with another form of roulette separation USPS referred to as "scoring," which was devised to allow a coil to be readily separated from an adjacent coil. The translucent outer wrapper of the sticks was also rouletted to allow postal clerks or customers to break off one coil at a time.

USPS said the new format would save space and would also eliminate the cut fingers that some postal clerks and customers had experienced with the transparent plastic "egg cartons" in which individual coil rolls were normally packaged and sold. The stamp stick concept also reduced the amount of plastic packaging needed, USPS pointed out. The outer wrapping, it said, was biodegradable, and the shipping container, which held 10 stamp sticks, was made of recyclable cardboard.

What the introduction of the stick meant for collectors was that, for the first time, coil stamps could be obtained in blocks of four — or, for that matter, blocks of any size up to and including a theoretical 1,000. Donald M. McDowell, director of the USPS Office of Stamp and Philatelic Marketing, told *Linn's Stamp News* that the scoring of the attached coils in a stick was designed to allow them to be broken readily. But he

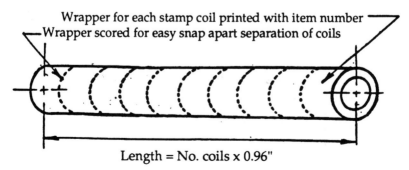

Wrapper for each stamp coil printed with item number
Wrapper scored for easy snap apart separation of coils

Length = No. coils x 0.96"

This USPS sketch depicts a 10-coil stick of stamps. The outer dimension of the 100-stamp coil is approximately 1 3/16 inches. The length of any stick equals the number of coils times 0.96 inches.

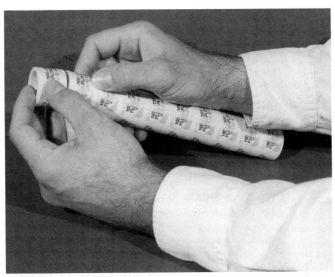

A principal benefit of stamp sticks, according to USPS, is that they can be separated easily into individual coils.

acknowledged that a stick could be unrolled as one unit. "You'd have to do it gingerly, but it could be done," he said.

The scoring between the coil rolls consisted of alternating long slits and very short "teeth," the parts of the paper that connected the coils together. Measured in inches, the slit was about 3¼ inches long, while the tooth was less than one-sixteenth of an inch. The teeth occurred about every fourth stamp, and their position between the coils was staggered.

Vertical pairs, although fragile, could be saved. Vertical strips could not be saved, because of the staggering of the position of the connecting teeth. As McDowell indicated, collectors who attempted to save pairs or blocks of the coils found that they had to handle the stamps with great care to avoid breaking the teeth that held the coils together. Blocks of 10 stamps, five wide by two deep, appeared to be more practical to collect, because they could be connected by two teeth.

Post offices also sold individual coils of 100 packaged in the conventional egg cartons. These were manufactured in stick format and broken off the sticks for packaging. The stamps were made in rows 13 deep, so three coils of 100 had to be trimmed off before the remaining 10 coils were packaged into stamp sticks.

Plate numbers occurred on every 33rd stamp. But because of the staggering of the teeth, the plate numbers didn't always fall between two teeth in such a way as to allow collectors to extract a block of 10 with the plate numbers centered.

The stick format was one that had previously been used by Canada Post, although Canada Post used conventional round-hole perforations between individual stamps on a roll.

USPS described both the use of rouletting for separating stamps and

209

the distribution of rolls in sticks as experimental. Its press release said the "national new-product test" of the rouletted stamps was "in response to years of requests from the mailing public for coil stamps that tear off the rolls easier than current round-hole perforated stamps."

Perhaps more to the point was USPS' acknowledgment that "the slit perforation process also is more economical than traditional round-hole perforation." USPS told *Linn's Stamp News* that the rouletting equipment used on the Flower coil cost an estimated one-fourth as much as conventional coil perforating equipment. The contractor for the stamp was Stamp Venturers, none of whose component companies had ever produced a coil stamp before.

USPS said it would "evaluate the public reaction to slit perforations before deciding whether to use them on future 100-stamp coils."

The rouletted stamps were issued only in 100-stamp coils for a practical reason. These small rolls are most often purchased for household use. Coils containing 500, 3,000 and 10,000 stamps typically are used by businesses with machinery that dispenses and applies the stamps directly onto cards and envelopes. These machines use the round-hole perforations to advance the coil through the mechanism.

Late in 1991, however, it was disclosed that Stamp Venturers had printed 150 million of the 29¢ Flower coil stamps with conventional round-hole perforations that were compatible with stamp-affixing machines. The perforated stamps, in rolls of 3,000, would be distributed as soon as USPS gave the word, Stamp Venturers managing director Richard Sennett told *Linn's Stamp News*.

Plans to issue a 29¢ Flower coil were first made public in the March-April 1991 issue of the Philatelic Sales Division's *Philatelic Catalog*, which gave order numbers for denominated Flower sheet, coil and booklet stamps and said they would be "available mid-April." However, the April 1 news release by USPS announcing the April 5 issuance of the sheet and booklet versions made no mention of the coil. (Ironically,

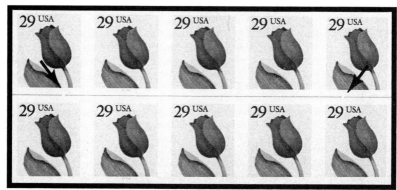

This block of 10 coil stamps is from the stamp stick. Although the stamp stick is fragile when unrolled, it can be collected in multiples. This piece is connected by the stamps at both ends, as indicated by the arrows.

however, the Flower stamp illustration that accompanied the April 1 news release showed a coil version — conventionally perforated!)

Ultimately, on August 2, USPS announced that the coil version would be released August 16. Long before that date, however, copies of the stamp had begun turning up in the mails. For instance, stamp dealer Henry Karen of North Woodmere, New York, showed *Linn's* a letter he had received from Marina Del Rey, California, postmarked July 29 and bearing a rouletted Flower coil stamp. The correspondent also included an unused copy of the stamp on an addressed reply envelope.

First-Day Facts

There was no first-day ceremony for the stamp, but a first-day cancellation was made available in Rochester, New York. Rochester also had been the first-day sale site for the 29¢ Flower sheet and booklet stamps April 5.

23¢ LUNCH WAGON (COIL)
TRANSPORTATION SERIES

Date of Issue: April 12, 1991

Catalog Number: Scott 2464

Color: blue (PMS 295U)

First-Day Cancel: Columbus, Ohio

FDCs Canceled: 115,830

Format: Coils of 100, 500 and 3,000. Printing sleeve of 864 subjects (18 across, 48 around).

Perf: 10.2 (Goebel stroke perforator)

Designer: Robert Brangwynne of Boston, Massachusetts

Art Director and Typographer: Richard Sheaff (CSAC)

Project Manager: Jack Williams (USPS)

Engravers: Gary Chaconas (BEP, vignette); Gary Slaght (BEP, lettering)

Printing: printed by BEP on 3-color intaglio C press (901)

Quantity Ordered: 441,000,000 (167,000,000 in coils of 100; 149,000,000 in coils of 500; 125,000,000 in coils of 3,000)

Quantity Distributed: 595,092,000 (356,480,000 in coils of 100; 121,300,000 in coils of 500; 117,312,000 in coils of 3,000)

Sleeve Number Detail: one sleeve number every 48th stamp

Tagging: prephosphored paper

The Stamp

On April 12, USPS issued its second Transportation series coil stamp of 1991. The stamp's 23¢ denomination covered the new first-class rate for each additional ounce after the first ounce.

Its subject was a lunch wagon of the 1890s, a forerunner of the fixed-location diners of the 20th century. The stamp was the ninth in the Transportation series to depict a type of "wagon," which has become the most common generic term in the series. It was preceded by a Mail Wagon (1981), an Oil Wagon (1985), a Bread Wagon (1986), a Milk Wagon (1987), a Conestoga Wagon (1988), a Patrol Wagon (1988), a Popcorn Wagon (1988) and a Circus Wagon (1990).

The Lunch Wagon stamp was the first Transportation coil to be issued on phosphor-coated paper. Unlike previous phosphor-coated stamps, it had dull gum. And, according to Stephen G. Esrati, writing in *Stamp Collector*, it was the first coil stamp on a new paper type, dubbed Type IV paper by Richard J. Nazar, principal investigator of paper types for the Plate Number Coil Study Group.

Nazar said the new paper, made to meet new USPS specifications for LP-713 paper, was made by Glatfelter Company of Spring Grove, Pennsylvania, which also made Type III paper, according to Esrati. The Glatfelter paper was finished by Ivex Corporation, formerly L&CP Corporation, which then supplied the paper to BEP.

This duplicated the chain of suppliers that had been used for Type III paper, Esrati wrote. However, Ivex Corporation lost its two-year contract to supply paper to BEP in 1990, and new paper was to come from Paper Corporation of the United States.

The characteristics of Type IV paper noted by Nazar were a thicker feel than previous coil papers and an extremely smooth gum. But the easiest way to tell it from earlier papers was that it was phosphor-coated, with no vertical tagging breaks visible on a roll when examined under shortwave ultraviolet light.

The idea for the stamp subject originated with Richard Sheaff, a design coordinator for the Citizens' Stamp Advisory Committee. Sheaff came across an illustrated description of vintage lunch wagons "at a time," he

This was Richard Sheaff's rough sketch made for the guidance of the designer, Robert Brangwynne. Note that the decade designation was originally 1900 rather than 1890s.

213

said, "when we were all scratching our heads about what else to put in the Transportation series." He hired Robert Brangwynne, an artist with whom he had worked on the 1990 Rhode Island Bicentennial stamp, to execute a design based on the reference material he had found. When Sheaff presented the idea to the committee, the members approved the subject for the series.

In its news release, USPS described the vehicle on the stamp as "a composite of the 18th and 19th century wagons that were used to deliver meals to the public in various American cities." USPS doubtless intended to say "19th and 20th century wagons," inasmuch as it had identified the subject vehicle as one dating from the 1890s. Moreover, the wagon shown wasn't really a composite, but a fairly close rendering of "The Owl," a night lunch wagon manufactured by Charles H. Palmer of Worcester, Massachusetts.

Charles Palmer had entered the lunch wagon business in 1889 by buying out one Sam Jones and his fleet of wagons. On September 1, 1891, Palmer received the first patent given for a lunch wagon design. According to Richard J.S. Gutman, a historian of the American diner, Palmer's patent described what was to become the standard configuration for nearly 20 years. His wagon had an enclosed body with the forward portion extending over a set of small front wheels and the rear made

Robert Brangwynne based his ink drawing of the lunch wagon on the lower engraving in this period advertisement.

narrower to stand between the tops of the high back wheels.

The rear of the wagon was the "kitchen-apartment," with a counter separating it from the "dining-room space," where customers could sit on stools to eat. Over one of the high rear wheels was a window for passing out food to those customers standing on the curb. The other side had a carriage window where a patron could drive up to place an order.

Palmer manufactured and sold two models. One was "The Star," a "fancy night cafe" with an elegant ornamental paint job and ringed with stained glass windows etched with stars. His other model, the one shown on the stamp, was "The Owl." It was described as a "night lunch wagon" and was much simpler in appearance, with fewer windows, and those etched with unpretentious designs. Evidently these enclosed carts were popular on cold and stormy nights, Gutman wrote, but during the summer the crowds preferred to stand out in the open air.

The Design

Robert Brangwynne based his pen-and-ink drawing of "The Owl" night lunch wagon on an engraving from a contemporary advertisement for Palmer's vehicles that Richard Sheaff had found illustrating a book titled *American Diner*, with text by Richard Gutman (Harper & Row, 1979). Brangwynne also referred to an illustration of a 1977 watercolor painting that was based on the same ad. The painting was reproduced in a book titled *Diners* by John Baeder (Harry N. Abrams).

Brangwynne's first drawing for the stamp closely followed the image in the advertisement and the painting, showing the wagon facing to the right, with a horse hitched to the shafts, and C.H. Palmer's name painted on the side of the vehicle. At the committee's request, he made some modifications. He flopped the wagon so it was facing left, removed the horse, removed Palmer's name to give the wagon a more generic character, and altered the shading and shadows.

Richard Sheaff said he was pleased with BEP's translation of Brangwynne's artwork into a finished stamp. "In order to do one of those Transportation series stamps successfully, you need a certain amount of detail for the engraving to show its stuff," Sheaff said. "If the artwork, or

Brangwynne's first version of the design, mocked up with dummy typography provided by Richard Sheaff, showed the wagon facing to the right, complete with horse.

the subject, is such that it's essentially an outline, then it isn't very interesting. It's just a white stamp with a white object that has a little outline about it. It has no presence.

"But on one where you can really get into it, and do some engraving, and have some detail, and have a nice solid 'something' — blue, in this case — on the stamp, that works much better. It's what people who LIKE engraving like ABOUT engraving. I've liked this one for that reason."

Varieties

Soon after the stamp was issued, an imperforate roll of 100 was purchased at a post office in Phoenix, Arizona. Jon Denney of M & M Southwest in Phoenix acquired the roll, and it was later sold to Dana Okey, a San Diego dealer specializing in errors. In June, Okey advertised pairs for sale at $895 apiece. According to Okey, the roll was mutilated in places. It contained 35 good pairs, one good strip with plate number 2,

A pair of Lunch Wagon stamps, imperforate between.

and two faulty strips of three with pieces missing. The whole roll was centered to the bottom, Okey said.

First-Day Facts

The Lunch Wagon stamp was issued at the Colopex stamp show in Columbus, Ohio, along with two other new varieties: the Wood Duck booklet printed by the Bureau of Engraving and Printing and the same booklet printed by KCS Industries. No formal first-day ceremony was held for the three stamps. USPS distributed generic blue folders in lieu of first-day ceremony programs.

On first-day covers serviced by USPS, the Postal Service affixed two 3¢ Conestoga Wagon coil stamps along with a Lunch Wagon stamp to equal the first-class rate of 29¢.

$5.80 WOOD DUCK BOOKLET (BEP)

Date of Issue: April 12, 1991

Catalog Number: Scott 2493 (single stamp); 2493a (booklet pane of 10)

Colors: magenta, cyan, yellow, black

First-Day Cancel: Columbus, Ohio

FDCs Canceled: 205,305 (includes BEP and KCS versions)

Format: 2 panes of 10 horizontal stamps, arranged horizontally, 5 across by 2 down. Gravure printing cylinders of 480 subjects (20 across, 24 around).

Perf: 10.2 (Goebel booklet machine stroke perforator)

Selvage Markings: cylinder numbers printed on each pane binding stub

Cover Markings: "© United States Postal Service 1991" and mailing information on inside of front cover. Universal Product Code (UPC) and promotion for USPS Souvenir Pages on outside of back cover. Coupon for Souvenir Pages on inside of back cover. Stamp picture on front cover is in black and white.

Designer: Robert Giusti of New Milford, Connecticut

Art Director: Derry Noyes (CSAC)

Project Manager: Joe Brockert (USPS)

Typographer: Bradbury Thompson (CSAC)

Printing: Stamps printed by BEP on 7-color Andreotti gravure press (601). Covers printed and booklets formed on Goebel booklet machine.

Quantity Ordered: 2,900,000,000 (144,700,000 booklets; 600,000 unfolded panes)

Quantity Distributed: 3,681,888,000 (183,774,900 booklets; 639,000 unfolded panes)

Cylinder Number Detail: 1 group of 4 cylinder numbers on each pane binding stub

Tagging: overall

The Stamp

A wood duck's head in profile was featured on 29¢ booklet stamps that were placed on sale April 12 at the Colopex 91 stamp show in Columbus, Ohio. These booklets followed by one week the denominated 29¢ Flower sheet and booklet stamps that were issued at another stamp show in Rochester, New York.

Each of the Wood Duck booklets contained 20 stamps in two panes of 10, but the booklets were provided by two different contractors: the Bureau of Engraving and Printing and KCS Industries of Milwaukee, Wisconsin. Although USPS had previously assigned Christmas and Love stamp issues to dual contractors — one for sheets and one for booklets — this was the first time it had employed two printers for a stamp that was issued in only one format.

"We knew going in that neither printer would be able to supply the full quantity that we required," explained Joe Brockert, USPS project manager for the stamps. BEP, in fact, had reduced its booklet-making capability in the preceding year by disassembling an off-line booklet-making section to make room for its new F press. The section had been installed in 1987 in response to a heavy demand for booklets.

The gravure-printed BEP version of the Wood Duck stamp displayed the "29 USA" inscription and the words "Wood Duck" in black. The KCS version, also printed in gravure, had the typography in red. The two booklet covers also were different: BEP's cover displayed an enlarged illustration of the stamp in black and white, and the KCS cover showed it in full color.

The printers made the stamps and booklets different on USPS' instructions, according to Brockert. "We wanted to build in a distinguishable difference, because we weren't sure there would be any other way to tell them apart once they had become individual stamps, or even panes separated from the covers," he said. "We saw no disadvantage to doing it, and we saw nothing but advantages, because the stamps are identifiable at all points along the chain, whether it's internally within the Postal Service or in the aftermarket with collectors.

"We knew that collectors were going to treat these as two different

218

varieties anyhow, because with two different printers there were bound to be at least subtle differences, so that making them visually different wasn't going to be viewed as intentionally creating a second variety to separate the collector from his or her money."

There turned out to be still another difference in the two varieties — an unwelcome one. As first reported in *Linn's Stamp News* for May 20, 1991, the ink on BEP-produced Wood Duck stamps was subject to flaking off when the stamps were soaked in water. The same phenomenon was also reported with the BEP-printed 19¢ Fawn stamp that had been issued March 11. Soaking, of course, is the standard method collectors use to remove used stamps from envelopes.

The flaking didn't occur spontaneously in every instance of soaking. However, any rubbing of the wet surface quickly destroyed the printed image. Cancellations also could be rubbed off easily — a fact that was obviously of great concern to the Postal Service.

Ira Polikoff, director of BEP's public affairs office, told *Linn's* that the unstable-ink problem was the result of a new paper contract with the IVEX Corporation of Troy, Ohio, which supplied coated gravure paper to the Bureau for use on its Andreotti press.

BEP is required by the U.S. Occupational Safety and Health Administration (OSHA) to use only water-based inks for employee health reasons, Polikoff said, and finding a suitable paper can be difficult. Previous gravure papers used with water-based inks by the Bureau often left "snowflaking" in the design, making the stamps look blotchy, he said. The new phosphor-coated paper developed by IVEX was more receptive to ink absorption, allowing a much clearer printed image.

But Polikoff said USPS didn't tell BEP that the new paper had to pass a soak test, so that issue wasn't addressed in the specifications. As a

These badly flaked specimens of the BEP Wood Duck stamp had been soaked in warm water (stamps at far left) and cold water. Bottom far left, an unsoaked BEP stamp; bottom left, a KCS booklet single that was unaffected by soaking.

result, Polikoff told *Linn's*, "the new paper is not only receptive to ink, but water as well."

The BEP spokesman said USPS had subsequently advised the Bureau that future gravure paper contracts would contain a soak-test specification. In the meantime, though, he said, BEP would have to use up its stock of gravure paper on hand, a process that could take several months.

USPS had a different view of the matter. Assistant Postmaster General Gordon C. Morison, in a letter to the chairman of the House Subcommittee on Postal Operations and Services replying to questions posed at the subcommittee's June 5 hearing on stamp production and procurement, noted that USPS was precluded from withholding payments from BEP for failure to meet required quality standards. "Had the Bureau manufactured its version of the Wood Duck booklet under the same contract that applied to the private-sector version, we would have been able to reduce our payment to the Bureau according to how many stamps we determined to have failed our 'soak test,'" Morison wrote. "If we had determined that just 10 percent of them were defective, we would have been able to reduce our payment by $793,000 . . . Such penalty clauses are not acceptable to the Bureau."

The Wood Duck booklet was the third U.S. definitive-stamp booklet with an ornithological subject. In 1988, after the first-class rate was increased to 25¢, USPS issued a booklet of stamps featuring the ring-necked pheasant, and followed it up a month later with a booklet containing two se-tenant varieties, showing the saw-whet owl and the rose-breasted grosbeak.

The wood duck, so named because it nests in natural tree cavities, is a common waterfowl of open woodland around lakes and along streams. Its range is the entire eastern United States and Canada, and the U.S. Pacific Northwest. The male is gaudily colored, with iridescent greens and purples along with spots, streaks and slashes of white. The dull-colored female has a white eye ring. Wood ducks fly swiftly, dodging with agility among the trees. They feed on plants and insects.

A pair of wood ducks in flight, painted by Stanley Galli, appeared on a 6¢ stamp of 1968 (Scott 1362) issued to publicize waterfowl conservation. Pairs of flying wood ducks were also depicted on the 1943-44 and 1974-75 Migratory Bird Hunting stamps (Scott RW10 and RW41).

The Design

Robert Giusti of New Milford, Connecticut, created the acrylic-on-

A pair of wood ducks was shown on this 1968 stamp (Scott 1362), designed by Stanley W. Galli, issued to publicize waterfowl conservation.

These pictures of the wood duck are Robert Giusti's preliminary sketch (left) and his pencil tracing over which he made his finished painting.

canvas painting used on the stamp. Giusti had completed an earlier design job for USPS that was scheduled to be released in 1992. Derry Noyes, the CSAC design coordinator who had given him the earlier assignment, asked him to prepare some illustrations of American wildlife for use on individual definitive stamps as they became necessary.

"I lean toward birds," Giusti said. "And for stamp purposes you want to keep the images as colorful as possible, so I thought, what could be more colorful than a wood duck's head? It's such a recognizable bird, and it seemed a natural choice."

Showing the head rather than the whole bird "was strictly a graphic preference on my part," Giusti said. "The head is really a beautiful part of the wood duck. A turkey, on the other hand, has a not very attractive face but a beautiful body. I decided to choose animals that I could really focus in on, zoom in on, and still keep the stamps colorful and pretty and fill the space. It also gave me room to show facial detail."

Giusti calls his approach to painting "a kind of stylized realism." "I try to keep these (stamp paintings) fairly realistic, but there is a tendency in all my work to be somewhat graphic-looking," he said. His commercial clients choose him, he added, because he gives them "a real crisp image that they feel is almost photographic and yet has the added quality of a sort of stylization, a simplification; a kind of graphic imagery."

Giusti's wood duck profile was a nicely composed piece of artwork. The crest at the back of the bird's head, with its upturned feathers at the tip, almost perfectly balanced the beak, while the arc of white at the throat provided a visual fulcrum.

"That was intentional," Giusti said. "I started out in this business as a graphic designer, so that basically this tendency to 'design' my images is ingrained in me. With the wood duck, since it was a profile against a white background, I wanted to use that white space nicely. I wanted to fill it attractively. To get a comfortable balance, sometimes I'll do a trick like 'whip up' the little hood on the wood duck in order to fill the image area."

For source material, Giusti referred to photographs of wood ducks, and also to the real thing — a group of the birds that visit a pond on his property in New Milford each spring and fall.

"You learn a lot from the attitude of the duck," he said. "Ducks have personalities, and each kind is a little different. Mallards act different from wood ducks. A wood duck is very shy, and very alert. It perks its head up a lot. It's very skittish, and it moves skittishly. Whereas a mallard sails along more, a wood duck darts along. So it helps to be able to observe them, and I do think I take from nature.

"It's easier when you do the whole bird, because then you can bring out the attitude more than you can with just a head. But even with that, they have that way of displaying that hood when they are alerted, or when they are preening, they whip the head around, and the feathers of the hood will curl up. You take what you can out of real life."

Giusti is a member of a highly exclusive club — father-and-son stamp design teams. His father, George Giusti, designed the 3¢ Atlantic Cable Centenary stamp of 1958 (Scott 1112) and the 8¢ Bowling stamped envelope of 1971 (Scott U563).

First-Day Facts

The two Wood Duck booklet varieties shared first-day honors at Colopex April 12 with the 23¢ Lunch Wagon coil stamp. Although USPS held no formal ceremony, the sponsoring Columbus Philatelic Club staged a brief ceremony. Among the speakers was Ken Crawford, Ohio's oldest active member of the conservation group Ducks Unlimited and a stamp collector. The club also produced its own program. USPS distributed its generic souvenir folder containing a booklet pane of 10 Wood Duck stamps and a Lunch Wagon coil pair with first-day cancellations.

Collectors had 60 days to obtain a first-day postmark by mail. For covers serviced by USPS, only full panes of 10 stamps at $2.90 each were affixed, and customers were required to send their orders to one of two addresses depending on whether BEP or KCS panes were wanted.

$5.80 WOOD DUCK BOOKLET (KCS)

Date of Issue: April 12, 1991

Catalog Number: Scott 2494 (single stamp); 2494a (booklet pane of 10)

Colors: magenta, yellow, cyan, black, line red

First-Day Cancel: Columbus, Ohio

FDCs Canceled: 205,305 (includes BEP and KCS versions)

Format: 2 panes of 10 horizontal stamps, arranged horizontally, 5 across by 2 down. Gravure printing cylinders of 400 subjects (20 across, 20 around) manufactured by Armotek Industries Inc., Palmyra, New Jersey.

Perf: 10.9 (L perforator)

Selvage and Other Markings: Cylinder numbers printed on each pane binding stub. Also, 20 percent of all panes show magenta cut mark at top or bottom edge of third stamp over (10 percent on upper stamp, 10 percent on lower stamp).

Cover Markings: "© United States Postal Service 1991 K" and mailing information on inside of front cover. Universal Product Code (UPC) and promotion for USPS commemorative panels on outside of back cover. Coupon for panels on inside of back cover. Stamp picture on front cover is in color.

Designer: Robert Giusti of New Milford, Connecticut

Art Director: Derry Noyes (CSAC)

Project Manager: Joe Brockert (USPS)

Typographer: Bradbury Thompson (CSAC)

Modeler: Richard Sennett, Sennett Enterprises

Printing: by Sennett Enterprises on Champlain gravure press at J.W. Fergusson and Sons, Richmond, Virginia, for KCS Industries Inc.

Quantity Ordered: 800,000,000 (40,000,000 booklets)

Quantity Distributed: 792,620,000 (39,631,000 booklets)

Sleeve Number Details: 1 group of 5 cylinder numbers preceded by the letter K on each pane binding stub

Tagging: phosphor-coated paper

The Stamp

Like the Bureau of Engraving and Printing version of the Wood Duck booklet, the KCS version was first placed on sale April 12 at the Colopex stamp show in Columbus, Ohio.

The KCS version was printed by Sennett Enterprises on the gravure press of J.W. Fergusson and Sons in Richmond, Virginia. In addition to the four standard process colors that BEP had used in printing its Wood Duck stamps, KCS used a line red for the ''29 USA'' logo.

With the KCS stamp, there were no reports of the kind of ink-flaking problem that plagued BEP's version of the Wood Duck stamp when it was soaked from an envelope.

Further details on the booklets, stamp design and first-day information can be found in the preceding chapter.

$2.90 FLAG WITH OLYMPIC RINGS BOOKLET

Date of Issue: April 21, 1991

Catalog Number: Scott 2528 (single stamp); 2528a (pane of 10)

Colors: red, blue, black, yellow, green

First-Day Cancel: Atlanta, Georgia

FDCs Canceled: 319,488

Format: 1 pane of 10 horizontal stamps arranged horizontally 5 across by 2 down. Gravure printing cylinders of 400 subjects (20 across, 20 around) manufactured by Armotek Industries Inc., Palmyra, New Jersey.

Perf: 10.9 (L perforator)

Selvage and Other Markings: Cylinder numbers printed on each pane binding stub. Also, 20 percent of all panes show blue cut marks at top or bottom edge of third stamp over (10 percent on upper stamp, 10 percent on lower stamp).

Cover Markings: "© United States Postal Service 1991 K" on inside of front cover. Universal Product Code (UPC) on outside of back cover. Domestic U.S. postage rates and other mailing information on inside of front cover and both sides of back cover.

Designer and Typographer: John Boyd of Anagraphics Inc., New York City

Art Director and Project Manager: Joe Brockert (USPS)

Modeler: Richard Sennett of Sennett Enterprises

Printing: By Sennett Enterprises on Champlain gravure press at J.W. Fergusson and Sons, Richmond, Virginia, for KCS Industries Inc., Milwaukee, Wisconsin. Formed into booklets at KCS.

Quantity Ordered: 600,000,000 (60,000,000 booklets)

Quantity Distributed: 592,080,000 (59,208,000 booklets)

Cylinder Number Detail: 1 group of 5 cylinder numbers preceded by the letter K on each pane binding stub

Tagging: phosphor-coated paper

The Stamp

Since 1957, when the first-class rate was 4¢, users of the U.S. mails have always had available for first-class letters a stamp showing the American flag in full color. Shortly after the 29¢ rate took effect February 3, 1991, USPS issued a coil stamp showing the flag over Mount Rushmore. On April 21, it followed with a booklet stamp featuring the flag and the five linked Olympic Games rings.

The stamp was the first definitive to bear the Olympic logo since USPS became an official worldwide sponsor of the 1992 Winter and Summer Games. It was issued in booklets containing one pane of 10 stamps and was produced by the gravure process by KCS Industries. This was the third KCS-made booklet, and the second within nine days. On April 12, USPS had issued two versions of its Wood Duck booklet, one of which was made by the Wisconsin company. KCS had also provided one version of the non-denominated F stamp booklet.

The first-day city for the Flag with Olympic Rings booklet was

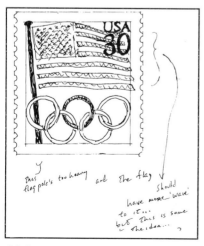

John Boyd's original sketch, along with his note to Joe Brockert: "This flagpole's too heavy and the flag should have more 'wave' to it . . . but this is somewhat the idea . . . what say?"

226

Atlanta, host city for the 1996 Summer Olympic Games.

"As part of the overall plan for the Olympic sponsorship, the Postal Service's Olympic Marketing Committee asked that one of our stamps show a flag accompanied by the Olympic rings," said Joe Brockert of USPS, project manager for the stamp. "We provided it."

The request was made in mid-1990, and the design process was worked out during the second half of the year. The typography couldn't be completed, however, until January 1991, when it was known that the new first-class rate would be 29¢.

Among a large quantity of Olympics-related commercial products that were marketed by USPS in 1991 were T-shirts and a sweatshirt bearing enlarged replicas of the Flag with Olympic Rings stamp. "No one should be without these basics . . . especially when it shows your support for our 1992 U.S. Olympic Team," the advertising flyer proclaimed. The stamp that was depicted on the shirts was perforated on all four sides, even though the actual stamps, being available only in booklets, each had at least one straight edge.

The Design

John Boyd of Anagraphics Inc. in New York City worked with Joe Brockert in developing the stamp's design. Boyd originally prepared a vertical sketch, but this format required a crowding together of the elements; the flagpole encroached on the Olympic rings, and the denomination encroached on the flag.

"John thought about it, and he said, 'I'm going to turn the thing sideways,' " Brockert recalled. "So he sent down another sketch and I said, 'That's better, let's concentrate on this approach.' "

Some Citizens' Stamp Advisory Committee members weren't convinced that the use of the five different colors of the Olympic rings would "hold" on the stamp in the small size, and asked to see how the design would look with rings of a single color. Brockert, using a color photocopier, offered them a version of Boyd's sketch with the rings in blue and the denomination in purple.

"The printers assured us that, yes, they could do it in multicolor, they

Here Boyd has translated his pencil sketch into color art, with the Olympic rings in five colors. But Boyd and Brockert were dissatisfied with the encroachment of the type on the flag and the pole on the rings, so Boyd designed an alternative in a horizontal format, and that became the design that was used.

could print the rings that small. It wouldn't be easy, but they could do it," Brockert said. "And we said, fine. The multicolored rings would be more attractive. And that was the final decision."

The replica of the stamp shown on the booklet cover — unlike the reproductions on the T-shirts and sweatshirts — accurately depicted it with one straight edge.

First-Day Facts

Assistant Postmaster General Deborah K. Bowker dedicated the stamp April 21 as part of the Atlanta Dogwood Festival celebration at 15th and Peachtree streets.

For covers completely serviced by USPS, only full panes of 10 stamps were affixed at a cost to the customer of $2.90. The original deadline for requesting first-day cancellations by mail was May 21, but later USPS extended the deadline to July 20.

$3.80 HOT-AIR BALLOON BOOKLET

Date of Issue: May 17, 1991

Catalog Numbers: Scott 2530 (single stamp); Scott 2530a (booklet pane of 10)

Colors: process magenta, process yellow, blue (PMS 285C), green (PMS 342C)

First-Day Cancel: Denver, Colorado

FDCs Canceled: 96,351. Combination Balloon-Piper FDCs, 167

Format: 2 panes of 10 vertical stamps arranged vertically, 2 across by 5 down. Gravure printing cylinders of 480 subjects (20 across, 24 around).

Perf: 10 by 10.2 (Goebel booklet machine stroke perforator)

Selvage Markings: cylinder numbers printed on each pane binding stub

Cover Markings: "© United States Postal Service 1991" and mailing information on inside of front cover. Universal Product Code (UPC) and promotion for USPS Souvenir Pages on outside of back cover. Coupon for Souvenir Pages on inside of back cover.

Designer: Pierre Mion of Lovettsville, Virginia

Art Director: Howard Paine (CSAC)

Project Manager: Jack Williams (USPS)

Typographer: Bradbury Thompson (CSAC)

Modeler: Clarence Holbert (BEP)

Printing: Stamps printed by BEP on 7-color Andreotti gravure press (601). Booklet covers printed and booklets formed on Goebel booklet forming machine.

Quantity Ordered: 610,000,000 (30,200,000 booklets; 600,000 unfolded panes)

Quantity Distributed: 375,138,000 (18,392,400 booklets; 792,000 unfolded panes)

Cylinder Number Detail: 1 group of 4 gravure cylinder numbers on each pane binding stub

Tagging: overall

The Stamp

On May 17, USPS issued a postcard-rate stamp in booklet form only, for use by tourists and vacationers. The 19¢ stamp depicted a colorful hot-air balloon. It was one of three face-different items making their debut at the Rompex 91 stamp show in Denver, Colorado.

The Balloon stamp was the second in a series of small, colorful definitives called "mini-scapes," which USPS planned to issue as the need and opportunity arose. The idea, in the words of Howard Paine, the Citizens' Stamp Advisory Committee design coordinator who helped implement the plan, was to show "generic landscapes" common to many sections of the country, or "tight little vignettes" of familiar objects and scenes. These would provide stamp users with cheerful, friendly alternatives to Great American and Flag definitives.

Paine commissioned three artists to prepare concept sketches. To one artist, Pierre Mion of Lovettsville, Virginia, Paine's list of suggestions included a hot-air balloon in flight, a child with an umbrella in the rain, and a piggy bank. Mion submitted colored-pencil sketches in double stamp size of these subjects, and added some sketches based on ideas of his own: a beach umbrella; the prow of a small boat of the kind used on the East Coast for oystering and crabbing; the end of a pier, and a boy on a carousel. At Paine's request, Mion then translated some of these sketches into finished art.

230

The first of the mini-scapes to be issued was a 15¢ postcard-rate stamp, produced solely in booklet form, bearing Mion's beach umbrella design. It became obsolete when the postcard rate increased to 19¢ February 3, 1991, and the Hot-Air Balloon booklet stamp became its replacement.

Balloons have been the subject of U.S. stamps in the past. In 1959 a 7¢ airmail stamp (Scott C54) commemorated the 100th anniversary of the carrying of mail by the balloon *Jupiter* from Lafayette to Crawfordsville, Indiana. It bore a posterlike picture of the *Jupiter* in flight over a cheering crowd. And in 1983 USPS issued a se-tenant block of four in connection with the 200th anniversary of the first manned balloon flight, made in France in 1783. The block honored two historic American balloons, the Union Army's hydrogen-filled *Intrepid* of 1861 and the National Geographic Society's helium-lifted *Explorer* II of 1935, and also celebrated the contemporary sport of hot-air ballooning.

The Design

Pierre Mion's gouache painting showed a bright yellow balloon, decorated with zig-zag stripes of red, white and blue and a red pinwheel design at the top, as seen from above, against a green backdrop of cultivated fields.

The source for the design, Mion said, was "photos in my own 'morgue,' and in my head." The pattern on the balloon was based on one of his photographs, he said, but he altered it to suit his own tastes. With

In these preliminary pencil sketches, Pierre Mion experimented with various viewing angles and patterns for the hot-air bag.

the mini-scape paintings, Mion added, an artist has considerable latitude: "They are fun to do."

In printing the stamps by gravure, the Bureau of Engraving and Printing used a green self-color for the fields, rather than mixing cyan and yellow process colors, which is the customary method of creating green in gravure or offset printing.

The booklet cover carried an enlarged reproduction of a stamp from inside the booklet, but the reproduction was in black and white, rather than in the bright original colors of the stamp itself.

First-Day Facts

USPS held no official first-day ceremony for the Hot-Air Balloon stamp and the other items that made their debut May 17 at Rompex: the 40¢ William Piper airmail stamp and the 45¢ Eagle aerogram, which was printed on two different colors of paper.

However, Rompex organizers staged a ceremony of their own at the show site in Denver. Among other things, they held an actual hot-air balloon flight at the show to salute the Balloon stamp, and featured a live golden eagle to help inaugurate the aerograms.

Rompex also furnished a program that contained single Balloon and Piper stamps, tied to the inside of the folder by a single strike of the first-day cancellation, as well as both versions of the aerogram with first-day cancels. Die-cut slots in the folder allowed for insertion of the aerograms. These were given free at the ceremony, and there were copies available afterward for sale at $5 apiece.

USPS provided 400 of the generic blue-and-gold first-day ceremony folders it had introduced earlier in the year. Each contained a full pane of the Balloon stamp and a single Piper stamp, both tied by a May 17 Denver cancel. In a pocket, the USPS folder had a first-day-canceled aerogram, but only the blue-paper version. These folders were distributed to showgoers on the second day of the show and were also mailed to program subscribers.

Collectors submitting covers bearing single copies of the Balloon stamp for first-day cancellation were reminded to add at least 10¢ additional postage to reach the first-class rate. For USPS-affixed stamps, only full booklet panes were provided, at $2.90 per cover.

5¢ CANOE COIL, BEP TRANSPORTATION SERIES

Date of Issue: May 25, 1991

Catalog Number: Scott 2453

Colors: brown, gray

First-Day Cancel: Secaucus, New Jersey

FDCs Canceled: 108,634. Canoe and Tractor-Trailer combination FDCs, 31,108.

Format: Coils of 500 and 3,000. Printing sleeve of 864 subjects (18 across, 48 around).

Perf: 10.2 (Huck rotary perforator)

Designer: Paul Calle of Stamford, Connecticut

Typographer: Bradbury Thompson (CSAC)

Engravers: vignette, Kenneth Kipperman (BEP); lettering, Gary Slaght (BEP)

Art Director and Project Manager: Jack Williams (USPS)

Modeler: Ronald C. Sharpe (BEP)

Printing: printed by BEP on 3-color intaglio C press (901)

Quantity Ordered: 628,076,000 (113,000,000 in coils of 500; 515,076,000 in coils of 3,000)

Quantity Distributed: 560,982,000 (112,950,000 in coils of 500; 448,032,000 in coils of 3,000)

Sleeve Number Detail: 1 intaglio sleeve number on every 48th stamp

Tagging: untagged

The Stamp

The February 3 rate change created a large number of new fractional rates for various categories of presorted bulk mail. In the past, USPS had attempted to cover many of its presort rates with individual stamps bearing the appropriate denominations. For non-profit mail, this had meant stamps in such denominations as 3¢, 3.1¢, 3.4¢, 3.5¢, 4¢, 4.9¢,

233

5.2¢, 5.3¢, 5.5¢, 5.9¢, 6¢, 7.1¢, 7.6¢, 8.4¢ and 8.5¢.

This time, however, the Postal Service chose to save itself production and inventory problems by issuing only a limited number of varieties, in round-number denominations. For non-profit bulk mailers, a 5¢ stamp was provided. The stamp could be used by all such mailers, regardless of the individual piece rate of their mailings. The difference between the 5¢ face value and the actual postage would be paid at the time the mail entered the mailstream, and this sum would be recorded by a meter strip, affixed to the mailer's post-office form, noting the total additional postage paid for that mailing.

This false franking (a term coined by postal-rate expert Henry W. Beecher) wasn't new. Mailers of presorted mail who wished to use postage stamps rather than printed indicia bearing their permit numbers had been doing it with USPS authorization for years. Sometimes, in fact, the total postage paid was an overpayment and resulted in a refund. In the past, USPS had created other stamps and stationery whose only practical purpose was false franking, e.g., the 3¢ Francis Parkman coil (Scott 1297b) overprinted with plain vertical lines in 1987. Never before, however, had it issued a stamp whose inscription noted that additional postage had been paid.

On May 25, however, two such stamps were issued: the 5¢ stamp for non-profit mail, and a 10¢ stamp for all commercial third-class and first-class presorts. Both were additions to the Transportation series of coil stamps, and both were considered precancels by USPS, with the engraved service inscriptions doubling as the "cancellation."

The new stamps required a change in the postal regulations. Previously, the service inscription on precanceled coil stamps had also stood as the required endorsement for the mail piece. The new service inscriptions, "Additional Nonprofit Postage Paid" and, on the 10¢ stamp,

Frederic Baraga, Michigan, 1835

Previous designs that depicted canoes included Stanley Galli's Father Marquette commemorative stamp of 1968 (Scott 1356), Dennis Luzak's Camp Fire stamp of 1986 (Scott 2163) and David Blossom's Father Baraga postal card of 1984 (Scott UX103).

"Additional Presort Postage Paid," still doubled as precancellations, but not as endorsements. This was a potential problem, mostly with the higher denominated stamp. It was impossible, looking at an envelope franked with a 10¢ stamp, to know whether it was a piece of first-class or third-class mail until an endorsement had been added.

The Postal Bulletin contained this instruction: "Pieces mailed at these rates must bear the appropriate endorsements, printed or rubber-stamped by the mailer above the delivery address and immediately below or to the left of the precanceled stamp." (Regardless of this wording, the mailer wasn't required to endorse a piece of mail in more than one place, according to *Classification Currents Communicator*, a newsletter from the USPS Office of Classification and Rates Administration.)

The 5¢ stamp depicted one of the large, lightweight bark canoes of the kind used by the voyageurs, the French fur traders and guides who roamed the wild "Up Country" of North America from Quebec to the Rocky Mountains in the 18th and 19th centuries. The French learned canoe-building techniques from the original Indian builders, the Algonkin, and later modified the vessels they built to suit their needs.

"Of all birchbark canoe forms, the most famous were the *canots du maitre* (also called north canoes, great canoes, or rebeskas) of the great fur companies of Canada," historians Edwin Tappan Adney and Howard I. Chapelle have written. "These large canoes were developed early . . . and remained a vital part of the fur trade until well toward the very end of the 19th century — 200 years of use and development at the very least . . . The great canoes of the Canadian fur trade must be looked upon as the national watercraft type, historically, of Canada and far more representative of the great years of national expansion than the wagon, truck, locomotive or steamship."

The Design

Paul Calle of Stamford, Connecticut, had never designed a Transportation series stamp before, although he had been responsible for the designs of a score of other U.S. stamps since 1967, and his son Christopher had done the artwork for three of the previous Transportation coils.

However, the senior Calle was very familiar with birchbark canoes of the 18th and 19th centuries, having worked over a 20-year period on a series of paintings of the fur trade from which limited-edition prints were marketed. He and his wife had recently done research on the subject in Canada and in the Grand Portage in Minnesota, a nine-mile land route between Lake Superior and the Pigeon River over which the fur traders and early explorers had carried their cargo, supplies and canoes. Here the Calles had seen reproductions of the original canoes, and Calle had obtained an eight-foot replica for his own collection. This design assignment, therefore, was a natural for him.

The canoe shown on the stamp was a large model, some 30 feet long, and its pointed stem-heads were characteristic of Algonkin Indian design. Calle made sketches of the vessel from various angles, then made a finished drawing of the image chosen by the Citizens' Stamp Advisory Committee. He did the drawing using an HB (medium) pencil on a plate-

This is Paul Calle's pencil sketch from which Bureau engraver Kenneth Kipperman made his intaglio die.

finish, four-ply paper of a kind ordinarily used for pen-and-ink work. His texture of tiny pencil strokes gave engraver Kenneth Kipperman of the Bureau of Engraving and Printing considerable guidance in creating the intaglio impression on a steel die.

The stamp bore the words "Additional Nonprofit Postage Paid" in two lines of small gray type.

First-Day Facts

The Canoe stamp and the 10¢ bulk-rate coil depicting a tractor trailer were placed on sale May 25 at the opening of Nojex 91, a stamp show sponsored by the North Jersey Federated Stamp Clubs at the Meadowlands Hilton Hotel in Secaucus, New Jersey. Nojex, rather than USPS, organized the ceremony and prepared the official first-day program, but Assistant Postmaster General Gordon C. Morison was on hand to dedicate the stamps.

For first-day covers wholly serviced by USPS, two Canoe stamps and one 20¢ Cable Car stamp were affixed, a total of 30¢ in postage.

236

5¢ CANOE COIL, STAMP VENTURERS
TRANSPORTATION SERIES

Date of Issue: October 22, 1991

Catalog Number: Scott 2454

Colors: red, black

First-Day Cancel: Secaucus, New Jersey

FDCs Canceled: 57,581

Format: Coils of 10,000. Gravure printing cylinders of 396 subjects (12 across, 33 around) manufactured by Armotek Industries Inc., Palmyra, New Jersey.

Perf: 10.2

Designer: Paul Calle of Stamford, Connecticut

Typographer: Bradbury Thompson (CSAC) (service inscription by Stamp Venturers)

Art Director and Project Manager: Jack Williams (USPS)

Modeler: Richard Sennett, Sennett Enterprises

Printing: Printed on a Champlain gravure press and perforated by Stamp Venturers at J.W. Fergusson and Sons, Richmond, Virginia. Coiled and finished at KCS Industries Inc., Milwaukee, Wisconsin.

Quantity Ordered: 120,000,000

Quantity Distributed: not available

Plate Number Detail: one pair of gravure cylinder numbers preceded by the letter S on every 33rd stamp

Tagging: overall

The Stamp

On October 22 USPS issued a new version of the 5¢ Canoe coil stamp that had originally appeared May 25. The original Canoe stamp had been printed by intaglio by the Bureau of Engraving and Printing in coils of 500 and 3,000. This one was gravure-printed by J.W. Fergusson & Sons for Stamp Venturers in coils of 10,000.

The canoe design was the second design in 1991 to be used on two different coil stamps produced by different printing processes. The first was the Flag Over Mount Rushmore, which was first featured on a BEP-printed intaglio stamp and later on a gravure version made by Guilford Gravure for the American Bank Note Company.

The gravure Canoe stamp had a somewhat different appearance from the intaglio version (see below). As such, it was the fifth face-different stamp in the Transportation coil series to bear the 5¢ denomination. Its predecessors were the 5¢ Motorcycle of 1983 (Scott 1899), the 5¢ Milk Wagon of 1987 (Scott 2253), the 5¢ Circus Wagon of 1990 (Scott 2452) and, of course, the 5¢ intaglio Canoe.

The Design

The new Canoe stamp was the first in the Transportation series produced by a process other than intaglio, and the first to be printed outside BEP. Though it used the same Paul Calle drawing of a birchbark *voyageur* canoe, it differed in appearance from the earlier intaglio stamp in several ways.

The gravure image, made up of minute dots of color, was less clearly defined than the intaglio image, which consisted of engraved lines. The coated gravure paper gave the new stamp a glossy surface. The canoe, lettering and numerals were in red, and the service inscription, "Additional Nonprofit Postage Paid," in black, whereas the prototype was printed in brown and gray.

Finally, the new stamp's service inscription had an altogether different appearance. With the Postal Service's permission, Richard Sennett of Stamp Venturers changed the original condensed typography to a somewhat bolder, more extended typeface. This made the inscription more readable in gravure, which prints a dot pattern that results in letters with edges that look ragged under magnification.

First-Day Facts

There was no first-day ceremony, but USPS offered a first-day postmark in Secaucus, New Jersey, where the original Canoe stamp had made its debut at the Nojex 91 stamp show. USPS also granted a 60-day grace period for mail orders. For covers completely serviced by USPS, two Canoe stamps and one 20¢ Cable Car coil stamp of 1989 were affixed, at a cost to the customer of 30¢.

10¢ TRACTOR TRAILER COIL TRANSPORTATION SERIES

Date of Issue: May 25, 1991

Catalog Number: Scott 2457

Colors: green, gray

First-Day Cancel: Secaucus, New Jersey

FDCs Canceled: 84,717

Format: Coils of 500 and 3,000. Printing sleeve of 864 subjects (18 across, 48 around).

Perf: 10.2 (Huck rotary perforator)

Designer: David K. Stone of Chapel Hill, North Carolina

Typographer: Bradbury Thompson (CSAC)

Engravers: Gary Chaconas, vignette (BEP); Gary Slaght, lettering (BEP)

Art Director and Project Manager: Joe Brockert (USPS)

Modeler: Ronald C. Sharpe (BEP)

Printing: printed by BEP on 3-color intaglio C press (901)

Quantity Ordered: 1,482,000,000 (375,000,000 in coils of 500; 1,107,000,000 in coils of 3,000)

Quantity Distributed: 893,254,000 (233,350,000 in coils of 500; 659,904,000 in coils of 3,000)

Sleeve Number Detail: 1 intaglio sleeve number on every 48th stamp

Tagging: untagged

The Stamp

The companion item to the 5¢ Canoe stamp for non-profit bulk mail was a 10¢ coil created for all third-class and first-class mailers who presorted their mailings. Like the 5¢ stamp, the 10¢ stamp, depicting a 1930s tractor trailer, was created as a false-franking item adaptable to various postage rates. At the time of mailing, users paid the difference between the 10¢ face value and the actual per-piece rate, which was determined by the class of mail and the degree of sorting.

239

However, after the plan was in place, it generated unexpected objections from the very mailers for whom the 10¢ stamp was created.

Mail Advertising Service Association International (MASA) pointed out that the new system ensured that stamped advertising mail would always carry a postage stamp with a denomination considerably lower than the fee actually paid. This, MASA said, would strengthen the public's belief that third-class mail had been and would continue to be subsidized by other classes of mail — an impression that was incorrect. For mailers who used the 10¢ stamp on presorted first-class mail, the gap between denomination and actual postage was even wider.

Accordingly, USPS announced July 9 that "mailers' specific needs have become clear" and that it would issue two new coil stamps in the fall: a 23¢ stamp to be used specifically for presorted first-class mailings, and a non-denominated bulk-rate stamp (see chapters on those stamps). The 5¢ Canoe and 10¢ Tractor Trailer stamps would remain in production, USPS said, although previously announced plans to offer the 10¢ stamp in coils of 10,000 would be abandoned.

To accommodate both bulk and first-class presorted mail, the Tractor Trailer stamp bore no service inscription — only the words "Additional Presort Postage Paid." For this reason, users were required to add an endorsement to each piece of mail bearing the stamps, so that postal clerks handling the mail en route to its destination would know whether it was third-class or first-class.

Several weeks after the 10¢ stamp was issued, specimens appeared in the mail with privately overprinted service designations. The first of these to be reported in *Linn's Stamp News* were on mailings from American Express and American Telephone and Telegraph Company, and bore the endorsement "Bulk Rate" and "First-Class."

The authority for this kind of private overprinting was given in two notices in the August 22 *Postal Bulletin*. The first stated: "The lack of an appropriate endorsement may cause confusion concerning the handling of undeliverable pieces. One temporary solution to this problem is for the mailer to print a First-Class endorsement on the stamp itself."

The second notice, appearing in a later announcement regarding the handling of unmarked mail, stated that in addition to using various denominations of precanceled postage stamps, "customers may precancel other denominations of stamps for that purpose." The announcement implied that mailers could mark their own stamps with whatever service designation was needed.

In the meantime, clerks were told to handle any apparently short-paid bulk mail as either fully prepaid first- or third-class mail and not attempt to collect postage due. Non-deliverable mail pieces without a first-class endorsement were to be treated as third-class mail, meaning that USPS wouldn't provide automatic, free forwarding and return services.

Tractor trailers of the kind depicted on the coil stamp are familiar sights on today's streets and highways. They consist of two separate units,

These two Tractor Trailer stamps bear privately applied service-indicator overprints that were authorized by USPS.

which are purchased separately and usually made by different manufacturers: the tractor, which contains the engine and driving compartment, and the semitrailer, which has wheels only under the rear end and rests at the front on the tractor. The two are attached by a round disc called a "fifth wheel," which permits the units to turn separately. Until the 1930s, trucks used gasoline engines exclusively, but today the diesel engine dominates long-distance trucking.

In 1953 the U.S. Post Office Department issued a 3¢ commemorative stamp (Scott 1025) in conjunction with the 50th annual convention of the American Trucking Association. The year also marked the 50th anniversary of the International Brotherhood of Teamsters, the union that represents over-the-road drivers.

The Design

Like most Transportation series stamps, the Tractor Trailer stamp was designed for use with whatever denomination and service inscription USPS might require at a given time. The artist was David K. Stone of Chapel Hill, North Carolina, who had previously designed eight other Transportation coils: Omnibus, Locomotive, Handcar, Star Route Truck, Bicycle, Hansom Cab, Surrey and Railroad Mail Car.

As USPS stated in its announcement, "the Tractor Trailer stamp design includes a composite drawing combining the most common features of tractor trailers of the early 1930s." From the beginning, artist Stone and Joe Brockert, the project manager and art director, had worked on the assumption that their truck should be at least 50 years old. Working from a variety of photographs, Stone made some sketches of different-looking vehicles, including one rather streamlined, almost art deco combination of tractor and trailer.

But he and Brockert settled fairly quickly on the basic look they wanted: a truck with the cab behind the engine rather than over it, an old-fashioned divided hood, a vertical windshield and radiator, and a trailer with paneled sides. Stone sketched this hybrid from various angles and

241

distances. In the fall of 1988, the Citizens' Stamp Advisory Committee selected one of the images, and Stone made the finished version in ink.

But not a completely finished version, it turned out. The truck was headed to the right, and CSAC decided belatedly that on the stamp it should be driving left — toward the center of the envelope, rather than off the edge. Before the drawing could be photographically reversed, however, Stone had to move the steering wheel and driver's-side mirror to the "wrong" side of the cab, so they would end up on the "right" side when it was flopped. He also converted what had been a passenger-side gasoline tank on the running board to a driver's-side tool kit.

"The trucks of that era were such composites anyhow that they had things all over the place," said Brockert. "They had doors on either side of the trailers; they had totally different configurations of door handles and rear-view mirrors and things on the fenders and so forth."

The Postal Service's desire to avoid depicting a specific make of truck had a historical antecedent. Back in 1953, in developing a design for the stamp to commemorate the 50th anniversary of the trucking industry, BEP artist William Schrage based his artwork on a photograph of a Reo

These are some of artist David Stone's preliminary sketches, including one showing a streamlined truck making a sharp turn. The typography in the sketches was for a non-existent 9.9¢ non-profit presort rate.

David Stone changed his finished ink drawing (left) by moving the steering wheel and exterior mirror and changing a running-board gasoline tank to a tool kit (right) so the drawing could be photographically reversed.

truck with an identifiable driver — Ben Winterberger of St. Louis, Missouri, a national driving champion — waving out the window. Except for removing the name "Reo" from the front of the vehicle and changing the horizontal grill openings to vertical ones, Schrage made virtually an exact copy of the truck in the photo. Columnist George Sloane, writing in *Stamps*, described what happened next:

"The bantering jubilance of Reo Motors' officials that a Reo truck was to be pictured on the new trucking stamp, whereas Postmaster General (Arthur) Summerfield, in private life, had been a Chevrolet dealer, was badly timed. The PMG had the Bureau redesign the model on the stamp, and it certainly is no Reo now. The stamp as issued disagrees with the advance photo of the design sent out for publicity. Innocent victim in the fast switch is the chauffeur who was to be shown on the stamp. He's away inside the cab now, not waving a greeting, and could be 'anyone.' "

First-Day Facts

The Tractor Trailer stamp, like the Canoe stamp, was issued May 25 at the Nojex 91 stamp show in Secaucus, New Jersey. For information, see the chapter on the Canoe stamp.

In the case of first-day covers processed completely by USPS, three Tractor Trailer stamps were affixed at a cost of 30¢. USPS declined requests to affix combinations of Canoe and Tractor Trailer stamps.

This 1953 3¢ commemorative stamp for the 50th anniversary of the trucking industry (Scott 1025) also depicted a generic truck. The design that was originally released had shown a truck that too closely resembled an actual Reo.

29¢ FLAGS ON PARADE

Date of Issue: May 30, 1991

Catalog Number: Scott 2531

Colors: red, blue, black, gray

First-Day Cancel: Waterloo, New York

FDCs Canceled: 104,046

Format: Panes of 100, horizontal, 10 across, 10 down. Gravure printing cylinders of 400 subjects (20 across, 20 around).

Perf: 11.2 (Eureka off-line perforator)

Selvage Markings: "© United States Postal Service 1991." "Use Correct ZIP Code ®."

Designers: Peter Cocci (BEP) from original art by Frank J. Waslick (BEP)

Art Director: Leonard Buckley (BEP)

Project Manager: Joe Brockert (USPS)

Typographer and Modeler: Peter Cocci (BEP)

Printing: printed by BEP on 7-color Andreotti gravure press (601)

Quantity Ordered: 900,000,000

Quantity Distributed: 607,370,000

Cylinder Number Detail: 1 group of 4 cylinder numbers alongside corner stamp

Tagging: overall

The Stamp

When is a commemorative stamp not a commemorative stamp? When it is issued "to coincide with" an anniversary that would not in itself qualify for a commemorative.

That was the case with the 29¢ Flags on Parade stamp, a definitive that was dedicated in Waterloo, New York, May 30, 1991, in the 125th anniversary month of the first Memorial Day celebration in that city.

Four years earlier, on behalf of his Waterloo constituents, Representative Frank Horton, Republican of New York's 29th District, had written to the Citizens' Stamp Advisory Committee asking for a commemorative stamp honoring Waterloo as the birthplace of Memorial Day. His request made no mention of any specific anniversary linkage. "Such a stamp would serve as a daily reminder to Americans everywhere of the tremendous sacrifices millions of men and women have made to preserve our freedom," Horton wrote. "I know you have the strictest regulations on the issuance of stamps — regulations that would normally preclude honoring a particular community. However, this is an extraordinary situation. It deserves your consideration."

CSAC took no action on the request. But Horton didn't give up, and Horton was no ordinary congressman in USPS' eyes. He was the second-ranking Republican on the House Committee on Post Office and Civil Service, the ranking Republican on the Postal Operations and Services Subcommittee, and the ranking Republican on the Government Operations Committee. His influence with USPS was such that his personal lobbying with Postmaster General Anthony M. Frank in 1988 was credited with winning approval of a Great Americans stamp for Chester Carlson, inventor of xerography and a late resident of Horton's hometown of Rochester, New York.

In 1990 Frank again found a way to accommodate Horton's wishes, and without violating CSAC guidelines. In a June 27, 1990, letter to the congressman, Frank informed him that a new American Flag stamp would be issued in Waterloo the following May 30. "Flag stamps are always among our most popular issues," the postmaster general wrote, "and the Waterloo first-day ceremony and postmark will provide a fitting tribute to the site where the first Memorial Day was observed 125 years ago." In a note at the bottom, Frank added: "See you there, I hope."

A USPS press release, dated August 3, 1990, reported the news to the public, noting that the stamp's issuance would "coincide with" the 125th anniversary of the first observance of Memorial Day. (Interestingly, the USPS release the following spring, which contained details about the stamp, used the word "commemorate" — a term that had been so carefully avoided earlier.)

Horton, in an announcement of his own, credited two Waterloo residents for their efforts in seeking postal recognition for the anniversary. "Joseph Donahue and Priscilla Suffredini are to be commended for their fine work as co-chairmen of the Waterloo Memorial Day Committee," his news release said. "I join the two co-chairmen in announcing our success in convincing the Postal Service of the importance of recognizing Waterloo as the birthplace of Memorial Day."

The new stamp, depicting three waving U.S. flags on staffs in parade formation, replaced the 25¢ Flag with Clouds definitive that had been issued in 1988, after the previous rate change. The Flag with Clouds had been produced in both sheet and booklet form. However, because a 29¢ Flag with Olympic Rings booklet was already available, the Flags on Parade stamp was printed in sheet form only.

Memorial Day, or Decoration Day, is a day set aside to honor Americans who gave their lives for their country. It is a federal holiday, observed since 1971 on the last Monday in May, and is also a legal holiday in most states. Most of the Southern states also have their own days for honoring the Confederate dead.

Although several communities claim to have originated Memorial Day, in 1966 Congress and President Lyndon Johnson declared Waterloo, in New York's Finger Lakes region, to be the birthplace of the holiday. Waterloo first observed Memorial Day on May 5, 1866, to honor soldiers who had died in the Civil War. Businesses were closed, soldiers' graves were decorated and flags were flown at half-mast.

Previous stamps issued on the traditional May 30 Memorial Day date were the 3¢ United Confederate Veterans commemorative of 1951 (Scott 998) and the 4¢ Lincoln Sesquicentennial stamp of 1959 (Scott 1116).

The Design

Finding new ways to present Old Glory is a challenge to designers and CSAC. "With the flag being repeated again and again on prime-rate stamps, you try to think, 'How do we see the flag?' " said Leonard Buckley, foreman of designers at the Bureau of Engraving and Printing and art director for this stamp. "We've seen it historically, we've seen it with fireworks, we've seen it in different parts of the nation, we've seen it here in the capital, flying over public buildings and monuments. As you use up these ideas, you ask yourself, 'How else can I show the flag?' "

The answer, in this case, was to depict not one but three flags. Credit

This is Frank J. Waslick's original watercolor painting of a group of seven rippling flags.

246

Peter Cocci took three of Waslick's flags and adapted them for this stamp design. CSAC then asked him to line up the flags as if they were passing in a parade.

for the design was divided between two BEP artists: Frank J. Waslick, who had retired some time before the stamp was issued, and Peter Cocci.

While Waslick was still on active service, he had developed a watercolor design for a future Flag stamp, featuring seven rippling flags in no particular formation. When the time came to select designs for new-rate definitives, Cocci used BEP's Electronic Design Center to create a new design, using three of Waslick's seven flags. CSAC liked the concept, but asked that the three flags be lined up in a staggered formation, as though passing the viewer in a parade.

Cocci also executed the typography for the stamp, using a Roman typeface called Palatino. Postmaster General Frank approved the design November 22, 1990.

First-Day Facts

Although Memorial Day was officially celebrated on Monday, May 27, the Flags on Parade stamp was dedicated the following Thursday, on the traditional May 30 date for the holiday.

More than 1,600 people attended the first-day ceremony at Waterloo Senior High School in what one USPS official described as "an un-air-conditioned gymnasium, where the temperature was probably over 100 degrees." The colors were presented by 16 members of the Waterloo Veterans Color Guard, followed by 50 Boy Scouts, each carrying a flag of one of the 50 states.

The stamp was dedicated by William T. Johnstone, assistant postmaster general, following a welcome by Mayor Lee Patchen of Waterloo and remarks by Representative Frank Horton and Priscilla Suffredini, chairman of the Waterloo Memorial Day Committee.

52¢ HUBERT HUMPHREY
GREAT AMERICANS SERIES

Date of Issue: June 3, 1991

Catalog Number: Scott 2190

Color: dark purple (PMS 532U)

First-Day Cancel: Minneapolis, Minnesota

FDCs Canceled: 93,391

Format: Panes of 100, vertical, 10 across, 10 down. Printing sleeve of 800 subjects (20 across, 40 around).

Perf: 11.2 (Eureka off-line perforator)

Selvage Inscription: "Hubert H. Humphrey/was born in 1911/and died in 1978." "He served four terms/as a U.S. Senator/from Minnesota." "From 1964 to 1968,/he served as the 38th/U.S. Vice President."

Selvage Markings: "© United States Postal Service 1991." "Use Correct ZIP Code ®." Register markings in corners.

Designer: John Berkey of Excelsior, Minnesota

Engravers: vignette, Thomas Hipschen (BEP); lettering, Richard Everett (BEP)

Art Director and Typographer: Howard Paine (CSAC)

Project Manager: Jack Williams (USPS)

Printing: printed by BEP on 3-color intaglio unit of 9-color offset-intaglio D press (902)

Quantity Ordered: 300,000,000

Quantity Distributed: 249,020,000

Sleeve Number Detail: single-digit intaglio sleeve number alongside corner stamp

Tagging: phosphor-coated paper

The Stamp

Hubert H. Humphrey, the 38th vice president of the United States and the unsuccessful presidential candidate of the Democratic Party in 1968, was shown on a stamp in the Great Americans series that was issued June 3 in Minneapolis. The stamp bore the 52¢ denomination, covering the two-ounce letter rate that took effect the preceding February 3.

In a year that saw many mishaps and much controversy befall the USPS stamp program, the Humphrey stamp created perhaps the most embarrassing moments of all for the Postal Service. This was because of a factual error — not in the design of the stamp, but in the selvage — which at one point appeared certain to cost USPS some $580,000 for a complete reprinting of the 300 million stamps already made.

As chronicled by *Linn's Stamp News*, the story began Friday, April 12, when Gary Griffith, Washington representative of *Linn's*, picked up the initial press release for the Humphrey stamp from USPS headquarters. In it was the wording of the biographical data that would appear in the sheet selvage, including this sentence: "From 1964 to 1968, he served as the 38th vice president." Humphrey's term as vice president actually began January 20, 1965, and ended January 20, 1969.

The following Monday, April 15, Griffith called the error to the attention of the Postal Service, which hadn't been aware of it. USPS spokesman Michael O'Hara told Griffith: "The years 1964 to 1968 were meant to include the year that he (Humphrey) was elected vice president." O'Hara said the stamp would be issued as it stood. He had no

The wrong dates for Humphrey's vice presidential term were given in the selvage and almost led to a $580,000 reprinting job.

249

comment on whether the mistake would be corrected on future printings.

On Wednesday, April 17, *Linn's* went to press with the error story. On Tuesday, April 23, *The Washington Post* carried a story about the mistake, saying that the Humphrey stamps "may be" destroyed and reprinted. Later that day, USPS, through O'Hara, issued this statement: "To maintain the integrity of the stamp program and to insure the historical accuracy of the selvage text, the Postal Service made the decision to correct and reprint the Humphrey stamps." The stamps would be reprinted by the Bureau of Engraving and Printing, which had done the originals, at a cost of $580,000.

The Associated Press sent stories over the wire on the afternoon of April 23 saying the stamps would be destroyed. On the same day, Representative Gerry Sikorski, D-Minnesota, a member of the House Post Office and Civil Service Committee, said he had written to Postmaster General Anthony M. Frank taking "strong exception" to the decision to reprint the stamps and asking that it be reconsidered.

The following morning, April 24, USPS officials let it be known that the reprint order might indeed be canceled. USPS spokesman O'Hara told *Linn's* that "our phone lines are going crazy." Late in the day, Postmaster General Anthony M. Frank announced that the stamps in fact would be issued as printed.

"If the information in the stamp design itself had been incorrect, we would not have issued it," Frank said in a statement. "Given the recent heightened visibility of the stamp, Americans will all the more remember HHH as the Great American he was.

"In actuality, the general public invariably discards the margin information, but some specialized stamp collectors save the margins."

A spokesman for Representative Sikorski, Steve Johnson, claimed "victory" over the Postal Service bureaucracy, according to an April 25 story in *The Washington Post*. Hubert Humphrey's sister, Frances Humphrey Howard of Washington, agreed with Frank's decision to use the stamps, *The Post* reported.

"They always accused Hubert of being a big spender," Frances Howard said. "Well, Hubert must have been giving Gerry Sikorski advice from on high. I'll bet he said, 'If there's money to be spent, it better be spent on people, by golly.' "

The postmaster general had ordered the reprint decision reversed after "weighing all the options," Dickey B. Rustin, manager of the USPS Stamp Product Development Branch, told *The Post*. "We can't avoid the economic realities of the cost of reprinting," Rustin said.

Also on April 25, the House Postal Operations and Services Subcommittee announced that it would hold a hearing June 5 on the production and procurement of postage stamps. The hearing would inquire into "the whole philatelic program," subcommittee staff director Debbie Kendall told *Linn's*, including the Humphrey stamp error and its handling.

Ironically, it was Postmaster General Frank's desire to provide postal customers with more information on stamp subjects that led indirectly to the Humphrey stamp embarrassment.

Until 1989, Great Americans stamps had shown only the subject's portrait and name, with no hint as to why the person was worthy of stamp honors. This tended to nullify one of the principal goals of the Great Americans series, which was to give recognition to achievers whose names weren't necessarily household words.

On orders from the postmaster general, the Office of Stamp and Philatelic Marketing began including a few words of description in the design of each Great Americans stamp. But the stamp office went further. It also began placing capsule biographies in the selvage of the sheets — not for only Great Americans, but for certain other stamps as well.

Because the first few stamps to get this treatment had already been researched and designed, the Great Americans designs had to be modified to accept additional wording. The selvage information didn't receive the kind of close attention from the staff and the Citizens' Stamp Advisory Committee that normally accompanied the development of stamps themselves. This produced some stylistic inconsistencies in the selvage wording and at least one factual mistake (in the selvage of the 40¢ Claire Chennault stamp of 1990; see the *1990 Linn's U.S. Stamp Yearbook*). But nothing caught the public's attention in the way the Humphrey error did.

Donald M. McDowell, director of the Office of Stamp and Philatelic Marketing, told the *Yearbook* the wording had been put together relatively quickly by himself and Jack Williams, the stamp project manager, on a word processor in McDowell's office, using "some standard reference works off the shelf."

"The thing that bit us was that you get in the habit of thinking the so-called 'Reagan years' were from election to election, and the 'Johnson years' were from election to election, and popularly thought of they were, but technically they were not; they were from the January following an election to the January following the next election," McDowell said.

"We blew it. And this is a case where an explanation is not an excuse. We made a human error, and we're human. They don't give you an infallibility inoculation when you go to work (in stamps)."

Hubert Horatio Humphrey was born May 21, 1911, in Wallace, South Dakota. He had to drop out of the University of Minnesota because of the Depression, but later returned and graduated Phi Beta Kappa and magna cum laude. In between, he studied pharmacy in Denver, Colorado, and worked as a pharmacist in his father's drugstore. In 1943, while he was assistant regional director of the War Manpower Commission, he ran for mayor of Minneapolis and lost, but in 1945, he won, and was re-elected in 1947. An outspoken liberal, known for his hard-hitting oratory, he helped found the Americans for Democratic Action during this period, and in 1948 captured national attention with a fervent speech at the Democratic National Convention in favor of a civil-rights plank. That fall he became the first Democrat elected to the U.S. Senate from Minnesota.

Humphrey sought the Democratic presidential nomination in 1960, but lost to John F. Kennedy. From 1961 to 1964, he was assistant majority leader in the Senate, and in 1964, President Lyndon B. Johnson chose him as his vice presidential running mate. The Johnson-Humphrey ticket won in a landslide. Four years later, after a growing national opposition to the Vietnam War had forced Johnson to drop plans to run for another term, Humphrey sought and won his party's presidential nomination. His identification with the Johnson Vietnam policy proved too heavy a handicap, and he lost the election by a close race to Richard M. Nixon.

In 1970 and 1976, he was again elected to the Senate. He died of cancer January 13, 1978, in Waverly, Minnesota.

Other men who served as vice president who have been pictured on U.S. stamps are John Adams, Thomas Jefferson, Martin Van Buren, John Tyler, Millard Fillmore, Andrew Johnson, Chester Alan Arthur, Theodore Roosevelt, Calvin Coolidge, Harry S. Truman and Lyndon B. Johnson. Hubert Humphrey was the first vice president who did not go on to become president to be portrayed on a stamp.

As an unsuccessful candidate for president, however, Humphrey had several predecessors on U.S. postage: Henry Clay, Daniel Webster, Winfield Scott, John Charles Fremont, Stephen A. Douglas, Horace Greeley, William Jennings Bryan, Charles Evans Hughes, Al Smith and Adlai Stevenson. Another past stamp subject was Republican Robert A. Taft, who sought his party's presidential nomination but didn't get it.

The Design

Howard Paine, art director for the stamp, asked a Minnesota artist and illustrator, John C. Berkey of Excelsior, to produce the artwork on which the engraving would be based. Berkey, who had more than 200 book covers to his credit along with many paintings for magazine covers and articles, movie posters and corporate illustrations, had previously designed the 1983 Christmas stamp that depicted Santa Claus.

Berkey contacted the vice president's son, Hubert "Skip" Humphrey III, attorney general of Minnesota, and asked for a suitable photograph from which to work. He was given a photo made in 1964 by Kurt F.G. Jafay, a professional photographer from Denver, Colorado. Using this as a model, Berkey made a pencil drawing of Humphrey.

"His image was very familiar to me, inasmuch as I grew up in Minnesota and he was in the news there for most of my adult life," said Berkey. "It wasn't as though I was trying to draw a stranger. I never met him, though. I'm probably one of the few people in Minnesota who had never talked to him!"

A news release by the Professional Photographers of America quoted Kurt Jafay's recollections of the day in Denver in 1964 when the portrait was made. According to Jafay, Humphrey arrived on time for the photo session, but his luggage was lost. Being very particular about his clothes,

Humphrey refused to be photographed wearing the same shirt he wore on the airplane. "By the time his aides returned from purchasing him a new shirt, we had one and one-half minutes to take the photo before he had to be off to his next appointment," Jafay said. Despite the problems, the sitting was a success, and Humphrey later had Jafay fly to Minnesota to take photographs of the vice president's family.

First-Day Facts

The stamp was dedicated by Edward E. Horgan Jr., associate postmaster general, at a ceremony at the Hubert H. Humphrey Institute on the University of Minnesota campus in Minneapolis.

The principal speaker was another former vice president and Democratic presidential candidate from Minnesota, Walter Mondale, who had been Humphrey's protege in the U.S. Senate. Also speaking was Hubert H. Humphrey III, the state attorney general.

Three distinguished Minnesotans gave unscheduled talks: Governor

This is the Kurt Jafay photograph that artist John Berkey used as a reference in designing the stamp.

Shown at the dedication of the Humphrey stamp are, from left, the late vice president's son, Hubert Humphrey III; Kurt F.G. Jafay, the photographer on whose portrait of Humphrey the stamp design was based; and Muriel Humphrey Brown, the honoree's wife.

Arne H. Carlson, who decided at the last minute to attend the ceremony; Muriel Humphrey Brown, the vice president's widow; and Harold Stassen, former Minnesota governor and frequent candidate for the Republican presidential nomination, who was introduced and delivered brief remarks from the audience.

1¢ KESTREL

Date of Issue: June 22, 1991

Catalog Number: Scott 2481

Colors: magenta, yellow, cyan, black

First-Day Cancel: Aurora, Colorado

FDCs Canceled: 77,781. Combination Bird FDCs, 120,615.

Format: Panes of 100, vertical, 10 across, 10 down. Printing plates of 400 subjects (20 across, 20 around).

Perf: 10.9 (L perforator)

Selvage Markings: "© USPS 1991." "USE CORRECT ZIP CODE ®."

Designer: Michael Matherly of Cambridge City, Indiana

Art Director and Project Manager: Joe Brockert (USPS)

Printing: printed by American Bank Note Company, Los Angeles, California (formerly Jeffries Banknote Division) on a Miller 4-color offset sheetfed press.

Quantity Ordered: 200,000,000 plus 350,000,000

Quantity Distributed: 550,000,000

Plate Number Detail: 1 group of 4 offset plate numbers preceded by the letter A alongside corner stamp

Tagging: untagged

The Stamp

One of the few things that can still be bought for a penny is a 1¢ postage stamp. Such a stamp is useful only for combining with other stamps to cover a particular rate, however, and few of them have been issued in recent years. Until 1991, the last one had been the re-engraved Omnibus coil stamp in the Transportation series, in 1986.

But on June 22, 1991, at the Topex 91 stamp show in Aurora, Colorado, USPS issued a new 1¢ definitive stamp, along with two other definitives, all in sheet format. All three pictured American birds. They were: 1¢, the American kestrel; 3¢, the Eastern bluebird, and 30¢, the cardinal.

The Kestrel and Bluebird stamps were developed from a group of five designs showing small, colorful specimens of wildlife that USPS had commissioned from artist Michael Matherly.

"We knew that we were headed toward offset printing for low values, and so we wanted to work with multicolored stamps," Brockert said. "We believed that wildlife would be the best kind of subject because of its popularity.

"Wildlife stamps tend to be well received by the public. They're not controversial. Commercial mailers will use them without worrying about what we're putting on them."

Matherly was asked to prepare his five designs in such a way that they could be printed by either offset or gravure and could be adapted to sheet, booklet or coil use as USPS needs dictated. The artist submitted a list of some 20 proposed design subjects, and from that list USPS and the Citizens' Stamp Advisory Committee chose five species that had the best design potential. Matherly then created concept sketches for all five, and later, at CSAC's request, he turned the sketches into finished art.

The fact that the Kestrel and Bluebird stamps were printed by offset made them the first U.S. denominated postage for general use to be produced by this printing method since World War I. (Earlier in 1991, the non-denominated Make-Up Rate stamp, with a face value of 4¢, had also been offset-printed.) U.S. Official Mail stamps had been printed by offset since 1988, when USPS concluded that the risk of counterfeiting of these controlled-use items wasn't great enough to preclude printing them by this less-costly method. Now, in 1991, the Postal Service made the same judgment in regard to low-value general-use stamps.

The Kestrel stamp was untagged, like other low-value stamps printed since the first of the year. It was also the first 1¢ stamp to have its denomination expressed in two digits (a zero plus the cent value), following a policy that USPS introduced in 1990 for stamps with denominations of less than a dime. One of the unexpected by-products of this policy now surfaced: a new form of postal-revenue abuse.

Linn's Stamp News editor Michael Laurence wrote in October that in recent weeks *Linn's* had seen numerous examples of covers on which "01" Kestrel stamps had been affixed at angles to make them read "10." (See illustration.) Even the absence of tagging, which would normally

256

cause the covers to be rejected by facer-canceler machines, didn't stop these pieces of mail from getting through without a postage-due charge. "This sort of abuse is widespread and growing," Laurence warned. "It promises to spread as the Kestrel stamp gains wider distribution. It won't stop until the Postal Service restores the cent sign to our stamps."

The American kestrel, or sparrow hawk, hadn't been previously depicted on U.S. stamps, although it had always been a natural. The male's slate blue and rust plumage, replete with streaks, spots and bars, makes it colorful and visually unique. The female, by contrast, is a dull reddish-brown color. The kestrel is the only falcon species in which the sexes are so different in appearance.

The bluejay-sized bird is the smallest and most frequently sighted falcon in the United States, ranging over most of North America. As kestrels search for the mice or insects that constitute their prey, they seem to dangle motionlessly above the ground in an unusual feeding style called "hover hunting."

Kestrels nest in natural tree cavities or those hollowed out by other animals. As trees disappear from their habitat, the birds are finding fewer natural places to live. But a growing number of kestrel lovers are erecting nest boxes as alternative housing near open areas where the birds like to hunt. Thanks to their efforts, reported Cheryl Lyn Dybas in *National Wildlife* magazine, "the kestrels' future is looking bright."

The Design

Michael Matherly is a Cambridge City, Indiana, wildlife artist and magazine illustrator. His painting for the 1¢ stamp showed a male kestrel

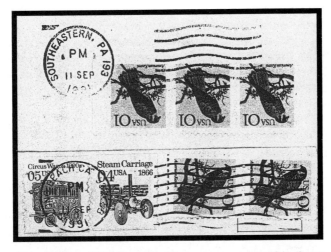

Above, three "01" Kestrel stamps are used upside down to appear to pay 30¢ in postage. Below, two "01" stamps are turned sideways to suggest two 10¢ stamps, supplemented by 4¢ and 5¢ Transportation coils to make the 29¢ rate.

sitting on a cedar branch. In his original work the kestrel faced to the right instead of the left, but USPS preferred to have the bird facing into the envelope when the stamp was used, and so the American Bank Note Company flopped, or reversed, the image. USPS also instructed ABNC to electronically remove some extraneous background to simplify the

This is Michael Matherly's original painting for the Kestrel stamp. USPS asked the printer to reverse the image and delete some of the branches in the background.

design and leave more room for typography.

Finally, the printer added a neutral background color that hadn't been in the original art. This was the result of a bit of serendipity. The USPS design staff customarily makes stamp-sized color photographs of stamp art and places them on envelopes so CSAC members will have an idea of what the finished product will look like when it fulfills its intended purpose. Sometimes these color reductions develop a background tone that wasn't in the original. In this case, the committee liked the effect of the tone behind the kestrel, and ABNC was told to create the same effect on the finished stamps.

As part of the typography, the identification line, "American kestrel," appeared in italics in the lower left. Some previous wildlife stamps, such as the Rose-breasted Grosbeak and Saw-whet Owl booklet stamps of 1988 (Scott 2284-85) and the $2 Bobcat of 1990, had carried no identification of the species (although the bobcat was identified in a selvage inscription). "A lot depends on the design," Joe Brockert explained. "If there's room, and if it doesn't detract from the image, we probably will go ahead and identify the bird or mammal on the stamp itself. If it doesn't make sense, if it doesn't fit, we won't."

First-Day Facts

The first-day ceremony for the Kestrel, Bluebird and Cardinal stamps was described by USPS as "unofficial." It took place at 9:30 a.m. June 22 at the Holiday Inn South, Denver Tech Center, in Aurora, Colorado, on the second day of the annual exhibition and convention of the American Topical Association.

Mary Ann Owens of Brooklyn, New York, a member of the Citizens' Stamp Advisory Committee and chairman of CSAC's Topical Subcommittee, was the featured speaker at the ceremony. Owens also served as chief judge for Topex 91.

First-day cover collectors wishing to have USPS affix stamps could get the 1¢ Kestrel stamp in only two ways: as a single, accompanied by a 29¢ Flag stamp, for a total of 30¢, or in combination with the 3¢ Bluebird and 30¢ Cardinal stamps, for a total of 34¢.

Date of Issue: June 22, 1991

Catalog Number: Scott 2482

Colors: magenta, yellow, cyan, black

First-Day Cancel: Aurora, Colorado

FDCs Canceled: 76,149

Format: Panes of 100, vertical, 10 across, 10 down. Printing plate of 400 subjects (20 across, 20 around).

Perf: 10.9 (L perforator)

Selvage Markings: "© USPS 1991." "USE CORRECT ZIP CODE ®."

Designer: Michael Matherly of Cambridge City, Indiana

Art Director and Project Manager: Joe Brockert (USPS)

Printing: printed by American Bank Note Company, Los Angeles, California (formerly Jeffries Banknote Division) on a Miller 4-color offset sheetfed press.

Quantity Ordered: 200,000,000

Quantity Distributed: 200,000,000

Plate Number Detail: 1 group of 4 numbers preceded by the letter A alongside corner stamp

Tagging: untagged

The Stamp

The 3¢ Bluebird stamp, which USPS issued June 22, along with the 1¢ Kestrel and 30¢ Cardinal, bore a denomination that has an honored place in U.S. postal history.

Three cents was the first-class non-local letter rate for the 20 years from 1863 to 1883; during World War I, and for the 26 years from 1932 to 1958. By 1991, however, the first-class rate had ballooned to nearly 10 times three cents, and a 3¢ stamp could be used only in combination with other stamps to make up a required amount of postage on a letter or parcel.

Like the 1¢ Kestrel, the Bluebird stamp expressed its denomination with a zero and a value digit, was offset printed for the American Bank Note Company by Jeffrey Banknote Company, and was untagged.

Its subject, the Eastern bluebird, is the state bird of Missouri and New York. As such it had been depicted on the stamps of those states on the 50-stamp State Birds and Flowers pane of 1982. A cousin, the Western bluebird, was shown on the Idaho and Nevada stamps of the 1982 pane and also on the Idaho Statehood Centennial commemorative of 1990.

The Eastern bluebird was pictured on the Missouri and New York stamps of the 1982 State Birds and Flowers pane.

The Eastern bluebird is a member of the thrush family. At about seven inches in length, it is smaller than its cousin, the robin. The male has deep blue upper parts, a red chestnut throat, neck and upper breast and a white lower belly, while the female is duller in color. Its range is the eastern half of North America from southeast Canada south through mid-Texas.

The bluebird was once an American icon, a sweet-singing symbol of hope and springtime whose name songwriters often wove into their lyrics, but it has become relatively rare. Bluebird populations have declined by up to 90 percent this century. One reason has been the loss of favored habitat, such as woodland edge, farm fields and orchards. The removal of dead trees and branches has reduced the number of available nest holes and increased the competition with more aggressive cavity-nesting species such as house sparrows and starlings. To check the species' decline, a large-scale bluebird nesting box project has been undertaken with promising results in many areas.

The Design

Artist Michael Matherly of Cambridge City, Indiana, painted both the American kestrel and Eastern bluebird as part of a series of five pictures

This is Michael Matherly's original painting for the Bluebird stamp. As with Matherly's painting for the 1¢ Kestrel stamp, USPS asked the printer to reverse the image and delete some of the background detail — in this case, some of the crab apple blossoms and leaves.

of small, colorful wildlife that USPS commissioned for stamp purposes.

Matherly's bluebird picture showed the bird sitting on a flowering crab apple tree branch. Like his kestrel painting, his bluebird originally faced right, or "off the envelope," and on the instructions of USPS the printers reversed the image when they processed the artwork electronically. They also removed some excess foliage in the background to simplify the design and leave ample room for typography, and added a neutral background color, both of which they had also done for the Kestrel stamp.

First-Day Facts

Details on the unofficial first-day ceremony for the three bird stamps at Topex 91 in Aurora, Colorado, can be found in the preceding chapter.

First-day cover collectors wishing to have USPS affix stamps to their covers could obtain the 3¢ Bluebird stamp in one of two ways: as a single accompanied by a 29¢ Flag stamp, for a total of 32¢, or as a single accompanied by single Kestrel and Cardinal stamps, for a total of 34¢.

262

30¢ CARDINAL

Date of Issue: June 22, 1991

Catalog Number: Scott 2489

Colors: yellow, red, blue, black

First-Day Cancel: Aurora, Colorado

FDCs Canceled: 101,290

Format: Panes of 100, vertical, 10 across, 10 down. Gravure printing cylinders of 400 subjects (20 across, 20 around) manufactured by Armotek Industries Inc., Palmyra, New Jersey.

Perf: 10.9 (L perforator)

Selvage Markings: "© USPS 1991." "USE CORRECT ZIP CODE ®."

Designer: Robert Giusti of New Milford, Connecticut

Art Director: Derry Noyes (CSAC)

Project Manager: Joe Brockert (USPS)

Printing: Stamps printed by Stamp Venturers on a Champlain gravure press at J.W. Fergusson and Sons, Richmond, Virginia. Stamps perforated, processed and shipped by KCS Industries, Milwaukee, Wisconsin.

Quantity Ordered: 200,000,000

Quantity Distributed: 200,000,000

Cylinder Number Detail: 1 group of 4 numbers preceded by the letter S alongside corner stamp

Tagging: phosphor-coated paper

The Stamp

When USPS issued a new 30¢ definitive on June 22, some collectors speculated that it did so to have an extra stamp of that denomination on hand in case USPS was able to obtain the 30¢ first-class rate it had sought previously without success from the Postal Rate Commission.

But Postal Service spokesmen denied that the 30¢ stamp was connected to its request for a rate reconsideration — a request that was formally filed July 2, 10 days after the stamp appeared. The stamp was issued to meet the new postcard rate to Canada and Mexico, they said. (An existing 30¢ definitive, the Frank Laubach Great Americans stamp of 1984, was also available for that purpose.)

The new stamp was a head-and-neck portrait of a male cardinal against a plain white background. It was designed by Robert Giusti of New Milford, Connecticut, who had designed the 29¢ Wood Duck stamp that was issued in two different booklet varieties earlier in the year. It was printed by the gravure process by J.W. Fergusson for Stamp Venturers.

On U.S. stamps, the cardinal has been an avian George Washington, appearing previously on these nine commemoratives — seven of them from the 1982 State Birds and Flowers pane.

264

The cardinal had been depicted so often in the past on U.S. stamps that it could be called the George Washington of birds. It appeared on one of the four Wildlife Conservation stamps of 1972 (Scott 1465), one of the eight Capex 78 souvenir sheet stamps of 1978 (Scott 1757a), and no fewer than seven of the stamps in the 1982 State Birds and Flowers 50-stamp pane (Scott 1965, 1966, 1969, 1985, 1987, 1998 and 2000). Why use this familiar bird again?

"Color," said Joe Brockert, the project manager. "Pure and simple. We told the artist to pick some nice, bright colorful birds. One of them was the cardinal. His treatments are so unique and so wonderfully well-rendered that we couldn't resist. We loved this. The cardinal had the little blueberry in its beak, and even though we had done many cardinals before, this one was unlike any of them. Basically, it was a unique way of looking at a familiar creature, rather than a new creature."

Cardinals are common the year round throughout the East, Midwest, Southeast and Southwest as well as Mexico. The bright red plumage of the male, with black face and throat, is unmistakable. Both male and female have pointed crests and thick red beaks. They eat seeds, berries, fruit and insects and are regular customers at backyard bird feeders. The song is a repetition of loud slurred whistles.

The Design

The Postal Service was pleased with Robert Giusti's artwork for the Wood Duck booklets and commissioned him to prepare three more

This is Robert Giusti's cardinal painting, which was used on the stamp with only minor changes.

wildlife stamp designs. The cardinal portrait was the first of the three. The other two, to be used later, were done in the same style as the duck and cardinal: tightly cropped "head shots."

Giusti's acrylic-on-canvas cardinal head was used as he had painted it, with only minor modifications. For instance, the printers who processed the artwork were told to "shave" the bird by removing tiny feathers

These pictures of the cardinal are Robert Giusti's preliminary sketch (left) and his pencil tracing over which he made his finished painting for the stamp.

around the beak, which USPS decided would look like printing flaws when reduced to stamp size.

The artist placed a berry in the bird's beak "just to add an interesting element," he said. "Then it isn't just a bird, a face, without any kind of personality and point of interest.

"I also added it because the painting was rather a monotone. The cardinal had a slight coloration in the wings, and in the neck area, the nape, but it was very subtle; it went into a mauve — at least it did on the original painting. But there was so much red, with just a hint of black, that I needed just a little touch of something else to set it off and give it a little more color interest. So I added a blueberry."

First-Day Facts

Details on the unofficial first-day ceremony for the three bird stamps issued at Topex 91 in Aurora, Colorado, can be found in the chapter on the 1¢ Kestrel stamp.

29¢ LIBERTY TORCH (ATM-VENDED SHEETLET)

Date of Issue: June 25, 1991

Catalog Number: Scott 2531A (single stamp); 2531Ab (sheetlet of 18)

Colors: green (PMS 569), gold (PMS 873), black, blue (PMS 283)

First-Day Cancel: New York, New York

FDCs Canceled: 68,456

Format: Self-adhesive. Pane of 18 vertical stamps arranged vertically, 3 across, 6 down. Gravure printing cylinders of 270 units, 15 across, 18 around. All perimeter selvage removed before distribution.

Perf: die cut, no perforations

Markings: "Peel here and Fold * Self-adhesive stamps * DO NOT WET * © USPS 1991" on removable strip across center of pane. "Self-adhesive * DO NOT WET * © USPS 1991 * Patent Pending," and an advertisement for USPS stamped envelopes with printed return addresses, printed on the back of the removable backing.

Designer: Harry Zelenko of New York, New York

Art Director: Joe Brockert (USPS)

Technical Manager: Joseph Y. Peng (USPS)

Modeler and Typographer: John Boyd of Anagraphics Inc., New York, New York

Printing: By Avery International, Pasadena, California, on an Avery-owned gravure press. Die-cutting done on USPS-owned Chesnut press.

Quantity Ordered: 36,000,000

Quantity Distributed: 53,442,000

Tagging: phosphor-coated paper

The Stamp

As it had promised to do, the Postal Service followed up its first generation of automatic teller machine (ATM) self-adhesive stamps with a second-generation stamp that was calculated to arouse fewer objections from persons concerned about the environment.

Both the 25¢ ATM stamp of 1990 and the F (29¢) ATM stamp that was issued early in 1991 had been made of polyester film, a material that could meet the exacting thickness standards required by the bank machines that were available for the marketing tests. The decision had generated criticism that, though not widespread, touched a sensitive nerve in the Postal Service. On June 25, USPS began selling a new pressure-sensitive ATM stamp made of paper.

"We needed to determine if customers would commingle stamp purchases with their banking transactions before we could proceed with research to develop a paper version of the stamp," said Gordon C. Morison, assistant postmaster general, in announcing the new product.

"Our consumer testing successfully demonstrated that customers enjoy the convenience of buying stamps through ATMs. This drove us to develop a new pressure-sensitive paper stamp that meets the same engineering criteria, can be vended through ATMs and is environmentally sound."

The new stamp was part of the continuing research and development effort on ATM-vended postage, said Donald M. McDowell, director of the Office of Stamp and Philatelic Marketing. Significant questions remained to be answered, he added. USPS needed to know, for instance, whether it could develop a stamp that would work reliably in a wide variety of automatic teller machines, regardless of their make and age.

"We have to be careful," McDowell said. "We can go to ATM manufacturers — and they've cooperated splendidly — and say, 'Bring us a hothouse flower for laboratory tests.' What we really need to do, however, is get out on a street corner in Sheboygan, with a vending machine that's grimy and has been on active duty for 15 years, and see whether that machine will vend this product.

"A banker will come in and say, 'I'm interested in knowing whether you've got something that will work in my machines.' We'll go to that bank and those machines and get a yes or no answer. If the answer is no, we'll ask ourselves, 'How can we change this thing so it will work?' "

The benefits to the Postal Service from the successful development of ATM stamps would be obvious, McDowell continued. "It costs us 7.9¢ to have to handle a stamps-only transaction in a post office lobby," he said. "It costs us nothing to do it with an ATM; it's like our stamps-on-consignment program.

"Today, if you total up post offices, branch stations, contract stations and Postal Service vending machines, we have 80,000 retail outlets. There are 80,000 ATMs out there. So this represents an opportunity to double our reach to the consumer with no capital investment on our part

268

other than what's required to make the product."

McDowell admitted to a touch of regret over the brief life and limited use of the polyester versions of the ATM stamp. "I absolutely believe that the polyester stamp was the best postage stamp the world has ever seen," he said, "and it's kind of crazy that it turned out to be just a way station on the way to something else.

"That was a postage stamp that you could put in the pocket of your swimming trunks and go swimming with and come back and it would work perfectly. It worked perfectly for mail processing. It worked perfectly for the customers. Obviously it worked very well in an ATM. It was an incredibly complex construction, very much a high-tech thing, and it's kind of ironic to think that we would have just passed through it quickly in the pursuit of the 'ultimate postage stamp.'"

Peel here and Fold • Self-adhesive stamps • DO NOT WET • © USPS 1991

This shows how a 12-stamp sheetlet with the larger stamp format would have looked. In this version of the design, the "USA" runs vertically.

USPS officially called the new product the EXTRAordinary Liberty Torch stamp. It was sold in dollar-bill-sized sheetlets with die-cut separation, as its two predecessors had been. But instead of being commemorative-sized, 12 to a sheetlet, the stamp was of the definitive size and was dispensed in 18-stamp multiples. The face value was $5.22, but the odd amount presented no problems because the machines automatically deducted the cost from the customer's bank account.

"The cost per thousand was rather high to begin with on self-adhesives, and we knew that any economies that we could get in the process would be greatly appreciated," said Joe Brockert, the project manager. "We decided that 18 stamps was about the optimum number you could get on something the size of a dollar bill. As it turned out, that size lent itself almost perfectly to 18 regular-issue sized stamps."

The stamps were arranged sideways on the sheetlet, with a vertical pull-off strip down the middle, the removal of which facilitated peeling the individual stamps from their liner. The earlier ATM sheetlets had not had such a strip — only the 12 abutting stamps — and some customers had complained of difficulty in getting the stamps off the backing.

The pull-off strip performed two other functions, as well. Its removal allowed the sheetlet to be folded for more convenient storage in a purse or billfold. And it bore the copyright notation, along with the essential message that the stamps were self-adhesive and shouldn't be moistened. This meant that the reverse liner didn't have to be entirely dedicated to this informational purpose.

Consequently, USPS was able to use the back of the sheetlet for a "house ad" promoting its stamped envelopes with custom-printed return addresses. That message was repeated four times on the back of each sheetlet. Brockert explained why:

This is the layout of the 18-stamp sheetlet in the small stamp format, as issued. In this version, however, the message on the peelable center strip contains more words than on the final version, and is in two lines instead of one.

"We didn't know whether the printers would be able to get a good front-to-back register, and by putting four messages on the back, no matter how it shifted, either up, down, or sideways, there would still be assurance of at least one complete message. As it turned out, they got absolutely perfect front-to-back registration. Assuming they are able to continue to do that, on the next generation of these stamps we'll probably put a much bigger and more elaborate advertisement on the back, and print it only once."

The stamp, like its polyester predecessors, was a materials "sandwich," consisting of eight layers: the phosphor coating; the ink with which the stamp was printed; the stamp paper, a lightweight experimental type; a water-soluble layer to permit the stamp to be soaked off its envelope; the pressure-sensitive adhesive; a silicone layer to prevent the adhesive from bonding to the backing paper; the backing paper itself, and the printing on the back.

Avery International of Pasadena, California, which had produced the first two ATM stamps, made this one as well. The plastic stamps had been printed and die-cut on a Chesnut gravure press that USPS owned and lent to Avery. For the paper stamp, however, Avery used its own gravure press for printing and the Chesnut press for die-cutting only.

270

THREE-DIMENSIONAL VIEW
OF ATM STAMP PAPER

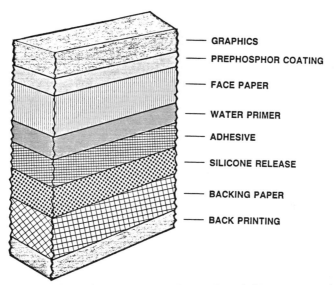

— GRAPHICS

— PREPHOSPHOR COATING

— FACE PAPER

— WATER PRIMER

— ADHESIVE

— SILICONE RELEASE

— BACKING PAPER

— BACK PRINTING

This Postal Service sketch shows the eight component layers of the Liberty Torch ATM stamp.

All margins with plate numbers and other markings were trimmed away in the process of cutting the large sheets into sheetlets for distribution.

These markings included a novel system for ensuring the front-to-back registration that had impressed Joe Brockert. On the back, in the light blue ink used to print the message, Avery printed a small bull's-eye to be lined up with a black circle printed on the front of the sheet. By looking through the translucent sheet margin, the printers could ascertain whether the two sides of the web were in register.

"Probably the most critical difference between printing the plastic stamp and the paper stamp was in the area of curl," said Alan Green, an Avery official. "Paper being moisture-sensitive, it is much harder to deal with in terms of keeping the layout consistent, and is subject to much more involvement on the part of the production people than plastic."

Because the stamp was produced under a research and development contract with Avery, it was subject to technical tinkering during its press run, and there was a possibility of physical changes in the stamp that would create new varieties or sub-varieties. However, as of this writing, none had come to stamp collectors' attention.

As part of the continuing consumer test program, the new paper stamp was sold at outlets of the participating banks: Seattle First National Bank (Seafirst) in Seattle, Washington; Equibank in Pittsburgh, Pennsylvania, and a new participant, First City Bank of Murfreesboro, Tennessee. Sheetlets were also available over the counter at philatelic centers

271

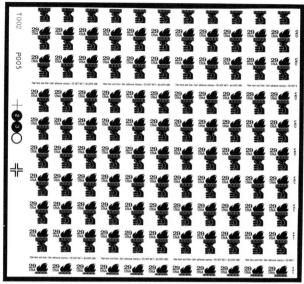

This is a portion of a cylinder proof of the Liberty Torch ATM stamp showing some of the marginal markings that were trimmed away in the production process.

throughout the country and by mail from the Philatelic Sales Division.

In April, *The Seattle Times* reported that Seafirst Bank would expand its sale of stamps from 170 ATMs in the Seattle area to nearly all of its 351 ATMs throughout the state of Washington.

The Design

Postmaster General Anthony M. Frank unveiled the design of the paper ATM stamp March 11 at an American Banking Association convention at Marco Island, Florida.

The image on the new ATM stamp was a stylized representation of the right hand of the Statue of Liberty holding her torch aloft. USPS officials had considered various color combinations — one particularly striking combination had a black torch, red flame and blue lettering — but finally decided to use more natural hues. The torch was green, a color suggestive of the patina that copper acquires with age, and the flame was gold. The USA 29 designation was in black.

Artist Harry Zelenko of New York City, who had made the stars-and-stripes design that was used on the first two ATM stamps, created this design as well. It was an adaptation of a sketch he had submitted at the same time he offered the stars-and-stripes design. His original Liberty torch had been in commemorative stamp size, but when USPS decided to make the paper ATM stamp in definitive size, Zelenko re-drew it, condensing the flame and cropping the hand just below the little finger.

Originally, the message that was prepared for the peelable center strip

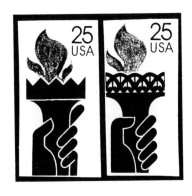

Harry Zelenko's first concept sketches for the Liberty Torch stamp were for a commemorative-size vertical stamp. Note the differing treatments of the flame and the holder in these two sketches.

on the front of the sheetlet was set in two lines. "We weren't sure how much latitude the printer was going to have to have for the die-cutting,"

In this second-stage sketch, the torch and hand were reversed, and the flame and holder were given still another look.

Joe Brockert said, "We figured it was safer to give them one line and more white space on either side in case the die cut 'floated.' "

First-Day Facts

No formal first-day ceremony was held when the stamp went on sale in New York City June 25. Collectors were given 60 days to submit pre-stamped covers, or covers plus 29¢ per stamp, for first-day cancellation.

19¢ FISHING BOAT COIL

Date of Issue: August 8, 1991

Catalog Number: Scott 2529

Colors: yellow, magenta, cyan, black

First-Day Cancel: Washington, D.C

FDCs Canceled: 82,698

Format: Coils of 500 and 3,000. Gravure printing cylinder of 684 subjects (19 across, 36 around).

Perf: 10.2 (platen perforator, designed and built by Guilford Gravure Division of George Schmitt and Company, Guilford, Connecticut)

Designer: Pierre Mion of Lovettsville, Virginia

Art Director: Howard Paine (CSAC)

Project Manager: Jack Williams (USPS)

Typographer: Bradbury Thompson (CSAC)

Modeler: CNW Incorporated, Cincinnati, Ohio

Printing: Printed by Multi-Color Corporation, Scottsburg, Indiana, for American Bank Note Company on a Schiavi 10-color webfed gravure press. Perforated and coiled at Guilford Gravure.

Quantity Ordered: 325,000,000 (175,000,000 in coils of 500; 150,000,000 in coils of 3,000)

Quantity Distributed: 294,625,000 (143,665,000 in coils of 500; 150,960,000 in coils of 3,000)

Cylinder Number Detail: 1 group of 4 gravure cylinder numbers preceded by the letter A on every 36th stamp

Tagging: phosphor-coated paper

The Stamp

When collectors read in the March-April 1991 issue of the Philatelic Sales Division's *Philatelic Catalog* that a 19¢ Fishing Boat coil, item number 7718, would be "available mid-April," they assumed that the stamp would be part of the long-running Transportation series.

April came and went without an official announcement of the stamp, however, and so did May. That didn't prevent the Philatelic Sales Division from listing the mysterious stamp in its May-June catalog — this time among the items that were immediately available. Those who ordered it from that listing, of course, were disappointed.

The May-June catalog also carried a note as part of its ordering information that the Fishing Boat coil would be gravure-printed and produced by the American Bank Note Company. That caused collectors to re-think their previous assumptions: All previous Transportation series coils had been intaglio-printed by the Bureau of Engraving and Printing. When *Linn's Stamp News* questioned Dickey Rustin, manager of the USPS Stamp Product Development Branch, he said: "I can't say what the Fishing Boat stamp will look like, but it will not look like the Transportation coils."

Finally, on July 24, USPS put out the word: The Fishing Boat coil would be issued August 8, and, as Rustin had indicated, wasn't part of the

These pencil sketches of pumpkins, a pier, a pelican and a seagull are among the ideas for mini-scape stamps that Pierre Mion turned into visible form.

Transportation series after all. It was actually a third stamp in the group of definitives that began with the Beach Umbrella booklet stamp of 1990 and continued with the Hot-Air Balloon booklet stamp issued earlier in 1991 — a group featuring simple, colorful scenes that the Citizens' Stamp Advisory Committee called "mini-scapes."

Both forerunners, like this one, were postcard-rate stamps. With the issuance of the Fishing Boat stamp, USPS customers now could choose a multicolor 19¢ stamp in one of three formats: coil, booklet and sheet (the latter being the Fawn stamp that had made its appearance March 11). One writer commented that the Fishing Boat didn't appear to have been made with vacationers in mind. It was offered only in coil rolls of 500 and 3,000, which weren't quantities that a tourist would be likely to slip into a purse or billfold before leaving home. However, the rolls were of the size widely used in vending machines at the largely automated post offices from which tourists would be mailing their cards.

The stamp was printed for ABNC by the Multi-Color Corporation of Scottsburg, Indiana. Perforating and coiling were done by George Schmitt and Company's Guilford Gravure Division of Guilford, Connecticut. The Fishing Boat was only the second coil stamp to be manufactured outside BEP, following by five weeks the first, the gravure version of the 29¢ Flag Over Mount Rushmore. Nevertheless, Rustin said, it wasn't production problems that had delayed the Fishing Boat's issuance. "We changed the release date because other stamps had higher demands," he said.

Multi-Color Corporation printed the stamp on a 19-row Schiavi press, which was a new press for plate number coil collectors. Also new was the 36-stamp interval between plate numbers. The company used 19½-inch-wide phosphored paper made by E.I. duPont de Nemours, gummed by BrownBridge and supplied by Paper Corporation of the United States.

The Design

Pierre Mion of Lovettsville, Virginia, created the simple picture of the

Pierre Mion made this rough preliminary sketch and this more developed pencil drawing as he worked toward the finished-painting stage of the Fishing Boat stamp.

276

prow of a fishing boat tied to a pier jutting from tranquil water near a marshy shoreline.

The idea grew out of a series of conversations and correspondence with Howard Paine, the Citizens' Stamp Advisory Committee design coordinator who developed the idea of the mini-scape designs. "We were doodling around with a lot of pencil sketches," Mion said. "I do a lot of landscapes and water scenes in addition to my illustrating work. It was my idea to do the front of a boat."

Like Mion's previous mini-scape designs, for the Beach Umbrella and Hot-Air Balloon booklet stamps, this painting was done in gouache (an opaque watercolor) and was based on what Mion termed "photos in my own 'morgue,' and in my head." "It's a small North Carolina-type work boat, an oyster or crabbing boat, powered by an outboard motor, with marsh grass in the background, reflected in the water," the artist said.

First-Day Facts

The stamp was issued in Washington, D.C., August 8. USPS held no formal dedication ceremony, but first-day postmarks were available at the city's main post office.

Collectors submitting addressed prestamped covers for first-day canceling were reminded that single Fishing Boat stamps on envelopes needed to be accompanied by at least 10¢ more in postage. For envelopes on which USPS affixed stamps, a 10¢ Canal Boat coil stamp from the Transportation series was used to supplement the Fishing Boat stamp.

23¢ FLAG FIRST-CLASS PRESORT RATE COIL

Date of Issue: September 27, 1991

Catalog Number: 2607

Colors: blue, red, black

First-Day Cancel: Washington, D.C

FDCs Canceled: 76,498

Format: Coils of 500 and 3,000. Gravure printing cylinders of 456 subjects (19 across, 24 around).

Perf: 10.2 (platen perforator, designed and built by Guilford Gravure Division of George Schmitt and Company)

Designer and Typographer: Terrence McCaffrey (USPS)

Art Director: Donald McDowell (USPS)

Project Manager: Joe Brockert (USPS)

Printing: Printed by Guilford Gravure for American Bank Note Company on an Andreotti 5-color webfed gravure press. Perforated and coiled at Guilford Gravure.

Quantity Ordered: 515,000,000 (35,000,000 in coils of 500; 480,000,000 in coils of 3,000)

Quantity Distributed: 515,000,000 (35,000,000 in coils of 500; 480,000,000 in coils of 3,000)

Cylinder Number Detail: 1 set of 3 cylinder numbers preceded by the letter A on every 24th stamp

Tagging: untagged

The Stamp

A 23¢ Flag stamp covering the first-class rate for presorted mail was issued in Washington September 27. It was initially sold in coils of 3,000, but USPS said coils of 500 would be available later.

The stamp bore the words "Presorted First-Class" prominently. Like

278

previous stamps that had carried that service inscription, most recently the 21¢ Railroad Mail Car coil stamp of 1988, this one was considered a precancel by USPS. Because it was designed for bulk mailings that bypassed post office facer-canceler machines, it was untagged. Postal regulations required a precancel permit for its use.

The 23¢ rate covered first-class mail sorted to the carrier route. But the stamp could also be used in false frankings for other categories of presorted first-class mail that carried higher rates, with the mailer making up the difference at the time of the mailing. These other categories were: ZIP plus 4, bar-coded, 5-digit sort, 23.3¢; ZIP plus 4, bar-coded, 3-digit sort, 23.9¢; ZIP plus 4 basic sort, 24.2¢, and basic sort, 24.8¢.

The stamp was issued to satisfy those users of first-class presorted mail who were unhappy with the 10¢ generic Tractor Trailer coil stamp, issued May 25, which bore the words "Additional Presort Postage Paid" (see chapter on the Tractor Trailer stamp). They argued that the use of a 10¢ stamp on a piece of mail for which they actually paid 23¢ or more gave the erroneous impression that the mail was excessively subsidized.

The new stamp also eliminated for mailers the nuisance of printing or rubber-stamping the required "Presorted First-Class" endorsement on envelopes (or on the stamps themselves, as some did with the 10¢ Tractor Trailer coil). The endorsement was part of the new stamp's design.

The announcement that this stamp would be issued was made July 9, along with news of a non-denominated coil stamp for regular bulk-rate mail. The two stamps would augment the 10¢ Tractor Trailer stamp and its counterpart for non-profit bulk mail, the 5¢ Canoe stamp, USPS said.

USPS explained that the first day of issue for the 23¢ Presort coil was timed to coincide with receipt of the stamps in the first post offices in the distribution system instead of the last offices.

"We first adopted this method of setting first-day issue dates during the most recent rate change," Assistant Postmaster General Gordon C. Morison said in the news release containing details about the stamp. "In previous rate changes, we received complaints internally and externally about stamps in our vaults that could not be sold because the first day of issue had not arrived.

"Our traditional method of setting first-day-of-issue dates was based on the receipt of stamps at the last post offices in the distribution chain. Meanwhile, the first offices in the chain had stamps that were vitally needed but could not be sold. With this method of establishing first-day-of-issue dates, we've solved that problem."

One consequence of this policy during 1991 was that USPS found it necessary to provide longer or extended first-day cancellation deadlines, while collectors waited for stamps to reach their local post offices.

The Design

The stamp was the fourth face-different definitive stamp of the year to include the American flag in its design. This one could be described as "flag over words," because the only other major design element was the two-line wording: "Presorted First-Class." Horizontal and vertical lines met in an "L" in the lower left corner to provide a partial border.

It was designed in an unusual way, and another unusual feature was the assigning of design credit to Donald M. McDowell, director of the Office of Stamp and Philatelic Marketing. "My contribution was more a technical contribution than a design contribution," McDowell said. "This was a stamp that you could describe as 'designed by omission.' We took an existing stamp design and subtracted elements from it.

"We had been discussing how we could, with the most dispatch, get a stamp out there for the major mailers who needed it. I suggested that we could convert a Mount Rushmore gravure coil stamp to a first-class presort stamp with some changes in the gravure cylinders. We could leave the flag exactly where it was, and remove the mountain scene and replace it with the necessary typography."

As the plan developed, the American Bank Note Company, which produced the 29¢ Mount Rushmore gravure stamp, was able to use the same red cylinder it had been using for the stripes on the flag over Rushmore, but had to redo the blue cylinder that had printed the flag's field in order to include the wording on the new stamp. ABNC also replaced the Rushmore stamp's brown cylinder with a black cylinder to print the L-shaped frameline and "USA 23."

The only conventional artwork that was made in the entire process was a pencil sketch by McDowell with which he showed his associates how the L-shaped line would provide the necessary design base.

"It was one of the fastest stamp design projects on record," McDowell said. "Afterward, we all sort of chuckled over the question, 'Who's going to get design credit?'" It turned out to be McDowell himself, his first such official acknowledgment in a long supervisory career in USPS stamp development and marketing.

The flag that was borrowed for the design had been created by Clarence Holbert of the Bureau of Engraving and Printing when he designed the original intaglio version of the Mount Rushmore coil.

First-Day Facts

No first-day ceremony was held, but first-day cancellations were provided. For covers that were completely serviced by USPS, one presort stamp and one 6¢ Walter Lippmann stamp from the Great Americans series were used to meet the 29¢ first-class rate.

$1 USPS OLYMPIC SPONSORSHIP

Date of Issue: September 29, 1991

Catalog Number: Scott 2539

Colors: red, yellow, blue, black, green, gold

First-Day Cancel: Orlando, Florida

FDCs Canceled: 69,241

Format: Panes of 20, vertical, 5 across, 4 down. Gravure printing cylinders of 180 subjects (15 across, 12 around) manufactured by Armotek Industries Inc., Palmyra, New Jersey.

Perf: 10.9 (L perforator)

Selvage Markings: "© USPS 1991"/36 USC 380"

Designer, Typographer, Art Director and Project Manager: Terrence McCaffrey (USPS)

Modeler: Richard Sennett, Stamp Venturers

Printing: Stamps printed by Stamp Venturers on a Champlain gravure press at J.W. Fergusson and Sons, Richmond, Virginia. Stamps perforated, processed and shipped at KCS Industries Inc., Milwaukee, Wisconsin.

Quantity Ordered: 60,000,000

Quantity Distributed: 60,000,000

Cylinder Number Detail: 6 gravure numbers preceded by the letter S alongside each of the 4 corner stamps

Tagging: phosphor-coated paper

The Stamp

On September 29, USPS issued what it described as a definitive stamp in the $1 denomination to publicize its sponsorship of the 1992 Winter and Summer Olympic Games.

Assistant Postmaster General Sherry A. Cagnoli unveiled the design July 29 in Tampa, Florida. She appeared at a news conference announcing the receipt by the U.S. Olympic Committee of the official invitations from the International Olympic Committee in Switzerland to participate in the 1992 Summer Olympic Games in Barcelona, Spain.

The stamp, in commemorative size arranged vertically, was issued in panes of 20 with plate numbers at all four corners, in the format that USPS has used for its high-value stamps since 1987. It was gravure-printed for Stamp Venturers by J.W. Fergusson and Sons of Richmond, Virginia.

The question of whether the stamp was really needed was raised by Michael Laurence, editor of *Linn's Stamp News*, in his column in *Linn's*. It was the third $1 definitive to be issued in little more than two years, the others being the Johns Hopkins sheet stamp of 1989 and the Seaplane coil of 1990. Laurence suggested that the new stamp's reason for being was the desire of USPS to recoup the millions of dollars it had invested in Olympic sponsorship by selling high-priced stamps to collectors.

Bill McAllister, stamp columnist for *The Washington Post*, asked Assistant Postmaster General Gordon S. Morison to comment on those points. Morison told him the stamp was needed.

The $1 Seaplane coil was created for large-volume mailers and for use in vending machines, Morison said. That left the Hopkins stamp as the only $1 sheet stamp available for use by the thousands of small post offices that lack postage meters. Supplies of the Hopkins were dwindling fast, Morison told McAllister, down to 10 million in September 1991. By October, he said, "we're going to be basically out of them."

The USPS procurement contract with the Bureau of Engraving and Printing made production of additional Hopkins stamps unwise, justifying a new $1 stamp, Morison said. "Since we're sponsoring the Olympics, it seems a natural thing" to promote the Games, he added. A stamp displaying the USPS and Olympic logos had been specifically requested by the Postal Service's Office of Olympic Marketing.

The stamp's Olympic theme, however, did represent a diversion from a plan USPS had announced only the year before for the "conversion of high-value sheet stamps from the Great Americans series to the colorful, commemorative-size Wildlife series." The announcement was made at the time a new $2 Bobcat definitive was issued. "Eventually the format of the $1 and $5 regular issues will follow in the tracks of the Bobcat stamp," USPS said. "Eventually," as it turned out, didn't mean 1991.

The Design

The stamp's design featured the USPS logo — a stylized drawing of a bald eagle with the words "United States Postal Service" in blue,

282

separated by a red horizontal bar — in the top one-third of the design. The letters USA, in red, and the five interlocking Olympic rings, in blue, yellow, black, green and red, appeared in the center of the design. The words "Official Sponsor of the 1992 U.S. Olympic Team," in blue, and "$1," in red, were in the lower third. A wide vertical border in metallic gold appeared on either side of the stamp.

In designing the stamp, USPS was constrained by guidelines established by the U.S. Olympic Committee for use of the Olympic rings in conjunction with the Postal Service logo. These guidelines dictated the relative size of the elements and their positioning in relation to each other.

For that reason, several designs that were worked up in definitive-stamp size by Richard Sheaff, a design coordinator for the Citizens' Stamp Advisory Committee, were found to be unsuitable. For one reason or other, they didn't meet the criteria. Eventually, Terrence McCaffrey of USPS developed a design that worked, but it was in commemorative size, arranged vertically, to accommodate the necessary vertical stacking of the logo elements and also to comfortably locate the denomination and the two lines of explanatory text.

The Olympic Marketing Division was emphatic in its request that the Olympic rings be printed in their natural colors, but this posed a potential printing problem. The black, green and yellow rings would be the only appearance of those colors on the stamp, and they were quite small. As

Richard Sheaff worked up these design concepts in definitive-stamp size before it was decided that a larger stamp would be necessary to accommodate all the design elements in the required size and relationship to each other.

283

Richard Sennett, head of Stamp Venturers, explained it, when very little of a specific color appears on a stamp, there may not be enough ink on that color's gravure cylinder to lubricate the doctor blades that wipe the excess ink away before the cylinder and paper web come together to create the printed image. For that reason, Sennett thought it might be necessary to print extra patches of the three colors along the vertical edges of the stamps and then cover them up with the metallic gold border. However, that step turned out to be unnecessary; the presses at Fergusson & Sons functioned satisfactorily without it.

The USPS logo had previously appeared on the 8¢ stamp (Scott 1396) issued July 1, 1971, to mark the creation of the U.S. Postal Service as the successor to the U.S. Post Office Department, and on the insignia of the three figures in the 25¢ Letter Carriers commemorative of 1989 (Scott 2420). It had also been shown many times as an auxiliary to stamp designs: in stamp selvage, for example, and on the reverse side of the 10¢ Postal People commemoratives of 1973 (Scott 1489-1498).

First-Day Facts

Associate Postmaster General Edward E. Horgan Jr. dedicated the stamp as part of the opening ceremony for the National Postal Forum exhibit hall at Marriott's Orlando World Center. The Postal Forum was a national conference of business mailers, trade suppliers and postal officials. Principal speaker at the event was Bruce Jenner, who won the gold medal in the Olympic decathlon in 1976.

USPS furnished a pictorial first-day handstamp depicting the USPS eagle logo and the five Olympic rings.

NONDENOMINATED (10¢) EAGLE AND SHIELD BULK RATE COIL

Date of Issue: December 13, 1991

Catalog Number: Scott 2604

Colors: blue, red, green, gold, black

First-Day Cancel: Kansas City, Missouri

FDCs Canceled: 31,341

Format: Coils of 500, 3,000 and 10,000. Gravure printing cylinders of 456 subjects (19 across, 24 around).

Perf: 10.2 (platen perforator designed and built by Guilford Gravure Division of George Schmitt and Company, Guilford, Connecticut)

Designer: Chris Calle of Ridgefield, Connecticut

Typographer: John Boyd of Anagraphics Inc., New York, New York

Art Director: Jack Williams (USPS)

Project Manager: Joe Brockert (USPS)

Printing: Printed by Guilford Gravure for American Bank Note Company on Andreotti 5-color webfed gravure press. Perforated and coiled at Guilford Gravure.

Quantity Ordered: 922,000,000 (228,000,000 in coils of 500; 594,000,000 in coils of 3,000; 100,000,000 in coils of 10,000)

Quantity Distributed: not available

Cylinder Number Detail: 1 group of 5 gravure cylinder numbers preceded by the letter A on every 24th stamp

Tagging: untagged

The Stamp

The last postal item of 1991 was a "fix-it" stamp — one of two late-blooming stamps issued to fix a problem that had developed from an innovation earlier in the year. It was a non-denominated coil for bulk mailers, and it officially went on sale December 13.

The February 3 rate change had brought with it more than a dozen fractional rates for bulk mail, depending on the degree to which the mailer

The Chris Calle eagle and shield design on the bulk-rate coil was originally proposed for the experimental self-adhesive stamp of 1989, for which Jay Haiden's design, shown here, was used.

presorted his mailings. USPS originally planned to produce only two stamps to accommodate those rates: a 5¢ stamp for non-profit mail and a 10¢ stamp for other types of third-class mail and presorted first-class mail. Because both these stamps had denominations lower than the lowest rate in the class, their use on mail would constitute a false franking, and the users were required to write a check with each mailing to cover the difference.

But, as explained previously (see chapters on Canoe, Tractor Trailer and Flag Presorted First-Class Rate stamps), the Postal Service's plan created an unforeseen problem for mailers. The problem had its roots in the very reason that non-profit and commercial mailers use stamps instead of the more economical imprinted envelopes or postage meters.

Market research told them that the public is more likely to open a letter bearing a stamp. And firms that send out large mailings are willing to pay more for stamp use because their fundamental need is to have their message read by the addressee. As Robert Rabinowitz, writing in *Stamp Collector*, noted:

"The public has the perception that bulk rate ('junk') mail travels for almost nothing. Part of the psychology of using a stamp is first to have the public believe it's 'just another letter' and, should the recipient note the postage employed, to get the feeling that the sender felt that the message was important enough to invest whatever the cost of that particular sort was.

"Today a third-class mailing with a basic sort really costs the mailer 19.8¢, but with the new stamps, the public sees only a 10¢ denomination.

Calle's original eagle had a small shield with only five red stripes and no stars.

286

The net result is that the message is cheapened in the eyes of the receiver."

Mail Advertising Service Association International (MASA) complained to the Postal Service about the 10¢ stamp. As a result, USPS agreed to issue a non-denominated bulk-rate coil stamp later in 1991. Mailers would buy the stamps at the per-stamp cost assigned by USPS, and would pay the balance of the postage due at the time they used the stamps for a bulk mailing. Because the stamps would carry no denomination, the public wouldn't be misled into thinking the mail was being handled at an absurdly low rate.

USPS formally announced on July 9 that the new stamp would be issued in the fall, along with the other "fix-it" stamp — a 23¢ stamp for presorted first-class mailings. The announcement made no specific reference to the MASA complaint, however. It noted only that the 5¢ and 10¢ stamps had been issued "for use while the stamp demand picture cleared after the February rate change" and that "mailers' specific needs" had now "become clear."

In its July 9 announcement, USPS said the non-denominated stamp would have a face value of 5¢. But later, when the details were disclosed, it turned out that the price would be twice that amount: 10¢ per stamp.

In the interim, Postal Service staffers had had second thoughts. There was no reason to set the denomination of the stamp below 10¢, they realized, because all bulk-rate categories called for per-piece payments higher than that. Charging a dime rather than a nickel meant that income from sales to collectors would be doubled. And there would be more revenue in the "float" — the period between the time the Postal Service sells a stamp and the buyer redeems it by using it on a piece of mail.

"We think this stamp can be used indefinitely," said Joe Brockert, the stamp's project manager. "Even when rates change, there's no reason why we can't continue to sell it for 10¢, and the mailers can't continue to pay the difference between that and postage. Now, the mailers may get

Calle based his eagle and shield design on this photograph of a model for a pedimental figure at the Illinois Merchant Bank, Chicago, by Henry Hering. Note that on the original there are oak and laurel leaves on either side of the sculpture, and the bank's monogram on the shield.

tired of using this after a year or two, and in that case we'll replace it, but it won't be because there's been a change in rates."

Interestingly, several of these points had been made earlier in a prescient article by postal-rate expert Henry W. Beecher in *The United States Specialist* for January 1991. In the article, titled "Are Discount-Rate Stamps Or Any Precancels Needed?" Beecher took note of the widespread use of false franking (a term that he had coined several years earlier) and the fact that mailers could pay discount-rate postage more cheaply by using permit imprints rather than stamps. He argued that discount-rate stamps should be eliminated altogether.

"I suggest that they be replaced by adhesive permit imprint labels provided by the Postal Service," Beecher wrote. "These labels could be in the same coil format as existing stamps, and in their designs, colors and method of printing be at least as attractive as the current Transportation series coils. Their inscriptions would include the legend 'USA Postage Paid' and a short designation of the subclass . . . The labels could be sold uniformly at a price sufficient to cover their cost of production and distribution, perhaps one or two cents each . . . Mailers should like them even better than the denominated labels: no longer would they be telling recipients of their mail that they paid 5.3¢ to mail a packet that would cost the casual mailer 85¢ . . . No longer would there be the problem of preparing stamps in new denominations required by a rate change . . . Philatelic sales outlets could sell these labels to collectors in any quantity at the same nominal price that mailers pay."

Although some of the details differed, Beecher's proposed permit label was quite close to what USPS actually came up with after its experiment with the 5¢ and 10¢ denominated bulk-rate coil stamps of 1991 proved unsuccessful.

The Design

Chris Calle's design subject was a Postal Service "golden oldie" — an American eagle fronted by a shield. The same subject, in various styles and configurations, has appeared on many U.S. stamps, going back to 1869. As the central image of the Great Seal of the United States, for instance, it has been featured on every one of the current series of Official Mail stamps, stamped envelopes and postal cards.

Calle had originally submitted his gold-colored eagle sketch for consideration for the 25¢ experimental self-adhesive stamp issued in 1989. For that stamp, however, Jay Haiden's somewhat different-looking eagle and shield was chosen. Because Calle's drawing was basically square, it would allow ample room at the top or bottom of a stamp for an endorsement inscription, and so USPS put it away for the day when a full-color stamp with endorsement would be needed. That day arrived.

USPS Postmaster General Anthony M. Frank approved the design for the bulk-rate stamp September 17, 1991. A few changes were made electronically in Calle's artwork during the modeling phase: The shield

288

was enlarged, the number of red stripes was increased from five to seven to correspond to the number on the American flag, and four stars were added to the shield's blue panel.

USPS considered printing the stamp in process colors, but didn't like the proofs that the printer, Guilford Gravure, made using four-color separations. Other options were the use of self-colors and the use of metallic gold ink.

"The printers found an appropriate yellow-orange self-color to give us a simulated gold," Brockert said. "That, with the black for detail, blue, red and green gave us the colors we needed.

"We decided we really didn't have enough time to test the metallic inks and be sure we had one that would be satisfactory when we got into full production. We found some good ones, and Guilford made some proofs, some with metallic on the eagle, some in which the entire stamp was printed on metallic-coated paper. But we didn't want to take the chance that it wouldn't work."

Calle had based his eagle and shield on a published photograph of a model by sculptor Henry Hering for a pedimental figure for the Illinois Merchant Bank in Chicago. The original sculpture had the bank's "IMB" monogram on the shield.

First-Day Facts

The stamp was released without ceremony December 13 in Kansas City, Missouri, which is the location of the USPS Philatelic Sales Division's principal facility.

Collectors were given until February 11, 1992, to order first-day cancellations. On covers completely serviced by USPS, one Eagle and Shield stamp and one 19¢ Fishing Boat coil stamp were affixed to each envelope to make the 29¢ first-class rate.

Like many other stamps of 1991, this one appeared on mail before the official issue date. The first reported pre-first day use of the Eagle and Shield stamp was on a cover dated December 6.

11¢ Caboose (Unprecanceled, Untagged)

On September 25, 1991, without prior notice, USPS placed into service an unprecanceled, untagged version of the 11¢ Caboose coil stamp in the Transportation series. The action, USPS said, was "in response to major mailers' needs under the postage rate structure implemented earlier this year."

The stamp was originally issued February 3, 1984. Printed on BEP's B press, it was the first Transportation coil to appear without joint lines. The sleeve number (1) appeared on every 52nd stamp, rather than at the standard 24-stamp interval on stamps printed on the old Cottrell presses.

At that time, the Caboose stamp, which had a "Bulk Rate" service inscription in its design, was printed both precanceled (with two continuous parallel black lines) and non-precanceled. The non-precanceled version, created for collectors, had block-over-vignette phosphorescent tagging to activate facer-canceler machines. This was necessary for use by collectors on first-class mail. The precanceled version was untagged.

The new version, printed on BEP's C press, was readily distinguishable from the old. It had no black precancel lines but, unlike the 1984 collector version, was untagged. Also, the sleeve number was 2, rather than 1, and appeared at 48-stamp intervals, rather than 52.

Other Tagging Varieties

A large number of tagging varieties of previously issued definitive stamps were created in 1991, primarily as a result of two policies. One was the decision of the Bureau of Engraving and Printing, announced in 1990, to produce all future stamps with "full-coverage tagging," meaning by applying overall tagging or by using prephosphored or phosphor-

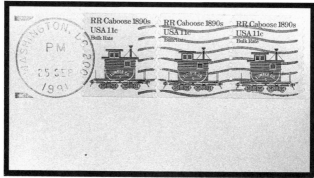

A cropped cover showing a first-day cancel of the reprinted and re-released 11¢ Caboose stamp of the Transportation series. Stamp on the left is the 1984 tagged collector version; pair on the right is the untagged reprint.

290

coated paper. The other was the Postal Service's decision, effective in January 1991, to stop tagging stamps with a face value below 10¢ (see chapter on 5¢ Steam Carriage coil).

Previously block tagged stamps that were found with overall tagging in 1991 were: 23¢ Mary Cassatt (Scott 2182); 45¢ Samuel Langley airmail (Scott C118), earliest known date of use January 22; 30¢ Frank Laubach (Scott 1864a), earliest known date July 23; 50¢ Chester Nimitz with bull's-eye perforations (Scott 1869a), July 15. The Nimitz stamp, when originally issued in 1985, was overall tagged, but was perforated on the L perforator, which leaves imperfect perforation intersections. Since 1986, it had been perforated on the Eureka (bull's-eye) perforator and had been block-tagged.

In addition, the 23¢ Cassatt and 10¢ Red Cloud (Scott 2176) were also produced on phosphor-coated paper, making a third variety of each of these Great Americans stamps. Red Cloud, like Cassatt, had previously been issued with both block and overall tagging. The earliest known use of the phosphor-coated Cassatt was on May 24.

Previously tagged stamps that were found untagged in 1991 were: 4¢ Father Flanagan (Scott 2171), earliest known date of use February 7; 1¢ re-engraved Omnibus coil (Scott 2225), March 6; 5¢ Circus Wagon coil (Scott 2452), August 27, and 5¢ Munoz Marin (Scott 2173).

AIRMAIL AND EXPEDITED MAIL

Four airmail stamps were issued in 1991, two of them in the Pioneers of Aviation series and one in the omnibus America series sponsored by the Postal Union of the Americas, Spain and Portugal. There was also a tagging variety of an older stamp, the Pioneers airmail honoring Samuel P. Langley. (This variety is described in the Revised Definitives chapter in the Definitives section of the *Yearbook*.)

In addition, 1991 saw three new expedited-mail items: a $2.90 Priority Mail stamp and $9.95 and $14 Express Mail stamps, the latter bearing the highest face value of any U.S. stamp ever issued for use by the general public. Each of the three displayed the five interlocking Olympic rings, which prompted charges that USPS, as an official Olympic Games sponsor, was going after extra dollars from collectors by making sports topicals out of mega-value stamps that had no inherent sports connection.

$9.95 EAGLE (EXPRESS MAIL)

Date of Issue: June 16, 1991

Catalog Number: Scott 2541

Colors: magenta, yellow, cyan, black (offset); black (intaglio)

First-Day Cancel: Sacramento, California

FDCs Canceled: 68,657

Format: Panes of 20, horizontal, semi-jumbo, 5 across, 4 down. Offset printing plates of 120 subjects (12 across, 10 around) and intaglio printing sleeves of 120 subjects (12 across, 10 around).

Perf: 10.9 (L perforator)

Selvage Markings: "© USPS 1991 36 USC 380"

Artist: Ned Seidler of Hampton Bay, New York

Designer, Typographer and Project Manager: Terrence McCaffrey (USPS)

Art Director: Joe Brockert (USPS)

Engraver: Armandina Lozano (American Bank Note Company)

Printing: printed by American Bank Note Company, Los Angeles, California (formerly Jeffries Banknote Division) on a Miller 4-color sheetfed offset press and a Giori Simplex 3-color sheetfed intaglio press

Quantity Ordered: 40,000,000

Quantity Distributed: 40,000,000

Sleeve/Plate Number Detail: in each of 4 corners, 1 intaglio sleeve number opposite corner stamp and 4 offset plate numbers preceded by the letter A in adjacent selvage

Tagging: untagged

293

The Stamp

On June 16, USPS issued its fourth stamp to prepay postage for its overnight Express Mail service. The denomination was $9.95, which covered the eight-ounce rate established February 3. Previous Express Mail stamps had sold for $9.35 (1983), $10.75 (1985) and $8.75 (1988).

The design was unveiled February 12 by Deborah K. Bowker, assistant postmaster general for communications, during a press conference at the U.S. Olympic Committee (USOC) headquarters in Colorado Springs, Colorado. The event had been called to announce the receipt by the USOC of the official invitations from the International Olympic Committee to participate in the 1992 Winter Olympic Games in Albertville, France.

The design of the new stamp, like those of its Express Mail predecessors, featured a bald eagle, but this one also had something new. As part of its promotional campaign as a corporate sponsor of the 1992 Olympic Games, USPS included in the stamp design the five interlocking Olympic rings. It was the first time these rings had appeared on a U.S. stamp that didn't directly commemorate the Games.

"Expedited mail is the category of our sponsorship," Michael O'Hara, a USPS spokesman, told *Linn's Stamp News.* "We determined it would be appropriate to put it on the Express Mail stamp."

Nevertheless, *Linn's* editorially criticized the design decision. Under the heading "Get Rid of Those Rings," the paper wrote in its March 4, 1991, edition:

"With this stamp, the United States Postal Service decisively steps backward into the ranks of stamp-issuing entities that crank out adhesives that have a strong topical hook and no earthly justification.

"No Olympic Games are currently under way . . . And, to the best of our knowledge, there are no Olympic Games for bald eagles. So why is this logo on the highest face-value regular U.S. postage stamp (sic) ever issued? The answer is that this is the first big step by the USPS towards recouping the estimated $10 to $15 million it agreed to ante up as an official sponsor of the 1992 Olympics . . .

"We have no quarrel in general with Olympic stamps, a popular specialty within the larger topic of sports philately . . . But a stamp with a face value of almost $10 and no Olympic connection other than the logo strikes us as cynical profiteering."

One *Linn's* reader, in rebuttal, termed the issue "a tempest in a teapot." "You should feel free to collect or not collect what you want," he wrote. "An Olympics topicalist should be able to decide whether to include a stamp that has no relation except some rings in his collection."

A few months before the new stamp appeared, USPS introduced a new Express Mail envelope designed for the convenience of business mailers. It turned out to be very inconvenient for stamp collectors, however.

On the new envelope, USPS form EP-13A, printed in September 1990, the square designated to receive the postage stamp lay across the

294

envelope's tear-strip opener. This meant that if a mailer properly affixed an Express Mail stamp to the envelope, the stamp would be destroyed by the act of opening the envelope.

Several collectors wrote to *Linn's* complaining that business sources from which they obtained used copies of Express Mail stamps were now supplying them with torn specimens. USPS officials told *Linn's* that the envelope wasn't intentionally designed to destroy stamps as a revenue-protection measure. They said the envelope was designed with aesthetics, not collectors, in mind, and promised that when the Express Mail envelope was next redesigned, officials would take into consideration the collectibility of the stamps affixed to it.

The Design

Young & Rubicam of New York, the advertising agency that handled Express Mail promotion for USPS, had designed the first two Express Mail stamps. In 1988, to design the third stamp, USPS had selected Ned Seidler of Hampton Bay, New York. The Expedited Mail Branch of USPS was so pleased with Seidler's stamp design that it commissioned him to design the new Express Mail envelopes previously mentioned.

Then, in 1990, when the Office of Stamp and Philatelic Marketing began the planning process for Express Mail and Priority Mail stamps to match the anticipated new rates, Expedited Mail sent over two of Seidler's eagle designs — one of an eagle in flight, the other of an eagle's

This is the result of an Express Mail envelope opened according to instructions: a ripped and destroyed Express Mail stamp.

295

Joe Brockert made this preliminary mockup, using the eagle head against a blue background that Ned Seidler had painted for Express Mail envelopes.

head — with the suggestion that the images be used on the new stamps.

"It turned into kind of a circular thing," said Joe Brockert, art director for the $9.95 Express Mail and $2.90 Priority Mail stamps.

The first three Express Mail stamps had shown the moon in the sky behind the eagle's head, but the Expedited Mail officials didn't want the moon used on the newer ones. To create the $9.95 stamp design, Brockert decided to adapt the Seidler head-and-shoulders eagle.

He did a quick pasteup of the artwork, roughing in the type and the Olympic rings and incorporating the blue background from the Express Mail envelope. Terrence McCaffrey, a USPS program manager for philatelic design, then reworked Brockert's design in pencil on onionskin paper. McCaffrey moved the type and rings elsewhere on the stamp, made them considerably larger, and converted the typeface for the USA and the denomination to the squarish letters and numbers prescribed by

This is Terrence McCaffrey's pencil sketch on tissue, made for the purpose of guiding graphics specialist John Boyd in putting together the finished design.

296

the U.S. Olympic Committee.

The Brockert mockup and the McCaffrey changes were then sent to John Boyd of Anagraphics Inc. in New York City, who photoset the type and rings and put together the finished product. On McCaffrey's instructions, Boyd also changed the background color to red. This change was made "for variety's sake," McCaffrey said (although the color was similar to the background hue used on the second Express Mail stamp, in 1985). Postmaster General Anthony M. Frank gave final approval to the design January 9, 1991.

The stamp was printed by a combination of offset and intaglio by the Jeffries Banknote Division of the American Bank Note Company in Los Angeles, California. It was the first offset-intaglio combination U.S. stamp to be printed outside the Bureau of Engraving and Printing. Though security engraving is a profession dominated by men, the engraver of this stamp was a woman, Armandina Lozano.

First-Day Facts

Harry Usher, president of the Los Angeles U.S. Olympic Festival Committee, was the principal speaker at the June 16 first-day ceremony on the steps of the California state capitol in Sacramento. Edward E. Horgan Jr., associate postmaster general, dedicated the stamp. The welcome was given by Heather Fargo, Sacramento's vice mayor.

At the end of the ceremony, the Olympic Festival torch was lit by a flame from a miner's lamp that was delivered "Express Mail" from U.S. Olympic Committee headquarters in Colorado Springs by former U.S. Olympian Shirley Babashoff, wearing a Postal Service carrier's uniform. The torch was then carried off on the first leg of its trip across California, via relay runners, to the Olympic Festival in Los Angeles. Also participating in the ceremony was Bob Mathias, former decathlon gold medalist for the United States.

USPS provided a pictorial handstamped first-day postmark, which, like the stamp, depicted an eagle's head and the five Olympic rings. The grace period for submitting covers for first-day cancellation was originally set at 30 days and eventually extended to 150 days (November 13) because of the difficulty collectors encountered in obtaining the stamps.

$14 EAGLE (EXPRESS MAIL)

Date of Issue: August 31, 1991

Catalog Number: Scott 2542

Colors: magenta, yellow, cyan, black (offset); red (intaglio)

First-Day Cancel: Hunt Valley, Maryland

FDCs Canceled: 54,727

Format: Panes of 20, horizontal, semi-jumbo, 5 across, 4 down. Offset printing plates of 120 subjects (12 across, 10 around) and intaglio printing sleeves of 120 subjects (12 across, 10 around).

Perf: 10.9 (L perforator)

Selvage Markings: "© USPS 1991 36 USC 380"

Designer: Timothy Knepp of Laurel, Maryland

Art Director, Typographer and Project Manager: Terrence McCaffrey (USPS)

Engraver: Dick Jones, American Bank Note Company

Modeler: Newell Colour Inc., Los Angeles, California

Printing: Printed by American Bank Note Company, Los Angeles, California (formerly Jeffries Banknote Division) on a 4-color Miller sheetfed offset press and 3-color Giori Simplex sheetfed intaglio press.

Quantity Ordered: 30,000,000, reduced to 5,166,000

Quantity Distributed: 5,166,000

Sleeve/Plate Number Detail: In each of 4 corners, 1 intaglio sleeve number opposite corner stamp and 4 offset plate numbers preceded by letter A in adjacent selvage.

Tagging: untagged

The Stamp

The second Express Mail stamp of 1991 was created for international mail and bore the denomination of $14.

The $14 rate was the highest of three rates established by USPS for Express Mail weighing up to one-half pound and bound for foreign

298

These are Timothy Knepp's first two color sketches for the high-value Express Mail stamp. The first one was short of detail and color. The second was more satisfactory but still needed additional refinement. (Knepp inadvertently omitted the Olympic rings from his second sketch.)

destinations. It applied to countries in rate groups 4, 5 and 6, which included Eastern Europe, the Soviet Union, Spain, Latin America, Africa and the Middle East.

The other rates were $11.50 for countries in rate group 1, which included Canada, Great Britain, Mexico and Northern Ireland, and $13 for countries in groups 2 and 3, which covered most of Western Europe and the Pacific Rim, including Germany, France, Japan and Korea.

Art Shealy, a USPS spokesman, told *Linn's Stamp News* that USPS chose the highest of the three rates for the new stamp because the volume to countries in rate groups 4, 5 and 6 made up 39 percent of all international Express Mail. "When the choice was to issue one stamp," he said, "it was logical to have it be the rate that is used for the majority of the countries."

Nevertheless, *Linn's* wondered why USPS hadn't put an $11.50 denomination on the stamp. Additional stamps could have been added as needed to make up the $13 and $14 rates, *Linn's* pointed out. Even so, the paper thanked USPS on behalf of collectors for issuing only one international Express Mail stamp instead of three.

The $14 denomination was by far the highest ever assigned to a U.S. stamp for general use. It topped the old record of $10.75 set by the domestic Express Mail stamp that was issued in 1985.

The new stamp was originally scheduled to be released September 6 in Indianapolis, Indiana. Later the date and place were changed, and the stamp was issued August 31 in Hunt Valley, Maryland, a Baltimore suburb, in conjunction with the Balpex stamp show. Its design wasn't made public until a few days before issuance, and most collectors didn't see a picture of the stamp until after the issue date.

The Design

Artist Timothy Knepp of Laurel, Maryland, had done some assignments for Terrence McCaffrey when McCaffrey worked in the USPS art department. These assignments included the Creatures of the Sea posters used to publicize National Stamp Collecting Month in 1990. When

McCaffrey became a program manager for philatelic design and was assigned to oversee the 1991 Express Mail and Priority Mail stamps, he decided to try Knepp on an eagle image for the $14 stamp.

Knepp collected eagle photographs, including some he made himself at the National Zoo in Washington, and then went to work. He first made several sketches of eagle heads, but eagle heads had already been selected for 1991's two earlier expedited-mail stamps, and McCaffrey asked for something different: a complete eagle, shown in flight. Knepp quickly came up with a color sketch that both men liked. It depicted a bird, wings spread fully, seen from above as it flew inland across a rocky coastline, to convey the idea of international mail.

"We didn't want to go the route that Young & Rubicam (the Postal Service's advertising agency) had gone, with the eagle soaring past the Eiffel Tower or some such landmark," McCaffrey said. "That would have been really international, but we wanted to make this an American stamp design."

However, the eagle Knepp had painted was dark, its feathers were undefined, and the land beneath was partly obscured by fog. "Too monochromatic," McCaffrey told the artist. "It needs some life." So Knepp came back with a sunlit scene, with more detail in the feathers and trees and more color.

This, with a few more modifications, became the accepted design.

"It was a matter of refining it until we got what we wanted," McCaffrey said. "It wasn't an easy assignment. For one thing, this view of an eagle, looking down from above, is an unusual one. There aren't any stock photographs taken from that angle. So Tim had to pretty much make a composite, working from a number of his own and other photos."

Postmaster General Anthony M. Frank approved the design June 5, 1991. The stamp was printed by a combination of offset and intaglio, with intaglio used for the the typography only.

First-Day Facts

USPS held no first-day ceremony for the stamp at the Balpex show. However, Balpex officials arranged first-day activities at the Marriott Hunt Valley Inn, site of the show. Designer Timothy Knepp, who lived nearby, was on hand to autograph covers and the generic first-day folders that USPS made available. USPS supplied a pictorial first-day handstamp featuring an eagle descending for a landing and the five Olympic rings.

Collectors were first given 60 days after the issue date to submit covers for first-day cancellation. Later an additional 30 days was allowed.

$2.90 EAGLE (PRIORITY MAIL)

Date of Issue: July 7, 1991

Catalog Number: Scott 2540

Colors: magenta, yellow, cyan, black (offset); black (intaglio)

First-Day Cancel: San Diego, California

FDCs Canceled: 79,555

Format: Panes of 20, vertical, 4 across, 5 down. Offset printing plates of 120 subjects (12 across, 10 around); intaglio printing sleeves of 120 subjects (12 across, 10 around).

Perf: 10.9 (L perforator)

Selvage Markings: "© USPS 1991 36 USC 380."

Designer, Typographer and Project Manager: Terrence McCaffrey (USPS)

Art Director: Joe Brockert (USPS)

Engraver: Armandina Lozano (American Bank Note Company)

Printing: Printed by American Bank Note Company, Los Angeles, California (formerly Jeffries Banknote Division) on a 4-color Miller offset sheetfed press and 3-color Giori Simplex sheetfed intaglio press.

Quantity Ordered: 70,000,000

Quantity Delivered: 40,000,000

Plate/Sleeve Number Detail: In each of 4 corners, 1 intaglio sleeve number alongside corner stamp and 4 offset plate numbers preceded by the letter A in adjacent selvage. Sleeve number is inverted in relation to plate numbers.

Tagging: phosphor-coated paper

The Stamp

On July 7 USPS issued a stamp bearing the $2.90 denomination to cover the rate that took effect February 3 for Priority Mail weighing up to two pounds to all delivery zones.

The stamp replaced the $2.40 stamp that had been issued July 20, 1989, to meet the then-current Priority Mail rate. Like its predecessor, the new stamp bore no inscription referring to Priority Mail service.

The earlier stamp had been issued in conjunction with the celebration of the 20th anniversary of the first manned moon landing, and bore a picture of two astronauts planting the American flag on the cratered lunar surface. At that time, USPS officials said that the topic of space exploration might be a continuing theme for Priority Mail stamps.

However, the new stamp featured not a space design but the head of a bald eagle. Thus USPS appropriated for Priority Mail the design theme it had already firmly established for its Express Mail stamps — a theme that had been restated three weeks earlier with the $9.95 Express Mail stamp that was issued on June 16.

The $2.90 Priority Mail and $9.95 Express Mail stamps had other things in common, as well. Both were printed by a combination of offset and intaglio by the Jeffries Bank Note subsidiary of American Bank Note Company. Both were designed by Terrence McCaffrey, a USPS program manager, philatelic design. Both vignettes were engraved by American Bank Note's Armandina Lozano.

And both displayed as a design element the five-ring Olympic Games symbol — a feature that *Linn's Stamp News* had criticized editorially after the Express Mail design was unveiled because it made a sports topical stamp out of a stamp with no sports connection (see chapter on $9.95 Express Mail stamp).

Unlike the Express Mail stamp, however, the new Priority Mail stamp was printed with a minor error that USPS decided to leave uncorrected. The intaglio sleeve number, which appeared in the selvage next to each of the four corner stamps on the 20-stamp panes, was printed upside down in relation to the four offset sleeve numbers in the adjoining selvage.

According to a Postal Service release, "Since the orientation of the plate numbers does not affect the stamps themselves, this orientation will not be changed and will continue on all future printings of this stamp to avoid creation of a philatelic variety." ("Aw, nuts," was *Stamp Collector's* ironic comment.)

Copies of the Priority Mail stamp that were used on the specially designed Priority Mail envelopes provided by USPS were doomed to almost certain destruction because of the envelope's design. The flap side of the cover was on the front instead of on the back, and the easy-open pull tab ran across the space designated for the stamps. Thus, a recipient who followed the printed instructions for opening the envelope ripped the stamp in two. The same problem was inherent in Express Mail envelopes unveiled by USPS in 1991 (see chapter on $9.95 Express Mail stamp).

302

The Design

Young & Rubicam, the New York advertising agency handling expedited mail services for USPS, suggested that two eagle paintings that it was using on Express Mail envelopes could also be used on stamps. Both were by Ned Seidler, the artist who had designed the $8.75 Express Mail stamp of 1988. USPS did adapt one of them for use on its first Express Mail stamp of 1991, and made an effort to incorporate the other — showing an eagle in flight — in its $2.90 Priority Mail stamp design.

Designer McCaffrey's first try at doing that placed the eagle in a horizontal semi-jumbo stamp format, with the Olympic rings in color, all

Ned Seidler's flying eagle was originally painted for use on Express Mail envelopes. Here, Terrence McCaffrey tried to adapt it to a Priority Mail stamp, but concluded that this treatment left too much empty space in the stamp design.

against a white background. "We felt there wasn't enough going on — the art was just lost. There was too much dead space," McCaffrey said.

He next tried a vertical format and an image that was tightly cropped so that only the head and part of the near wing appeared, against a red background, with the typography and rings in dropout white. "It was still too empty," said the designer. "There wasn't enough eagle, enough image there to make it work."

Next, he employed a square format that would include more of the eagle, and changed the background to blue so the stamp wouldn't resemble the new Express Mail stamp too closely. But that, too, was

Next, designer Terrence McCaffrey tried to shoehorn the flying eagle into a vertical semi-jumbo and a square format, also with unsatisfactory results.

303

Allstock Inc. furnished the photo of a fierce eagle, which McCaffrey incorporated in this stamp design. Then it was decided that this particular photo had been used by too many of Allstock's other customers and that the Postal Service should seek another, albeit similar pose.

judged to be unsatisfactory.

"At that point, we decided we were trying to shoehorn an image that had been created for something else into a stamp shape, and it just wasn't working," McCaffrey said. "So we had to do a scramble."

McCaffrey had been working with other photographs of eagles on some non-stamp-related art projects for USPS, and he came across a photo of a fierce-looking eagle, in profile, in the catalog of Allstock Inc., a stock photo house in Seattle, Washington. USPS frequently uses Allstock pictures for such products as its commemorative mint set booklets, but it had never used one on a stamp before. Now McCaffrey quickly made a stamp design of the eagle photo, setting the bird's white head against a black background and adding red lettering and Olympic rings. He showed it to the Citizens' Stamp Advisory Committee. The committee liked the design and approved it.

Then McCaffrey learned that the photo he had used was a popular one that other Allstock customers had also ordered from the catalog. Not wanting to share an identical subject with a host of commercial users, McCaffrey asked to see similar photographs, and was sent other poses of the eagle by the same photographer, Kevin Schaefer.

McCaffrey picked a pose that showed the bird's head in a slightly more upright position, and turned slightly more forward, than in the first picture. He moved the type from the bottom of the stamp to the top to show more of the dark feathers of the eagle's body. The resulting design was OK'd by Postmaster General Frank March 27, 1991.

For reproduction rights, USPS paid Allstock the standard $3,000 fee it pays stamp designers. USPS staffers thought at first that the use of the picture on a stamp design would mean they would have to require Allstock to "retire" it from its inventory. But after due consideration, they decided this wouldn't be necessary. The intaglio treatment of the eagle's head on the stamp would alter the image enough so that use of the photo elsewhere wouldn't be a problem, they concluded.

304

The offset plate numbers and intaglio sleeve number appear inverted in relation to each other on all 20-stamp panes of the $2.90 Priority Mail stamp.

First-Day Facts

The Priority Mail stamp was dedicated by Michael S. Coughlin, deputy postmaster general, in a public ceremony July 7 at the main post office in San Diego, California. The principal speaker was U.S. Olympian Shirley Babashoff, who had also played a prominent role in the first-day ceremony of the $9.95 Express Mail stamp in Sacramento June 16. USPS provided a pictorial handstamp first-day postmark showing an eagle in flight and the five Olympic rings.

Because many collectors found it difficult to obtain the stamp, USPS twice extended the deadline for submitting covers for first-day cancellations, first from 30 to 60 days after the issue date and later to 120 days.

50¢ HARRIET QUIMBY (AIRMAIL)
PIONEERS OF AVIATION SERIES

Date of Issue: April 27, 1991

Catalog Number: Scott C128

Colors: magenta, cyan, yellow, black

First-Day Cancel: Plymouth, Michigan

FDCs Canceled: 154,789

Format: Panes of 50, horizontal, 5 across, 10 down. Gravure printing cylinders of 200 (10 across, 20 around) manufactured by Armotek Industries Inc., Palmyra, New Jersey.

Perf: 10.9 (L perforator)

Selvage Markings: "© United States Postal Service 1991 36 USC 380." "Use Correct ZIP Code ®." USPS Olympic logo.

Designer: Howard Koslow of East Norwich, New York

Art Director and Typographer: Howard Paine (CSAC)

Project Manager: Jack Williams (USPS)

Modeler: Richard C. Sennett, Stamp Venturers

Printing: Stamps printed by Stamp Venturers on a Champlain gravure press at J.W. Fergusson and Sons, Richmond, Virginia. Stamps perforated, processed and shipped by KCS Industries, Milwaukee, Wisconsin.

Quantity Ordered: 250,000,000

Quantity Distributed: 250,000,000

Cylinder Number Detail: 1 group of 4 cylinder numbers preceded by the letter S alongside corner stamp

Tagging: phosphor-coated paper

The Stamp

Harriet Quimby, the first woman in America to receive a pilot's license and the first woman to fly solo across the English Channel, was honored on a 50¢ airmail stamp issued April 27 at the Plymouth Show, a stamp exhibition in Plymouth, Michigan. The denomination matched the half-ounce overseas airmail rate that went into effect the previous February 3.

The stamp was the 13th in USPS' Pioneers of Aviation series, which has honored 12 different people as part of nine different issues. All 13 stamps have been denominated for overseas airmail use.

The series began with the 1978 release of two se-tenant 31¢ airmails depicting Wilbur and Orville Wright. Since then the following people have been recognized: Octave Chanute (two stamps), Wiley Post (two stamps), Blanche Stuart Scott (the only other woman besides Quimby in the series), Glenn Curtiss, Alfred Verville, Lawrence and Elmer Sperry (on a single stamp), Samuel Langley and Igor Sikorsky.

Though size and printing techniques have varied for these stamps, all had a similar format. Each Pioneer of Aviation has been shown with the aircraft with which he or she was most closely associated. And all except the Sikorsky stamp have carried the phrase "Aviation Pioneer," "Aviation Pioneers" or "Pioneer Pilot." The Quimby stamp, like the one for Blanche Stuart Scott, bore the latter wording.

"The most celebrated of America's (early) pioneer women fliers was the beautiful and tantalizingly mysterious Harriet Quimby," wrote historian Valerie Moolman. "A willowy, green-eyed brunette, she was reported variously to have been born in Massachusetts, Michigan or California — and into families of either solid wealth or rural poverty."

On this latter point, stamp collector Harry C. Winter wrote in a letter to *The Airpost Journal*: "A very widespread error, which was actually perpetrated by Harriet Quimby and her mother, was that she was born in California in 1884. Actually, incontrovertible evidence from census and other records establishes that she was born in Coldwater, Michigan, on May 1, 1875."

Quimby's public history began in 1902 when she emerged as a drama writer for newspapers in San Francisco. A year later she moved to New York as drama critic for *Leslie's Weekly*. After attending a flying show, she resolved to learn to fly herself, and took lessons at the Moisant Aviation School at Hempstead, Long Island. She qualified for her Aero Club license (number 37) August 1, 1911.

She then toured the United States and Mexico with the Moisant exhibition team, wearing a self-designed elegant flying suit that quickly became her trademark: wool-backed plum-colored satin with a monklike hood. Newspapers dubbed her the Dresden-China Aviatrix, but she was in fact a dedicated pilot who worked hard to promote aviation and persuade women to fly.

During this time, she developed her plan to fly the English Channel, as Louis Bleriot had first done in 1909. In March 1912 she sailed for Europe and arranged with Bleriot for the loan of a Bleriot monoplane, which she shipped secretly to Dover, England. Bad weather hampered her preparations, and she was advised against making the attempt. Nevertheless, heavily dressed and with a hot water bottle tied to her waist, she took off from Dover early on April 16, 1912. Fog rolled in, and she was forced to use her compass. A deviation from course would have put her over the North Sea on a no-return trip. But when the fog parted 20 minutes later, she saw land beneath her; it was France. She landed on the beach beside a fishing village, and excited spectators brought coffee to her in the plane.

Her achievement would normally have caused excitement around the world, but the news of it was overwhelmed by a far greater story. Two days earlier the *Titanic* had struck an iceberg and sunk with the loss of 1,513 lives. The papers, naturally, were full of news of this great disaster.

Harriet Quimby's own life ended tragically a few weeks after her flying triumph. On July 1, 1912, 11 months to the day after she earned her license, at an aviation meet in Boston, she took a passenger, meet

This front-page story in the July 2, 1912, New York Times told of Harriet Quimby's tragic death.

308

manager William A.P. Willard, for a short flight in her brand-new 70-horsepower white Bleriot monoplane. As they flew 1,000 feet above Dorchester Bay, the plane dove abruptly. Incredibly, in those days flyers did not customarily use safety belts, and both occupants were flung out. As spectators watched in horror, Quimby and Willard plunged into shallow water 200 feet from shore and were killed instantly. Ironically, the plane, empty of its human cargo, landed intact in the water. The accident was witnessed by Quimby's friend Blanche Stuart Scott, who was aloft in her own plane, competing for an endurance prize. The press reported that Scott collapsed in her seat after bringing the aircraft down for a safe landing.

Quimby, at 37, was the fourth woman to be killed in an aviation mishap. "Ambitious to be among the pathfinders," wrote *The Boston Post*, "she took her chances like a man and died like one."

The Design

For artist Howard Koslow, this was the second design assignment in the Pioneers of Aviation series. He had previously designed the 39¢ Lawrence and Elmer Sperry stamp of 1985.

Using this Smithsonian photograph as a reference, Koslow painted the hood, goggles and scarf that frame Quimby's face on the stamp portrait.

His design for the Quimby stamp showed a glamorous-looking aviator in her trademark purple jacket and hood, goggles pushed up over her eyes, smiling at the viewer. A side view of a Bleriot monoplane fills the background space.

There was no shortage of pictures of the photogenic flyer from which to work. Looking over the material, Howard Paine, the stamp's art director, said to Koslow, "Oh, boy, we've got movie-star quality here." Koslow obtained several photographs from the files of the Smithsonian Institution, including some good closeups. Most depicted Quimby in her satin flying togs, but one striking picture showed her wearing a long dress, with a stylish hat and elbow-length gloves, holding a furled parasol.

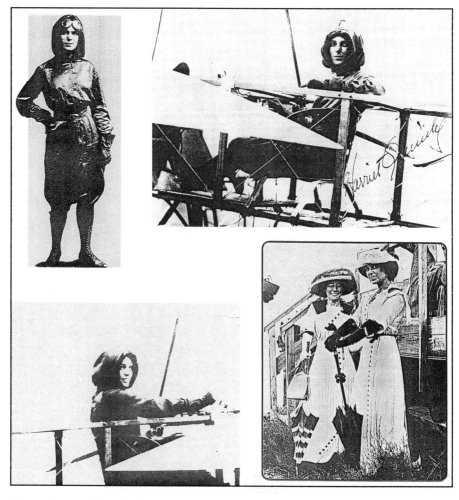

These four additional photos of Quimby were part of Howard Koslow's reference material in preparing the design. In the photo showing her in dress, hat and gloves, she is standing beside Matilde Moisant, America's second licensed female pilot.

310

This is a portion of a full-color poster showing Quimby standing in front of her plane. Koslow worked from a transparency of the fragile original, which is in the Smithsonian Institution. The face on the stamp portrait is primarily based on this image.

The researchers also found in the Smithsonian's Archives a color poster, based on a painting of Quimby. In it she is standing in front of her monoplane, wearing her purple flying costume, with what appears to be a necklace around her neck. The print was very fragile, but Jack Williams, the project manager, obtained a transparency from the Smithsonian for Koslow to use.

Koslow did three color sketches. On two of them, he based the portrait

Designer Howard Koslow made this pencil sketch before executing his final painting. He has tilted Quimby's head and shoulders to her left, at the suggestion of art director Howard Paine.

311

These three color sketches by Koslow show two different portraits of Harriet Quimby, based on a poster and a photograph, combined with two different views of the Bleriot monoplane.

on a photograph that showed her face at a slight angle and with goggles pushed up above her eyes. The third used the face from the color poster, without goggles but with necklace. Two of the designs had in the background a side view of the Bleriot monoplane, taken from a photo-

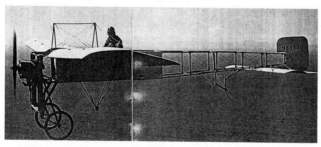

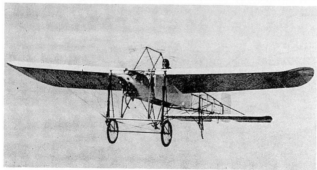

The plane on the stamp was based on this side-view photograph of a replica of Louis Bleriot's Channel-crossing Type XI monoplane, which appeared in All Color World of Aircraft (Octopus Books Ltd., London, 1978). Koslow also had tried a front-end view of the Bleriot plane based on a photo in Flying magazine for November 1964.

graph in a reference book. The other showed a frontal view of the plane.

For his finished painting, Koslow combined some of the earlier design elements. The Quimby face appears to be the one from the poster, but the headgear and goggles resemble those in the photographic portrait. At the suggestion of art director Paine, Koslow tilted the face and shoulders slightly to her left and showed more of her right shoulder, thus filling the space in the lower left part of the design. He used the side view of the Bleriot aircraft, which more effectively filled the background than the frontal view would have done.

Varieties

In July 1991, Bob Dumaine of Sam Houston Philatelics reported that a horizontally imperforate pane of 50 Quimby stamps had been purchased at a Cleveland, Ohio, post office. The pane was separated vertically into two sections before the error was noticed. Dumaine said he had bought the pane and sold it privately for an undisclosed price.

First-Day Facts

USPS held no first-day ceremony for the Quimby stamp.

In his letter to *The Airpost Journal*, Harry C. Winter, an Ann Arbor, Michigan, resident, wrote: "We collectors in Michigan are still wondering if the USPS researched Harriet Quimby sufficiently to learn of her obscure Michigan origins, or whether it was just dumb luck that caused them to select The Plymouth Show in Plymouth, Michigan, as the site for the first day of issue. In any event, that selection was fortunate and permitted at least one cachetmaker to hotfoot it to Coldwater, Michigan, on Saturday morning and obtain a number of unofficial first-day cancellations from the town of her birth."

40¢ WILLIAM T. PIPER (AIRMAIL)
PIONEERS OF AVIATION SERIES

Date of Issue: May 17, 1991

Catalog Number: Scott C129

Colors: yellow, magenta, cyan, black

First-Day Cancel: Denver, Colorado

FDCs Canceled: 107,817

Format: Panes of 50, horizontal, 5 across, 10 down. Gravure printing cylinders of 200 subjects (10 across, 20 around) manufactured by Armotek Industries Inc., Palmyra, New Jersey.

Perf: 10.9 (L perforator)

Selvage Markings: "© United States Postal Service 1991." "Use Correct ZIP Code ®." "36 USC 380." USPS Olympic logo.

Selvage Inscription: "William T. Piper/1881-1970/aviation pioneer." "Maker of the/famous Piper Cub/light airplane." "Widely known as/ the 'Henry Ford/of aviation.' "

Designer: Ren Wicks of Los Angeles, California

Art Director and Project Manager: Jack Williams (USPS)

Typographer: Bradbury Thompson (CSAC)

Modeler: Richard Sennett, Sennett Enterprises, for American Bank Note Company

Printing: Stamps printed for American Bank Note Company on a leased Champlain gravure press at J.W. Fergusson and Sons, Richmond, Virginia, under the supervision of Sennett Enterprises, Fairfax, Virginia. Stamps perforated, processed and shipped by ABNC, Bedford Park, Illinois.

Quantity Ordered: 175,000,000 plus 7,400,000

Quantity Distributed: 182,400,000

Cylinder Number Detail: 1 group of 4 cylinder numbers preceded by the letter A alongside corner stamp

Tagging: overall

The Stamp

On May 17, USPS issued a 40¢ airmail stamp honoring William T. Piper, founder of the Piper Aircraft Corporation and a man known as "the Henry Ford of aviation," who during his lifetime built more airplanes than anyone else in the world.

USPS, in announcing the Piper stamp, explained that its 40¢ denomination "pays the one-ounce airmail rate to Canada." Actually, there was no separate airmail rate to Canada; 40¢ was the required postage for first-class mail to the Dominion, which, like first-class mail in the United States, normally would go by air if the distance was of appropriate length.

What the stamp obviously was intended to cover was the international airmail rate for postcards to countries other than Canada and Mexico. As rate specialist Henry Beecher pointed out in a letter to *Stamp Collector*, this had been the case with three of the Piper stamp's predecessors in the Pioneers of Aviation series, the 28¢ Blanche Stuart Scott (Scott C99), the 33¢ Alfred V. Verville (Scott C113) and the 36¢ Igor Sikorsky (Scott C119). "When those stamps were current, their denominations matched the rate for international airmail postcards, but did not correspond to any other common rate," Beecher wrote. "It is merely a coincidence that there is such a correspondence in the case of the 40¢ Piper stamp."

The Piper stamp was the 14th in the Pioneers series, and followed the 13th, for Harriet Quimby, by less than a month. It shared its first-day date and place with two other postal items: the 19¢ Hot-Air Balloon booklet stamp and the 45¢ Eagle aerogram.

William Thomas Piper was one of several key figures in the development of American aviation whose names had been proposed for eventual stamp honors by a subcommittee of the Citizens' Stamp Advisory Committee headed by the late Emerson Clark, an aeronautical engineer and one-time president of the American Philatelic Society. Piper's greatest contribution to aviation was the famous Piper Cub, the light, cheap, durable and forgiving airplane that put flying within easy reach of thousands who had never before had the money or skills to become pilots.

The Cub was, as Piper liked to call it, "the nursery in which aviation grew up." By 1940, four out of five qualified pilots had learned to fly in a Cub. More than three-fourths of all pilots trained for World War II service received basic instruction in the plane.

Piper was nearly 50 years old before he was in any way identified with the aviation industry. He was born January 8, 1881, at Knapps Creek, New York, grew up in Bradford, Pennsylvania, and attended Harvard University. In 1928, as a successful oil-company executive in Bradford,

315

he became a board member of the local Taylor Brothers Aircraft Corporation and encouraged development of a glider, from which the first of the Cubs evolved.

First flown September 2, 1930, the Cub was first called Brownbach Tiger Kitten because of its tiny two-cylinder, two-cycle engine. The experimental model was unsatisfactory, and on June 15, 1931, it was replaced by the 37-horsepower model E-2 Cub. The plane sold for $1,325, a price maintained until the late 1930s.

Although the little yellow planes were slow, drafty, frail and uncomfortable, they sold well — but not enough to prevent Taylor Brothers from going bankrupt. In the reorganization that followed, Piper became company treasurer, and in 1936 he bought a controlling interest.

The next year a fire wiped out the plant. Borrowing money to get a new start, Piper moved the company to an abandoned silk mill in Lock Haven, Pennsylvania, and by the end of 1937 Cub production had reached a record 687. The following year the plane design was modified into the J-3 model, dubbed "the putt-putt" and "the flivver of the air," and now considered the classic Cub.

As World War II drew near, the Army discovered the value of the Cub

The stamp portrait of Piper was based on this photograph from the collection of William T. Piper Jr.

The number on the Piper Cub shown on the stamp — N6233H — was borrowed from a Cub that was once regularly flown by USPS' Donald M. McDowell.

as an artillery spotter, and began ordering the planes by the hundreds. By V-J Day, Piper had sold 5,673 Cubs to the armed forces, for use not only for spotting and pilot training but also for aerial photography, reconnaissance and medical evacuation.

After the war, Piper sales climbed with the introduction of new twin-engine model planes and the acceptance by businessmen of Piper's belief that "it's as easy for you to fly an airplane as it is to drive a car — and a plane gets you there faster." He insisted that the controls on his aircraft be simple. "I'm a poor pilot myself," he said, "but any fool can fly a Piper. I planned it that way."

Piper didn't learn to fly himself until 1931, when he was 50. In two weeks, he soloed. He continued to pilot his own plane until 1957, when he was 76. He died in Lock Haven January 16, 1970, at the age of 89.

CSAC members were dissatisfied with these two Piper portraits, which were done in pencil by the first artist commissioned by the Postal Service to prepare concept sketches.

The Design

Ren Wicks' stamp design showed a smiling William Piper, the sun highlighting his face and bushy eyebrows, his white hair blowing in the wind. In the background, a yellow Model J-3 Cub soared over a bank of clouds.

Wicks based his Piper portrait on a photograph that was used as a frontispiece for the book *Mr. Piper and his Cubs* by Devon Francis (Iowa State University Press, 1973). The picture was originally from the private collection of Piper's son, William T. Piper Jr.

Unfortunately, the younger Piper was unable to ascertain who had taken the photograph or when. He did report, however, that the same photograph had been used by the late Milton Caniff, the cartoonist who created the "Terry and the Pirates" and "Steve Canyon" comic strips, for a charcoal sketch

317

Ren Wicks' first pencil sketch with the portrait that was finally chosen had the plane on the left and Piper's face on the right.

of Piper that Caniff made for the Aviation Hall of Fame in Dayton, Ohio.

At the beginning of the stamp project, another artist had been commissioned to do concept sketches, but his portraits of Piper "just weren't working," said Jack Williams, the stamp's art director and project manager. So Wicks was hired. The Citizens' Stamp Advisory Committee found his sketches, based on other photographs, much more to its liking.

The tiny serial number on the plane's fuselage, distinguishable with a strong magnifying glass, is N6233H. To guarantee authenticity, the artist used the number of an actual Cub — one located in Texas that Donald M. McDowell, director of the USPS Office of Stamp and Philatelic Marketing, had piloted at one time.

This alternative design by Wicks showed a bespectacled Piper in a business suit.

"I just happened to know where a Piper Cub lived that was owned by somebody who wouldn't scream in outrage if the numbers appeared on the stamp," explained McDowell. "The last thing in the world we wanted was to run the risk that the designer would take the letter N and pull some numbers out of the air and throw them on there and it would turn out to be, for example, an American Airlines 747's registration number. The very quick and easy way was to make sure we had the N number of a real Piper Cub."

USPS had taken a similar precaution with the Banking and Commerce se-tenant pair of 1975 (Scott 1577-1578), which included in its design magnetic-ink code numbers and characters of the kind used in automated checking. To avoid the inadvertent use of numbers from some citizen's actual bank account, McDowell provided the designer with the coding of an inactive account he himself had once used.

318

First-Day Facts

The Piper stamp was issued May 17 at the opening of the Rompex 91 stamp show at the Holiday Inn/Holidrome Trade Convention Center in Denver, Colorado. The 19¢ Hot-Air Balloon definitive booklet stamp and the 45¢ Eagle aerogram made their debut at the same time. No first-day ceremony was held for any of the items, although a dedication ceremony in Lock Haven for the Piper stamp had been proposed by Ray C. Noll Jr., an executive of the Piper Aviation Museum in that city.

Collectors were given until June 16 to submit covers for first-day cancellation. Later, USPS extended the deadline to July 16.

50¢ ANTARCTIC TREATY (AIRMAIL)

Date of Issue: June 21, 1991

Catalog Number: Scott C130

Colors: aqua, red, blue, black

First-Day Cancel: Washington, D.C.

FDCs Canceled: 114,452

Format: Panes of 50, horizontal, 5 across, 10 down. Gravure printing cylinders of 200 subjects (10 across, 20 around) manufactured by Armotek Industries Inc., Palmyra, New Jersey.

Perf: 10.9 (L perforator)

Selvage Inscription: "1991 marks the 30th/anniversary of the/ratification of the/ Antarctic Treaty." "The pact dedicated/Antarctica for/ peaceful purposes/rather than military." "The Treaty has fostered/peaceful cooperation/and scientific research/by thirty-nine countries."

Selvage Markings: "© United States Postal Service 1991." "Use Correct ZIP Code ® 36 USC 380." USPS Olympic logo.

Designer: Howard Koslow of East Norwich, New York

Art Director and Typographer: Howard Paine (CSAC)

Project Manager: Jack Williams (USPS)

Modeler: Richard Sennett, Stamp Venturers

Printing: Stamps printed by Stamp Venturers on a Champlain gravure press at J.W. Fergusson and Sons, Richmond, Virginia. Stamps perforated, processed and shipped by KCS Industries, Milwaukee, Wisconsin.

Quantity Ordered: 115,000,000

Quantity Distributed: 113,000,000

Cylinder Number Detail: 1 group of 4 cylinder numbers preceded by the letter S alongside corner stamp

Tagging: phosphor-coated paper

The Stamp

USPS issued a 50¢ airmail stamp June 21 in Washington, D.C., to mark the 30th anniversary of the effective date of the Antarctic Treaty, which dedicated the frozen continent at the bottom of the world to peaceful purposes and guaranteed freedom of scientific research.

Thirty years was an unusual milestone for stamp commemoration. In fact, the published guidelines of the Citizens' Stamp Advisory Committee read: "Events of historical significance shall be considered for commemoration only on anniversaries in multiples of 50 years." Moreover, the new stamp represented a repeat commemoration within an unusually brief time. On June 23, 1971, the U.S. Post Office Department had marked the 10th anniversary of the treaty with an 8¢ stamp (Scott 1431) — the last stamp, in fact, that the department issued before it metamorphosed into the U.S. Postal Service.

When *Linn's Stamp News* asked USPS spokesman Frank Thomas to comment on the first point, he said: "Most of the guidelines have been

Howard Koslow also designed this 1971 commemorative for the 10th anniversary of the Antarctic Treaty.

broken at one time or another." As for the reason for commemorating the event again, Thomas said there was great interest in Antarctica now "because the international community is working to help preserve the environment there rather intensely." In fact, for several months in 1991 the treaty powers met in Madrid to develop a long-term policy barring mining and drilling in the Antarctic.

The USPS announcement that a new Antarctic Treaty stamp would be issued was made nearly a year ahead of time, in July 1990. Australia Post was among those joining the commemoration, issuing two stamps for the Australian Antarctic Territory to mark the treaty's 30th anniversary.

In addition to Scott 1431, previous U.S. stamps with Antarctic themes were a 3¢ commemorative issued in 1933 honoring Richard E. Byrd's second Antarctic expedition (Scott 733), and a se-tenant block of four stamps in 1989 depicting U.S. Antarctic explorers Byrd, Nathaniel Palmer, Charles Wilkes and Lincoln Ellsworth (Scott 2386-89).

For many years, the scientific climate in Antarctica was unsettled by disputes among nations over sovereignty. At one point the United States had advanced a plan for internationalizing the continent under the auspices of the United Nations, but it came to nothing.

321

In 1957-58, however, some 10,000 scientists and technicians from 67 nations took part in a coordinated scientific program called the International Geophysical Year, which included cooperation in Antarctic research. To help preserve the momentum of IGY, President Dwight D. Eisenhower in 1959 invited delegates from the nations concerned to "confer with us to seek an effective joint means of keeping Antarctica open to all nations to conduct scientific or peaceful activities there."

The resulting conference met in Washington in October 1959. It produced the Antarctic Treaty, which was signed by 12 nations December 1, 1959, and which took effect June 23, 1961. Fourteen more nations later subscribed to the document and acquired full voting rights at meetings of the treaty powers.

The treaty's six principles were: Antarctica is to be used for peaceful purposes only; the freedom of scientific investigation and cooperation which characterized the IGY is to continue; scientific observations shall be made freely available and scientific personnel exchanged; all political claims are frozen for 30 years; nuclear explosions and disposal of radioactive waste in Antarctica are banned, and all nations and equipment are open to the inspection of duly-appointed observers.

The 1991 negotiations were successfully concluded in October when 24 Treaty nations, including the United States, signed a protocol to the pact banning mineral and oil exploration in Antarctica for 50 years.

The Design

Howard Koslow had designed the first Antarctic Treaty commemorative back in 1971 — it was the first of many stamp assignments for this prolific artist — and so it was appropriate that he was chosen to design the new one as well.

Because the earlier design had been graphic, showing a polar-projec-

Howard Koslow prepared these color sketches of Mount Erebus, a live Antarctic volcano, with penguins, a "Sno-Cat" vehicle and researchers in the foreground.

tion map of Antarctica, Koslow and Howard Paine, the art director, decided that the new one should be illustrative. Koslow prepared three color sketches showing Mount Erebus, the 13,202-foot live volcano on Ross Island, and a fourth that had as its central element a nunatak — polar parlance for a rock thrusting through an ice field — with the sea in the foreground. To each sketch he attached a tab that could be folded over the picture to add an alternative design element, such as a red "Sno-Cat" vehicle or, for the offshore view, a red research ship. (Paine described these appendages as "now-you-see-it-now-you-don't" flaps.)

The Citizens' Stamp Advisory Committee liked the offshore picture with the red ship, and Koslow prepared a finished acrylic painting. Some time later, however, he got a call from Jack Williams of USPS, the stamp's project manager, telling him that the ship he had depicted was unsuitable. A State Department official, in examining the reference material Koslow had used, noticed that the vessel wasn't American, but Danish — a ship called the *Magga Dan*. It would have to be replaced with an American ship, Williams said.

Koslow, it turned out, had copied his ship from a photograph he had found in *The National Geographic* magazine accompanying an article entitled "Antarctica: Icy Testing Ground for Space" (text by Samuel W. Matthews, photographs by Robert W. Madden, October 1968). The photo had been taken at Antarctica's McMurdo Station and showed the *Magga Dan* lying at anchor in McMurdo Sound with a prominent elevation called Observation Hill in the background. The text, which Koslow hadn't studied closely, explained that the *Magga Dan* was Danish and was, at the time the article was written, a touring vessel, chartered to a New Zealand firm. The 21 passengers it had brought to McMurdo Station constituted the first tour group ever to arrive at that remote outpost.

To replace the *Magga Dan* in the stamp design, the State Department provided USPS with a picture of an appropriate alternative ship, the U.S. Coast Guard icebreaker *Glacier*. Although now out of service, the *Glacier*, built as a Navy ship and commissioned in 1955, had done Antarctic duty during the 30-year life of the treaty. Koslow found additional pictures of the *Glacier* at his local library and, working from these sources, "whited out" the *Magga Dan* in his painting and painted the proper Yankee vessel in its place.

Howard Koslow's first version of the finished design showed the Danish tour ship **Magga Dan**. *He subsequently replaced the foreign vessel with the U.S. Coast Guard icebreaker* **Glacier**.

For his landscape, Koslow turned to another source — a photograph of a nunatak that appeared in a book titled *The Antarctic* by Richard Harrington (1976, Alaska Northwest Publishing Company). The caption, on page 76, described the scene as being near U.S. Palmer Station on Anvers Island, on the Antarctic Peninsula. Unfortunately, the use by the artist of two different photo sources led to another problem: a mixup in the official USPS description of the stamp design.

In preparing the news release on the stamp, USPS staffers duly noted that the ship photograph to which Koslow had referred was taken at McMurdo Station, and wrongly assumed that this was the setting for the entire picture. As a result, the release said the stamp "features a dramatic view of McMurdo Sound, the operational and scientific hub of American activities in Antarctica. Observation Hill on Ross Island is in the background."

The mistake became public after Bob Allen, an employee of the U.S. Geological Survey in Reston, Virginia, telephoned *Stamp Collector* to challenge the information the newspaper had published with its picture of the stamp. Allen, who had been doing Antarctic work for more than 30 years, said that Observation Hill was a cinder cone not usually covered with snow. Moreover, he said, McMurdo Station, the largest U.S. research base in Antarctica, was situated at the base of the hill, and there was no ice shelf like the one shown on the stamp. The caller suggested — correctly, as it turned out — that the picture more closely resembled the area near Palmer Station, which is some 2,500 miles from McMurdo.

Stamp Collector then took its information to Frank Thomas, the USPS spokesman, who confirmed that the original press release had been in error. USPS subsequently issued a correction.

First-Day Facts

Lawrence Eagleburger, deputy secretary of state, and Robert Corell of the National Science Foundation were principal speakers at a public first-day ceremony at the State Department's Dean Acheson Auditorium. Robert Rutford, president of the University of Texas at Dallas and chairman of the National Academy of Science Polar Research Board, gave the welcome and introduced the distinguished guests. Assistant Postmaster General Thomas E. Leavey dedicated the stamp.

50¢ FIRST AMERICANS (AIRMAIL) AMERICA SERIES

Date of Issue: October 12, 1991

Catalog Number: Scott C131

Colors: magenta, yellow, cyan, black, red, green

First-Day Cancel: Anchorage, Alaska

FDCs Canceled: 88,086

Format: Panes of 50, horizontal, 5 across, 10 down. Gravure printing cylinders of 200 subjects (10 across, 20 around).

Perf: 11.2 (Eureka off-line perforator)

Selvage Inscription: PUASP logo. "Postal Union/of the Americas,/Spain and Portugal." "Union nations agreed/to issue stamps in/the AMERICA series/with a common theme." "Pre-Columbian/Voyages of Discovery/is the 1991 theme."

Selvage Markings: "Use Correct/ZIP® Code." "©/United States/Postal Service/ 1991/36 USC 380." USPS Olympic logo.

Designer: Richard Schlecht of Arlington, Virginia

Art Director and Typographer: Richard Sheaff (CSAC)

Project Manager: Joe Brockert (USPS)

Modeler: Clarence Holbert (BEP)

Printing: printed by BEP on 7-color Andreotti gravure press (601)

Quantity Ordered: 50,000,000

Quantity Distributed: 15,260,000

Cylinder Number Detail: 1 group of 6 gravure cylinder numbers alongside corner stamp

Tagging: phosphor-coated paper

The Stamp

In 1991, for the third consecutive year, USPS participated in an omnibus stamp issue sponsored by what is now called the Postal Union of the Americas, Spain and Portugal (PUASP). The omnibus issue was one of an annual series leading up to the 1992 celebration of the 500th anniversary of Christopher Columbus' first voyage to the New World.

When the project began, the organization was known as the Postal Union of the Americas and Spain (Portugal joined in 1990). Each of the 24 member countries at that time agreed to issue stamps in 1989 with the common theme of pre-Columbian peoples and their customs, images and traditions. In 1990 the theme was natural wonders that the early European explorers might have seen. In each of those years, USPS contributed two stamps to the program, one for first-class mail and the other for international airmail.

But the Postal Service's enthusiasm for the project was never more than lukewarm, and in 1991, when the common theme prescribed by PUASP was the voyages of exploration, USPS skipped the first-class rate stamp and issued only a 50¢ airmail stamp as its contribution to the America series.

In choosing a design subject, the Citizens' Stamp Advisory Committee interpreted the word "voyages" to include any kind of travel of discovery. This cleared the way for CSAC to focus on the widely held scientific belief that the two American continents were originally peopled long ago

These concept sketches by two other artists were submitted to CSAC. The committee liked the sketch depicting a mastodon or mammoth hunt, but some members were afraid it would offend animal lovers.

by Asian natives who migrated across a land bridge that once spanned what is now the Bering Strait.

During the Ice Age, about one million years ago, the ocean level was lower than it is today because much of the earth's water was frozen in great sheets of ice that covered much of the Northern Hemisphere. Land that had been submerged — and is submerged now — became dry. One such area lay between Siberia and Alaska, where the Bering Strait now separates Asia and North America by about 50 miles. This land bridge, known today as "Beringia," existed one or more times during the Ice Age.

Plants grew on the new land, and animals began to cross Beringia in both directions. Some people of Siberia followed the animals that they hunted eastward into the Americas, a New World that until then had no human occupants. These migrants were the ancestors of the American Indians. The date of the first crossing is unknown, but authorities say it was probably more than 20,000 years ago. By 6000 B.C., humans were living at the southern tip of South America.

The Design

USPS commissioned three artists to submit concept sketches depicting the people who took part in the great migration across the land bridge.

One artist's dramatic vertical sketch depicted two hunters attacking a fierce mammoth or mastodon with spears. The committee liked this one graphically, but turned it down after some members expressed the fear that it would offend postal customers who were opposed to the killing of animals. Other sketches showed travelers on the move, on foot or by

Richard Schlecht, the artist who prepared the final design for the stamp, also had made these earlier concept sketches of migrants traveling by water and land, and a map of the Bering land bridge beside a Clovis point or fluted flint arrowhead.

In October 1990, Schlecht made this preliminary sketch, which CSAC approved for development into finished art.

umiak, a boat made of animal skins. Some of the designs incorporated maps, and one showed a Clovis point, or fluted flint arrowhead, of the type used by early arrivals in North America.

Eventually, the committee chose an evocative sketch by Richard Schlecht of Arlington, Virginia, and Schlecht prepared a finished version in watercolor. It showed a family of travelers standing on a ridge overlooking a broad river valley, with mountains in the background. The father was seen in profile in the left foreground and other family members and their dog stood on a rocky outcrop behind him.

Schlecht based the costuming on illustrations in a book, *Crossroads of Continents* by William Fitzhugh and Aron Crowell. The book, published by the Smithsonian Institution in 1988, grew out of an exhibit at the Smithsonian. Much of the remaining detail came from his own ideas of what might be appropriate for that vanished place and that time many millenia ago.

The features of the man in the foreground were based on photographs of present-day natives of the Alaskan and Siberian coastal areas. "I just wanted to make sure he had features that were more or less Siberian, or what we think Siberian features would have looked like then," Schlecht said. The flat landscape with its meandering river was characteristic of tundra. The dog resembled a modern-day husky or malamute.

Schlecht consulted anthropologist Dennis Stanford at the Smithsonian for advice on such details as the beadwork on the man's costume, the man's face, and whether dogs would have accompanied the migrants. The artist had proposed including a travois, or crude animal-drawn sledge of the kind used later by Plains Indians, but Stanford advised him that it wouldn't have been appropriate for the period.

Although explanatory text was to be provided in the selvage, officials decided that the stamp also had to explain itself to a certain extent with its own wording. Art director Richard Sheaff's layout called for the words to wrap across the top and down the right side. For the type, Sheaff chose a clean-looking Roman face called Stone Serif, which had been created specifically for computer use.

Sheaff offered CSAC a selection of phrases whose words had been carefully chosen and letter-counted to fit the allotted space. Some of these used the word "Beringia" for the long-lost land bridge, but the committee decided — no doubt correctly — that the term would baffle postal customers. Finally the committee settled on this wording: "THE FIRST

328

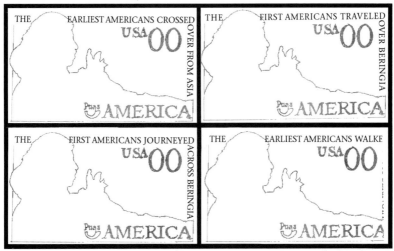

Art director Richard Sheaff prepared these alternative combinations of wording for CSAC's consideration.

AMERICANS CROSSED OVER FROM ASIA."

Back when the four-year America omnibus issue was in the planning stage, the Postal Union of the Americas and Spain had specified that participating countries should include in their stamp designs the PUAS logo, a stylized post horn with initials. USPS had done so with its first two annual stamp sets, even though the cryptic piece of graphic art meant nothing to the stamp-using public. On the 1991 stamp, the logo was omitted. (It was reproduced, however, on the stamp selvage, along with the full name of the organization.)

"The committee and the Postal Service had been very ambivalent about that requirement from the beginning," said Sheaff. "Somewhere along the line with this stamp we decided that it would be difficult to make the logo show up well where we had planned to put it, at the bottom of the design. We decided that it was just visual clutter, and that we should be done with it and stop using it."

Richard Schlecht's previous design work for USPS had included the five-stamp Steamboats booklet of 1989 and several coil stamps in the Transportation series.

First-Day Facts

The America stamp, like its predecessors in the series, was first placed on sale October 12, Columbus Day. The public ceremony was held at the Performing Arts Center in Anchorage, Alaska.

William T. Johnstone, assistant postmaster general, dedicated the stamp. Principal speakers were David Ames, associate director of the National Park Service's Alaska District, and Willie Hemsley, president of the NANA Development Corporation.

OFFICIAL STAMPS

The current series of Penalty Mail (Official Mail) stamps is the third wave of such stamps in U.S. postal history.

The first consisted of a separately identified set of stamps for each of nine departments of government — Agriculture, Executive, Interior, Justice, Navy, Post Office, State, Treasury and War. These first went into use July 1, 1873, after Congress had abolished the franking privilege.

They consisted of 120 separate items that are now listed in the Scott stamp catalog, and ranged in denomination from 1¢ to the $10 and $20 stamps issued for the State Department. There were also 69 Official stamped envelopes issued for use by the Post Office and War Departments during this period.

The stamps, which are highly regarded by collectors, and the envelopes were supplanted on May 1, 1879, by penalty envelopes and, on July 5, 1884, were declared obsolete. They were apparently never actually demonetized or declared invalid for Official postage.

The second group of Official Mail stamps was a set of six varieties issued in 1910-1911 for the transmission of free mail resulting from administration of the brand-new Postal Savings system. Three varieties of stamped envelope also were issued for this purpose. After less than four years, these separate postal items were discontinued.

The third — and current — Official Mail stamps made their debut January 12, 1983, with seven denominations, 1¢ through $5. Their purpose was to provide a better accounting of actual mail costs for official departments and agencies.

The phrase "Penalty for private use $300" is inscribed on all current Official Mail stamps, thus explaining the designation "Penalty Mail." That $300 fine has been unchanged since Congress set it in legislation approved March 3, 1877. Considering what inflation has done in the intervening years, it is probably not the deterrent it once was.

Fourteen Official Mail stamps have been added since 1983. Five of these were issued in 1991 to meet new rate requirements, of which two were printed by a private contractor, the first Officials of the current series to be made outside the Bureau of Engraving and Printing.

F (29¢) OFFICIAL MAIL COIL

Date of Issue: January 22, 1991

Catalog Number: Scott O144

Colors: blue, red, black

First-Day Cancel: Washington, D.C. (no first-day ceremony)

FDCs Canceled: 88,137

Format: Coils of 100. Offset printing plates of 432 subjects (18 across, 24 around).

Perf: 10.2 (Goebel stroke perforator)

Designer and Typographer: Bradbury Thompson (CSAC)

Art Director and Project Manager: Joe Brockert (USPS)

Printing: printed by BEP on 6-color Goebel Optiforma offset press (043)

Quantity Ordered: 30,000,000

Quantity Distributed: 26,440,000

Plate Number Detail: no plate numbers

Tagging: phosphor-coated paper

The Stamp

One of five non-denominated postage items issued by USPS January 22 in preparation for the increase in the first-class rate to 29¢ February 3 was an F coil stamp for Official Mail.

The stamp was the fourth Official Mail stamp to be issued in connection with a rate change and carrying a letter representing a denomination. Its predecessors were a coil stamp bearing the inscription "Domestic Letter Rate D" (22¢) and a sheet stamp with the inscription "Postal Card

331

Rate D" (14¢), both issued February 4, 1985, and a coil stamp inscribed "Domestic Mail E" (25¢), which appeared March 22, 1988.

On the F stamp, the wording was "For U.S. Addresses Only." This phrase was used on the other F items as well, in an attempt by the Postal Service to make it as clear as possible to users that the stamps weren't valid for mail to foreign addresses.

The Bureau of Engraving and Printing printed the stamp by the offset process, the printing method used for all Official Mail stamps since 1988.

As with previous Official Mail stamps, the F stamp could be purchased by collectors only through the Philatelic Sales Division.

The Design

Bradbury Thompson's F stamp design, patterned after the Great Seal of the United States, was the same design that had appeared on all Official Mail stamps since the use of that category of stamp was resumed in 1983. The capital letter F was in the lower right corner, in the same place the letter D had appeared on the non-denominated first-class rate and postcard rate Official Mail stamps of 1985. (On the E stamp of 1988, the capital letter had been centered at the bottom.)

First-Day Facts

No first-day ceremony was held for the stamp, but Washington, D.C., first-day postmarks were available. Customer affixing of stamps to covers wasn't permitted for this item; all stamps were affixed by USPS. Addressed envelopes submitted were required to bear the following return address: US POSTAL SERVICE, WASHINGTON DC 20066-9998, OFFICIAL BUSINESS, printed, typed or rubber-stamped in three lines in the upper left corner. Gummed address labels could also be used, but the return address couldn't be written in longhand. Items submitted without the return address were returned unserviced.

Collectors were given 60 days after the issue date, rather than the customary 30, to submit their orders.

4¢ OFFICIAL MAIL

Date of Issue: April 6, 1991

Catalog Number: Scott O146

Colors: blue, red, black

First-Day Cancel: Oklahoma City, Oklahoma

FDCs Canceled: 101,627

Format: Panes of 100, vertical, 10 across, 10 down. Offset printing plates of 400 subjects (20 across, 20 around).

Perf: 11.2 (Eureka off-line perforator)

Selvage Markings: "© USPS 1982."

Designer and Typographer: Bradbury Thompson (CSAC)

Art Director and Project Manager: Joe Brockert (USPS)

Printing: printed by BEP on 6-color Goebel Optiforma offset press (043)

Quantity Ordered: 30,000,000

Quantity Distributed: 13,550,000

Plate Number Detail: no plate numbers

Tagging: phosphor-coated paper

The Stamp

The second Official Mail stamp of the year bore the makeup rate of 4¢ — the amount a user had to add to the old first-class rate of 25¢ to equal the new one of 29¢. It was issued April 6, 1991, at the Okpex stamp show in Oklahoma City, Oklahoma.

The stamp was printed by the Bureau of Engraving and Printing by the offset process and issued in panes of 100. It was the second 4¢ stamp in the current Official Mail series. The first, which was printed by intaglio, was part of the initial seven-stamp set that made its debut in Washington, D.C., January 12, 1983.

This earlier 4¢ stamp was removed from sale by the Philatelic Sales Agency June 30, 1991, nearly three months after its successor was issued.

The Design

The stamp had the same basic design as previous stamps in the current Official Mail series. It differed from the previous 4¢ stamp in the series, however, in that its denomination was given as "04" rather than "4c." This was consistent with the Postal Service's current way of expressing denominations of less than a dime.

First-Day Facts

There was no first-day ceremony for the 4¢ Official Mail stamp or for the other postal item that made its debut at Okpex April 6, a 29¢ Official Mail stamped envelope.

First-day covers bearing Postal Service-affixed 4¢ stamps could be ordered by mail for 29¢ each. USPS affixed one of the new stamps and one 25¢ Official Mail stamp to each envelope. Collectors were required to add the following return address to their addressed envelopes: "US POSTAL SERVICE, OKLAHOMA CITY, OK 73125-9998, OFFI-CIAL BUSINESS" in three lines in the upper left corner.

19¢ OFFICIAL MAIL

Date of Issue: May 24, 1991

Catalog Number: Scott O147

Colors: red, blue, black

First-Day Cancel: Seattle, Washington

FDCs Canceled: 76,758. Official Stamp combination FDCs, 14,312

Format: Panes of 100, vertical, 10 across, 10 down. Offset printing plates of 400 subjects (20 across, 20 around).

Perf: 10.9 (L perforator)

Selvage Markings: "© USPS 1983"

Designer and Typographer: Bradbury Thompson (CSAC)

Art Director and Project Manager: Joe Brockert (USPS)

Printing: printed by American Bank Note Company on a 2-color Harris offset sheetfed press at ABNC, Bedford Park, Illinois

Quantity Ordered: 30,000,000

Quantity Distributed: 30,000,000

Plate Number Detail: no plate numbers

Tagging: phosphor-coated paper

The Stamp

On May 24, USPS issued its first two Official Mail stamps of the modern era to be printed outside the Bureau of Engraving and Printing. Bearing the 19¢ and 23¢ denominations, they were offset-printed in sheet form by the American Bank Note Company in suburban Chicago.

The stamps had their first-day sale at Pipex, a stamp show in Seattle, Washington, sponsored by the Northwest Federation of Stamp Clubs.

335

Making their debut on the same occasion were two other Official Mail items: a 29¢ coil stamp and a 19¢ postal card.

The 19¢ stamp was also intended for postcard use. For that purpose it replaced the 15¢ Official Mail coil stamp of 1988.

The Design

The design of the 19¢ stamp was the same as that used on all the modern-day Official Mail stamps: a blue rectangular vignette displaying the Great Seal of the United States, with red wording along the top and bottom and the denomination, in black, centered beneath the vignette.

A comparison of the ABNC-produced 19¢ stamp with the BEP-produced 15¢ stamp of 1988, also printed in offset, shows that the new stamp was printed in a lighter shade of blue, with what appeared to be a coarser screen for its solid-color background. The vignette on the ABNC stamp was also slightly wider and deeper than the BEP vignette. The red lettering on the ABNC stamp was thicker, but the black numerals were thinner than on its BEP counterparts.

First-Day Facts

USPS held no first-day ceremony for the Official Mail items at Pipex.

Collectors submitting addressed envelopes and payment for first-day cancellations were required to print or type the following return address: US POSTAL SERVICE, SEATTLE WA 98109-9998, OFFICIAL BUSI-NESS in three lines in the upper left corner. USPS affixed one 19¢ Official Mail stamp and three 4¢ Official Mail stamps (at a cost of 31¢ to meet the first-class rate of 29¢) on each envelope.

23¢ OFFICIAL MAIL

Date of Issue: May 24, 1991

Catalog Number: Scott O148

Colors: red, blue, black

First-Day Cancel: Seattle, Washington

FDCs Canceled: 68,918

Format: Panes of 100, vertical, 10 across, 10 down. Offset printing plates of 400 subjects (20 across, 20 around).

Perf: 10.9 (L perforator)

Selvage Markings: "© USPS 1983"

Designer and Typographer: Bradbury Thompson (CSAC)

Art Director and Project Manager: Joe Brockert (USPS)

Printing: printed by American Bank Note Company on a 2-color Harris offset sheetfed press at ABNC, Bedford Park, Illinois

Quantity Ordered: 40,000,000

Quantity Distributed: 40,000,000

Plate Number Detail: no plate numbers

Tagging: phosphor-coated paper

The Stamp

The 23¢ Official Mail stamp issued at Seattle's Pipex stamp show on May 24 was created to meet the rate for the second ounce of first-class mail. Like the 19¢ stamp issued on the same occasion, it was produced by the American Bank Note Company in sheet form, printed by the offset method at ABNC's Bedford Park, Illinois, facility.

The Design

The design, based on the Great Seal of the United States, was the same design Bradbury Thompson had created for the Official Mail series in 1983. This design has been used on all stamps in the series since then.

First-Day Facts

As with previous Official Mail issues, USPS affixed the stamps on all first-day covers that it serviced by mail. Two 4¢ Official Mail stamps were placed beside a single 23¢ stamp on each cover for a total cost to the customer of 31¢.

29¢ OFFICIAL MAIL COIL

Date of Issue: May 24, 1991

Catalog Number: Scott O145

Colors: blue, red, black

First-Day Cancel: Seattle, Washington

FDCs Canceled: 79,414

Format: Coils of 100. Printing plates of 432 subjects (18 across, 24 around).

Perf: 10.2

Designer and Typographer: Bradbury Thompson (CSAC)

Art Director and Project Manager: Joe Brockert (USPS)

Printing: printed by BEP on 6-color Goebel Optiforma offset press (043)

Quantity Ordered: 25,000,000

Quantity Distributed: 18,720,000

Plate Number Detail: no plate numbers

Tagging: phosphor-coated paper

The Stamp

USPS provided a 29¢ Official Mail coil stamp May 24 to replace the F stamp it had issued January 22 for the new first-class rate. The stamp first went on sale at the Pipex stamp show in Seattle, Washington, along with Official Mail stamps of two other denominations and an Official Mail postal card.

The stamp, like all previous first-class stamps in the current Official

Mail series, was issued in coil form. The coils of 100 were offset-printed by the Bureau of Engraving and Printing.

The Design

The design of the 29¢ stamp was the standard Great Seal of the United States design that Bradbury Thompson had created for the first of the current Official Mail stamps in 1983. Except for the "29," it was indistinguishable from its denominated predecessor, the 25¢ Official Mail coil stamp of 1988.

First-Day Facts

Unlike the other two Official Mail stamps that made their debut at Pipex May 24, the 29¢ stamp required no additional postage on first-day covers to meet the first-class rate.

$15 MIGRATORY BIRD HUNTING (DUCK) STAMP 1991-92

Date of Issue: June 30, 1991

Catalog Number: Scott RW58

Colors: magenta, yellow, cyan, brown (offset); black (intaglio); black (flexographic back plate)

First-Day Cancel: June 30, 1991, Washington, D.C.; July 1, 1991, East Dorset, Vermont

Format: Panes of 30, horizontal, 5 across, 6 down. Offset printing plates of 120 subjects (12 across, 10 down); intaglio printing sleeves of 240 subjects (12 across, 20 around); flexographic back plate of 120 subjects (12 across, 10 down).

Perf: 11.2 by 11.1 (Eureka off-line perforator)

Selvage Markings: sleeve number

Artist: Nancy Howe of East Dorset, Vermont

Stamp Designer and Modeler: Peter Cocci (BEP)

Engraver: Gary Chaconas (BEP)

Printing: printed by BEP on 6-color offset, 3-color intaglio D press (902)

Quantity Ordered: 4,800,000

Quantity Distributed: 3,822,000

Sleeve Number Detail: 1 intaglio sleeve number alongside corner stamp

Tagging: untagged

The Stamp

The 1991-1992 Federal Migratory Bird Hunting and Conservation stamp was the 58th in the series, the first to cost $15, the first to depict the king eider — and the first to be designed by a woman.

Nancy Howe of East Dorset, Vermont, won the contest to create the artwork for the 1991 duck stamp. The 40th annual competition was held in Washington, D.C., November 6 and 7, 1990.

Howe's acrylic painting of a pair of king eiders in the subarctic tundra was named winner over 625 other entries after the judges broke a three-way tie for first place. Second place went to Wilhelm Goebel of New Jersey for his painting of black scoters, and third went to Cynthie Fisher of Washington state for her spectacled eiders.

After the judging, Manuel Lujan, secretary of the Interior, telephoned Howe to give her the news and invite her to Washington to meet President Bush the following afternoon. She arrived at the White House with her husband Jim Russell and their sons, Ryan, 8, and Tyler, 7, for a 10-minute chat with the president.

Howe, 39, was not only a wildlife artist but also a sheep farmer and a model for the catalogs of Vermont's Orvis Company. A graduate of Middlebury College with a major in art, she had been painting since childhood. She was an active member of Ducks Unlimited and had

Nancy Howe and her family met President Bush at the White House November 8, 1990, the day after she won the Duck stamp contest. Left to right are: Manuel Lujan Jr., secretary of the interior; Norma Opgrand, chief, Federal Duck Stamp Office; President Bush; Nancy Howe and her husband, Jim Russell; Constance Harriman, assistant secretary of the Interior; and S. Scott Sewell, principal deputy assistant secretary of the Interior. Nancy and Jim's sons, Tyler and Ryan, are standing at front.

exhibited her work with that organization as well as in many other art shows.

She had entered the duck stamp contest at least 13 times without success, and was almost ready to give up. "The format is so limiting," she said. "You're working on what will be a tiny stamp, and you're required to do a particular species, and you have to leave room for writing on the design. I got tired of seeing paintings win that I didn't particularly care for, and I wondered how I was going to proceed if I would never do something that looked like those paintings.

"My husband and I talked about whether I should enter again, because it just wasn't fun any more. I decided that it was still worth taking a shot, but that I would do a piece that would look more like a detail from one of my larger paintings, so that if I didn't win I could take it to a gallery and sell it as a miniature, and it wouldn't look like a duck stamp. That way, I figured, I would do something I would really like, and if the judges didn't like it I'd have a saleable piece of work.

"And that was what seemed to appeal to the public and the judges — that it looked like a little painting, it was subtle, it didn't strike you that 'This is a duck stamp entry.' It made it more fun for me to do, and I think that was the quality that perhaps helped to separate it from the other entries." In pleasing herself, she also pleased the others who counted.

Howe's father had encouraged her to enter the contest — and to persist, "He kept saying I was going to be the first woman to win, that I should keep trying," she said. He died in 1979, more than a decade before his prediction came true.

Howe eventually sold all her previous contest paintings except an early "rather primitive-looking" one and the red-breasted merganser she had submitted in 1989. "It was technically nice but it had no heart to it at all," she said of the 1989 painting. "In fact, that was why I got so soured on the duck stamps. When I finished that one I thought, well, I'll ship this out, but I don't really care about it. It just had nothing that appealed to me as a painting. Technically, the bird was quite attractive. But I just didn't feel it had any other quality that drew you into the picture. So that one is hanging in my son's bathroom right now."

The first federal duck stamp, in 1934, had a face value of $1. Over the years Congress has periodically increased the cost, which went from $12.50 to $15 in 1991. All hunters aged 16 and over must buy a current duck stamp in order to hunt waterfowl. The Department of the Interior says that 98¢ of each dollar raised through the sale of stamps goes directly to purchase migratory waterfowl habitat. To date, nearly four million wetland acres have been bought with the more than $350 million generated by the program.

For the first few years, the duck stamp artwork was commissioned, but the policy changed with the first contest in 1949. The idea for the competition came from Bob Hines, who had painted the picture used for the 1946-1947 duck stamp and who in 1949 began a long career as an illustrator for the U.S. Fish and Wildlife Service. During the contest for the 1991-1992 stamp design, the Interior Department presented Hines with a certificate of appreciation and displayed a collection of his artwork in the department museum.

The federal government provides no monetary prize for the contest winner. However, the winner is free to market limited-edition prints of the design, and this privilege has earned several past winners more than $1 million in royalties apiece. In Nancy Howe's case, she and her print publisher, Voyageur Art, agreed to donate some of the proceeds from the art prints to waterfowl conservation — reportedly, the first time this had been done. Her prints were sold for a basic price of $150 each.

Winning the federal contest also gives an enormous boost to an artist's reputation. Additional commissions come from conservation groups, from states that issue their own duck and other wildlife stamps, and, recently, from foreign governments. For example, Nancy Howe, like the two previous federal contest winners, was signed to paint the picture for the following year's Australian duck stamp.

Judges for the contest won by Howe were Susan Bournique, photo editor for The Nature Conservancy's magazine; James Gordon Jude, Sydney, Australia, stamp dealer and executive director of the Australian Wildlife Fund; Robert J. Koenke, publisher and editor of the magazine *Wildlife Art News*; Dolores "Sissy" George LaVigne, wildlife art collector and hunter, and Romi Myers Perkins, outdoorswoman, conservationist and wildlife art collector. The alternate judge was Jack Elrod, writer-illustrator of the "Mark Trail" comic strip.

The contest for the 1991 duck stamp design, like the two before it, required competitors to choose their subjects from among five species specified by the Fish and Wildlife Service from a list of North American waterfowl that hadn't previously been pictured on the stamps. For the 1992 stamp competition, which was judged in November 1991, the king eider was dropped from the list and the surf scoter was added. By 1997, through the process of elimination, duck stamps will have depicted all 42 species of waterfowl whose ranges include the contiguous United States and Alaska, plus Hawaii's nene goose.

King eiders are at home in Arctic coastal waters and range from Siberia and northwestern Alaska to Labrador and Greenland. They winter along the Atlantic and Pacific coasts as far south as New Jersey and California, and sometimes on the Great Lakes.

The male is characterized by a short orange or red-violet bill, a yellow or orange frontal shield outlined in black and a pale blue crest. Its body is mostly black, with a white front, and a black V outlines the throat. The female is a tawny brown with dusky brown crescent-shaped bars.

The Design

"I wanted to paint a species I hadn't done before," Nancy Howe said. "I would have liked to pick one that was local to my area, but the only one on the list was the red-breasted merganser, and I had already done that.

"I found the king eider attractive to do — it's odd-looking but it's stunning in coloration — and we have a local museum that had a mounted male specimen that I could work from for details of feathering.

"To come up with positions of both the birds, I had to resort to published photographs. Usually it takes a number of photographs; you take the head from one, for instance, and the leg position from another, to get it the way you want it. Actually, the female's position in the painting was one of a goose that I had seen, and I adapted it.

"Usually when I do a picture with a number of birds in it, I work on the composition of the birds and do the background afterward. So I spent a lot of time picking positions that I liked and putting them on tracing paper, and then moving them around to get the best composition. When I had what I wanted I transferred the tracing to the painting surface."

In designing her background, Howe used an artistic technique she had seen used in another artist's shore-bird scene. Her picture had the kind of lighting in which the viewer doesn't actually see the sky but gets an inference of it by its reflection in the water. She did the water in "sunup or sundown colors, sort of an aqua color with those orangey pinks that you get at dawn or dusk," she said.

Howe had never visited the tundra, and she looked for photographs in books and old *National Geographic* magazines. The tundra in her painting consisted of "last year's grasses, somewhat colored by the sky, and with some shoots of new green to make it obvious it's early spring," she said. She spent as much time on this background as on the birds, using a fine-tipped brush for the elaborate detail. "There's quite a lot of layering of colors there," she said. "Each blade may have three or more different colors in it, depending on whether it's in the dark or the light." People have an impression that tundra is "brown, dreary and lifeless," she said,

Nancy Howe's contest-winning acrylic painting of a male and female king eider.

"and I wanted to show how much richness of color there actually is there."

Even so, the brightly colored male king eider stood out boldly against its environment. The more drably patterned female, however, tended to blend in. Howe solved this artistic problem by placing enough of the watercourse behind the female so that the bird was silhouetted. "The rest of the job was just working the water areas to make a nice design, to make it pleasing to the eye and draw you into the birds," she said.

Howe was proud of her finished work. "There was a black duck I had submitted a number of years ago, and a lesser scaup, both of which I thought would have made really nice stamps," she said. "But this year's design was probably the strongest piece of all, so I'm glad it won."

First-Day Facts

Each year the first sheet of duck stamps off the Bureau of Engraving and Printing presses is signed by a number of federal officials and the artist. For the 1991 stamp, this event occurred May 6.

As in past years, there were two widely separated ceremonies heralding the actual sale of the duck stamps: a first-day ceremony at the Smithsonian Institution's National Museum of American History and a second-day ceremony in the artist's home state.

The first-day ceremony took place Sunday, June 30, in the Smithsonian's

The signers of the first sheets of 1991-1992 duck stamps at the Bureau of Engraving and Printing May 7, 1991, were, left to right: Gary Chaconas, engraver; Susan Bournique and Dolores "Sissy" LaVigne, contest judges; Peter Daly, BEP director; John Turner, director, Fish and Wildlife Service; Catalina Vasquez Villalpando, treasurer of the United States; Robert Koenke, contest judge; Manuel Lujan Jr., secretary of the Interior; Norma Opgrand, chief, Federal Duck Stamp Office; Frank Bracken, deputy secretary of the Interior; Nancy Howe, contest winner; Senators Patrick J. Leahy, D-Vermont, and James Jeffords, R-Vermont; Romi Perkins, contest judge; Representative Bernard Sanders of Vermont; and Jim Russell, Nancy Howe's husband.

Carmichael Auditorium. The speakers included Christopher Koss, president of the J.N. "Ding" Darling Foundation (named for the Iowa editorial cartoonist whose enthusiastic advocacy of conservation helped create the duck stamp program), and James Bruns, acting director of the National Postal History and Philatelic Museum. Washington was the only city where the stamps were available June 30.

What the Interior Department calls the "first day of sale" ceremony was held Monday, July 1, at a tiny white clapboard cabin that serves as the post office in Nancy Howe's hometown of East Dorset, Vermont. Besides Howe, participants included Governor Richard A. Snelling; U.S. Senator Patrick J. Leahy, D-Vermont; Frank A. Bracken, deputy secretary of the Interior; John Turner, director of the U.S. Fish and Wildlife Service, and Don Kelpinski, head of USPS operations in Vermont. Norma Opgrand, chief of the Federal Duck Stamp Program, was mistress of ceremonies.

USPS had arranged to furnish two different pictorial cancellations, one at the Smithsonian June 30, the other at the "King Eider Station" in East Dorset July 1. But the cancellation device failed to arrive in East Dorset on time, so covers for the collectors on hand were canceled with the regular East Dorset postmark. The pictorial device, featuring a feather, arrived the next day and was put to use on mailed-in first-day cover requests. Of the two varieties, the regular East Dorset postmark was reportedly much more scarce. As usual, covers were required to carry first-class postage in addition to the duck stamp.

POSTAL STATIONERY

The 11 varieties of stamped envelope that were issued in 1991 included a new Love envelope, a Country Geese envelope designed to appeal to household mailers, and two aerograms with the same design but printed on different colors of paper.

No new hologram envelope was produced during the year, but the window-and-patch manufacturing technique developed by USPS for its first two hologram envelopes — depicting a Space Station and professional football's Lombardi Trophy — was used to create a multicolor envelope commemorating the 250th anniversary of a cherished Postal Service customer, the magazine industry.

Among the 11 postal cards were four in the Historic Preservation series — three of which marked the anniversaries of institutions of higher education — and one in the America the Beautiful series. A card commemorating the ratification of the Bill of Rights brought to an end the Postal Service's extended celebration of the Bicentennial of the U.S. Constitution, which began in 1987.

F (29¢) OFFICIAL MAIL SAVINGS BOND ENVELOPE

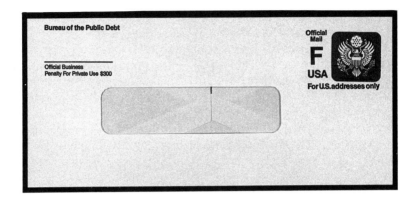

Date of Issue: January 22, 1991

Catalog Number: Scott UO83

Colors: blue, black

First-Day Cancel: Washington, D.C. (no first-day ceremony.)

FDCs Canceled: 30,549

Size: 7₁₅⁄₁₆ inches by 3₉⁄₁₆ inches, with window

Watermark: eagle and recycling symbol

Markings: Under flap: "© USPS 1988." At front upper left: "Bureau of the Public Debt" and penalty notation. On outside of flap: "GOOD NEWS!/U.S. Savings Bonds . . . Now Tax Free for Education/Save today for college tomorrow./To see if you qualify/-get IRS Form 8818-."

Designer and Typographer: Bradbury Thompson (CSAC)

Art Director and Project Manager: Joe Brockert (USPS)

Modeler: John Boyd of Anagraphics Inc., New York, New York

Printing: Westvaco-USEnvelope Division in 2-color flexography on a VH machine. Recycled paper used.

Quantity Ordered: 2,200,000

Quantity Distributed: 3,523,500

Tagging: square bar to left of indicium

The Envelope

As was the case when postal rates were last changed in 1988, USPS in 1991 issued a non-denominated version of its Official Mail Savings Bond envelope to cover the new first-class rate but didn't do so for its regular Official Mail envelope. The Savings Bond envelope was one of a group of F series postal items issued in Washington, D.C., January 24.

"The demand for regular Official Mail envelopes is such that we thought the agencies could get by with the old envelopes plus makeup postage," said Joe Brockert, project manager and art director for the Savings Bond envelope. "The regular envelopes are used much less heavily than the Savings Bond envelopes. We thought that a three-month gap was acceptable. The Savings Bond people in the Treasury Department thought that kind of gap wasn't acceptable, however. Their program is ongoing. They are mailing out bonds weekly and they are also ordering envelopes weekly."

The Savings Bond envelopes are used to mail individual bonds to purchasers whose addresses are not (yet) entered into a computerized sort sequence: purchasers of single bonds from banks, purchasers who are just starting payroll savings accounts and those submitting changes of address. After the information is entered, the bonds are mailed at the appropriate presort discounts in properly endorsed penalty envelopes.

Like its predecessors, the new Savings Bond envelope was issued in one size only, 3 9/16 inches deep by 7 15/16 inches long, which was tailored to the size of the bonds it was made to hold, and had an address window. Because of the envelope's odd size, Westvaco-USEnvelope Division's VH envelope-forming machine wasn't capable of embossing the indicium. All printing was done by flexography. The envelope's specialized usage precluded any USPS concern about the possibility of counterfeiting.

At the request of the Bureau of Public Debt, USPS changed the promotional message printed on the back flap. The 25¢ Savings Bond envelope had carried the wording: "Buy and Hold U.S. Savings Bonds/ The Great American Investment/Call 1-800-US-BONDS." The message on the new Savings Bond envelope was "GOOD NEWS!/U.S. Savings Bonds . . . Now Tax Free For Education/Save today for college tomorrow./To see if you qualify/-get IRS Form 8818-."

This is a drawing of the new watermark used on the F-series and 29¢ Official Mail Savings Bond stamped envelopes. The watermark is drawn as seen from the back of the envelope front, as stamp watermarks are viewed from the back of the stamp, which is why the recycling arrows are going counterclockwise.

USPS announced that the new envelope would be the first U.S. stamped envelope made out of recycled paper. The paper, made by Westvaco, bore an appropriate watermark: an eagle and shield encircled by four arrows, the symbol of recycling. It was the first new watermark design to be seen on U.S. stamped envelopes since 1968, and the first pictorial envelope watermark since the Columbus-Liberty profiles that were used on the 1893 Columbian series.

The Design

The indicium was similar to that of the 25¢ Savings Bond envelope of 1988. The Great Seal of the United States was superimposed on a solid blue square at the right; to the left, in black, was the inscription "Official/Mail/F/USA," and beneath was the line that is necessary on non-denominated mail items, "For U.S. addresses only."

First-Day Facts

There was no first-day ceremony. Collectors wishing first-day covers were instructed to send a peelable return address label and 34¢ for each cover desired to the postmaster in Washington, D.C. Sixty days was allowed for ordering.

29¢ STAR ENVELOPE

Date of Issue: January 24, 1991

Catalog Number: Scott U619

Colors: blue, red

First-Day Cancel: Washington, D.C. (no first-day ceremony)

FDCs Canceled: 33,025

Size: number 6¾, number 10, both sizes with and without windows

Watermark: USA and star (number 49)

Markings: "© USPS 1991" under flap

Designer and Typographer: Richard Sheaff (CSAC)

Art Director and Project Manager: Jack Williams (USPS)

Printing: Westvaco-USEnvelope Division by flexography and embossing on a VH machine

Quantity Ordered: 160,000,000

Quantity Distributed: 640,663,000

Tagging: square bar to left of indicium

The Envelope

On January 24, without advance notice, USPS issued a 29¢ stamped envelope to cover the first-class rate that would take effect February 3.

The design was quite basic, consisting of a large, solid star in blue and the inscription "USA 29" in two lines of red. Like all previous definitive first-class envelopes, this one had an embossed element, although one that was virtually invisible. It consisted of two colorless horizontal bars, about 1⅜ inches long, above and below the printed indicium.

The new envelope, along with a new 19¢ postal card issued the same day, went into hurried production beginning January 4 after the Postal Rate Commission had announced its recommendation of a 29¢ letter rate and a 19¢ postcard rate. It was manufactured in two sizes, number 6¾ and number 10, with and without windows.

In the past, USPS had specified that embossing be used in the printing process as a security feature. Now officials found another rationale for it: as a sales promotion device.

A flyer went out to businesses from Westvaco's Marketing and Communications section touting "printed, embossed stamped envelopes" as "a sure way for your business mail to stand out from other correspondence." "Nothing leaves as good an impression," the message said. "The bright, colorful printed stamp stands out in any stack of mail, and the unique embossing sets up a quality image which carries over to the contents of your correspondence. In essence, no matter how carefully your envelope is typed, it simply can't look as professional or distinctive as a printed, embossed stamped envelope."

The printed return addresses — including a mandatory ZIP+4 Code — could contain up to seven lines of up to 47 characters and spaces each, including two advertising/slogan lines. The maximum number of lines was five if the customer asked for a Postal Service endorsement, such as "Address Correction Requested." The Stamped Envelope Unit offered these customized envelopes in quantities of 500 or 50, with prices

The Pentagon stamped envelope, sold in error by the Philatelic Sales Division, had a return address printed by the same flexographic plates used to print the stamped area.

This is Richard Sheaff's basic Star design, which, with modifications to the star and lettering made by the manufacturer, became the envelope indicium. The horizontal bars, instead of being printed in color on the envelope, were blind embossed.

ranging from $156.40 for 500 number 6¾ windowless (31.28¢ apiece) to $17.50 for 50 number 10 windows (35¢ apiece). Single, non-customized envelopes sold for 34¢ each.

In the July-August issue of the Philatelic Sales Division's *Philatelic Catalog,* an unannounced item appeared under the category ''Official Mail Envelope.'' It was item 2136, described as ''Dept. of Defense,'' selling for 34¢. The same listing was carried in the September-October catalog but was gone when the November-December issue came out.

The mystery item, it turned out, was a 29¢ Star envelope, number 10 size, without window, with a return address depicting a stylized pentagon and two lines of type reading: ''Department of Defense/Official Business.'' It further turned out that the item had been erroneously listed and sold by the Philatelic Sales Division, not only by mail order but at several USPS philatelic centers.

''It was just a mistake,'' USPS spokesman Francis Richter told *Linn's Stamp News.* ''It was just a private order by the Department of Defense for a preprinted envelope.''

Richter said an employee of the Stamped Envelope Agency, which printed the envelope, assumed that it was a new variety and notified the Philatelic Sales Division accordingly.

Richard Sheaff developed this assortment of single-star envelope indicium designs in red and blue or red, blue and gray, using his Macintosh computer.

This Star indicium, with lines that would wrap around to the back of the envelope, was prepared for a non-denominated F envelope that wasn't issued.

In fact, the envelope could well be considered a collectible variety, even though it was not intended to be made available to collectors. Unlike other envelopes printed with return addresses — such as those that USPS was vigorously promoting in the flyer quoted above — the Pentagon envelope's additional printing, in blue, was done by the same flexographic plate used to print the blue star in the indicium.

Although the envelope was marked "Official Business," it carried no penalty notification of the kind that is standard on Official Mail envelopes, and individual envelopes could be legally used by anyone who bought them, not just by Defense Department personnel.

The Design

The Star design was one of a large number of envelope designs that Richard Sheaff of Needham Heights, Massachusetts, a CSAC design coordinator, had created for USPS to keep in reserve. Sheaff had produced this particular one on his Macintosh computer in the fall of 1990. He was disappointed, he said, at the way it was translated into a finished product.

"It originally had a nice, crisp five-pointed star that actually had points on it," he said. "It had bars with a certain kind of a weight, with rounded ends, and typography that was carefully done. And somehow it came out of the printing process at Westvaco with type of a different weight and in a different place.

"It turns out that their flexography process, with a rubber plate, can't reproduce pointed stars, or pointed anything; it rounds them off. So they re-drew the star with rounded points on it, to make it easier for themselves. They gave us three samples. They said, 'We can round them just a little, or a little more, or a lot more.' And we said, 'Well, if you have to round them, round them the minimum amount.' And they went ahead and rounded them about three times as much."

Sheaff's design had included horizontal bars above and below the indicium that could have been printed in color as a graphic element to frame the star and typography. USPS chose instead, as we have seen, to have them blind-embossed, which left the printed elements visually afloat on the corner of the envelope.

First-Day Facts

No first-day ceremony was held for the two postal stationery items issued January 24. However, first-day cancellations from Washington,

355

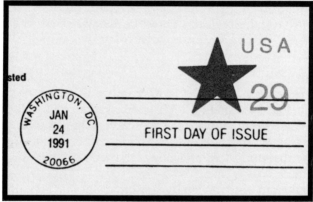

First-day cancels photographically cropped from two 29¢ Star embossed stamped envelopes. Top, a machine cancel applied by a rotating steel die hub on a high-speed Pitney Bowes Model D canceling machine. Bottom, a so-called hand-cancel applied by a rubber composition device mounted on the drum of a Kirk-Rudy printer at Philatelic Sales Division headquarters.

D.C., were made available. Collectors were given 60 days, to March 25, to submit their addressed Star envelopes for canceling or to send peelable return-address labels plus 34¢ per item for USPS-supplied envelopes.

29¢ OFFICIAL MAIL ENVELOPE

Date of Issue: April 6, 1991

Catalog Number: Scott UO84

Colors: blue, black

First-Day Cancel: Oklahoma City, Oklahoma

FDCs Canceled: 27,841

Size: number 10, with and without window

Watermark: USA and star (number 49)

Markings: "© USPS 1988" under flap. "Official Business/Penalty For Private Use $300" at upper left corner.

Designer and Typographer: Bradbury Thompson (CSAC)

Art Director and Project Manager: Joe Brockert (USPS)

Modeler: John Boyd of Anagraphics Inc., New York, New York

Printing: Westvaco-USEnvelope Division in 2-color flexography and embossing on a VH machine

Quantity Ordered: 2,500,000

Quantity Distributed: 5,715,000

Tagging: square bar to left of indicium

The Envelope

On April 6, USPS issued a 29¢ Official Mail envelope for the general use of federal agencies. The envelope, which had its first-day sale at the Okpex stamp show in Oklahoma City, Oklahoma, replaced the 25¢ Official Mail envelope of 1988. It was issued in the number 10 size, with and without windows.

The item was one of only two envelopes issued in 1991 to have old-fashioned embossing in its indicium. (The other was the 29¢ Star definitive envelope that was issued January 24). For a century or so, embossing was a standard element in the manufacture of U.S. stamped envelopes, but since the mid-1980s USPS has made an increasing number of envelopes by flexography only, or a flexo-offset combination. Even the Official Mail envelopes created specifically for mailing savings bonds have been printed without embossing.

The Design

The basic indicium was the old familiar Great Seal of the United States on a solid blue background, the design used on all Official Mail stamps, postal cards and envelopes since the current series began in 1983. However, the arrangement of design elements in the upper right corner was different from the arrangement on previous Official Mail envelopes.

Previously, the typography had been grouped to the left of the indicium, with "Official Mail" in two lines and the denomination and "USA" in two more lines beneath. On the new envelope, "Official Mail" was placed in one line above the indicium, and the space those words had formerly occupied was left blank. The purpose was to leave space for FIMs — facing identification marks, used to identify pre-bar-coded mail to automated postal equipment — in case some government mailer should have occasion to use them.

In addition, the order of the "USA" and denomination was reversed, with the latter now placed at the bottom. This was another concession to automation. It was insurance against the possibility, admittedly a small one, that post office Optical Character Readers (OCRs) might try to read the smaller "USA" line as part of an address. The larger denomination numerals were deemed to be too big to confuse the OCRs. "We try to eliminate any possibility that our mail processing people will tell us that we've designed something that's affecting their processing capabilities," said Joe Brockert, the envelope's project manager and art director.

First-Day Facts

There was no first-day ceremony for the envelope or the 4¢ Official Mail stamp that also made its debut at Okpex. Collectors wishing first-day covers were instructed to send peelable return address labels, plus 34¢ for each envelope ordered, to the postmaster at Oklahoma City. USPS then added the official government return address, affixed the label and canceled the envelope. Sixty days was allowed for ordering.

29¢ OFFICIAL MAIL SAVINGS BOND ENVELOPE

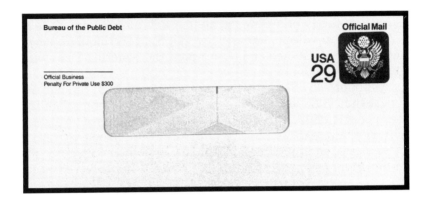

Date of Issue: April 17, 1991

Catalog Number: Scott UO85

Colors: blue, black

First-Day Cancel: Washington, D.C. (no first-day ceremony)

FDCs Canceled: 25,563

Size: 7¹⁵⁄₁₆ inches by 3⁹⁄₁₆ inches, with window

Watermark: eagle and recycling symbol

Markings: Under flap: "© USPS 1988." At front upper left: "Bureau of the Public Debt" and penalty notation. On outside of flap: "GOOD NEWS!/U.S. Savings Bonds . . . Now Tax Free For Education/Save today for college tomorrow./To see if you qualify/-get IRS Form 8818-"

Designer and typographer: Bradbury Thompson (CSAC)

Art Director and Project Manager: Joe Brockert (USPS)

Modeler: John Boyd of Anagraphics Inc., New York, New York

Printing: Westvaco-USEnvelope Division in 2-color flexography on a VH machine. Recycled paper used.

Quantity Ordered: 3,000,000

Quantity Distributed: 3,576,000

Tagging: square bar to left of indicium

The Envelope

The 29¢ version of the Official Mail Savings Bond envelope was issued April 17 in Washington, D.C. It replaced the non-denominated F envelope that USPS had made available to the Treasury Department's Bureau of the Public Debt before the February 3 rate change.

The new envelope, like the F version, was printed on recycled paper supplied by Westvaco and bore a pictorial watermark showing an eagle and shield and the circular-arrows recycling symbol.

Although USPS had been making Official Mail Savings Bond envelopes since 1988, not all branches of the Bureau of the Public Debt used them consistently. A *Linn's Stamp News* reader from Pittsburgh, Pennsylvania, reported in mid-1991 that for more than a year his bonds had been mailed to him in a plain window envelope with a penalty notation in the upper left corner and an Official postage meter imprint.

The Design

The design elements of the 29¢ Savings Bond envelope were changed somewhat from those of the F and the 25¢ Savings Bond envelopes of 1988. The words "Official Mail" were moved from the left side of the Great Seal indicium to a line above it, and the "USA 29" logo, which remained on the left side, was moved downward. The purpose was to open a space at the top of the envelope for Facing Identification Marks (FIMs), which expedite automatic sorting of mail, in case the Bureau of the Public Debt should want to add them to the envelopes in the future.

The same change had been made on the 29¢ Official Mail envelope that had been issued 11 days earlier for general use by federal agencies. However, that envelope's indicium could be distinguished from the indicium of the Savings Bond envelope by the fact that its Great Seal design element was embossed rather than printed by flexography.

First-Day Facts

There was no first-day ceremony. Collectors wishing first-day covers were instructed to send a peelable return address label and 34¢ for each envelope desired to the postmaster in Washington, D.C. Fifty-eight days were allowed for ordering.

11.1¢ BIRDS NON-PROFIT ENVELOPE

Date of Issue: May 3, 1991

Catalog Numbers: Scott U620

Colors: blue (PMS 300), red (PMS 186)

First-Day Cancel: Boxborough, Massachusetts

FDCs Canceled: 20,720

Size: number 6¾, number 10, each with and without windows

Watermark: star below USA (Type 49) or star above USA (Type 50)

Markings: "© USPS 1991" under flap

Designer and Typographer: Richard Sheaff (CSAC)

Art Director and Project Manager: Joe Brockert (USPS)

Printing: Westvaco-USEnvelope Division in 2-color flexography on a VH machine

Quantity Ordered: 5,300,000

Quantity Distributed: 9,788,000

Tagging: untagged

The Envelope

On May 3, USPS issued a stamped envelope for non-profit bulk third-class mail. It bore a denomination of 11.1¢, matching the new basic rate. The envelope had its first-day sale in Boxborough, Massachusetts, in conjunction with the opening of Philatelic Show 91, sponsored by the Northeastern Federation of Stamp Clubs.

The envelope was available in both number 6¾ and number 10 sizes and with and without windows. It replaced the 8.4¢ embossed envelope of 1988 that depicted the Navy frigate *Constellation* in its indicium.

Like the *Constellation* envelope and the *USS Constitution* non-profit envelope that preceded it, this one was precanceled, with the cancellation markings incorporated into the design. In this case, the precancel consisted of three parallel lines representing utility wires, with a flock of birds perched on the wires or fluttering around them.

But like other, more recent stamped envelopes, this one wasn't embossed, but printed entirely by flexography, with security afforded in part by a wraparound of the three parallel lines onto the back of the envelope. Tagging, which can offer an additional security feature, was omitted, inasmuch as the envelopes weren't intended to go through facer-canceler machines.

Non-profit bulk mailers who presorted their mail to five digits enjoyed a discount from the 11.1¢ rate, to 9.8¢; those who presorted to the carrier route paid only 7.4¢ per item. In planning the envelope, USPS considered the possibility of making the item usable by all non-profit bulk mailers, regardless of the level of sortation, by placing a low basic rate on it — 4¢, 5¢ or 6¢ — and then charging the users, at the time of mailing, whatever additional postage was required. Designer Richard Sheaff actually made some models of the envelope bearing the service inscription "Additional Non-Profit Postage Paid." Although in the end this approach wasn't used with the envelope, it was used with the 5¢ Canoe coil stamp that was issued three weeks later.

The Design

The design was one of literally dozens of envelope concepts that Richard Sheaff had prepared in recent years for possible use by USPS. Among these were several that incorporated what Sheaff called a "postmark-looking way" of dealing with non-profit indicia — designs (like the birds on the wires) that made use of parallel lines that suggested cancellation bars. One sketch, for example, showed a longhorn steer behind a fence.

Sheaff said his inspiration for the birds image was "a scrap of ephemera from the 1880s or 1890s" — possibly a book jacket — that he had come across at one time but whose identity he had forgotten. He first worked up an envelope design using pen and ink, but later created the finished product on a Macintosh computer. The birds, he admitted, were generic, not based on any particular species.

First-Day Facts

USPS sponsored no first-day ceremony for the envelope at Boxborough, but the Northeastern Federation of Stamp Clubs prepared a first-day program that was distributed at its show at the Boxborough Host Hotel.

Collectors requesting first-day cancellations were required to provide

362

These sketches by Richard Sheaff envisioned using the birds-on-a-wire design theme on a first-class rate envelope and also on an envelope for non-profit bulk mailers who would pay the required additional postage at the time of mailing.

an additional 18¢ postage on their envelopes to make up the first-class rate. In cases in which USPS was asked to furnish the envelope, 36¢ was charged, and a 19¢ Fawn stamp was affixed beside the indicium. A 60-day grace period was provided for first-day cancellation requests.

29¢ LOVE ENVELOPE

Date of Issue: May 9, 1991

Catalog Number: U621

Colors: red (PMS 213), purple (PMS 259), indicium; light blue (envelope exterior)

First-Day Cancel: Honolulu, Hawaii

FDCs Canceled: 40,110

Size: number 6¾, number 10

Watermark: unwatermarked

Markings: "© USPS 1991" under flap

Designer: Salahattin Kanidinc of Jackson Heights, New York

Art Director and Project Manager: Joe Brockert (USPS)

Typographer: Bradbury Thompson (CSAC)

Modeler: John Boyd of Anagraphics Inc., New York, New York

Printing: Westvaco-USEnvelope Division by flexography on a VH press and offset on a two-color Jet press

Quantity Ordered: 4,000,000 number 6¾; 4,000,000 number 10

Quantity Distributed: 22,630,000 total

Tagging: vertical bar to right of indicium

The Envelope

USPS' second Love stamped envelope was one of the four Love postal items that were dedicated May 9, 1991, in Honolulu, Hawaii.

This envelope, like the prototype in 1989, bore an indicium that featured an unusual treatment of the word "Love." But whereas the 1989 envelope was issued in the number 9 size only, making it useful for RSVPs by persons mailing invitations in a number 10, this one was made

364

available in two standard sizes, number 10 and number 6¾.

The envelopes were sold for 34¢ each, 5¢ more than their 29¢ face value. They were also available with custom-printed return addresses for $17.20 per box of 50 number 6¾ envelopes (34.4¢ apiece), or $17.40 per box of 50 number 10s (34.8¢ apiece).

In a first-ever form of product promotion, USPS also produced 80,000 of the Love envelopes with the imprint "— Sample —" defacing the denomination. These envelopes — 40,000 of each size — were distributed to post offices across the country by the U.S. Stamped Envelope Agency, a division of the Westvaco Corporation.

The envelope variety was the first so-called specimen postal item to be officially produced by the United States since two War Savings stamps were handstamped with the word "Specimen" in 1917. Historically, stamps that were so overprinted had been produced by the U.S. Post Office Department to distribute as samples to prospective printing bidders. In some cases, specimens were given to dignitaries and Universal Postal Union representatives.

The Love envelopes with the "Sample" imprint had a different purpose: to promote the preprinted return address service. The letter accompanying the envelopes, dated May 1991, advised postmasters that by displaying the specimen items and making information available to postal customers they could boost their office's revenue "100 percent by the end of the fiscal year." Revenue generated by the sale of preprinted stamped envelopes was credited to post offices according to ZIP Code, the letter explained.

Normally, return addresses on stamped envelopes were printed on the finished envelopes by a plate prepared by a computer-driven linotype machine. For the specimen envelopes, however, the sample return address, and the word "Sample" as well, were printed from the same offset plate that created the purple denomination figure.

This number 6¾-size specimen Love envelope was mailed to each of 40,000 U.S. post offices, along with a number 10-size envelope.

Kanidinc's talent for calligraphy was put to good use on this multicolored United Nations postal card (Scott UX8) and this personalized signature.

Specimen stamps and envelopes have always been considered collectible, even though they are invalid for postage. In the case of the Love envelopes, a number of the samples were obtained by collectors through their post offices, and in November these items were reported to be selling in the $30 range. This led to complaints from other collectors who were unable to secure copies.

As a result, USPS unexpectedly disclosed that it would reprint the sample envelope in both sizes and offer them to collectors through the Philatelic Sales Division. The November-December issue of the *Philatelic Catalog* listed the items at the same 34¢ price as the mint envelopes and appended this explanatory note: "Because some reached collectors, we are making them available through the catalog."

There was a major catch, however. The new sample envelopes were made in a different way — by overprinting existing stamped envelope stock — and thus were distinguishable from the originals. There was ink overlap on the new samples where the horizontal defacing line crossed the denomination, and there was also the probability of "floating" overprints, rather than the fixed-position elements existing on the first batch of specimens.

In addition, according to John Shultz, editor of *The Catalogue of the 20th-Century Envelopes and Wrappers of the United States*, the defacement lines were of different lengths and line quality than on the originals.

Complicating things still further for collectors was the fact that a third, or "provisional," type of specimen envelope had been created between printings, when a need arose at post offices for more samples. Stamped Envelope Agency personnel took existing stock of Love envelopes, printed a return address on a computer-driven linotype machine and hand-defaced the denominations with a pink pen.

The Design

The envelope was designed by Salahattin Kanidinc of Jackson Heights, New York, a Turkish-born U.S. citizen who specialized in calligraphy. Kanidinc had previously designed a 1978 United Nations stamp and a

366

Salahattin Kanidinc submitted this calligraphic Love stamp sketch to USPS in 1986.

1982 U.N. postal card in which fancy script lettering comprised the principal design elements. Like the first U.S. Love envelope, its indicium design evolved from a proposal for a Love stamp.

In 1986 Kanidinc submitted to USPS, unsolicited, a design for a stamp in which the script word "Love" formed part of a heart-shaped figure on a square background. At that time, USPS was considering adding Love envelopes to its product line, and Kanidinc's design was deemed suitable for consideration for such an envelope.

"We told him his submission was interesting," said Joe Brockert, the USPS project manager. "We asked him to see if he could re-do it in a couple of other ways."

The artist returned with a rectangular sketch on which the heart was omitted and flowing, horizontal curved lines were added above and below the word "Love." This was approved for use in the indicium.

At one point, when it was thought that the design would be embossed, technicians at Westvaco-USEnvelope Division modified the design by thickening the lines to a width they considered necessary for embossing. But the ultimate decision to use offset printing allowed the use of the lighter, more delicate lines that Kanidinc had drawn.

Westvaco applied the blue tint to the paper and printed the copyright line on the back of the envelope by flexography on its VH machine. The envelopes were then formed and passed through a two-color offset Jet press to receive the carmine rose and purple indicium.

"They did a tremendous job of coming up with a pale tint," Brockert said. "What I wanted was an extremely pale blue, and I got exactly what I wanted. I had given them a sample of one of our aerograms that was printed on a pale blue paper, and asked them to match it.

"They had a heck of a time getting it to print right — some of the earlier

Kanidinc later produced this variation on his earlier sketch, with flowing, curved lines above and below the word "Love."

This 29¢ Love stamped envelope bears a rubber-composition-device cancel from a Kirk-Rudy machine at Philatelic Sales Divison headquarters. No steel die hub first-day cancel was available for this and several other 1991 stamp items.

impressions of their blue were terribly mottled, badly screened-down versions of a darker color — but they finally got the right combination of ink and screen.

"We didn't know whether the manufacturer could leave the area behind the indicium uncolored so that the word 'Love' would read on pure white. But that would have created a registration problem, so we decided to allow the blue to show through. That was one of the reasons we wanted the blue to be as pale as possible, so the design would show up better."

First-Day Facts

Details on the first-day ceremony can be found in the chapter on the 29¢ Love sheet stamp.

45¢ EAGLE AEROGRAM

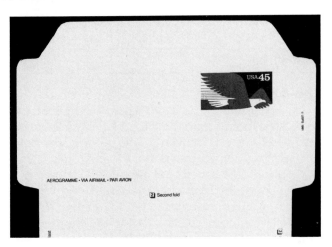

Date of Issue: May 17, 1991

Catalog Numbers: Scott UC63 (blue paper); UC63a (white paper)

Colors: red, gray, blue (indicium, inscriptions)

First-Day Cancel: Denver, Colorado

FDCs Canceled: 19,941

Size: 7½ by 3⁹⁄16 inches folded

Format: Die cut into single aerograms. Printing plates of 4 subjects (2 across, 2 around).

Paper: two varieties, one on white paper, one on blue paper

Watermark: none

Markings: "© USPS 1991." "AEROGRAMME . VIA AIRMAIL . PAR AVION." "Do not use tape or stickers to seal . No enclosures permitted." "(1) Fold first at notches." "(2) Second fold." "(3) Seal top flap last." (twice). "Additional message area:"

Designer: Howard Koslow of East Norwich, New York

Art Director and Project Manager: Joe Brockert (USPS)

Typographer: Bradbury Thompson (CSAC)

Modeler: Ronald C. Sharpe (BEP)

Printing: printed by BEP on 6-color Goebel Optiforma offset press (042)

Quantity Ordered: 21,500,000 (10,415,000 on white paper, 11,085,000 on blue paper)

Quantity Distributed: 17,910,000 (7,500,000 on white paper, 10,410,000 on blue paper

Tagging: bar

The Aerogram

The rate for aerograms, which are thin-paper, no-enclosure stationery items used for international airmail correspondence, was raised from 39¢ to 45¢ February 3. On May 17, an aerogram for the new rate was issued.

The aerogram, with an indicium showing a stylized eagle in flight, was of the kind USPS calls "standard." It offered a maximum amount of writing space unobstructed by extra design elements like those used on commemorative aerograms — for example, the 1989 aerogram that honored Montgomery Blair. In the past, commemorative aerograms had generated complaints from customers that there wasn't enough writing room in the message area for all that they wanted to say, or in the address area for the sometimes-lengthy overseas addresses. As a result, USPS had concluded that it must always have available an aerogram of simple generic design, without cachets or other supplemental decorations, to meet the needs of those customers.

On the new item, the left front cachet area and the part making up the back of the folded aerogram were left blank. Unfolded, the item consisted of three equal segments; the third or bottom segment was folded inside before sealing, and both sides of this segment could be used as the message area.

The aerogram was made on two different colors of paper, white and light blue. Blue is the traditional aerogram color, both in the United States and overseas, but USPS had used white paper on most recent aerograms to achieve cleaner, sharper design reproduction. However, some customers had complained that their writing showed through the white paper. So with the new aerogram, the Postal Service asked the Bureau of Engraving and Printing to return to the blue — specifying a lighter blue than that which had been used in the past. The blue paper didn't arrive until the press run was partially completed.

The Design

Veteran stamp designer Howard Koslow of East Norwich, New York, created the flying eagle design used on the aerogram's indicium. Koslow had actually done the acrylic painting in the early 1980s, and it was first considered for use on a 28¢ airmail postal card.

"For some reason, it wasn't used, but everybody loved the artwork," recalled Joe Brockert, the project manager. "So we put it on the shelf for future contingencies."

The next opportunity to use the design came in 1988, when USPS was

370

This is Howard Koslow's original flying eagle sketch, made in the early 1980s.

preparing to make a second attempt to issue a practical self-adhesive stamp (the first try had produced the ill-fated Christmas "precancel" of 1974). The fact that the eagle would have been simple to print was a strong selling point. However, Brockert said, "when we decided that we wanted the self-adhesive to have an aspect ratio closer to that of definitive stamps, we knew that Howard's design wouldn't work, so we went with Jay Haiden's eagle and shield design instead."

Simplicity of printing is also a plus with the paper used for aerograms, and when the need arose for a new aerogram, USPS finally found a suitable use for the design. Koslow himself wasn't aware that his artwork was going to go public at last as a postal-stationery indicium until he read the news, accompanied by an illustration, in the philatelic press.

"It was a nice change of pace," Koslow said of the original assignment, "because it gave me an opportunity to get away from the representational eagles I've done so many times." (Most recently, Koslow had painted a "representational eagle" for the Desert Storm commemorative stamp issued by the Republic of the Marshall Islands in 1991.)

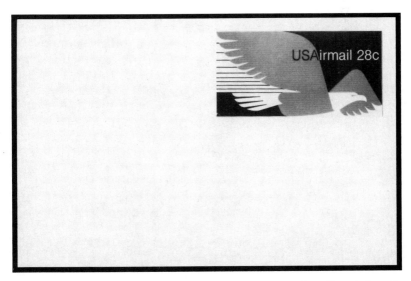

The flying eagle was originally mocked up as a 28¢ airmail postal card.

371

Howard Koslow's eagle design was considered for use on the 1989 self-adhesive stamp. This is how it would have looked.

As an artist, Koslow said he greatly preferred the appearance of the white-paper version of the aerogram. "The blue doesn't look good," he said. "It cuts down on the contrast of the red and the blue in the image. If you look at the two of them, it's much cleaner, much sharper-looking on the white."

First-Day Facts

The aerogram was one of three postal items with flight themes that made their debut May 17 at the opening of the Rompex 91 stamp show in Denver, Colorado. The others were the 19¢ Hot-Air Balloon stamp and the 40¢ William Piper airmail stamp.

USPS held no first-day ceremony. Collectors wishing first-day cancellations on the aerogram were given 30 days to submit their prepurchased aerograms or their addressed labels and remittance, at 45¢ per item, to the postmaster in Denver, the city named on the postmark.

29¢ STAR SECURITY ENVELOPE

Date of Issue: July 20, 1991

Catalog Number: Scott U623

Colors: blue, red

First-Day Cancel: Washington, D.C.

FDCs Canceled: 16,038

Size: number 9, with and without window

Watermark: unwatermarked

Markings: "© USPS 1991" under flap; security design inside.

Designer and Typographer: Richard Sheaff (CSAC)

Art Director and Project Manager: Joe Brockert (USPS)

Printing: Westvaco-USEnvelope Division in 2-color flexography on a VH machine

Quantity Ordered: 4,200,000

Quantity Distributed: 4,061,000

Tagging: square bar to left of indicium

The Envelope

On July 20, with only a few days' prior announcement, USPS issued a 29¢ security envelope for use by mailers wishing to send checks, money orders and important documents. It contained a liner with a pattern of blue lines and dashes to protect the contents from outside detection.

The item was the second security envelope bearing first-class postage to be provided by the Postal Service. It replaced the 25¢ envelope that had been issued July 10, 1989.

Like its predecessor, it was manufactured in the number 9 size, which at 87/8 by 37/8 inches falls between the two standard USPS envelope sizes, number 63/4 and number 10. It was available with or without window. Unlike the first envelope, however, it was made in only one window format. USPS had created two window versions of its first security envelope: a standard envelope and a special one with the window close to the right edge to meet the specific mailing needs of the Arizona Department of Economic Security.

The Design

The indicium of the security envelope bore essentially the same design that had been created by Richard Sheaff for the Star definitive envelope issued in January for general use: a solid blue star and red "USA 29." However, in place of the blind-embossed horizontal lines above and below the star and typography were thin blue lines that wrapped around the right side of the envelope and extended for three-fourths of an inch on the back. This made the envelope readily identifiable to postal clerks.

The VH envelope-forming machine used by Westvaco-USEnvelope Division can emboss only when the two standard sizes of envelope are being made, and so no embossing was used on the security envelope. USPS believed that the wraparound feature of the indicium and the presence of the patterned liner, along with the tagging, provided adequate protection against counterfeiting.

First-Day Facts

There was no first-day ceremony for the security envelope, but first-day cancellations were provided at the Washington, D.C., main post office. Mail-order customers were given 30 days after the issue date to order first-day covers.

374

29¢ MAGAZINE INDUSTRY ENVELOPE

Date of Issue: October 7, 1991

Catalog Number: Scott U622

Colors: black, yellow, blue, red, green, gray

First-Day Cancel: Naples, Florida

FDCs Canceled: 26,020

Size: number 10

Watermark: unwatermarked

Markings: "© USPS 1991" under flap

Designer: Bradbury Thompson (CSAC)

Typographer: John Boyd (Anagraphics, New York, New York)

Art Director: Terrence McCaffrey (USPS)

Project Manager: Joe Brockert (USPS)

Printing: Westvaco-USEnvelope Division used VH machine to print envelopes by flexography, die-cut windows, affix indicia and form envelopes. Indicia printed in rolls by flexography by Packagings System Corporation, Danielson, Connecticut.

Quantity Ordered: 4,500,000

Quantity Distributed: 3,776,000

Tagging: vertical bar to right of indicium

The Envelope

The Postal Service has been happy to accommodate the magazine industry in recent years, particularly through the issuance of stamped envelopes. For example, it created one variety of envelope — the Bison precancel of 1986 — to accommodate *Reader's Digest*, and another variety — the Christmas envelope of 1988 — for *TV Guide*.

Thus it was consistent with past policy for USPS to issue a commemorative stamped envelope October 7, 1991, to mark the 250th anniversary of American magazines, and to dedicate it at a closed ceremony at the American Magazine Conference. So willing was USPS to cooperate with the industry that it made a change in the envelope's wording to suit the preference of the Magazine Publishers of America, even though production had begun and the change imposed an extra cost. (The cost was "minimal," according to the USPS announcement. Donald M. McDowell, director of the Office of Stamp and Philatelic Marketing, said it was "less than $10,000.")

A reason for Postal Service solicitousness wasn't hard to find. Magazine publishers are among USPS' biggest customers, but they were being wooed by competition in the form of so-called alternative delivery services. After USPS increased its second-class postal rates by an average of 22 percent in February 1991, private firms such as Publisher's Express and Alternate Postal Delivery looked even more attractive than before to magazine executives seeking to cut their mailing costs.

In the summer of 1990, Donald D. Kummerfeld, president of the Magazine Publishers of America, asked Postmaster General Anthony M. Frank for a stamp the following year to mark the industry's anniversary — an anniversary that the Association itself had belatedly realized was coming. Frank replied that the commemorative stamp program was filled but that a stamped envelope could be provided.

In producing the envelope, the manufacturer, Westvaco-USEnvelope Division, used the same patch-in-a-window technique it had used on the two hologram envelopes issued by USPS, the Space Station (1989) and Professional Football (1990). The indicium was printed by flexography by a subcontractor, Packaging Systems Corporation of Danielson, Connecticut, on an offset paper with a clay coat on one side, supplied by the Champion Paper Company. The high-gloss finish on this paper was capable of accepting much finer printing than ordinary paper used for stamped envelopes.

The printed indicium was patched into a die-cut window in the envelope's upper-right corner. The manufacturing job was easier than the job of assembling the earlier hologram envelopes, said Richard Salois of Westvaco, because the holograms had been made on a metallized film, which created adhesion problems. With the Magazine envelope, the patching was paper to paper and could be accomplished using a standard adhesive, Salois said.

The "USA 29" inscription was printed by flexography to the left of the window, on the envelope itself. Below the window were the words "Creating a Brighter World." It was this latter inscription that USPS changed after the actual envelope production had begun in order to satisfy the Magazine Publishers of America.

The original inscription drafted by USPS had read "Recording a Brighter World." P. Robert Farley, executive vice president and general manager of the Magazine Publishers, recalled what had happened:

"The slogan 'Recording a Brighter World' originally was shown to us in early 1991. At that point we called down to Washington and asked if it would be possible to change it to 'Creating a Brighter World,' because 'Recording' connotes another medium. They said it could be done.

"But apparently they forgot about it, or somebody was transferred, and they didn't do it. And they sent us up an enlarged picture of the stamped envelope not long before the first-day event, and it had 'Recording' on it. We called up about it, and they said they were sorry, they made a mistake, but there was nothing they could do about it.

"And then, three or four days later, they said they were changing it! Which made us very happy."

As Donald M. McDowell of USPS recalled it, the change requested by the Association had been "a constructive suggestion." "We agreed that the suggestion made sense and changed it," he said.

The envelopes were issued only in number 10 size, without windows, and sold for 34¢ each. They could be ordered with a preprinted return address of up to four lines in boxes of 50, at 34.8¢ per envelope, or boxes of 500 at 32¢ each.

Most experts credit Benjamin Franklin with conceiving the first magazine in the colonies, but Franklin actually lost the race to publish first. His old commercial rival Andrew Bradford got wind of Franklin's plans and set about to beat him. Bradford published *The American Magazine* ("A Monthly View of The Political State of the British

Richard Sheaff put together these two design concepts, one for a stamp, the other for an envelope, using the covers of the first two American magazines. The Citizens' Stamp Advisory Committee felt they were too detailed to be effective.

Terrence McCaffrey mocked up this indicium, using the magazine industry's anniversary logo.

Colonies") in Philadelphia on February 13, 1741, three days before the appearance of the first issue of Franklin's *The General Magazine* ("and Historical Chronicle, For all the British Plantations in America"). As one historian noted, "A great tradition of American magazines — the missed deadline — was born at the same time; both publications bore a January cover date."

Neither magazine lasted long enough to make an impact. Bradford was out of business in three months, Franklin in six. In fact, all through the rest of the 18th century, magazines came and went with great frequency. There was, for instance, *The Pennsylvania Magazine*, edited by Tom Paine, which lasted only a year but went out in style; its last issue in 1776 contained the text of the Declaration of Independence.

Today, more than 11,000 magazines chronicle the people and topics that shape U.S. society, and almost 500 new magazines on average appear each year.

The Design

Although the late request by the Magazine Publishers of America

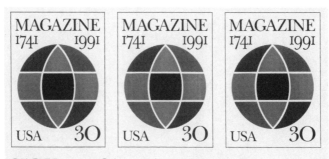

This is Bradbury Thompson's first design approach, using three identical multicolored magazine covers.

American Magazines
Recording a Brighter World

In this modification, Bradbury Thompson made the first magazine in gray and black, the second in gold and the third in multicolor, to suggest the evolution of color printing capabilities.

made a stamp impractical, Richard Sheaff, a Citizens' Stamp Advisory Committee design coordinator, worked up an initial design concept in both stamp and envelope format. The design displayed the covers of *The American Magazine* and *The General Magazine*, along with a block of explanatory type.

However, officials "felt there was just too much going on" in this design, and that it would be difficult to comprehend when reduced to stamp or indicium size, said Terrence McCaffrey of USPS, the art director.

Other approaches were then examined. The Magazine Publishers of America offered a special anniversary logo that New York designer Walter Bernard had created for the organization's stationery and promotional materials — an American flag, folded so as to resemble three magazines standing side by side. McCaffrey developed an envelope indicium from it. The committee turned it down.

"They thought it was just another flag icon, and that it didn't 'say' American magazines as quickly as some of the other design ideas did," McCaffrey said.

One of these other ideas, offered by CSAC's Bradbury Thompson, depicted three identical magazine covers, each bearing a multicolored, stylized globe to suggest the universality of magazines. "But no one could really figure out why there were three globes in a repeat pattern," McCaffrey said.

Thompson also provided a similar design that was intended to emphasize the progress in color printing capabilities over 250 years. The first of the three magazine covers was dated "1741" and was in gray and black, the second was dated "1866" and was in black and a single color, and the third, "1991," was multicolor.

"The committee liked that idea, but they weren't completely satisfied. They didn't think it was working yet," McCaffrey said. "They thought

379

MAGAZINE
1741   1991

American
Magazines

USA 29

Recording a Brighter World

This design is similar to the finished product, with the left half of the globe in gray and the right half in five colors. Eventually, "American Magazine" was placed inside the indicium and "Recording" was changed to "Creating."

there were just too many magazines.

"So Brad went back and worked up another design that used a single magazine and combined the first element, black and white, and the third element, full color, and dropped the second element, single color. And that's what we ended up with."

Was it necessary to print the design on a patched-in piece of coated stock? No; it could have been printed on the envelope paper itself, in the conventional way, McCaffrey said. However, the mat finish of the paper would have given the colors a flatter appearance, and the result would have been an envelope with much less visual impact.

First-Day Facts

Postmaster General Anthony M. Frank dedicated the envelope October 7 at the American Magazine Conference in Naples, Florida. The ceremony, at the Ritz-Carlton Hotel, was an early item on the schedule of the first full day of the conference, and was open only to members of the Magazine Publishers of America and The American Society of Magazine Editors. Reginald K. Brack Jr., chairman of the Magazine Publishers of America, was an honored guest at the dedication.

The cover of the first-day program reproduced the first issue of Benjamin Franklin's *The General Magazine*, one of the two magazines that had originally been considered for use in the design of the envelope.

Collectors ordering first-day covers were allowed 30 days to send their addressed, stamped envelopes, or addressed pressure-sensitive labels plus remittance, to the postmaster at Naples for servicing.

380

29¢ COUNTRY GEESE ENVELOPE

Date of Issue: November 8, 1991

Catalog Number: U624

Colors: blue, yellow

First-Day Cancel: Virginia Beach, Virginia

FDCs Canceled: 21,031

Size: number 6¾

Watermark: star below USA (Type 49) or star above USA (Type 50)

Markings: "© USPS 1991" under flap

Designer: Marc Zaref of New York, New York

Art Director and Project Manager: Joe Brockert (USPS)

Typographer: Bradbury Thompson (CSAC)

Modeler: John Boyd, Anagraphics Inc., New York, New York

Printing: offset lithography (indicium) and flexography (copyright notation, tagging) by Westvaco-USEnvelope Division

Quantity Ordered: 3,000,000

Quantity Distributed: 2,018,000

Tagging: square bar to left of indicium

The Envelope

On November 8, USPS issued a 29¢ stamped envelope with an indicium reflecting a popular American country craft design: an adult goose, wearing a blue bow, leading three goslings on a stroll. Although the envelope was a late addition to the 1991 program — it wasn't announced until late September — it had been in the works since 1988, and its design took final form in early January of 1989.

The envelope was created to appeal to what USPS called "the household market," as opposed to business and organizational mailers, the largest users of stamped envelopes. It was issued originally only in the standard number 6¾ size, without window.

The selling price was 34¢ apiece, or $154 for boxes of 500 (30.8¢ apiece). Country Geese envelopes could also be ordered from the Stamped Envelope Agency with preprinted return addresses in boxes of 50 for $17.20 per box, which was only 20¢ more than the cost of buying 50 individual envelopes.

"Once we had the flexibility to make 50-packs of personalized envelopes, we knew that we had to come up with something that would appeal to the household mailer," said Joe Brockert, the project manager and art director for the Country Geese envelope. "So we were looking at different kinds of home decor and things like that that would appeal to households. One of the themes that we didn't seem able to escape was the country theme, which has been extremely popular in recent years."

The Country Geese envelope could be purchased only at philatelic centers and by mail from the Philatelic Sales Division and the USPS Stamped Envelope Agency. At the time the envelope was ordered, the Postal Service was still hoping for a 30¢ first-class rate before the end of the year, and the uncertainty of what the rate would be caused officials to limit the print order.

The Design

The goose with a bow around its neck is a popular country motif, and is found on many commercial products, such as paper towels, napkins and disposable cups. Its exact origin is unclear, however, according to Marc Zaref, the New York City graphic designer who had researched folk-art objects in preparation for creating the envelope indicium.

The stenciled flower pattern that Zaref placed beneath the geese on the

This is Marc Zaref's original sketch, showing a single adult goose against a square background of solid blue.

envelope was evocative of the stenciling done in rural America in the 19th century by traveling craftsmen, he said. These artisans carried leather stencils in a variety of figures and applied the decorations to walls, furniture and other farmhouse surfaces.

One of Zaref's early concept sketches showed a single adult goose in a square-shaped indicium with a decorative stenciled border. The Citizens' Stamp Advisory Committee then asked Zaref to submit another sketch depicting a family of geese. The resulting image was chosen for use on the envelope.

The outlines of the geese, the row of flowers and "USA 29" were printed in blue, and the beaks and feet of the birds were yellow. Zaref chose what he called "a light, dusty blue" in keeping with his understanding of the kind of muted colors used by the early stencilers. Also, he said, a brighter blue would have given the image "the commercial feeling" he was trying to avoid.

The envelopes were formed on a VH machine at Westvaco-U.S. Envelope Division in Williamsburg, Pennsylvania, and the tagging and copyright notation beneath the flap were applied by flexography. Then the indicium was printed on the formed envelopes by a Jet offset press.

Before full production began, Westvaco ran some trial printings, and adjustments were made, including a strengthening of the lines on the offset plates to ensure that the outlines of the birds didn't break up at some stage in the manufacture.

First-Day Facts

The Country Geese envelope was issued November 8 in conjunction with the Vapex 91 stamp show in Virginia Beach, Virginia. There was no first-day ceremony, but the Postal Service provided showgoers with its now-familiar generic blue souvenir folder containing an envelope with the first-day cancellation.

Collectors ordering first-day covers by mail were given 60 days to submit addressed envelopes, or addressed pressure-sensitive labels plus remittance, to the postmaster at Virginia Beach.

19¢ FLAG POSTAL CARD

USA 19

Date of Issue: January 24, 1991

Catalog Number: Scott UX153

Colors: red, blue, black

First-Day Cancel: Washington, D.C. (no first-day ceremony)

FDCs Canceled: 26,690

Format: Printed in 80-card sheets. Printing plates of 80 subjects (8 across, 10 around). Available in 40-card sheets and banded 5-card vending machine packs.

Size: 5½ by 3½ inches

Markings: "© USPS 1991"

Designer and Typographer: Richard Sheaff (CSAC)

Art Director and Project Manager: Jack Williams (USPS)

Printing: U.S. Government Printing Office (GPO) on a 5-color Roland Man 80 sheetfed offset press

Quantity Ordered: 456,000,000

Quantity Distributed: 222,531,000

Tagging: vertical bar to right of stamp

The Card

On January 24, USPS issued a 19¢ definitive postal card to meet the new card rate that was scheduled to take effect February 3. The action came with only one day's advance notice and two days after the USPS

Board of Governors had accepted the new rate recommended by the Postal Rate Commission.

No F cards had been ordered because of the relative speed with which denominated cards can be prepared and printed on the Government Printing Office's Roland Man offset press. After the Rate Commission had made its recommendations on January 4, Postmaster General Anthony M. Frank said that acceptance of the rates was virtually certain, and USPS stamp officials felt confident enough to order quick production of the cards bearing the 19¢ denomination.

The Design

The indicium of the card was a rectangular, borderless box containing a detail of a stylized billowing American flag, with portions of all 13 stripes visible, along with a corner of the blue field and four white stars.

Richard Sheaff, a Citizens' Stamp Advisory Committee design coordinator, adapted the design from one that he had developed in 1990 for a possible Flag stamp. Sheaff had created two versions of the stamp design: one, a vertical in definitive size that showed only 11 stripes and three stars; the other, a horizontal in commemorative size with 13 stripes and three stars. USPS officials decided that the latter design concept would be suitable for the new postal card, and asked Sheaff to adapt it to that purpose. He developed both an F version that wasn't issued and a 19¢ denominated version that was. In the process, he added a fourth star to the flag detail.

First-Day Facts

No first-day ceremony was held for the new card, which went on sale January 24 in Washington, D.C. Collectors were given 60 days in which to submit their addressed stamped cards for first-day cancellations, or to send peelable return address labels plus 19¢ per card desired for Postal Service-provided canceled cards.

The 19¢ postal card design was an adaptation of a design idea that Richard Sheaff had developed in July 1990 for a future Flag stamp. Shown here are two variations done with a stamp in mind.

38¢ FLAG DOUBLE REPLY POSTAL CARD

Date of Issue: March 27, 1991

Catalog Number: Scott UY40

Colors: red, blue, black

First-Day Cancel: Washington, D.C. (no first-day ceremony)

FDCs Canceled: 25,562

Format: Printed in 80-card sheets, 40 impressions on each side, but available only as individual double reply cards, rouletted between cards. Printing plates of 40 subjects (8 across, 5 around).

Size: 5½ by 7 inches (5½ by 3½ inches when folded)

Markings: "© USPS 1991"

Designer and Typographer: Richard Sheaff (CSAC)

Art Director and Project Manager: Jack Williams (USPS)

Printing: U.S. Government Printing Office (GPO) on a 5-color Roland Man 80 sheetfed offset press

Quantity Ordered: 20,500,000

Quantity Distributed: 14,248,000

Tagging: vertical bar to the right of stamp

The Postal Card

Since 1892, USPS has made available double postal cards, fastened together but easily separable. The buyer — usually a business — could use one for the message, and the addressee could use the other for a reply. The Scott stamp catalogs list these items in a separate section, apart from the single postal cards, with their own numbering system.

In the early years, paid reply postal cards had their own distinctive designs, with the reply card differing from the message card in wording and/or picture. But since 1956, the cards have borne the same designs as the single cards that were then current, with no difference between the reply and message units. The cards are printed on opposite sides of the paper, so that when they are folded along the scored line between them, the reply card is on the inside.

On March 27, USPS issued a double-reply card version of the 19¢ definitive card it had issued the preceding January 24. The indicium used on the two attached cards was the same as the one on the single card: a stylized detail from the American flag, designed by Citizens' Stamp Advisory Committee design coordinator Richard Sheaff.

The Government Printing Office produced the reply cards from 80-unit offset plates, as it does single cards, but in this case the plates were laid out with only 40 units — what GPO refers to as "40-up" — with cards and blanks alternating. When the sheets were turned over to be printed on the other side, the blank spaces became the reverse side of printed cards. Afterward, the sheets were moved to the GPO's Uno cut-pack system to be cut into pairs of cards, scored, counted, packaged and banded.

The item replaced the 15¢ America the Beautiful double-reply cards, issued in 1988, showing bison grazing on a prairie. The Flag card had its first-day sale in Washington, D.C., without a ceremony. Collectors wishing first-day cancellations were told to buy the cards, address them and send them in a larger envelope to the Washington postmaster, or else send a peelable return address label and 38¢ for each double reply postal card wanted. In a complaint of the type often heard in 1991, one collector reported in a letter to *Linn's Stamp News* that she was unable to obtain the cards before the May 26 deadline for first-day cancellations, although she had tried at two New Jersey philatelic centers and at the Nojex show in Secaucus, New Jersey.

19¢ POSTAL BUDDY POSTAL CARD

Date of Issue: February 3, 1991

Catalog Number: Scott 2 (under heading Computer Vended Postage/Postal Cards)

Colors: black, red, blue

First-Day Cancel: none

FDCs Canceled: none

Format: sheets of four

Size: 5½ by 4¼ inches

Perf: extremely fine sawtooth

Markings: "PATENTS PENDING, U.S. AND FOREIGN. © 1990 POSTAL BUDDY CORPORATION, SAN DIEGO, CA 92117-4328." "Postal Buddy™ Authorized United States Postal Service change-of-address station" (in repeat pattern).

Designer, Art Director and Project Manager: Joe Brockert (USPS)

Typographer: John Boyd of Anagraphics, Inc., New York, New York

Printing: computerized printing by Postal Buddy vending machine

Tagging: untagged

The Postal Card

On July 5, 1990, USPS and a private company, the Postal Buddy Corporation of San Diego, California, began a six-month market test of an automated change-of-address system that for the first time delivered a U.S. postage item with a fixed denomination that was printed by a laser printer on demand.

The item was the Postal Buddy postal card, with a 15¢ indicium, which customers could use to notify correspondents of address changes or send meeting notices or other messages. The Postal Buddy machines were installed in 30 locations in Northern Virginia in 1990. Early in 1991 they were placed in the post office at USPS headquarters in Washington, D.C., and six other Northern Virginia locations, and discontinued in six of the original sites.

Meanwhile, USPS decided to expand the experimental program to one year, and seek bids for a nationwide electronic change-of-address network based on the lessons learned in the market test. And on February 3 the Postal Service and its private partner created a new variety of the Postal Buddy card.

The Postal Buddy machines were programmed to convert the card denomination from 15¢ to 19¢ at 12:01 a.m. February 3 as the new postcard rate took effect. The new card, featuring the USPS eagle logo in its indicium, was identical to the old one except for the change of denomination.

Although February 3 was a Sunday, the new cards were available to the public on that day from many of the interactive vending machines in the experimental area of Northern Virginia that had 24-hour access or were located in retail stores that were open on Sunday. Collectors seeking the new cards could obtain them without messages from the machines.

Cards purchased on the first day, February 3, were provable because the laser printer in the machine printed, below the indicium, a series of numbers that encoded the machine number, the year, the day of the year and the transaction number that day. They could also be mailed that day for a postmark, of course, although, unlike postage meters, which are also custom-printed on demand, Postal Buddy cards could be mailed on any date and from any location.

It wasn't until July that the Philatelic Sales Division of USPS offered the new cards in mint sheets of four through its catalog, by mail order only. The year before, the 15¢ cards had been available over the counter at philatelic centers, either mint or with a first-day cancellation from Merrifield, Virginia. This time, however, the PSD didn't create cards with first-day cancels for collectors, and the only cards that exist with the February 3 datestamp are ones actually mailed by individuals on that day.

The new Postal Buddy cards, like the originals, were untagged. That meant that the facing of the cards by automated post office equipment was haphazard, and cancellations were often misplaced or missing.

The first Postal Buddy card was so novel that it wasn't listed in the

389

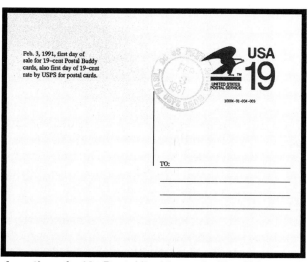

A portion of a 19¢ Postal Buddy card with a February 3, 1991, first-day cancel. Few such Postal Buddy first-day covers are known.

1991 *Scott Specialized Catalogue of United States Stamps.* However, the 1992 edition included both cards, under the heading: "Computer Vended Postage/Postal Cards."

Postal Buddy — a trademarked name — was a computerized change-of-address and instant printing terminal that was developed by entrepreneur Sidney R. Goodman, president of the Postal Buddy Corporation.

Customers used the Postal Buddy computer keyboard to print their change-of-address information or other messages onto the front of the cards. The machine could access a ZIP+4 database to provide the correct nine-digit ZIP Code for the customer's new address. Cards emerged from the machine with the indicium, coded number line and customized message printed in place, and a series of ruled lines on which the buyer could write the recipient's address.

The card's reverse side carried a border containing the USPS logo and the words "Postal Buddy (TM)" in blue and "Authorized United States Postal Service change-of-address station" in red, all of which was then repeated twice. The remainder of the side was blank and usable for a message if desired. The cards were dispensed in sheets of four, separated by minuscule perforations, at a cost of 37¢ per 19¢ postal card.

The machine also dispensed receipts, furnished free on request the USPS Change of Address Form 3575 for the customer to use to notify his postmaster of a pending address change and sold preprinted return address labels. At no charge, it electronically sent address-change information to USPS and to any of scores of companies that were on-line with the system, and sent confirmation cards to the individuals involved to guard against unauthorized changes. After the initial tests, the capability was added to order newspapers, magazines and mail-order catalogs.

The Design

As reported in the 1990 *Linn's U.S. Stamp Yearbook,* USPS officials had originally considered using a penalty indicium on the Postal Buddy cards and had even mocked up a sheet of four cards that way. However, they realized that this would be impractical, given the certainty of a rate change during or shortly after the test period. So the decision was made to use denominated postage. An essay was made using the new USPS logo with the Olympic rings and the official sponsorship line, but the width-to-depth ratio of the indicium was unsatisfactory, and officials settled on the conventional eagle logo, USA and the denomination.

First-Day Facts

As noted above, there was no advance notice that the Postal Buddy machines would begin producing 19¢ cards February 3, and USPS created no after-the-fact first-day covers for collectors by canceling sheets of cards with a February 3 postmark. Therefore, those first-day covers that exist are genuine and are quite rare.

19¢ CARNEGIE HALL POSTAL CARD
HISTORIC PRESERVATION SERIES

Carnegie Hall Centennial 1991

Date of Issue: April 1, 1991

Catalog Number: Scott UX154

Colors: magenta, yellow, cyan, black

First-Day Cancel: New York, New York

FDCs Canceled: 27,063

Size: 5½ by 3½ inches

Format: Printed in 80-card sheets, but available only in single cards. Printing plates of 80 subjects (8 across, 10 around).

Markings: "© USPS 1991"

Designer: Howard Koslow of East Norwich, New York

Art Director and Project Manager: Jack Williams (USPS)

Typographer: Bradbury Thompson (CSAC)

Printing: U.S. Government Printing Office (GPO) on a 5-color Roland Man 800 sheetfed offset press

Quantity Ordered: 20,000,000

Quantity Distributed: 20,000,000

Tagging: vertical bar to the right of stamp

The Postal Card

An old joke. A tourist in New York City asks an elderly man with a violin case, "How do you get to Carnegie Hall?" His reply: "Practice, practice." Carnegie is the dream destination of performers everywhere, and on April 1, 1991, USPS marked this storied building's 100th anniversary with a postal card in the Historic Preservation series.

Plans to issue the card had been announced more than two years earlier from the Carnegie Hall stage by Norma Pace, a member of the USPS Board of Governors. The occasion was the first-day ceremony March 25, 1989, for a stamp honoring conductor Arturo Toscanini, who had conducted the New York Philharmonic Orchestra there. Violinist Isaac Stern was described as "visibly moved" by Pace's announcement, as well he might have been; it was Stern who had led the effort to rescue the Hall from developers in 1960 and raise the $60 million it took to restore the place to its original state.

Carnegie Hall's opening festival in May 1891 featured Piotr Ilyich Tchaikovsky conducting his own *Marche Sollenelle*. It was the American debut for Tchaikovsky, the first major foreign composer to make an appearance in the United States. Ever since, Carnegie Hall, with its magnificent acoustics, has had a reputation for musical firsts.

A Polish pianist, Ignace Jan Paderewski, was virtually unknown when he performed at Carnegie in its first season. Jascha Heifetz was a 16-year-old prodigy when he played his violin there in 1917. These things also happened at Carnegie Hall: George Gershwin's jazzy Piano Concerto in F was premiered in 1925; black and white musicians first played together in concert, in Benny Goodman's 1938 tribute to swing; Leonard Bernstein, at 25, made his conducting debut in 1943 as a fill-in for an ill Bruno Walter, and years later conducted his televised Young People's Concerts; Vladimir Horowitz came out of retirement in 1965; and Charlie Parker, Dizzy Gillespie and Ella Fitzgerald first brought bop to the concert arena. Popular idols like the Beatles, Rolling Stones and Bob Dylan all did their musical thing here, and speakers from Mark Twain to Dr. Martin Luther King Jr. held forth from its stage.

Carnegie Hall was conceived on the high seas. Walter Damrosch, a conductor and music promoter, had been seeking financial backing for a hall for his Oratorio Society and the New York Symphony, when he met steel magnate and philanthropist Andrew Carnegie on a voyage to Scotland. By the time they returned to New York, Carnegie had pledged $2 million to build the new hall.

The site Carnegie chose was Seventh Avenue and 57th Street, then far uptown. For it, William Burnet Tuthill designed a six-story Italianate palazzo of brick and terra cotta. On opening night, May 5, 1891, all 2,247 seats and 63 boxes were sold, and carriages bearing the cream of New York society were lined up for a quarter of a mile. "There was no coming and going of dandies and mouthpieces," *The New York Herald* noted with approval. "All was quiet, dignified, soft, slow and noiseless as

393

The view chosen for the finished painting was based on this photograph, made by Koslow himself. On the stamp, the artist omitted the traffic light and sign, suspended at the left, to simplify the picture.

became the dedication of a great temple." Damrosch led a chorus of 400 voices in *Old Hundredth* to give the hall its musical baptism.

The Design

The Carnegie Hall card was the first postal card design assignment for Howard Koslow, although he had been creating the artwork for U.S. stamps for 20 years.

Koslow had less lead time for the assignment than for most stamps, he said. "I knew exactly what had to be done," he said. "It had to be the

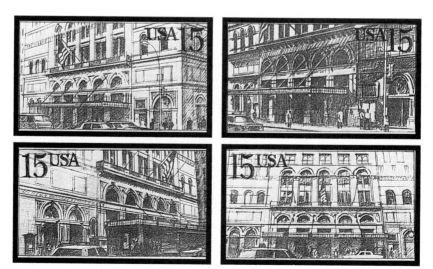

Howard Koslow made these four pencil sketches, based on photographs, for consideration of the Citizens' Stamp Advisory Committee.

facade of the building." He didn't want to do an interior view, like the design of 1990 Chicago Orchestra Hall card, which could have shown "any balcony." "I wanted the picture to say Carnegie Hall," he said.

Koslow visited the Carnegie Hall publicity department, which furnished him with slides, photographs and other reference material. He then went outside and took Kodacolor pictures of his own. "I was climbing on some scaffolding on a building across the street, on the northwest corner of 57th Street and Seventh Avenue, to get some elevation, because otherwise you're blocked by traffic," he recalled. "I couldn't get permission from the doorman to go up one flight of stairs to the work area. He said, 'You call the owner.' Well, I wasn't about to do that. So I went up on the scaffolding."

Back in his studio, Koslow made pencil sketches showing four different views of the building and submitted them to the Postal Service. Later, Jack Williams, the project manager, called him and told him the Citizens' Stamp Advisory Committee had chosen a view looking at an angle toward the main entrance from the corner of 57th and Seventh, with the viewer's eye level slightly above the entrance canopy. Koslow then proceeded to paint the scene in his customary medium, acrylic.

His picture showed the building's brick-red facade, with an American flag, flanked on either side by a Carnegie Hall Centennial banner,

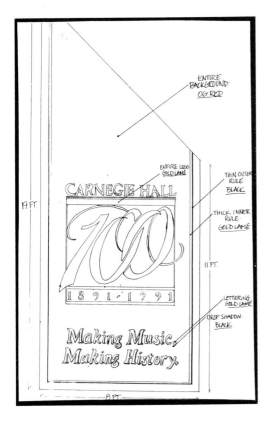

Koslow used this drawing of the Carnegie Hall centennial banner from the institution's files as a reference in adding the banners to his painting.

hanging over the entrance. At the time he made his painting, the centennial banners hadn't been deployed, and he had to improvise them by referring to a sketch of the banner's design furnished by Carnegie Hall. For the first time in the Historic Preservation series, human activity was shown: the tops of a van, taxicab and sedan were seen in the foreground, and pedestrians walked along the sidewalk. "Our feeling was that the building should have activity around it," Koslow said. "To me, it was so indicative of the tempo of that area, of New York City. The street is constantly busy, and I felt that the 'busyness' belonged."

The artist also eliminated elements that would have intruded on his design. "There was a horrible big traffic light and suspended sign coming in from the left side," Koslow said. "It would have obliterated the flags and just made a mess. So I just took those things out. Otherwise, the picture is a faithful reproduction of what is there." A traffic signal on a vertical pole at the right, being unobtrusive, was included in the painting.

First-Day Facts

Isaac Stern was an unexpected guest and spoke briefly at the first-day ceremony, held on the main stage of Carnegie Hall March 27. He had previously indicated he would be unable to attend. The card was dedicated by Richard J. Strasser Jr., senior assistant postmaster general for marketing and customer services, and the welcome was given by James D. Wolfensohn, chairman of the Hall's board of trustees.

19¢ OFFICIAL MAIL POSTAL CARD

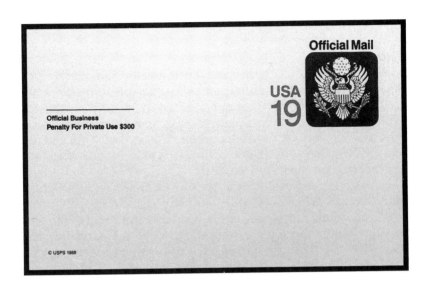

Date of Issue: May 24, 1991

Catalog Number: Scott UZ5

Colors: red, blue, black, gold

First-Day Cancel: Seattle, Washington

FDCs Canceled: 23,097

Size: 5½ by 3½ inches

Format: Printed in 80 card sheets, but available only in single cards. Printing plates of 80 subjects (8 across, 10 around).

Markings: "© USPS 1988" at lower left corner. "Official Business/Penalty For Private Use $300" at upper left corner.

Designer and Typographer: Bradbury Thompson (CSAC)

Art Director and Project Manager: Joe Brockert (USPS)

Printing: U.S. Government Printing Office (GPO) on a 5-color Roland Man 800 sheetfed offset press

Quantity Ordered: 5,000,000

Quantity Distributed: 1,248,000

Tagging: vertical bar to right of stamp

The Postal Card

A 19¢ Official Mail postal card was issued May 24 at the Pipex stamp show in Seattle, Washington, along with 19¢, 23¢ and 29¢ Official Mail stamps. The card was the fourth to be issued since USPS resumed issuance of Official Mail stamps and postal stationery in 1983. It replaced the 15¢ card issued June 10, 1988.

The Design

When Bradbury Thompson, design coordinator for the Citizens' Stamp Advisory Committee and designer of all USPS Official Mail postal items of the modern era, created the design for the 15¢ Official Mail postal card of 1988, he made the design elements bigger and bolder than those he had incorporated in the 13¢ card of 1983 and the 14¢ card of 1985. He also added three colors — red, black and gold — to the blue he had used on those earlier cards.

For the 19¢ card of 1991, Thompson made additional changes. He made the words "Official Mail" still larger, and moved them from a place to the left of the blue square containing the Great Seal of the United States to a line above the square. This was part of a general rearrangement of elements on Official Mail postal stationery to leave room for Facing Identification Marks (FIMs) at the top of the envelope or card if government agencies wished to use them.

And he expanded the use of red and black — previously limited to the typography — to the indicium itself for better effect. This time the details of the Great Seal were black and the vertical stripes on the eagle's shield were red, instead of blue as in the past.

As on the 15¢ card, the stars were gold, and again the gold was a standard Pantone color rather than metallic. "There's more danger of flaking with a metallic ink than with a regular ink," explained Joe Brockert, the card's project manager, "and because the stars were so small we were afraid metallic gold would flake, especially at the points."

First-Day Facts

No first-day ceremony was held for the Official Mail items at Pipex. Collectors wishing first-day cancellations on the postal card were instructed to send a return address label and 19¢ for each card ordered to the Seattle postmaster. USPS then added the official government return address, affixed the customer's label and postmarked the card. A 60-day period was allowed for requesting this service.

19¢ OLD RED POSTAL CARD
HISTORIC PRESERVATION SERIES

Date of Issue: June 14, 1991

Catalog Number: Scott UX155

Colors: yellow, magenta, cyan, black

First-Day Cancel: Galveston, Texas

FDCs Canceled: 24,308

Format: Printed in 80-card sheets, but available only in single cards. Printing plates of 80 subjects (8 across, 10 around).

Size: 5½ by 3½ inches

Markings: "Old Red/The University of Texas/Medical Branch at Galveston/© USPS 1991"

Designer: Don Adair of Richardson, Texas

Art Director: Derry Noyes (CSAC)

Project Manager: Joe Brockert (USPS)

Typographer: Bradbury Thompson (CSAC)

Printing: U.S. Government Printing Office (GPO) on a 5-color Roland Man 800 sheetfed offset press

Quantity Ordered: 20,000,000

Quantity Distributed: 20,000,000

Tagging: vertical bar to right of stamp

The Postal Card

On June 14, USPS issued its second Historic Preservation series postal card of the year and its 19th, by the Postal Service's count, in the 14-year run of the series.

The card was issued in conjunction with the centennial celebration of the University of Texas Medical Branch at Galveston, and depicted "Old Red," UTMB's original classroom building, which was still in use 100 years after its opening. Old Red — formally named the Ashbel Smith Building, after the first president of the university's Board of Regents — is the oldest U.S. medical school structure west of the Mississippi River, and is listed on the National Register of Historic Places.

Coincidentally, the first Historic Preservation card, in 1977, also showed a Galveston landmark, the old Federal Building, which was completed in 1861.

As has often been the case with postal cards in the Historic Preservation series, the Old Red card originated with a request for a postage stamp.

In 1988, UTMB officials began making plans for the school's 100th anniversary and, among other things, asked USPS for a commemorative stamp. They were told that Postal Service guidelines precluded stamps for institutional anniversaries, but that a postal card would be considered. The subject was an obvious one: Old Red.

Letters from UTMB President Thomas N. James went out to the school's alumni and friends, state legislators, members of Congress and others, asking them to support a postal recognition of the centennial. In 1990 the campus community learned that Old Red had been approved as a postal card subject.

"We had a lot of people working on our behalf," said Vicki Saito, UTMB assistant vice president for external affairs. "We're fortunate that the Postal Service chose Old Red to be part of the Preservation series. Actually, we're probably more delighted with the card than we would have been with a stamp."

In 1881 the Texas Legislature authorized the establishment of the University of Texas and a U.T. Medical Department. A statewide referendum later that year selected Austin, the state's capital, and Galveston, its largest city and leading commercial center, as the sites.

Nicholas C. Clayton, the first professional architect in Texas and Galveston's most prominent architect in the late 1880s, was commissioned to design the medical classroom building. He toured East Coast medical schools to obtain the latest ideas, then returned home to create a structure in Romanesque Revival style. The building got its nickname from his choice of construction materials: red pressed brick from Cedar Bayou, red Texas granite and sandstone. The building was completed in 1890, the same year the adjacent John Sealy Hospital opened. The U.T. Medical Department held its first classes October 5, 1891, with a faculty of 13 and an enrollment of 23 students.

Old Red sits 12 feet off the ground on a series of massive piers. Its exterior features a series of three-story arches containing the windows and, above them, an arcade of small windows that forms an effective finish for the circular wings and main front. The brickwork above the arches and in the spandrels between the main and second levels is unusual; every other brick juts out to create a uniformly rough surface.

A spacious flight of steps leads to an ornate portico that gives direct entrance to the first floor of the building. Above it is a large central arch surmounted by a Texas Lone Star in bas-relief. Under the main entrance porch, Clayton provided a covered drive-through for carriages and other vehicles. Inside, a grand central staircase provides access to the second and third floors.

Like many other Galveston buildings, Old Red was damaged by the great hurricane of 1900, one of the greatest natural disasters to strike the United States. The storm swept out of the Gulf of Mexico across the city, which had no seawall at that time to protect it, and left in its wake massive destruction and an estimated 6,000 dead.

Old Red still stood after the storm, but much of the roof was gone, including a central octagonal turret above the entry and decorative fleches on the top of each towerette. These were not replaced, and many architects today are said to believe that the simplified, less ornate roofline is actually more attractive than Clayton's original design.

As the decades went by, new buildings were added to the campus. By the 1970s Old Red, though still structurally sound, was showing its age. A successful fund drive led to a restoration, which began in 1982 and was completed in 1985. In 1986 Old Red was officially rededicated and commissioned again for service in the training of medical professionals. Today it houses administrative offices, an amphitheater (one of two that were in the original building), which is used as a lecture hall, and an anatomy dissection laboratory.

In its 100 years, UTMB has graduated more than 17,000 doctors, nurses and other health science professionals. The Medical Branch has grown from one hospital and one school to seven hospitals, four schools

These two pictures show Old Red as it looked in the 1890s, before the great storm of 1900 knocked down the central octagonal turret above the entry and destroyed much of the roof, and as it looks today, after the restoration project of 1982-85.

and two institutes that today occupy 71 buildings on 64 acres.

The Design

Don Adair of Richardson, Texas, a commercial illustrator and designer, was asked by art director Derry Noyes to submit sketches of Old Red for the postal card. Adair had previously designed the Republic of Texas Sesquicentennial stamp of 1986.

UTMB sent slides and photographs to USPS for use in the design process. In addition, Adair visited Galveston in the summer of 1990 to examine the building, mix some paint samples that he could match to the color of the actual stones, and make his own photographs.

Adair submitted three pencil sketches showing Old Red from different angles. The Citizens' Stamp Advisory Committee chose a ground-level view of the building from the left, and Adair made a finished painting in watercolor on Strathmore Bristol board. Like most artists who depict old buildings for the Historic Preservation series, Adair commented afterward on the difficulty of conveying the idea of elaborate detail — windows, arches, ornamentation — in the small five-times-up painting that USPS requires.

With Old Red, USPS returned to its practice of placing a brief descriptive inscription in the lower left corner, or cachet area. Three lines of small type disclosed that the subject of the card was "Old Red/The University of Texas/Medical Branch at Galveston." This placement of information, which had been used frequently on past commemorative postal cards, had been omitted from the first such card of 1991 (Carnegie Hall) because officials were afraid that typography in that location would confuse the optical address-scanning machines used to sort mail. However, by the time the Old Red card was designed, they were satisfied that this wouldn't be a problem.

"The printing orders for commemorative cards are low. Most of them are used by individuals rather than businesses, and so they would have handwritten rather than printed addresses," said Joe Brockert of USPS. "The information printed on the cards is in cyan ink and is in very small characters. We've concluded that it won't mislead the OCRs (optical character readers).

Adair made these two pencil sketches of Old Red as seen from the right, in addition to the sketch that formed the basis for the finished design.

402

"The cachet area is a useful place for us to provide information on the subject of the card. We can say far more there than we can put in or around the indicium without cluttering the design or encroaching on the card's address area."

Designer Don Adair's brother Ron, also an artist, had himself previously designed four stamps, the Everett Dirksen and John Hanson commemoratives and the Margaret Mitchell and Mary Lyons definitives in the Great Americans series.

First-Day Facts

The first-day ceremony was originally announced for June 12, but was later moved to June 14 to coincide with the UTMB convocation, which was the highlight of the centennial year. The postal card event was at 11 a.m. in Levin Hall; the convocation followed at 2 p.m.

Southern Regional Postmaster General Jerry K. Lee Sr. dedicated the card. President James of UTMB was the featured speaker.

Date of Issue: June 28, 1991

Catalog Number: Scott UXC25

Colors: cyan, magenta, yellow, black

First-Day Cancel: Flushing, New York

FDCs Canceled: 24,865

Size: 5½ by 3½ inches

Format: Printed in 80-card sheets, but available only in single cards. Printing plates of 80 subjects (8 across, 10 around).

Markings: "© USPS 1991" at lower left corner

Designer: Chuck Hodgson of Newhall, California

Art Director and Project Manager: Jack Williams (USPS)

Typographer: Bradbury Thompson (CSAC)

Printing: U.S. Government Printing Office (GPO) on a 5-color Roland Man 800 sheetfed offset press

Quantity Ordered: 5,000,000

Quantity Distributed: 3,594,000

Tagging: vertical bar to right of stamp

The Postal Card

On June 28, USPS issued a 40¢ airmail postal card depicting Pan American Airways' *Yankee Clipper*, the Boeing 314 flying boat that in 1939 launched the first scheduled commercial air service between North America and Europe. The card had its first-day sale in Flushing, New York, near the *Yankee Clipper's* original takeoff point.

The denomination covered the new rate for international air postcards and replaced the 36¢ postal card of 1988 that featured a Douglas DC-3 passenger and cargo aircraft.

USPS, in its announcement of the new card, said the *Yankee Clipper* "flew the world's first trans-Atlantic airmail on May 20, 1939." This was incorrect. Individual planes and pilots had carried mail across the Atlantic as far back as Alcock and Brown in 1919. Earlier in the 1930s, German and French airlines began providing mail service across the South Atlantic between West Africa and the "hump" of Brazil. But the *Clipper* put passenger and mail service over the North Atlantic Ocean on a regular basis.

Pan American, under its dynamic president, Juan Trippe, had inaugurated transpacific mail and passenger service in 1935 with the *China Clipper*, a Martin M-130 seaplane. Three and a half years later, the company was ready to span the Atlantic. On January 29, 1939, Boeing made its first delivery to Pan American of the plane that would do the job.

The Boeing 314, at 42 tons, was 1½ times the size of the *China Clipper* and carried twice the payload. Four 1,500-horsepower Wright Cyclone engines were tucked under its outstretched wings. Its flight deck, where the 12-man crew worked, was equal to the entire cabin space of a Douglas DC-3. For passengers, there were three lounges, a dining room and 35 sleeping berths aligned behind the main cabins. The transatlantic fare was set at $375 one way, $675 round trip, about the same as the price of a cabin on the French liner *Normandie*.

The first two 314s were sent to Pan American's Pacific fleet. The third was flown to Baltimore by way of San Francisco, where it was displayed at the Golden Gate International Exhibition. On March 3, at Anacostia in Washington, First Lady Eleanor Roosevelt christened it the *Yankee Clipper* with a bottle that reportedly contained waters of the seven seas.

Preparations for the first flight took several weeks. On May 20, the 12th anniversary of Charles Lindbergh's solo flight to Europe, the *Yankee Clipper*, loaded with 1,800 pounds of mail, took off from Long Island's Manhasset Bay, turned toward the New York World's Fair and passed 500 feet over the heads of the fair's thousands of Saturday visitors. Then she headed east for Marseilles on a flight that would take just over 26½ hours, with stops in the Azores and Lisbon, Portugal.

Four days earlier, the U.S. Post Office Department had issued a 30¢ stamp to be used on transatlantic airmail (Scott C24). Its design featured the winged globe used on several previous airmail stamps, with the addition of oceanscape and the word "Trans-Atlantic."

This 30¢ Transatlantic stamp was issued May 16, 1939, in time to frank letters carried by the Yankee Clipper *May 20.*

The first transatlantic paying passengers left New York on another 314, the *Dixie Clipper*, for Marseilles June 28. During the summer of 1939, when Europe was sliding toward war, Pan American Boeing 314s made two weekly round trips between New York and London and Marseilles by way of Lisbon. Eastward flew socialites and dress manufacturers for the seasonal rituals of sport and high fashion. Westward went cargoes of fall designs from the Paris haute couture and the first wave of immigrants who could afford to arrive in America by air, the wealthy refugees from the Third Reich.

On August 28, U.S. flags were painted on the *Yankee Clipper* as marks of neutrality in the world war that was then less than one week away.

The Design

Chuck Hodgson of Newhall, California, a veteran designer of aircraft stamps and postal cards, was chosen to design the *Yankee Clipper* card. Hodgson's credits included two items issued in 1985, to mark the 50th anniversary of transpacific airmail: a 33¢ airmail postal card and a 44¢ airmail stamp, both depicting the Martin M-130 *China Clipper*. He also designed the DC-3 airmail postal card of 1988 and a $1 Transportation coil stamp of 1990 that pictured a 1914 Benoist airboat.

Hodgson painted three different views of the *Yankee Clipper*, using his own research sources. The Citizens' Stamp Advisory Committee chose a view of the plane in flight, seen from ahead and below, against a cloud-filled sky. In Hodgson's first artwork the plane's right wingtip was cropped off by the rectangular frame of the indicium, but the committee decided the image would be more dramatic if the entire wing was shown by projecting it outside the frameline.

This same technique had been used previously with the 1978 airmail postal card depicting the Curtiss Jenny biplane and the 1982 card

These two side views of the Yankee Clipper *prepared by veteran designer Chuck Hodgson were turned down in favor of a more dramatic view of the aircraft from below.*

406

On the first version of the finished postal card, the left wingtip of the plane was cut off by the frame.

showing gliders in flight. Its use this time was facilitated by the conclusion of USPS officials that there was no longer any real need for international airmail stationery to have a distinctive border of alternating red and blue lozenges, and the *Yankee Clipper* card was issued without that customary design accessory.

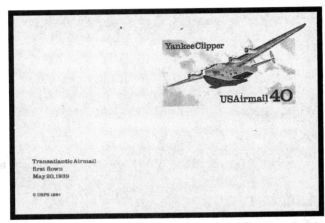

At CSAC's request, designer Hodgson extended the wingtip to the edge of the card. In this version, however, the words "Transatlantic Airmail" are still in the cachet area rather than inside the indicium.

First-Day Facts

No dedication ceremony was held for the *Yankee Clipper* postal card, but the card and first-day postmark were available June 28 in the rotunda of the Pan Am Marine Air Terminal at New York City's LaGuardia Airport and the main post office in Flushing.

Ironically, on December 4, a little over five months after the card was issued, Pan American World Airways stopped flying permanently after suffering years of losses. The death blow came the day before in U.S. Bankruptcy Court, when Delta Air Lines backed out of participating in an emergency reorganization plan for Pan Am.

30¢ NIAGARA FALLS POSTAL CARD
AMERICA THE BEAUTIFUL SERIES

America the Beautiful   USA 30

Date of Issue: August 21, 1991

Catalog Number: Scott UX158

Colors: yellow, magenta, cyan, black

First-Day Cancel: Niagara Falls, New York

FDCs Canceled: 29,762

Size: 5½ by 3½ inches

Format: Printed in 80-card sheets, but available only in single cards. Printing plates of 80 subjects (8 across, 10 around).

Markings: "© USPS 1991"

Designer: Wendell Minor of New York, New York

Typographer: Bradbury Thompson (CSAC)

Art Director and Project Manager: Joe Brockert (USPS)

Printing: U.S. Government Printing Office (GPO) on a 5-color Roland Man 800 sheetfed offset press

Quantity Ordered: 3,500,000

Quantity Distributed: 2,362,000

Tagging: vertical bar to right of stamp

The Card

On August 21, USPS issued a postal card in its America the Beautiful series depicting Niagara Falls. The denomination was 30¢, which covered the air postcard rate to Canada and Mexico.

The card was the 11th in the series. The first six cards depicted different kinds of generic landscapes: prairie, desert, wetlands, mountains, seashore and woodlands. The more recent cards have focused on scenes in specific places: Philadelphia, Baltimore, New York City, Washington, D.C., and now Niagara Falls.

USPS originally listed the card as part of its 1990 program. On July 3, 1990, however, it announced that the item had been "deferred." Its inclusion in the July-August 1991 *Philatelic Catalog* of USPS' Philatelic Sales Division signaled that it would soon be forthcoming. On July 23, 1991, USPS released the design, date of issue and other information. By then, however, copies of the card had already entered the mailstream in some locations (see below).

At one point, officials had discussed making the card a picture postal card, with perhaps a night view of the falls on the picture side and a day view in the indicium, or vice versa. Two major considerations convinced them to issue a conventional card, however. First, USPS had been unable to find a way to properly market its earlier picture postal cards, which sold for a premium over face value. Second, a 30¢ card was needed for mail to Canada, and the Niagara Falls image seemed to be a natural for it.

One of the world's great natural wonders, Niagara Falls has been a tourist attraction, not to mention a destination for honeymooners, for more than a century and a half. Here the Niagara River, which drains Lake Erie and the upper Great Lakes into Lake Ontario, makes a spectacular vertical plunge of 160 feet into a broad gorge.

The Falls consist of two principal cataracts, separated by Goat Island: the narrower American Falls, on the U.S. side, and Horseshoe Falls, which are Canadian. More than two million visitors every year come to the adjacent New York state and Ontario provincial parks to climb observation towers, visit the spray-soaked Cave of the Winds at the foot of the American Falls, or ride the *Maid of the Mist*, one of four diesel-powered boats of that name that ply the lower river and carry passengers deep into the embrace of the Horseshoe Falls.

Niagara Falls had been depicted postally several times before. The U.S. Pan-American Exposition series of 1901 commemorated a world's fair that was illuminated with hydroelectric power from Niagara. Its 5¢ value (Scott 297) bore a picture of the Falls View Bridge — at the time, the longest single-span steel bridge in the world — with the Falls visible through the graceful arch. That bridge endured until 1938, when an ice jam destroyed it.

A view of the American Falls from Goat Island was shown on the 25¢ stamp of the 1922-31 series (Scott 568, 699). In 1948, a 3¢ stamp marking a century of friendship between the United States and Canada (Scott 961) depicted the old Niagara Railway suspension bridge, and again the Falls was visible in the background. And one of three 6¢ postal cards issued in 1972 for the Tourism Year of the Americas showed Niagara Falls in a montage of scenes on the reverse (Scott UX61).

Canada showed the Horseshoe Falls on a handsome 20¢ pictorial stamp of 1935 (Scott 225). Interestingly, the view was from the same spot as that shown on the 1991 U.S. postal card — Prospect Point, on the American side — but was from a higher elevation so as to focus more directly on the Canadian portion of the Falls.

Despite this reasonably full philatelic record, for the past 20 years one of the most persistent one-man stamp campaigns in history had been waged on behalf of a U.S. stamp depicting Niagara Falls. Herbert C. Force, a retired school custodian and amateur photographer living in Niagara Falls, New York, wrote thousands of letters to postal officials, politicians, editors and others, advocating a Niagara Falls stamp that would show the Falls at night, bathed in colored lights, or, as a second choice, in the daytime with a rainbow in the mist.

As new stamps by the hundreds appeared with no sign of his beloved Niagara, Force's frustration grew. He pointed out that the Statue of Liberty, a man-made icon, showed up frequently on stamps, but not Niagara, "the original national symbol." Flag stamps? Why not the Flag over Niagara? Love stamps? Why not depict the honeymoon capital of North America? An "F" stamp? Why did USPS decide the F should stand for Flower instead of Falls?

Some of Force's campaign ploys were, to say the least, ingenious. When a newspaper in Buffalo published a photograph of the American Falls in 1987 in which both the brink of the waterfall and the railing along the observation area described "S" curves, Force sent photocopies to editors around the country, pointing out the message: The S meant "we need a 'S'tamp." His crusade received wide publicity. Columnist Andy Rooney wrote about him, and in 1986 a *Wall Street Journal* article featured the Force campaign under the whimsical headline: "How About a Stamp That Honors The Postal Service's Biggest Pest?"

After the 30¢ postal card was issued, Force told a writer for *Stamp Collector* that it wasn't good enough. The indicium design should have been based on a photograph, he said, rather than an artist's rendering.

The Design

Bart Forbes of Dallas, Texas, had designed all the previous America the Beautiful postal cards, but the Niagara Falls assignment went to another artist. He was Wendell Minor of New York City, who had previously designed the North Dakota Statehood stamp of 1989.

Minor did a variety of concept sketches in color. One was a night view of the American Falls, seen from the Canadian side. Fireworks sparkled overhead, mauve lights played on the mist below, and the skyline of Niagara Falls, New York, was visible in the background. Another was a

410

America the Beautiful   USA 15

Wendell Minor also submitted these color sketches of the American Falls at night, seen from the Canadian side, with fireworks overhead and mauve lights reflecting off the mist, and in the daytime, seen from the observation platform on the U.S. side.

day view of the same American Falls, but from a point corresponding to the observation platform that juts out from the U.S. side.

A third concept, which the Citizens' Stamp Advisory Committee asked Minor to transform into finished artwork, showed the American Falls as seen from the New York state shoreline at Prospect Point, where the water plunges over the brink. In the background at the left was Goat Island, and in the far distance could be seen the Horseshoe Falls, with a rainbow visible in the surrounding mist.

First-Day Facts

No first-day ceremony was held for the Niagara Falls postal card, but August 21 first-day cancellations from Niagara Falls, New York, were available by mail.

This card was one of the many 1991 postal items that were prematurely sold by various post offices because of lack of adequate information from USPS headquarters. Cards were reported with postmarks as early as July 5, nearly seven weeks before the official release date.

19¢ BILL OF RIGHTS RATIFICATION POSTAL CARD
CONSTITUTION BICENTENNIAL SERIES

Date of Issue: September 25, 1991

Catalog Number: Scott UX156

Colors: red, blue, black

First-Day Cancel: Richmond, Virginia

FDCs Canceled: 27,457

Format: Printed in 80-card sheets but available only in single cards. Printing plates of 80 subjects (8 across, 10 around).

Size: 5½ by 3½ inches

Markings: "© USPS 1991"

Designer and Typographer: Mark Zaref of New York, New York

Art Director: Terrence McCaffrey (USPS)

Project Manager: Joe Brockert (USPS)

Modeler: John Boyd of Anagraphics, Inc., New York, New York

Printing: U.S. Government Printing Office (GPO) on a 5-color Roland Man 800 sheetfed offset press

Quantity Ordered: 15,000,000

Quantity Distributed: 13,341,000

Tagging: vertical bar to right of stamp

The Postal Card

The final item in a series of stamps and postal cards commemorating the bicentennial of the U.S. Constitution was a 19¢ card that marked the 200th anniversary of the ratification of the Constitution's first 10 amendments, known collectively as the Bill of Rights.

The card was dedicated September 25 in Richmond, Virginia, on the opening day of the 1991 Virginia State Fair. Virginia was the state whose concurrence in the amendments brought the number of states ratifying to 11 — three-fourths of the total number then in the Union — and made them officially part of the Constitution.

The Constitution Bicentennial series began May 25, 1987, with a postal card (Scott UX116) celebrating the convening of the Constitutional Convention in Philadelphia in 1787. In all, it comprised 24 stamps and three cards.

When the Constitution itself was submitted to the states in September of 1787, much of the opposition to the document from so-called antifederalists centered on its lack of a Bill of Rights. At the Massachusetts ratifying convention, and in the state conventions that followed, the backers of the Constitution were able to win critical votes by promising to support the desired amendments as soon as the new Congress was seated. These bargains saved the Constitution from defeat.

James Madison, a member of the first House of Representatives, led the process by which more than 200 amendments suggested by the states were distilled into 10 guaranteeing basic liberties. The amendments were approved by Congress September 25, 1789, and sent out for ratification. (The 200th anniversary of this event was marked by a 25¢ commemorative stamp, Scott 2421, issued September 25, 1989.)

The package of amendments actually consisted of 12, but two of them, concerning the size of the House of Representatives and congressional salaries, have never received sufficient state ratifications to be adopted. The remaining 10 amendments guarantee every U.S. citizen specific personal liberties, including freedom of speech, religion, assembly and the press, protection from illegal search and seizure, the right to a fair and

Another quill pen — in an eagle's beak — was featured on this 1989 commemorative stamp marking the 200th anniversary of the enactment of the Bill of Rights.

413

speedy trial and a safeguard against cruel and unusual punishment.

On November 20, 1789, less than two months after Congress enacted the amendments, New Jersey ratified 11, rejecting the amendment dealing with the size of the House. One day later, North Carolina, which had refused to ratify the Constitution without a Bill of Rights, voted to ratify the basic document and became the 12th state. Within another month, Maryland and North Carolina ratified all 12 proposed amendments, and by June 1790 a total of nine states had ratified the 10 amendments that would become the Bill of Rights.

When on January 10, 1791, Vermont joined the original 13 states in the Union, it became necessary to secure ratification in 11 states to make an amendment part of the Constitution. Vermont became the 10th state to approve the Bill of Rights November 3, 1791, and on December 15, 1791, Virginia followed suit. It was then official.

Three of the original states didn't get around to ratifying the Bill of Rights until the 150th anniversary of the approval of the amendments in Congress. These super-procrastinators were Massachusetts (March 2, 1939), Georgia (March 18, 1939) and Connecticut (April 19, 1939).

The Design

Artist Marc Zaref, the head of a New York City graphic design studio, created the graphic work for the card's rectangular indicium.

A white quill pen and parts of two others were superimposed on a red rectangle. To the right was explanatory text in white on a blue background: "December 15, 1791, the states complete ratification of 10 of the 12 amendments submitted by Congress in September 1789." The type was a modification of Baskerville, an elegant 18th-century typeface.

These two proposed designs for the Bill of Rights commemorative both incorporated a text block outside the indicium. One of the indicia showed quill pens against a red background, the same as on the approved design. The other featured a single quill against a black-on-yellow representation of a portion of the actual Bill of Rights.

Black script lettering below the design read: "Ratification of the Bill of Rights," with "USA 19" in red at the lower right.

Before arriving at this final design, Zaref produced numerous rough sketches — some done at the library during his research — and a few ideas that he brought to an advanced state of development. Among the latter were a detail from a stylized American flag in which quill pens represented the stars. Another design focused on lines of text from the Bill of Rights.

In a press release, Zaref analyzed the design process and its results. "The ratification of the Bill of Rights is an abstract concept," he said, "and the challenge was to develop a visual interpretation of the idea. Any type of pictorial representation of the document tended to compete with the simplicity of the design, as well as to focus the emphasis onto the Bill of Rights itself, rather than on the ratification process."

Because the concept was abstract, Zaref felt that explanatory text was essential to the viewer's understanding of what was being commemorated. Zaref wrote the original text block, which was modified slightly by USPS after consultation with the Commission on the Bicentennial of the United States Constitution.

Zaref said he tried to develop subtle visual references to familiar images to relate to the ideas behind the ratification. The quill pen symbolized the signing of the document; the quill shapes were designed to suggest that they continued out beyond the indicium in a repeating pattern, to indicate that ratification was a process repeated by each state.

"The white quills on a red ground suggest qualities of the American flag, and the uneven density of the alternating red and white stripes might suggest motion, like a flickering flag," he said. "Balancing this level of abstraction is the text on a blue background, which might be seen as the flag's white stars on a blue field."

These are four of many rough pencil sketches made by Marc Zaref in the process of working out a suitable design for the Bill of Rights postal card.

The line of script across the bottom had a hand-drawn quality that referred to the calligraphic nature of the actual document, Zaref said. He said the final design "reflected the integration of the different elements, each developed to create specific visual references."

Postmaster General Frank approved the design April 18, 1991.

Quill pens had been a recurring motif in the Constitution Bicentennial series. Howard Koslow's 22¢ stamp (Scott 2360) celebrating the signing of the document showed a hand holding a quill pen. And Lou Nolan's design for the 25¢ stamp (Scott 2421) for the enactment of the Bill of Rights depicted a stylized eagle, in silhouette, with a quill pen in its beak.

First-Day Facts

The State Fair of Virginia, with the theme "Celebrate Freedom," opened at 5 p.m. September 25. As part of the opening ceremonies, LeGree S. Daniels, a member of the USPS Board of Governors, dedicated the postal card. The principal speaker was L. Douglas Wilder, governor of Virginia. Warren E. Burger, former chief justice of the United States and chairman of the Commission on the Bicentennial of the United States Constitution, had been scheduled to speak, but sent a replacement.

USPS furnished an elaborate pictorial first-day handstamp depicting an eagle grasping a star-bedecked ribbon.

19¢ MAIN BUILDING AT UNIVERSITY OF NOTRE DAME POSTAL CARD
HISTORIC PRESERVATION SERIES

Date of Issue: October 15, 1991

Catalog Number: Scott UX157

Colors: magenta, yellow, cyan, black

First-Day Cancel: Notre Dame, Indiana

FDCs Canceled: 34,325

Format: Printed in 80-card sheets but available only in single cards. Printing plates of 80 subjects (8 across, 10 around).

Size: 5½ by 3½ inches

Markings: "Notre Dame/Sesquicentennial/1842-1992/© USPS 1991"

Designer: Frank Constantino of Winthrop, Massachusetts

Art Director and Typographer: Richard Sheaff (CSAC)

Project Manager: Joe Brockert (USPS)

Printing: U.S. Government Printing Office (GPO) on a 5-color Roland Man 800 sheetfed offset press

Quantity Ordered: 15,000,000

Quantity Distributed: 8,060,000

Tagging: vertical bar to right of stamp

The Postal Card

Many years ago, the U.S. Post Office Department stopped issuing commemorative stamps for the anniversaries of American colleges and universities. Since then, however, the department and its successor, the U.S. Postal Service, have found indirect ways of giving postal recognition to such events. Recently, a favored way to honor a college has been to issue a Historic Preservation series postal card depicting a landmark building or other architectural feature at the institution.

The first of these was the Healy Hall card, issued January 23, 1989, in conjunction with the 200th anniversary of Georgetown University. One person who took special note of this card was Richard "Digger" Phelps, a member of the Citizens' Stamp Advisory Committee and, at the time, men's basketball coach at the University of Notre Dame.

"I knew Notre Dame had a 150th anniversary coming up, and that our administration building was historically significant," Phelps said. "Everyone knows the gold dome — that's the one landmark on the campus that stands out in everyone's mind. So I presented it to the committee, and the committee felt it would be a good subject for a postal card."

On October 15, 1991, a 19¢ Historic Preservation series card depicting the gold-domed administration building was placed on sale. The structure, known on campus as the Main Building, wasn't identified on the card, which bore the wording "Notre Dame/Sesquicentennial/1842-1942." The card was the 18th in the Historic Preservation series and the third card in the series to be issued in 1991.

At least two previous postal items had been associated with Notre Dame. Nearly a century earlier, in 1893, the 10¢ stamp of the Columbian Exposition series had reproduced a painting by Luigi Gregori, *Return of Columbus and Reception at Court*, which is owned by the university and hangs in the Main Building. And in 1988 a stamp honored Knute Rockne, the coach who made the school a football power in the 1920s.

The University of Notre Dame is an independent, national Catholic research university in Notre Dame, Indiana, adjacent to the city of South Bend. It enrolls approximately 10,000 students in four undergraduate colleges and two graduate schools.

It was founded in November 1842 by a French priest of the Congregation of Holy Cross, the Reverend Edward Sorin, and chartered by the Indiana legislature January 15, 1844. Father Sorin's original land grant of several hundred acres was the site of an early mission to native Americans, but included only three small buildings in need of repair. The school's classical collegiate curriculum never attracted more than a dozen students a year in the early decades. Nevertheless, the timing and location of Notre Dame was propitious: The 1840s and 1850s saw the opening of the Midwest by railroads and canals and also the great pre-Civil War immigration of Europeans, mostly of the Catholic faith.

The first Main Building, a six-story structure that housed virtually the entire university, was built in 1865 and destroyed by fire in April 1879.

This elevated view, seen from the level of the statue of the Virgin Mary atop the Gold Dome, would have shown more of the building's eclectic architecture.

A replacement drive was quickly organized, led by the university's president, the Reverend William J. Corby, and its founder, Father Sorin. Architect Willoughby J. Edbrooke, a 30-year-old Episcopalian from Chicago, won a competition to design the new building, and 300 laborers worked at breakneck speed that summer to fulfill Father Corby's pledge that the structure would be up by September 1. On that date, though it still lacked its east and west wings and dome, the Main Building was ready for the fall semester.

Edbrooke called his building an example of "modern Gothic" architecture, while others have classified its riot of turrets, gables, angles, corners and oversized dome and rotunda as "modern Sorin," after the university's founder. The dome itself wasn't erected until 1882, was gilded at Father Sorin's insistence (university officials argued for a less-expensive paint job), and was topped by its 19-foot, two-ton statue of the Virgin Mary in 1888. As Digger Phelps said, it is the universally known symbol of the university: graduates are known as "Domers," and the yearbook is titled simply *The Dome*. For many years student folklore had it that a freshman occupying a dormitory room facing the gold dome was guaranteed academic success.

Architect Edbrooke went on to build many other public buildings, including the Post Office in Washington, D.C., which was depicted on a Historic Preservation series postal card of 1983 (and was partially shown on the District of Columbia Bicentennial stamp that was issued just a few weeks before the Notre Dame card).

The Design

Art director Richard Sheaff obtained some photographs of the Administration Building from the university and turned them over to artist Frank Constantino of Winthrop, Massachusetts. Working from the photographs, Constantino made several sketches of the building, including one from an elevated level that would have fully displayed the building's eccentric and eclectic architecture. Ultimately, however, he and Sheaff decided that a ground-level view would show the gold dome to best advantage, and this was the view on which Constantino based his final

419

watercolor painting.

The limitations of the five-color Roland Man offset press at the Government Printing Office affected the choice of colors to be used on the card. One station on the press was reserved for the taggant, which left four colors available for the indicium. On most postal cards, these turn out to be the standard process colors: magenta, yellow, cyan and black. USPS officials discussed the use of a metallic gold for the dome, which would have yielded a striking effect, but to do it they would have had to omit process black. "We didn't want the detail lines and the edges to drop out," said Joe Brockert, the project manager, "and when we looked at the design separated out in three rather than four colors, without black, it just wasn't as good.

"We also couldn't find the right combination of self-colors. We thought we might be able to find a tan and use various screen values of that tan to form every color in the building, and find a green and use it for all the greenery around the building, and find a blue for the sky; and if we could have identified three colors which, with screening, could have made up that whole scene, we would have done that. But — knowing that we needed green and blue — we couldn't identify a single color that would make up everything that we needed in the building.

Frank Constantino based his painting for the postal card on this photograph of the Notre Dame Administration Building. He artistically trimmed back some of the foliage on either side of the walkway to show more of the building.

Notre Dame Administration Building

In this preliminary painting, the wording "Notre Dame Administration Building" is incorporated in the indicium.

"So we couldn't create it out of self-colors, we couldn't do it in only three process colors, and we finally dropped the idea of doing the dome in metallic gold."

For the same reason, GPO was told to print the "19 USA" in the upper left corner of the design in black, rather than the dark blue that the artist had originally specified. The blue would have had to be an additional color that couldn't be accommodated.

Artist Constantino had previously designed the 15¢ Isaac Royall House postal card of 1990.

First-Day Facts

The postal card was dedicated October 15 in the Monogram Room of the Joyce Athletic and Convocation Center at Notre Dame, the same building where then-President Ronald Reagan had dedicated the Knute Rockne stamp some 3½ years earlier. The principal speaker was Digger Phelps. The Reverend Edward A. Malloy, president of the university, welcomed the audience and introduced the honored guests, and John G. Mulligan, regional postmaster general, dedicated the card.

The university obtained 10,000 cards with first-day cancellations and sent one to every student currently enrolled on the home campus.

19¢ THE OLD MILL AT THE UNIVERSITY OF VERMONT POSTAL CARD
HISTORIC PRESERVATION SERIES

Date of Issue: October 29, 1991

Catalog Number: Scott UX159

Colors: black, cyan, magenta, yellow

First-Day Cancel: Burlington, Vermont

FDCs Canceled: 23,965

Size: 5½ by 3½ inches

Format: Printed in 80-card sheets, but available only in single cards. Printing plates of 80 subjects (8 across, 10 around).

Markings: "The Old Mill/University of Vermont/Bicentennial/© USPS 1991"

Designer: Harry Devlin of Mountainside, New Jersey

Art Director and Typographer: Bradbury Thompson (CSAC)

Project Manager: Jack Williams (USPS)

Printing: U.S. Government Printing Office (GPO) on a 5-color Roland Mann 800 sheetfed offset press

Quantity Ordered: 10,000,000

Quantity Distributed: 8,473,000

Tagging: vertical bar to right of stamp

The Postal Card

1991 proved to be a banner year, philatelically, for Vermont. One of the first postal items of the year was a 29¢ stamp commemorating the bicentennial of Vermont statehood, and one of the last of the year was a 19¢ postal card marking the bicentennial of the state university.

The latter was definitely an add-on. Stamp collectors had no indication that the three Historic Preservation series postal cards that had been scheduled for 1991 would be followed by a fourth one until the September-October *Philatelic Catalog* of the Philatelic Sales Division appeared, listing an "Old Mill" card. Later, USPS disclosed that Old Mill was a building on the campus of the University of Vermont in Burlington, Vermont, and that the card would be issued October 29 at Burlington in connection with the celebration of the university's 200th anniversary.

The card resulted from the initiative of John J. Broza of Glen Cove, New York, a stamp collector, an English teacher at Schreiber High School of Port Washington and a University of Vermont alumnus (Class of 1960). Broza wrote to the Citizens' Stamp Advisory Committee October 4, 1990, asking consideration for a postal card in 1991 honoring his alma mater on its 200th anniversary. "The Old Mill at the University of Vermont is the school's oldest building, its cornerstone having been laid by the Marquis de Lafayette," Broza wrote. "Wouldn't you agree that an item of postal stationery perhaps depicting the Old Mill as a symbol of the University of Vermont's bicentennial would be justified?"

"He did it on his own," said Jean Holt, the university's bicentennial coordinator. "It was really very wonderful. He didn't even let us (at the university) know until he had a sense that there was some interest on the part of the Postal Service." CSAC obtained detailed information about the building from the university, and subsequently approved the project.

University officials were reasonably sure the postal card would be forthcoming when artist Harry Devlin arrived on the campus in May of 1991 to photograph the Old Mill and take notes on colors. But they didn't get official word of the approval until August.

On November 3, 1791, the University of Vermont was chartered by the same general assembly that only 10 months earlier ratified the U.S. Constitution and set the stage for Vermont's admission as the 14th state. A 50-acre parcel of wilderness forest overlooking Lake Champlain, donated by Ira Allen, younger brother of Revolutionary War hero Ethan Allen, would become the campus of the first college chartered in Vermont and the fifth in New England.

The Old Mill symbolizes the growth and development of the University of Vermont. The present building, constructed between 1825 and 1829 as three closely spaced buildings, was designed by John Johnson to replace the original 1802 college building that burned in 1824. When the three sections were connected in 1846, it was said to be the largest building in the state. Long and narrow, the Old Mill received its nickname in the mid-19th century because of its similarity to the brick mill buildings that housed New England's rapidly expanding textile industry.

In 1975 the Old Mill was listed on the National Register of Historic Places. The university currently uses its upper floors as a dormitory and the main floor for exhibitions and other purposes.

The Design

Harry Devlin, an architectural artist and illustrator from Mountainside, New Jersey, created the oil-on-gesso painting from which the Old Mill card's indicium was made. Devlin had been the designer of the previous year's American Papermaking commemorative postal card, which depicted the Rittenhouse paper mill in Germantown, Pennsylvania.

Although the university supplied reference photographs, Devlin worked from color slides that he made on a visit to the campus with his son. "It's very important that I do that," he said. "I look for certain things when I paint a building. I need bright sunlight, to give me a contrast between dark side and light side. That gives it punch and drama — a 'posteresque quality' that you're looking for.

"As it turned out, I had exactly 11 seconds of sunlight to make my pictures. My son will bear witness. In that time, I made four photographs, bracketing the correct exposure with an overexposure and an underexposure. There had been a long stretch of rainy days, but the Weather Bureau expected a fair day on the day we drove up there from New Jersey. When we arrived it was totally overcast, but we stuck around, and between 3 and 4 in the afternoon there was a little patch of blue in the sky, heading right for the place. We stood out there in the rain, and I had my camera all set to go, and there was a sudden burst of sunlight. So I got what I wanted, and it started to rain hard again and rained all the next day. We were very fortunate."

The long shadows in the painting testified to the lateness of the hour

The University of Vermont furnished this photograph of the Old Mill to the U.S. Postal Service.

when the photograph was made. Devlin photographed and painted the building from ground level, as seen from the right side. He had thought that the "USA 19" was going to be placed in the upper left corner of the indicium, he said, adding: "I would have shot it from the other angle if I had known they were going to put it on the right-hand side."

In an unusual bit of cropping, the artist cut off the top of the steeple at the frameline. "Had I included it all, the building would not have fit that (indicium) shape very well," he explained. "You're limited to a specific, predestined shape. To get the entire building in, I would have had to include way too much foreground, and the building itself would have been too diminished in size. It would have been blocked off by trees, too, because there were a lot of trees back of where I stood."

Even with the building filling the indicium, some of the detail that Devlin included in his artwork was unavoidably lost in the printing process. For instance, he reproduced each of the building's dozens of window panes and mullions on his 14-inch-wide painting, but because of the small size of the indicium and the screening necessary to make the offset plates, the detail was impossible to fully appreciate.

CSAC was shown a mockup of the card as a picture postal card, with the painting filling the picture side as well as the smaller indicium space. "We do this with these buildings cards sometimes, to show another way it could be done," said Jack Williams, the card's art director and project manager. "The committee decided against making it a picture card, and it was never discussed with the university."

After CSAC saw Devlin's painting, its only request was that he remove a small portion of a neighboring building that showed on the left side and that might have been mistaken for an extension of the Old Mill.

Like the three Historic Preservation cards issued earlier in 1991, this one didn't bear the words "Historic Preservation." The last card to carry that inscription was the Chicago Orchestra Hall card of 1990.

First-Day Facts

The card was dedicated by Michael J. Shinay, executive assistant to the postmaster general, at a public ceremony October 29 in the Recital Hall of the Music Building on the university's Redstone Campus.

George H. Davis, the president of the university, had resigned that post just days before the ceremony, and the duty of extending the welcome fell to another university official, Dalmas A. Taylor. Principal speakers were Deborah Ripley, another pinch-hitter (she substituted for Vermont's governor, Howard Dean), and Thomas D. Visser of the university's Historic Preservation Program.

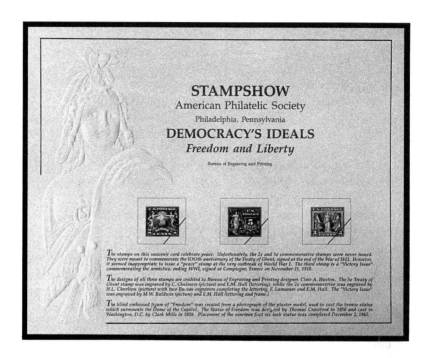

Date of Issue: August 22, 1991

Catalog Number: Scott 131

First-Day Release: Philadelphia, Pennsylvania (Stampshow 91) and Washington, D.C. (BEP Visitors' Center)

Colors: Brown (PMS 4645U), black (offset); red (PMS 186U), blue (PMS 294U), purple (intaglio); metallic gold (letterpress)

Size: 10 by 8 inches

Conceptual Design: Steve Manset (BEP)

Designer and Modeler: Clarence Holbert (BEP)

Paper Stock: LP 686 Artificial Parchment 100 percent rag ivory

Printing: 6-color Miller offset sheetfed press; foil stamping and sculptural embossing on Kluge letterpress; intaglio die stamper

Quantity: 8,500

The Card

The Bureau of Engraving and Printing's only philatelic souvenir card of 1991 was issued in connection with the American Philatelic Society's Stampshow 91, held August 22 through 25 in the Philadelphia Civic Center in Philadelphia, Pennsylvania. The card bore the words "Democracy's Ideals: Freedom and Liberty," which was the theme for the year of BEP's philatelic and numismatic cards.

The Stampshow card was unusual in that it featured intaglio die imprints of two U.S. stamps that had been prepared but never issued, along with a third stamp that actually was issued. The card also bore a blind embossed head-and-shoulders impression of "Freedom," the bronze statue that stands atop the dome of the U.S. Capitol in Washington.

The images were explained in the card's text:

"The stamps on this souvenir card celebrate peace. Unfortunately, the 2¢ and 5¢ commemorative stamps were never issued. They were meant to commemorate the 100th anniversary of the Treaty of Ghent, signed at the end of the War of 1812. However, it seemed inappropriate to issue a 'peace' stamp at the very outbreak of World War I. The third stamp is a 'Victory Issue' commemorating the armistice, ending WWI, signed at Compiegne, France on November 11, 1918.

"The designs of all three stamps are credited to Bureau of Engraving and Printing designer, Clair A. Huston. The 5¢ Treaty of Ghent stamp was engraved by C. Chalmers (picture) and E.M. Hall (lettering), while the 2¢ commemorative was engraved by H.L. Chorlton (picture) with two Bureau engravers completing the lettering, F. Lamasure and E.M. Hall. The 'Victory Issue' was engraved by M.W. Baldwin (picture) and E.M. Hall (lettering and frame).

"The blind embossed figure of 'Freedom' was created from a photograph of the plaster model, used to cast the bronze statue which surmounts the Dome of the Capitol. The Statue of Freedom was designed by Thomas Crawford in 1856 and cast in Washington, D.C. by Clark Mills in 1858. Placement of the nineteen foot six inch statue was completed December 2, 1863."

The die imprints of the three stamps were printed in red (2¢ Ghent) and blue (5¢ Ghent), the colors that had been chosen for those unissued items, and a light purple (3¢ Victory), the actual color of that stamp (Scott 537). Each was "canceled" with a diagonal black line across the lower right, a practice BEP has followed with its philatelic cards in recent years.

The designs of the two unissued stamps of 1914 had been known to collectors. They had been included, for example, in Max G. Johl's works on 20th-century U.S. stamps. Actual die imprints were something few people had seen, however. Both stamps were of the small size, arranged horizontally. The 2¢ value showed two female figures on either side of a globe clasping hands across the Atlantic Ocean. The one at the left represented America, with an American flag, and the one at the right represented Britannia, holding a British flag. The 5¢ stamp showed a

427

winged female figure as an allegory of peace, with a dove of peace flying before her. Both bore the word "Peace" and the dates "1814-1914." Although the dies were completed, no printing plates were ever made, Johl reported.

The 3¢ Victory commemorative, issued March 3, 1919, was also a small, horizontally arranged stamp. Like the unissued pair of 1914, it was allegorical in design, showing a female Liberty Victorious encased in armor and holding a sword and the scale of Justice. Behind her were the flags of the United States and its four allies, Great Britain, Belgium, Italy and France. It was widely criticized for reasons summed up by Max Johl: "The design was too crowded and fine detail was lacking. The use of a shaded background tended to give the design a blurred and unsatisfactory appearance. The poor quality of the ink obtainable and the fast presses

1991-92 DUCK STAMP SOUVENIR CARD (FISH AND WILDLIFE SERVICE)

Date of Issue: June 30, 1991

Catalog Number: none

First-Day Release: June 30, Washington, D.C.; July 1, East Dorset, Vermont

Colors: process yellow, magenta, cyan and black; brown (PMS 412), green (PMS 342) and gray (PMS 430), all offset; gold foil (letterpress); black (offset) text on back of card

Size: 10 by 8 inches

Designer, Typographer and Modeler: Peter Cocci (BEP)

Paper Stock: Poseidon Perfect

Printing: 6-color Miller offset sheetfed press (4-subject plates); Kluge letterpress for gold foil stamping

Quantity: 10,000, of which 750 are numbered in gold

The Card

For the fifth consecutive year, the National Fish and Wildlife Foundation, a non-profit organization chartered by Congress to support wildlife conservation projects, sponsored a duck stamp souvenir card to help fund its programs.

The card, offset-printed by the Bureau of Engraving and Printing, bore an enlarged full-color replica of the 1991 Duck Stamp showing king eiders, with simulated perforations around the stamp's edges, against a green background. The card carried the signatures and the agency seals or logos of Manuel Lujan, secretary of the Interior; John Turner, director, U.S. Fish and Wildlife Service, and James Range, chairman, National Fish and Wildlife Foundation, plus the signature of duck stamp designer Nancy Howe of East Dorset, Vermont.

Ten thousand cards were printed. These cards, along with a copy of the $15 duck stamp itself, were sold for varying prices. The least expensive were 8,250 cards without serial numbers or cancellations. Their cost was $20 each.

The remaining 1,750 cards had first-day cancellations, from Washington, D.C., where the cards went on sale June 30, and East Dorset, Vermont, where they were first sold July 1. Of these canceled cards, 1,000 bore no serial numbers and sold for $25 each, and 750 were numbered in gold and sold for $150 each (numbers 1 through 10), $75 each (11 through 100) or $50 each (101 through 750). The gold numbers were applied by letterpress.

The $15 cost of the stamp was deducted from the proceeds of each card, and the Washington-based Foundation retained the balance. After paying BEP for the printing costs, the Foundation used the funds for its conservation programs.

Rates Revised: USPS Request For 30¢ Stamp Rejected

Less than three years after the last general rate increase, USPS implemented another broad overhaul of its rate structure, which featured an increase in the price of a first-class stamp from 25¢ to 29¢.

The new rates took effect February 3, 1991, following a decision by the USPS Board of Governors January 22 to approve most of the increases recommended January 4 by the independent Postal Rate Commission.

However, the governors approved the 29¢ first-class rate only "under protest." They had asked the PRC for a 30¢ first-class rate, arguing that without it the Postal Service would continue to lose money.

The PRC, when it trimmed the Postal Service's first-class rate requests, also recommended a 25-percent hike in third-class postage, as opposed to the 17-percent increase USPS had planned.

Postmaster General Anthony M. Frank took every opportunity during the year to criticize the 29¢ first-class rate. He called it "penny foolish" and declared that "our market research and any number of paper editorials suggest that a lot of Americans would prefer the 'roundness' of the 30¢ stamp we proposed."

In testimony before Congress March 21, Frank proposed that USPS be given more independence to set its own rates. He complained of the PRC's "predispositions," including "an apparent intent to sock it to the third-class mailers, come hell or high water."

On July 2, the Board of Governors unanimously rejected the new rates and asked PRC for a reconsideration. By now USPS was already suffering a major revenue shortfall, and the agency ended fiscal 1991 in September with a loss of $1.6 billion. Among the causes, Postmaster General Frank said, were the recession, additional retiree cost burdens placed on USPS by Congress — and the PRC-imposed rate structure.

On October 4, the PRC again turned down the 30¢ rate. At this point, the Board of Governors could have overruled the PRC by a unanimous vote. However, at its November meeting, it could muster only a 6-3 tally in favor of the 30¢ rate. The effective result, the postmaster general said, was that the rate would stay at 29¢ at least until 1994.

Among the rate changes that took effect February 3 were these (old rates in parentheses):

First-class mail, each additional ounce, 23¢ (20¢); postcards, 19¢ (15¢); postcards to Canada and Mexico, 30¢ (21¢ and 15¢); letter mail to Canada, one ounce, 40¢ (30¢); letter rate to Mexico, one-half ounce, 35¢, and one ounce, 45¢ (25¢); airmail rate to all other countries, one-half ounce, 50¢ (45¢); aerograms, 45¢ (39¢); airmail postal cards, 40¢ (36¢).

Priority Mail, $2.90 ($2.40); Express Mail (letter, to addressee), $9.95 ($8.75).

Following are some of the many new bulk-mail rates:

Unsorted ZIP+4, 27.6¢ (24.1¢); letters sorted to three or five digits, 24.8¢ (21¢); ZIP+4 presort, 24.2¢ (20.5¢); basic bulk rate, 19.8¢ (16.7¢); bulk mail sorted to five digits, 16.5¢ (13.2¢); bulk mail sorted by carrier route, 13.1¢ (10.1¢); basic non-profit, 11.1¢ (8.4¢); sorted non-profit, 9.8¢ (7.6¢); non-profit sorted by carrier route, 7.4¢ (5.3¢).

In its January 1991 rate decision, the Postal Rate Commission proposed that USPS offer for the first time an "automation discount" to private citizens for using envelopes bearing Facing Identification Marks (FIMs) and bar codes incorporating the addressee's nine-digit ZIP Code. Such mail should move for 27¢, the PRC said.

The USPS Board of Governors accepted this "Public Automation Rate," or PAR, under protest. However, as 1991 went by USPS made no effort to implement it. Postal officials said privately that a two-tier rate system of this kind would present enormous problems of customer education and Postal Service monitoring.

House Holds Hearing Into Stamp Production

On June 5, 1991, the House Subcommittee on Postal Operations and Services of the Committee on Post Office and Civil Service held a one-day hearing on the production and procurement of postage stamps by the U.S. Postal Service.

The hearing, according to introductory remarks by the chairman, Representative Frank McCloskey, D-Indiana, was held to take testimony on various reported problems, including "instances of shoddy manufacturing, inadequate supply, and management errors" which McCloskey said had cast doubt on the Postal Service's ability to provide postal customers with "quality stamps in adequate numbers."

Among those who testified before the House committee June 5 were Peter Daly (left), director of BEP; Carl D'Alessandro (center), also of BEP, and Gordon C. Morison (right), assistant postmaster general.

McCloskey also cited other incidents (which are described in detail elsewhere in this *Yearbook*). These included the printing of wrong dates in the selvage of the Hubert Humphrey definitive stamps; the unsatisfactory perforating of the first batch of William Saroyan commemoratives; the problem with unstable ink on the BEP-printed Wood Duck booklet stamps, and the controversy over the printing of the Dennis Chavez definitive in Canada. It all added up, the chairman said, to "an ignominious and impressive list of fiascoes in terms of stamp quality and management oversight."

The hearing was held before an audience of more than 100 persons and was covered by television and the Washington press. Witnesses included, for the Postal Service, Assistant Postmaster General Gordon C. Morison and A. Keith Strange, director of the Office of Procurement; for the Bureau of Engraving and Printing, Peter H. Daly, director, and Carl D'Alessandro, chief operating officer; for the United States Bank Note Corporation and American Bank Note Company, Stanley Kreitman, president of both entities, and Tom Harris, senior vice president; for the U.S. General Accounting Office, L. Nye Stevens, and, representing stamp collectors, Kenneth Lawrence, a Jackson, Mississippi, stamp writer and outspoken critic of the diversion of stamp printing from the BEP, and Charles L. Jones III, a USPS employee from Phoenix, Arizona.

Statements, letters and supplemental materials from these and other interested parties were placed in the record, including an explanation from Richard C. Sennett of Sennett Enterprises of his roles as a subcontractor to private companies supplying stamps to USPS and as a prime contractor as the managing director of a partnership, Stamp Venturers.

Detailed and sometimes conflicting testimony was taken on the cost-effectiveness, quality outcomes and other consequences of the Postal Service's policy of diversifying its sources of stamps through contracts with private printers. Representative McCloskey remarked on the "pejorative" tone of Assistant PMG Morison's criticism of BEP as a stamp supplier, and told him the relationship between USPS and BEP "obviously . . . needs more work." He and Representative Gerry Sikorski, D-Minnesota, also expressed concern over the past and present linkages of a number of the private firms involved in bidding on stamp contracts. "You have got all these subcontracts collapsed down into not many," Sikorski told the USPS officials.

No conclusions were reached, but on June 27 the subcommittee asked the General Accounting Office to conduct a full audit of U.S. stamp printing. Assistant PMG Morison had told reporters after the hearing that he would "welcome" such an audit. The review would include the corporate interrelations of the contractors and the degree of competitiveness of their bidding. GAO was also asked to look into BEP's pricing and costs and suggest "ways to improve the partnership in the production of postage stamps by the Bureau." "The hearing record is replete with inconsistent factual information provided by private industry, Bureau and Postal Service officials,'' McCloskey wrote in his audit request.

Senators Call for Replacement of CSAC

Following the well-publicized disclosures that the Dennis Chavez stamp was printed in Canada and the Hubert Humphrey stamp contained the wrong dates in the selvage, U.S. Senator Ted Stevens, R-Alaska, introduced a bill that would replace the USPS Citizens' Stamp Advisory Committee with a 15-person committee appointed by the president. The committee would select stamp subjects and approve final stamp designs. The bill, co-sponsored by Senator David Pryor, D-Arkansas, would also prohibit printing U.S. stamps outside this country.

Stevens, ranking Republican on the Senate Subcommittee on Federal Services, Post Office and Civil Service, of which Pryor was chairman, said in an April 24 statement that stamp design was becoming too commercialized and that too many issues contained inaccuracies. An independent committee would ensure that ''only truly great Americans who have made contributions of national significance are honored by stamps,'' his release stated.

Defenders of CSAC quickly rallied. The American Philatelic Society's board of directors on May 15 approved a resolution saying APS ''fully supports the CSAC as the sole means of determining the selection of subjects for commemoration on United States postage stamps and other emissions of the (USPS).'' The American Stamp Dealers Association took a similar position. No action was taken by Congress on the senators' bill in 1991, nor were any hearings scheduled for early 1992.

USPS Holds Second Printers' Conference

The second USPS Stamp Printers' Conference was held in Washington November 18 and 19, drawing some 300 representatives from 78 companies in the United States, Europe and Japan.

Assistant PMG Gordon Morison told a press briefing that nearly 20 billion non-denominated ''G'' stamps were in production in anticipation of the next rate change. Of this total, some 14.7 billion would be produced by the private sector over a two-year span ending in 1993, Morison said. Another non-denominated Makeup Rate stamp will also be provided when the rate goes up again, he added.

Meanwhile, Morison said, private vendors were figuring in a major way in ongoing 1992 stamp production. Their projected stamp volume for fiscal 1993 was 4.81 billion sheet stamps, 3.352 billion coil stamps, 3.498 billion booklet stamps and 2.718 billion pressure-sensitive stamps, for a total of 14.378 billion stamps.

Looking ahead, the assistant PMG told reporters the future would hold more pressure-sensitive stamps, with three contracts already awarded; more booklet stamps, some of them pressure-sensitive; and linerless coils, meaning pressure-sensitive coil stamps wound on a roll without backing paper, like transparent adhesive tape.

434

Lighthouses Win in Stamp Popularity Polls

The five se-tenant Lighthouse stamps issued in booklet form were voted the most popular U.S. stamps of 1990 in both the *Linn's Stamp News* and *Stamp Collector* annual polls. 1990 was the 20th consecutive year in which a se-tenant issue had won *Linn's* popularity contest.

The Lighthouses, designed by Howard Koslow, won 17½ percent of the votes in *Linn's* "favorite stamp" category and 21 percent in *Stamp Collector's* equivalent category. In both polls the three runners-up, in the same order, were the Indian Headdresses booklet of five se-tenant designs, the Creatures of the Sea block of four (a joint issue with the Soviet Union) and the Classic Films block of four.

Other results of the two polls included:

Linn's: Commemoratives, best design, Lighthouses booklet; worst design, 25¢ contemporary Christmas (Christmas tree); most important, Creatures of the Sea block; least necessary, Classic Films block. Definitives, best design, $2 Bobcat; worst design, 25¢ Flag ATM (plastic) stamp; most important, ATM stamp; least necessary, ATM stamp. Postal stationery, best design, American Papermaking postal card; worst design, 15¢ Postal Buddy postal card; most important, 15¢ Literacy postal card; least necessary, 25¢ Football hologram envelope.

Stamp Collector: Commemoratives, best favorite, Lighthouses booklet; least favorite, Classic Films block. Definitives, best favorite, $2 Bobcat; least favorite, 5¢ Luis Munoz Marin. Postal stationery, best favorite, 15¢ Paper Mill postal card; least favorite, 25¢ Football hologram envelope.

Bruns Named to Head National Postal Museum

James H. Bruns, acting director of the Smithsonian Institution's National Postal Museum, was named permanent director of the new facility. The $15 million museum, which is scheduled to open to the public in July 1993, will be located in the former Washington, D.C., city post office near Union Station on Capitol Hill. It will be operated as part of the Smithsonian Institution's National Museum of American History and will have additional guidance from the U.S. Postal Service, which is providing much of the funding. Bruns, 44, has been philatelic curator at the Smithsonian since 1983.

Sununu's Stamp Trip Gets Him in Trouble

John Sununu, who as White House chief of staff was the best-known stamp collector in the Bush administration, drew heavy criticism and comedians' gibes in June 1991 for having a White House limousine transport him from Washington to a Christie's stamp auction in New York City. At the auction Sununu reportedly spent $4,851 as the winning bidder for 14 lots of U.S. stamps, including a used 5¢ Franklin of 1847 (Scott 1) and a set of unused Zeppelin airmails (Scott C13-C15).

Sununu, in his defense, said he used the limousine trip for work and needed to be in "secure" contact with the White House at all times. In

December 1991 Sununu resigned as chief of staff and at about the same time was named to the 15-member advisory board of the Smithsonian's National Postal Museum.

Postal Service Discontinues Sale of T-Shirts, Trinkets

In November USPS set for itself a deadline date of February 1, 1992, to get rid of its controversial non-stamp-related gift items, including T-shirts, teddy bears and coffee cups.

A memo sent to field division managers stated that the merchandise was being discontinued because of increasing customer criticism that led to congressional criticism of the practice, as well as poor media relations.

According to the memo, even independent USPS marketing research confirmed that customers didn't like to see apparel and merchandise sold at the same counter as core products and services.

Under the new policy, post offices and philatelic centers were permitted to continue to sell any merchandise that contained actual postage stamps, and stamp pins.

VARIETIES

1972 Mount McKinley Color-Missing Error

A single mint copy of the 15¢ Mount McKinley commemorative from the 1972 National Parks Centennial issue (Scott 1454) was reported with the offset yellow missing. The error received a March 14, 1991, certificate from the Philatelic Foundation.

The discoverer was Stan Goldfarb, an error dealer from Potomac, Maryland. Goldfarb told *Linn's Stamp News* he had originally found the stamp about three years earlier in a lot of discount postage he had purchased. He spotted it while looking for a normal copy to accompany a color shift. He set the error stamp aside for a lengthy time, and finally sent it to the Philatelic Foundation in April 1990.

The stamp was printed on the Bureau of Engraving and Printing's Giori press by a combination of offset and intaglio.

1976 Christmas Stamp Color-Missing Error

A previously unreported 15-year-old error on the 1976 contemporary Christmas stamp (Scott 1703), depicting Nathaniel Currier's 1855 lithograph *Winter Pastime*, was auctioned September 11 through Christie's in New York City.

The item was a complete pane of 50 stamps. On four of them, the red color was completely missing, leaving the stamps with a greenish appearance. Another eight stamps were partly affected by the color omission, which, according to the Philatelic Foundation certificate issued for the pane, was caused by a wiping error. At least two of the eight freak stamps were nearly missing the red.

The affected stamps were the lower-left vertical strip from a right-side pane. The red cylinder number that should have appeared in the lower right corner of the pane was absent.

The stamps were printed by the gravure process by the Bureau of Engraving and Printing on its A press, which the Bureau retired and disassembled in 1991. The A press was capable of printing in gravure, intaglio or a combination of the two.

Christie's said the stamps were bought in New York in December 1976. The buyer purchased a single pane, noticed the error later, and

Shown at right is a 15¢ Mount McKinley commemorative with the offset yellow color missing.

returned to the post office hoping to find more, but was unsuccessful. The buyer then put the sheet away for 14 years, Christie's said.

1982 Stagecoach Coil, Tagged, Imperforate

The first imperforate examples of the tagged 4¢ Stagecoach coil stamp of 1982 (Scott 1898A) to be found imperforate were reported in 1991, nearly six years after they had been postally used.

The stamps were printed on the Bureau of Engraving and Printing's Cottrell press. A strip of three of the error stamps, bearing a Providence, Rhode Island, postmark dated May 18, 1985, was found in an on-paper mixture by an Ohio collector. Accompanying the canceled strip in the same mixture was an uncanceled imperforate line pair, plate number 1. The two pieces were apparently not only from the same coil but, because the ends seemed to match, were separated from each other. Probably the uncanceled, ungummed line-and-number pair was affixed below the strip of three on the envelope — the whole comprising the 22¢ first-class rate — and the pair then was skipped by the canceling machine.

Previously, only a few copies of the untagged, precanceled 1982 Stagecoach stamp, from plates 5 and 6, were known imperforate.

Dealer Jacques Schiff sold the canceled strip of three at auction February 8 for $1,400, plus the 10-percent buyer's fee, and sold the line pair at auction in May for $1,900, plus 10 percent.

1989 Bill of Rights Intaglio-Missing Error

Single copies of the 1989 Bill of Rights Bicentennial commemorative stamp (Scott 2421) with the black intaglio impression missing were offered for sale in March by J. Nalbandian Inc., of Warwick, Rhode Island, for $299. The stamp was printed by BEP by a combination of offset and intaglio, with the only intaglio portion being the "USA 25" inscription.

1990 Beach Umbrella Color-Missing Error

Copies of the 15¢ Beach Umbrella booklet stamp without the dark blue gravure color ("USA 15") were offered for sale by dealer B. Nolan of Closter, New Jersey, for $275. No details were available on the error, which was listed as 2443b in the 1992 Scott specialized catalog.

This canceled strip of three Cottrell-printed, tagged, imperforate Stagecoach stamps was found in an on-paper mixture by an Ohio collector.

Shown here are a normal 25¢ Bill of Rights stamp (far left) and a specimen with the intaglio inscription missing (left).

$2 Bobcat Intaglio-Missing Error

Published reports in 1991 told of at least two discoveries of $2 Bobcat stamps of 1990 (Scott 2476) with the intaglio black ("$2 USA") missing. Tom Pullin, a North Carolina postal employee, told *Linn's Stamp News* he had bought a partial pane of 13 of the stamps from the postmaster in his local Rolesville, North Carolina, post office. Later, the stamps were confiscated by postal inspectors, who reportedly told Pullin they suspected him of stealing the error stamps from stock that was marked for destruction. The disposition of the case wasn't known as of this writing.

In September, according to a report in *Stamp Collector*, error dealer Jack Nalbandian Inc. of Warwick, Rhode Island, purchased a full pane of 20 of the Bobcat stamps with the intaglio portion missing. The pane was found by a collector in "the Michigan area," Nalbandian said.

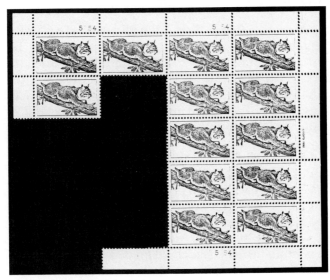

This partial pane of 1990 $2 Bobcat stamps containing 13 possible color-missing errors was found in a North Carolina post office.

439

Shown here is a left-margin block of four Creatures of the Sea stamps with the black intaglio denomination, "USA" and creature names omitted.

1990 Eisenhower Imperforate

An imperforate pane of 40 stamps issued in 1990 to commemorate the 100th anniversary of the birth of Dwight D. Eisenhower (Scott 2513) was found among a group of panes of the Eisenhower stamp purchased in central California, according to error dealer Jacques Schiff, who sold the pane privately through his firm.

The Eisenhower stamps were printed by gravure by the American Bank Note Company.

1990 Creatures of the Sea Intaglio-Missing Error

A small number of the 1990 Creatures of the Sea block of four commemoratives (Scott 2508-2511) were found without the black intaglio impression, consisting of the 25¢ denomination, "USA" and the names of the creatures. The find was made in Santa Rosa, California. The stamps were printed by the Bureau of Engraving and Printing in a combination of offset and intaglio.

1988 25¢ Official Mail Coil, Imperforate

A used pair of the 25¢ Official Mail stamp of 1988 (Scott O141) was found early in the year. Later a partial roll of mint stamps containing 40 imperforate pairs was discovered.

The used pair was found by Russ Burkhard, 39, a Navy administration specialist, while he was soaking stamps for a Springfield, Virginia, Stamp Club youth project. Burkhard made a regular practice of bringing discarded covers bearing Official Mail stamps and naval cancellations to weekly club meetings.

"I was soaking a group of 200 covers with 20¢ and 25¢ Official Mail stamps to be distributed to juniors in the area," Burkhard told *Linn's*

This used pair of imperforate 25¢ Official Mail coil stamps was found by a collector in Virginia.

Stamp News. "I cut the stamps off the envelope, soaked them and had them laid out on paper towels on my kitchen counter. I was inspecting the group for damaged stamps when I found what I thought was part of a label. When I turned it over, I was pleasantly surprised."

From its postmark, Burkhard traced the stamps to the Naval Reserve Center in Grand Rapids, Michigan. The unit's postal representative told him that he had had a roll of 100 of the stamps, completely imperforate, but that he finally cut them apart and used them for postage from September through mid-November of 1990. Most were used in multiple strips on large flats because the clerk didn't want to spend the time to cut them all, Burkhard was told.

A short time after Burkhard reported his find, Bob Dowiot of J. Nalbandian Inc. of Warwick, Rhode Island, told *Linn's* that the firm had bought a partial roll from an individual in Virginia containing 40 imperf pairs. One pair was poorly cut, leaving 39 good pairs. According to Dowiot, the entire roll of 100 had been imperf, but the non-collector who had found it had already used the other 20 stamps for postage.

1946 Duck Stamp Color Error

Two singles and a block of 16 of the 1946 federal duck stamp (Scott RW13) were reported to exist in a color that the 1992 *Scott Specialized Catalogue of United States Stamps* described as "bright rose pink" instead of the normal red brown. The 1992 edition was the first to list this variety. Bob Dumaine of the Sam Houston Duck Company wrote that when a specimen of the color variety stamp is placed next to a normal stamp, "it isn't close to the same color. The error stamp is basically red and devoid of any hint of brown." Dumaine said 17 of the 18 known copies of the stamp were mint with full gum; the other had been hinged.

1990 Duck Stamp Without Message on Back

At least 42 1990 duck stamps (Scott RW57) without the conservation message in gray ink that normally appeared on the reverse were found in and near Richmond, Virginia.

Twenty-four of the missing-message stamps were bought by a Richmond, Virginia, collector at his local post office. He originally obtained a partial pane of 17 of the $12.50 stamps. Then, as an afterthought, he hastened back to the post office and was able to purchase seven additional loose stamps. The error was from an upper left pane bearing plate number

186307, according to Bob Dumaine of the Sam Houston Duck Company, which acquired the stamps.

Another Richmond area collector purchased six of the error stamps and sold them to Richmond's Colonial Stamp Shop. Still another 12 stamps were bought in Hood, Virginia, near Richmond.

According to Dumaine, no similar error had been reported for any previous duck stamp. The first 12 stamps in the program (Scott RW1-RW12) were issued without back inscriptions. Beginning in 1946, inscriptions were added directly to the stamp paper and then gummed over. A change in the printing process in 1954 (Scott RW21) allowed the inscription to be printed on top of the gum.

Double-Printed America the Beautiful Postal Cards

Two examples of the 15¢ America the Beautiful (The Prairie) postal card of 1988 (Scott UX120) with a faint doubling of the entire four-color design and tagging were reported by a collector who owned them. One was submitted to *Linn's Stamp News* for inspection.

The cards were printed on the older, hi-brite paper stock, which has a smooth appearance and glows brightly under longwave ultraviolet light.

George Whitman, supervisor of postal card production at the Government Printing Office, told *Linn's* the doubled cards were probably make-ready cards, printed either when the Roland Man offset press was set up for a printing run or when the press was cleaned.

Such cards, which are routinely pulled and destroyed, often bear multiple impressions because reusing them saves paper. The cards in collectors' hands were probably accidentally released, since the doubling was not too extreme.

Shown is a double-printed America the Beautiful postal card. The entire design and phosphorescent tagging are slightly doubled. A blown-up inset is shown to help highlight the doubling, which is difficult to capture on film.

PLATE NUMBERS

Transportation Coils (not precanceled)

Scott number	Stamp	Plate number	Tagging type
1897	1¢ Omnibus (1983)	1,2,3,4,5,6	overall
2225	1¢ Omnibus (1986)	1,2	block
2225a	1¢ Omnibus (1991)	2	untagged
1897A	2¢ Locomotive (1982)	2,3,4,6,8,10	overall
2226	2¢ Locomotive (1987)	1	block
1898	3¢ Handcar (1983)	1,2,3,4	overall
2252	3¢ Conestoga Wagon (1988)	1	block
2123	3.4¢ School Bus (1985)	1,2	overall
1898A	4¢ Stagecoach (1982)	1,2,3,4,5,6	overall
2228	4¢ Stagecoach (1986)	1	block
2228a	4¢ Stagecoach (1990)	1	overall
2451	4¢ Steam Carriage (1991)	1	overall
2451b	4¢ Steam Carriage (1991)	1	untagged
2124	4.9¢ Buckboard (1985)	3,4	overall
1899	5¢ Motorcycle (1983)	1,2,3,4	overall
2253	5¢ Milk Wagon (1987)	1	block
2452	5¢ Circus Wagon (1990)	1	overall
2452a	5¢ Circus Wagon (1991)	1	untagged
1900	5.2¢ Sleigh (1983)	1,2,3,5	overall
2125	5.5¢ Star Route Truck (1986)	1	block
1901	5.9¢ Bicycle (1982)	3,4	overall
2126	6¢ Tricycle (1985)	1	block
2127	7.1¢ Tractor (1987)	1	block
1902	7.4¢ Baby Buggy (1984)	2	block
2128	8.3¢ Ambulance (1985)	1,2	overall
2129	8.5¢ Tow Truck (1987)	1	block
1903	9.3¢ Mail Wagon (1981)	1,2,3,4,5,6	overall
2257	10¢ Canal Boat (1987)	1	block
2130	10.1¢ Oil Wagon (1985)	1	block
1904	10.9¢ Hansom Cab (1982)	1,2	overall
1905	11¢ Caboose (1984)	1	block
2131	11¢ Stutz Bearcat (1985)	1,2,3,4	overall
2132	12¢ Stanley Steamer (1985)	1,2	overall
2133	12.5¢ Pushcart (1985)	1,2	block
2134	14¢ Iceboat (1985)	1,2,3,4	overall
2134b	14¢ Iceboat (1986)	2	block
2260	15¢ Tugboat (1988)	1, 2	block
2260a	15¢ Tugboat (1988)	2	overall
1906	17¢ Electric Auto (1981)	1-7	overall
2135	17¢ Dog Sled (1986)	2	block
2262	17.5¢ Racing Car (1987)	1	block
1907	18¢ Surrey (1981)	1 through 18 complete	overall
1908	20¢ Fire Pumper (1981)	1 through 16 complete	overall

443

Scott number	Stamp	Plate number	Tagging type
2263	20¢ Cable Car (1988)	1,2	block
2263b	20¢ Cable Car (1990)	2	overall
2464	23¢ Lunch Wagon (1991)	2,3	phosphor-coated paper
2136	25¢ Bread Wagon (1986)	1 through 5 complete	block
2468	$1 Seaplane (1990)	1	overall

Transportation Coils (precanceled)

Scott number	Stamp	Plate number	Tagging type
2123	3.4¢ School Bus (185)	1,2	untagged
1898A	4¢ Stagecoach (1982)	3,4,5,6	untagged
2124	4.9¢ Buckboard (1985)	1,2,3,4,5,6	untagged
2453	5¢ Canoe (1991)	1	untagged
2454	5¢ Canoe (gravure) (1991)	S11	untagged
1900	5.2¢ Sleigh (1983)	1,2,3,4,5,6	untagged
2254	5.3¢ Elevator (1988)	1	untagged
2125	5.5¢ Star Route Truck (1986)	1,2	untagged
1901	5.9¢ Bicycle (1982)	3,4,5,6	untagged
2126	6¢ Tricycle (1985)	1,2	untagged
2127	7.1¢ Tractor (1987)	1	untagged
2127a	7.1¢ Tractor (1989)	1	untagged
1902	7.4¢ Buggy (1984)	2	untagged
2255	7.6¢ Carreta (1988)	1,2,3	untagged
2128	8.3¢ Ambulance (1985)	1,2,3,4	untagged
2231	8.3¢ Ambulance (1986)	1,2	untagged
2256	8.4¢ Wheel Chair (1988)	1,2,3	untagged
2129	8.5¢ Tow Truck (1987)	1,2	untagged
1903	9.3¢ Mail Wagon (1981)	1,2,3,4,5,6,8	untagged
2457	10¢ Tractor Trailer (1991)	1	untagged
2130	10.1¢ Oil Wagon (1985)	1,2	untagged
2130a	10.1¢ Oil Wagon (1988)	2,3	untagged
1904	10.9¢ Hansom Cab (1982)	1,2,3,4	untagged
1905	11¢ Caboose (1984)	1	untagged
not yet assigned	11¢ Caboose (1991)	2	untagged
2132	12¢ Stanley Steamer (1985)	1,2	untagged
2132b	12¢ Stanley Steamer (1987)	1	untagged
2133	12.5¢ Pushcart (1985)	1,2	untagged
2258	13¢ Patrol Wagon (1988)	1	untagged
2259	13.2¢ Coal Car (1988)	1,2	untagged
2261	16.7¢ Popcorn Wagon (1988)	1,2	untagged
1906	17¢ Electric Auto (1981)	1,2,3,4,5,6,7	untagged
2262	17.5¢ Racing Car (1987)	1	untagged
2264	20.5¢ Fire Engine (1988)	1	untagged
2265	21¢ Railroad Mail Car (1988)	1,2	untagged
2266	24.1¢ Tandem Bicycle (1988)	1	untagged

Great Americans Sheet Stamps

Scott number	Stamp	Plate number	Perf type	Tagging type
1844	1¢ Dix	1 floating	bull's-eye	block
		1,2 floating	L perf	block
2168	1¢ Mitchell	1	bull's-eye	block
1845	2¢ Stravinsky	1,2,3,4,5,6	L perf	overall
2169	2¢ Lyon	1,2	bull's-eye	block
1846	3¢ Clay	1,2	L perf	overall
2170	3¢ White	1,2,3	bull's-eye	block
1847	4¢ Schurz	1,2,3,4	L perf	overall
2171	4¢ Flanagan	1	bull's-eye	block
		1	bull's-eye	untagged
1848	5¢ Buck	1,2,3,4	L perf	overall
2172	5¢ Black	1,2	bull's-eye	block
2173	5¢ Marin	1	bull's-eye	overall
		2	bull's-eye	untagged
1849	6¢ Lippmann	1 floating	L perf	block
1850	7¢ Baldwin	1 floating	L perf	block
1851	8¢ Knox	3,4,5,6	L perf	overall
1852	9¢ Thayer	1 floating	L perf	block
1853	10¢ Russell	1 floating	L perf	block
2176	10¢ Red Cloud	1	bull's-eye	block
		1	bull's-eye	overall
		2	bull's-eye	phosphor-coated
1854	11¢ Partridge	2,3,4,5	L perf	overall
1855	13¢ Crazy Horse	1,2,3,4	L perf	overall
1856	14¢ Lewis	1 floating	L perf	block
2177	14¢ Howe	1,2	bull's-eye	block
2178	15¢ Cody	1	bull's-eye	block
		2	bull's-eye	overall
		3	bull's-eye	block
		3	bull's-eye	overall
1857	17¢ Carson	1,2,3,4,13,14,15,16	L perf	overall
2179	17¢ Lockwood	1,2	bull's-eye	block
1858	18¢ Mason	1,2,3,4,5,6	L perf	overall
1859	19¢ Sequoyah	39529, 39530	L perf	overall
1860	20¢ Bunche	1,2,3,4,5,6,7,8,10,11,13	L perf	overall
1861	20¢ Gallaudet	1,2,5,6,8,9	L perf	overall
1862	20¢ Truman	1 floating	L perf	block
		2	bull's-eye	block
		3	bull's-eye	overall
2180	21¢ Carlson	1	bull's-eye	block
1863	22¢ Audubon	1 floating	L perf	block
		3	bull's-eye	block
2182	23¢ Cassatt	1	bull's-eye	block
		1	bull's-eye	overall
		2	bull's-eye	prephosphor

Scott number	Stamp	Plate number	Perf type	Tagging type
2183	25¢ London	1,2	bull's-eye	block
2184	28¢ Sitting Bull	1	bull's-eye	block
1864	30¢ Laubach	1 floating	L perf	block
		2	bull's-eye	block
		2	bull's-eye	overall
1865	35¢ Drew	1,2,3,4	L perf	overall
2185	35¢ Chavez	S1,S2 (six positions)	L perf	phosphor coated
1866	37¢ Millikan	1,2,3,4	L perf	block
1867	39¢ Clark	1 floating	L perf	block
		2	bull's-eye	block
1868	40¢ Gilbreth	1 floating	L perf	block
		2	bull's-eye	block
2186	40¢ Chennault	1	bull's-eye	overall
2188	45¢ Cushing	1	bull's-eye	block
		1	bull's-eye	overall
1869	50¢ Nimitz	1,2,3,4	L perf	overall
		1,2	bull's-eye	block
		2	bull's-eye	overall
2190	52¢ Humphrey	1	bull's-eye	prephosphored
2191	56¢ Harvard	1	bull's-eye	block
2192	65¢ Arnold	1	bull's-eye	block
2194	$1 Revel	1	bull's-eye	block
2194A	$1 Hopkins	1	bull's-eye	block
		1	bull's-eye	overall
2195	$2 Bryan	2	bull's-eye	block
2196	$5 Bret Harte	1	bull's-eye	block

Notes:
Plate positions: Floating plate number positions are left or right, either blocks of six or strips of 20 (number must be centered in selvage in a block of six. All other plate number positions consist of upper left, upper right, lower left and lower right, with the following exceptions: 35¢ Chavez, which has positions of upper left, center upper right, upper right, lower left, center lower right and lower right. (Traditional corners have plate numbers to the side of the stamps; center positions have plate numbers above or below stamps.)
Tagging types: Block: tagging block centered over design of stamp; no tagging in selvage.
Overall: tagging applied to entire pane, generally leaving an untagged strip at outer edge of large margin selvage.
Phosphor-coated: paper with coating of phosphor applied before stamps are printed.
Prephosphored: paper with phosphor built into structure of paper.

ITEMS WITHDRAWN FROM SALE IN 1991

Commemoratives: $5 25¢ Steamboats booklet (6/30)
25¢ Letter Carriers (2/28)
25¢ Drafting Bill of Rights (4/30)
25¢ Prehistoric Animals (4/30)
25¢ America, 1989 (4/30)
25¢ Idaho Statehood (4/30)
25¢ Wyoming Statehood (4/30)
25¢ Supreme Court (4/30)
25¢ Ida B. Wells (4/30)
$5 25¢ Lighthouses booklet (8/31)
25¢ Marianne Moore (6/30)
25¢ Rhode Island Statehood (6/30)
$5 25¢ Indian Headdresses booklet (8/31)
25¢ Eisenhower (10/31)
25¢ America, 1990 (10/31)
25¢ Creatures of the Sea (10/31)
25¢ Micronesia-Marshall Islands (10/31)

Special Stamps: 25¢ Love, 1988 (6/30)
45¢ Love, 1988 (6/30)
$3 25¢ Special Occasions booklet (6/30)
25¢ Christmas Traditional sheet stamp, 1989 (4/30)
25¢ Christmas Contemporary sheet stamp, 1989 (4/30)
$5 25¢ Christmas Traditional booklet, 1989 (2/28)
$5 25¢ Christmas Contemporary booklet, 1989 (2/28)
$5 25¢ Love booklet, 1990 (8/31)
25¢ Christmas Traditional sheet stamp, 1990 (10/31)
25¢ Christmas Contemporary sheet stamp, 1990 (10/31)
$5 25¢ Christmas Traditional booklet, 1990 (10/31)
$5 25¢ Christmas Contemporary booklet, 1990 (10/31)

Definitives: 19¢ Sequoyah (6/30)
20¢ Harry S. Truman (6/30)
30¢ Frank Laubach, "A" press (8/31)
40¢ Lillian M. Gilbreth (6/30)
$4.40 22¢ Seashells booklets, packet of 7 (6/30)
6¢ Walter Lippmann (8/31)
1¢ Margaret Mitchell (8/31)
3¢ Paul Dudley White (8/31)
17¢ Belva Ann Lockwood (6/30)
40¢ John Harvard (out of stock, September)
$2 William Jennings Bryan (6/30)
4¢ Stagecoach coil, re-engraved "B" press (8/31)
17.5¢ Racing Car coil (8/31)
$1.50 25¢ Jack London booklet (6/30)
$3 25¢ Jack London booklet (4/30)
25¢ Flag Over Yosemite prephosphored (10/31)
25¢ Flag With Clouds sheet stamp (6/30)
$3 25¢ Flag With Clouds booklet (6/30)
$5 25¢ Owl and Grosbeak booklet (6/30)
25¢ Honeybee coil (6/30)
5.3¢ Elevator coil (8/31)
7.1¢ Tractor coil, 1989 (8/31)
7.6¢ Carreta coil (8/31)
8.4¢ Wheel Chair coil, "B" press (8/31)
8.4¢ Wheel Chair coil, "C" press (10/31)
10.1¢ Oil Wagon coil, 1988 (8/31)
13.2¢ Coal Car coil (8/31)
16.7¢ Popcorn Wagon coil (8/31)
20¢ Cable Car coil (8/31)
20.5¢ Fire Engine coil (8/31)

21¢ Railroad Mail Car coil (8/31)
24.1¢ Tandem Bicycle coil (8/31)
25¢ Eagle and Shield self-adhesive, booklet and strip (10/31)
$3 15¢ Beach Umbrella booklet (8/31)

Airmail and Expedited Mail: 36¢ Igor Sikorsky (8/31)
45¢ Samuel P. Langley (8/31)
$8.75 Express Mail (8/31)
$2.40 Moon Landing Priority Mail (10/31)
$10.75 Express Mail stamp and booklet (8/31)
45¢ America, 1990 (10/31)

Official Stamps: 1¢ 1983 (6/30)
4¢ 1983 (6/30)
13¢ 1983 (6/30)
17¢ 1983 (6/30)
20¢ coil 1983 (6/30)
15¢ coil 1988 (6/30)
25¢ coil 1988 (6/30)

Duck Stamps: $10 Snow Goose, 1988 (8/31)

Stamped Envelopes: 25¢ Stars, all versions (4/30)
8.4¢ Frigate Constellation, all versions (6/30)
25¢ Official, all versions (6/30)
25¢ Savings Bonds, with and without wording on back (4/30)
39¢ Graphic Design aerogram, 1988 (8/31)
25¢ Christmas Snowflake (4/30)
25¢ Security, plain and window (4/30)
25¢ Security, "Arizona" variety (4/30)
25¢ Philatelic Mail (6/30)
45¢ Official (6/30)
45¢ Official, self-sealing (6/30)
65¢ Official (6/30)
65¢ Official, self-sealing (6/30)
25¢ Football hologram (10/31)
29¢ Defense Department envelope (removed without notice)

Postal Cards: 15¢ Official (4/30)
15¢ The Prairie (4/30)
15¢ Northwest Territory (4/30)
15¢ The Prairie, double reply card (4/30)
36¢ DC-3 airmail card (8/31)
28¢ Yorkshire (8/31)
15¢ The Desert (4/30)
15¢ The Wetlands (4/30)
15¢ The Woodlands (4/30)
15¢ The Seashore (4/30)
21¢ The Mountains (6/30)
15¢ Philadelphia Cityscape (4/30)
15¢ Washington Cityscape (4/30)
15¢ Postal Buddy card (removed without notice)
15¢ Literacy (6/30)
15¢ Isaac Royall House (8/31)
15¢ George Caleb Bingham art card (8/31)
15¢ American Papermaking (6/30)
15¢ Quad at Stanford (8/31)
15¢ Orchestra Hall (10/31)

Souvenir Cards: London 1990, mint and canceled (10/31)

448